Access to Justice for Vulnerable People

About The Advocate's Gateway

The Advocates' Gateway, affectionately and widely known as 'TAG', exists to promote excellence in the justice system's approach to vulnerable witnesses and defendants, and to develop collaboratively research-led best practice. It provides a central source of practical guidance and information for advocates and others working with witnesses and defendants with communication needs, and delivers education and training.

www.theadvocatesgateway.org

Access to Justice for Vulnerable People

edited by

Professor Penny Cooper
and Linda Hunting

WS
&H

Wildy, Simmonds & Hill Publishing

Copyright © The editors and authors severally 2018.

Access to Justice for Vulnerable People

ISBN 9780854902675

British Library Cataloguing in Publication Data
A catalogue record for this book is available from the British Library

The right of Penny Cooper and Linda Hunting to be identified as the editors
of this Work has been asserted by them in accordance with the Copyright,
Designs and Patents Act 1988.

Cover Image courtesy of Penny Cooper.

First published in 2018 by

Published by
Wildy, Simmonds & Hill Publishing
London

Printed and bound by CPI Group (UK) Ltd, Croydon, CR0 4YY

For Lord Justice Nicholas Green
for his unfailing support of the work of TAG.
But for his support and vision,
the International Conferences of The Advocate's Gateway
would not have become a reality.

ACKNOWLEDGEMENTS

The editors would like to thank the many individuals and organisations who have contributed to the work of The Advocate's Gateway since its inception in 2012. They would particularly like to thank those who have shared their expertise at the second International Conference held in London June 2017 *Access to Justice for Vulnerable People*. Without the dedication of these individuals to research and support the needs of vulnerable people, the development of this book (arising out of that conference) would not have been realised. Grateful thanks go to the conference committee and to the management committee of The Advocate's Gateway - they know who they are - and they have provided much faith and support throughout. We are also very grateful for the financial and administrative support of the Council of the Inns of Court for the 2017 and the 2015 conferences. Lastly, we would like to thank Wildy, Simmonds and Hill Publishing for their commitment and guidance in compiling this book. The editors are grateful for the patience and wise counsel of Dr. Brian Hill who has assisted greatly with both this book and our 2016 publication.

Thank you for your interest in the work of The Advocate's Gateway by purchasing this book. Long may discussion with professionals working in these areas of vital importance improve justice and fairness to many more vulnerable people.

THE EDITORS

Professor Penny Cooper

Penny designed and pioneered the well-known and successful English witness intermediary role as well as the ground rules hearing approach which was written into court rules on her recommendation. She co-founded and has led The Advocate's Gateway ('TAG') since inception. Penny's research is widely published and cited; she has written judicially endorsed guidance for advocates and witness intermediaries. She has trained and assessed all accredited intermediaries in England, Northern Ireland and New South Wales, Australia and has trained judges and practitioners in more than ten jurisdictions. Penny practices as a barrister at 39 Essex Chambers, London advising on effective participation of witnesses in a wide range of serious, complex and high value cases. Penny leads grant-funded research at the Institute for Criminal Policy Research, Birkbeck, University of London.

Linda Hunting

Linda is a visiting lecturer in criminology and law at the University of West London and University of Roehampton and has worked as a consultant developing materials for undergraduate courses. Formerly the research and development coordinator at the Inns of Court College of Advocacy, and now a member of the TAG management committee. Linda played a pivotal role in the development and promotion of The Advocate's Gateway from its inception in 2012 and has contributed to its toolkits on mental health.
Linda was called to the Bar of England and Wales at Gray's Inn in 2012, and holds a LL.M in criminal law, a Post Graduate Diploma in Professional Legal Skills, and an LL.B (Hons). She sits on Referral Order Panels for young offenders across three boroughs in London and has been active with many Pro-Bono initiatives including; advice and representation in Equality, Disability, Benefit and Housing Law. Linda is a member of the Criminal Bar Association, The Howard League for Penal Reform, Association of Women Barristers and The Ealing Equality Council. She also sits as a member of the Editorial Board for the Journal of Intellectual Disabilities and Offending Behaviour.

This is the second publication Professor Penny Cooper and Linda Hunting have co-edited with Wildy, Simmonds and Hill Publishing. The first; *Addressing Vulnerability in Justice Systems* was published in 2016.

CONTENTS

Foreword

This is the second volume addressing access to justice for vulnerable people produced by The Advocate's Gateway (TAG) and edited by Professor Penny Cooper and Linda Hunting. The first volume of papers was published in December 2015, as Nick Green (now Lord Justice Green) said in his introduction, the previous collection of papers offered profound insights into how issues of vulnerability interact with the justice system and the need to improve and adapt practice and procedure to enable vulnerable parties and witnesses to give their best evidence. This new collection is similarly valuable; it reflects international developments and collaboration between practitioners and academics.

The "toolkits" on TAG are invaluable and, as a judge, I have seen the marked improvement both in the evidence given to the court and the ability of advocates to elicit clear evidence through their use in numerous cases. These have included criminal as well as family cases; and cases involving parties with multiple difficulties in communication, for example one where a parent who suffered PTSD and who needed a language interpreter as well as the assistance of an intermediary. Without the advocates use of the toolkit it is doubtful any useful evidence would have been adduced. Unfortunately, my observation is that while the use of the toolkits and advocacy training is plain in criminal cases the training for advocates in family proceeding continues to lag behind; family cases so often involve vulnerable parties caught up in highly emotional and difficult situations so it the need for the use of appropriate "tools" and their training in the use of those tools is not only desirable but necessary if the requirements of practice directions and Family Procedure Rules 2010 are to be properly implemented.

As discussed by Professor Cooper in her paper in the previous volume, the former President of the Family Division spoke of the need for a sea change in the Family Court's approach to the issues concerning vulnerable witness and set up a Working Group to make recommendations which, eventually resulted in Part 3A of the FPR 2010 coming into force; this rule placed a duty on the Family Court to consider and provide for the participation of, and the provision of measures for, vulnerable parties and witnesses. The Working Group had also made recommendations regarding the greater involvement and participation of children in family proceedings concerning them, regrettably and unfortunately for the voice of the child, the Ministry of Justice announced its decision not to implement the proposed rule change. It would appear that, nonetheless, the number of children giving evidence in the Family Court has increased and so the need for the assistance of TAG in respect of child witnesses is greater than ever.

The Hon. Ms Justice Alison Russell
Royal Courts of Justice
October 2018

Contributing Authors
(IN ALPHABETICAL ORDER)

Dr. Clare Allely

Clare is a Reader in Forensic Psychology at the University of Salford in Manchester, UK, and is an affiliate member of the Gillberg Neuropsychiatry Centre at Gothenburg University, Sweden. Clare is also an Honorary Research Fellow in the College of Medical, Veterinary and Life Sciences affiliated to the Institute of Health and Wellbeing at the University of Glasgow. Dr. Allely holds a Ph.D. in psychology from the University of Manchester and has previously graduated with an MA (hons.) in Psychology from the University of Glasgow, an MRes in Psychological Research Methods from the University of Strathclyde, and an MSc degree in Forensic Psychology from Glasgow Caledonian University. Between June 2011 and June 2014, Dr. Allely worked at the University of Glasgow as a postdoctoral researcher. Current research projects and interests include the path to intended violence in mass shooters; autism spectrum disorders in the criminal justice system (police, courts, prisons); the psychology of terrorism and research into brain injury or neurodevelopmental disorders in forensic populations.

Dr. Hugh Asher

Hugh is the project manager of the KeyRing 'Equal and Fair Project', a Comic Relief-funded project which provides learning disability and autism awareness training to front-line staff in the criminal justice system. As part of this project, Hugh also coordinates and chairs the Working for Justice Group (WfJ) in collaboration with the Prison Reform Trust. The WfJ group is a reference group comprising people with learning disabilities and autism who have first-hand experience of the criminal justice system. Hugh is also working on a Prison Reform Trust project researching the experiences of women with learning disabilities in the criminal justice system.

Professor Ray Bull

Ray is Professor of Criminal Investigation at the University of Derby. In 2005 he received a Commendation from the London Metropolitan Police for "Innovation and professionalism whilst assisting a complex rape investigation". In 2008 Professor Bull received the 'Award for Life-time Contribution to Psychology and Law' from the European Association of Psychology and Law. In 2010 was elected an Honorary Fellow of the British Psychological Society for the contribution made to the discipline of Psychology. In 2012 he was made the first Honorary Life Member of the International Investigative Interviewing Research Group. In 2014 Professor Bull became President of the European Association of Psychology and Law. He also regularly acts as an expert witness and conducts workshops and training on investigative interviewing around the world.

Chantelle de la Croix

Chantelle was born profoundly deaf and attended a school where children were taught using the oral method and were not allowed to use sign language. She left school with no qualifications and attended Derby College to improve her English and Maths. Her first qualification was an NNEB in Nursery Nursing and this was achieved through interpreter provision at college.

Around 20 years ago, Chantelle was a witness in a court case along with two other deaf people and observed how they really struggled to follow and respond in the correct way. In working with families, she came across a lot of family cases and observed many deaf people facing the same barriers. From this, she decided to train and become a qualified Intermediary for deaf people, striving to improve access to proceedings for deaf witnesses and defendants and assist the court in dealing with the complexities of working in BSL and across cultures.

Dr. Alan Cusack

Alan is a graduate of University College Cork (BCL, LLM, PhD), University College Dublin (Dip. Emp) and the Law Society of Ireland (Solicitor, 2012). In 2017, Alan completed a PhD at University College Cork in the area of access to justice for victims of crime with intellectual disabilities. In pursuit of his studies, Alan was awarded a Government of Ireland PhD scholarship from the Irish Research Council as well as a PhD Scholarship from University College Cork. Alan is a qualified solicitor and, subsequent to commencing his doctorate, practiced with Arthur Cox solicitors in Dublin. In 2017, Alan was appointed as Lecturer in Law at the University of Limerick. He is a professional member of The Law Society of Ireland

and is also a member of the Society of Legal Scholars. In 2015 Alan was an Academic Visitor at the Centre for Criminology at the University of Oxford.

The Rt Hon. Lady Dorrian, Lord Justice Clerk

Lady Dorrian was appointed a Judge of the Supreme Courts in 2005, having served as a Temporary Judge since 2002. She was appointed to the Inner House in November 2012 and was appointed The Lord Justice Clerk in April 2016. Lady Dorrian is a graduate of the University of Aberdeen (LLB). She was admitted to the Faculty of Advocates in 1981 and was Standing Junior Counsel to the Health and Safety Executive and Commission between 1987 and 1994. Lady Dorrian served as Advocate Depute between 1988 and 1991, and as Standing Junior to the Department of Energy between 1991 and 1994. Lady Dorrian was appointed Queen's Counsel in 1994. Between 1997 and 2001 she was a member of the Criminal Injuries Compensation Board.

Professor Louise Ellison

Louise is a Professor of Law in the School of Law, University of Leeds and Director of the School's Centre for Criminal Justice Studies. She is the author of The Vulnerable Witness and the Adversarial Process (2001, Oxford University Press) and numerous journal articles addressing the criminal justice response to victims of crime. As a member of an expert panel she has advised government on rape law reform and was part of an expert advisory group which developed guidance for the Crown Prosecution Service in cases involving witnesses with mental health conditions. She has conducted funded projects examining the impact of educational guidance and special measures on juror decision making in rape cases and the influence of witness preparation on witness accuracy in criminal cases. Her recent research has explored the effects of trauma on victims of crime and implications for victims' engagement with the criminal justice process.

Felicity Gerry QC

Felicity is an international barrister who also leads an Indigenous Justice and Exoneration Project in the Northern Territory of Australia (NT) dealing with issues relating to Indigenous incarceration. Several volunteers and students from the Project contributed to this chapter. Felicity has specialised in complex cases involving vulnerable people: She researches justice reform at Charles Darwin University, is on the Management Committee of The Advocate's Gateway and was the expert on an MDAC project in 2016/7 to train lawyers across all EU Member States on the rights of children with mental disabilities.

Penelope Gibbs

Penelope worked in radio production and at the BBC before being inspired to influence social change in the third sector. She set up the Voluntary Action Media Unit at TimeBank before joining the Prison Reform Trust to run the Out of Trouble – a five-year campaign to reduce child and youth imprisonment. In 2012 Penelope set up Transform Justice, a charity which advocates for a fairer, more open, more humane and more effective justice system in England and Wales. Penelope has researched and written several publications for Transform Justice including: *Justice denied? The experience of unrepresented defendants in the criminal courts; Magistrates: representatives of the people?* and *Defendants on video - conveyor belt justice or a revolution in access?* Penelope has also volunteered in the justice system – she sat as a magistrate for three years and is currently deputy chair of the Standing Committee for Youth Justice.

The Rt Hon. Sir John Gillen

Lord Gillen was educated at Methodist College and Queen's College, Oxford. He was called to the Bar of Northern Ireland in 1970, took Silk in 1983, and was appointed a High Court Judge in January 1999. In January 2001 he was assigned as the Family Judge and held this position and that of Chairman of the Children Order Advisory Committee until December 2006. In September 2008 he was assigned as the Senior Judge of the Queen's Bench Division. He was sworn in as a Lord Justice of Appeal in September 2014. In September 2015 The Lord Chief Justice commissioned a Review of Civil and Family Justice, led by Sir John. Sir John retired on 7 November 2017.

Dr. Andy Griffiths

Andy is a Research Fellow at the University of Portsmouth, UK, Associate Tutor at the College of Policing, and international Consultant. He is both a former Senior Investigating Officer (SIO) and head of major crime for a UK police force, having completed thirty years' service specializing in interviewing and investigation, and during which he led numerous major crime investigations. Throughout his police career he also contributed to UK national policy and training on investigative interviewing, as a member of the national council advising all police forces. He was awarded his PhD for research on the effectiveness of training on real life major crime suspect and witness interviews and has numerous publications in this field. He has contributed to miscarriage of justice investigations in the USA, New Zealand and the UK on a pro bono basis and lectured in many different countries.

John Horan

John is a passionate advocate of anti-discrimination and the rights of disabled people. He is a barrister at Cloisters chambers, and himself disabled. John was responsible for the recent ground-breaking judgement in the matter of Rackham and Galo. He writes and lectures for UK, European and International audiences including government, professional bodies and the legal profession, as well as disabled people themselves.

Dr. Jessica Jacobson

Jessica is Director of the Institute for Criminal Policy Research (ICPR) and a Reader in Criminal Justice at Birkbeck, University of London. She was formerly a researcher in the Home Office and also worked for many years as an independent policy researcher/consultant. Jessica undertakes research and publishes widely on many different aspects of the criminal justice system including prisons, sentencing, and the work of the criminal courts more widely. Her recent publications include *Inside Crown Court: Personal experiences and questions of legitimacy* (Policy Press, 2015, with Gillian Hunter and Amy Kirby) and *Imprisonment Worldwide: The Current Situation and an Alternative Future* (Policy Press, 2016, with Andrew Coyle, Helen Fair and Roy Walmsley). She is currently co-investigator on a project funded by the Nuffield Foundation which is examining the treatment of vulnerability in the courts and tribunals system of England and Wales.

Lore Mergaerts

Lore obtained a Bachelor of Criminology at KU Leuven, a Master of Laws in Forensics, Criminology and Law (Maastricht University) and a Master of Science in Psychology and Law (Maastricht University). After four years of being a teaching assistant in the Criminology program, she currently is a PhD researcher at the Leuven Institute of Criminology at the Faculty of Law at KU Leuven. Her research project is funded by the research fund Flanders (FWO) and concerns the role of the criminal defence lawyer in the pre-trial investigation with regard to (identification of) vulnerable suspects.

Dr. Sue O'Rourke

Dr O'Rourke qualified as a Clinical Psychologist in 1989 and specialises in mental health and deafness. She has worked in NHS mental health services for deaf people, including at Rampton hospital, working with offenders in maximum security. From 2004 she worked developing specialist secure services for deaf offenders with mental health needs and now works as an independent practitioner. Dr. O'Rourke has carried out research relating to deaf people in the criminal justice system, on behalf of the Department of

Health. She has several publications relating to mental health and deafness and has presented at national and international conferences. Over the last 20 years Dr O'Rourke has carried out many medico-legal assessments and works as an expert witness in relation to criminal, personal injury and family proceedings. She has particular expertise assisting the courts in relation to vulnerable witnesses and defendants. Dr. O'Rourke is lead author of the Advocates Gateway's toolkit on deafness and is a qualified sign language interpreter.

Dr. Anton van Dellen

Dr van Dellen is a member of Goldsmith Chambers and represents registrants, claimants and appellants in wide range of Courts and Tribunals. He has a Bachelor of Medicine and Surgery (MBBCh) from the University of the Witwatersrand, Johannesburg; a Doctor of Philosophy (DPhil) from the University of Oxford and a Bachelor of Arts (Law) from Trinity College, University of Cambridge. Anton worked as a Registrar in Neurosurgery and was a Fellow at Christ Church, University of Oxford, as well serving in a number of senior management roles in the NHS. He delivers the expert witness training course for the Royal Society of Medicine. He is a member of Inner Temple's Bar Liaison, Remuneration, Library and Archive Committees. He is also an elected member of the Bar Council and sits on the Legal Services and Education and Training Committees.

Mr. Mw. K.G.M. van Dijk – Fleetwood-Bird

Mr. K.G.M. van Dijk – Fleetwood-Bird is a lecturer/researcher at the Erasmus School of Law, department of Healthlaw at the Erasmus University in Rotterdam, Netherlands. She has been working as a Speech- and language therapist for 20 years in the Rotterdam area. She has worked with young people with (severe) speech- and language difficulties in the primary care. This chapter is based on the developing dissertation of van Dijk – Fleetwood-Bird: 'Caught by language', Oral language competence of young offenders and the implications for the Dutch Youth Justice System. Promotores: Prof. M.J.A.M. Buijsen, Prof. P.C. Snow & mr. dr. J. uit Beijerse.

Introduction

Access to Justice for Vulnerable People: Change in Scotland

The Rt Hon. Lady Dorrian, Lord Justice Clerk[1]

Thank you very much for inviting me to speak at The Advocate's Gateway international conference. The first of these conferences, two years ago, played a significant part in providing some of the momentum for change in Scotland, as delegates from North of the Border got together here to discuss how to take back the messages being so powerfully presented - the messages that positive action to take account of the needs of the vulnerable brings real benefits both to those whose needs are met and to the wider justice system. As I hope to outline to you today, one of the most important features behind the progress we have made in recent years has been the fact we have sought out the good practice and innovative thinking in other jurisdictions and applied that learning to develop solutions for our own jurisdiction. So, events like these can prove to be transformative well beyond the confines of the conference hall.

I'd like to start with an admission. It is an admission made freely, under no duress and with full recognition of its consequences. The admission is that, in respect of measures designed to make the experience of child and vulnerable witnesses less traumatic, "Scotland is still significantly lagging behind those at the forefront in this field." It is an admission actually made in a report, entitled the Evidence and Procedure Review, which the Scottish Court Service published in 2015 and for which I and the current Lord Justice General, Lord Carloway, were members of the Steering Group.

As you may know, it is still a requirement under Scots Law, that evidence must be corroborated. Unfortunately, our admission was all too easy to corroborate. The Evidence and Procedure Report referred to the

---

[1] Lady Dorrian is the second most senior judge in Scotland. This introduction is based on her keynote address delivered on Friday 2nd June 2017 at the Second International Conference of The Advocate's Gateway held at The Law Society, 133 Chancery Lane, London WC2A 1PL.

unreported case of *Akram*, in which a commission was arranged to take the evidence of a 5 year old girl, who was the complainer of a sexual assault that was alleged to have occurred twelve months earlier. The commission lasted for 2 days. During that time, unsurprisingly, the child's attention wandered, she repeatedly tried to leave the room where she was being filmed, and she often refused to answer questions. In upholding the appeal against conviction – primarily on other grounds - Lord Eassie said: "It appears to us from what we saw of the video that at least by the second day, if not earlier, the child had been rendered incapable of engaging meaningfully with the process of giving evidence."

It was, in fact, very unusual at the time for a commission to have been held at all. The vast majority of child witnesses in criminal trials, even in the High Court, were required to give their evidence at the trial itself, either by remote TV link or in Court itself with a supporter and behind a screen. What is certain is that the advocates examining and cross-examining child witnesses would have received little, if anything, by way of training or guidance in how to ask questions appropriate to the child's age. They would certainly expect to put the defence case directly to the child witness, to be able to accuse them of lying and to seek to undermine their credibility in court. On the rare occasion where a commission was deemed to be appropriate, there was little by way of protocols or established good practice to ensure that the witness' evidence, in pre-recorded form, was taken in the right way and in the right environment.

The publication of the Report of the Evidence and Procedure Review in March 2015, however, was the catalyst for a debate and a programme of work designed to return Scotland and its criminal justice system to the forefront of practice in this field. It is far too soon to say that we have got there; but we have started to take the steps that will not only bring us more in line with the good practice in place here in England and in other jurisdictions, but could actually take us to a far more radical approach.

The first of those steps has been a decision to increase and promote the use of pre-recorded examination and cross-examination for child and other vulnerable witnesses. This has been embodied in a High Court Practice Note on taking Evidence by a Commissioner. We have a Commission Procedure that does provide a pre-existing statutory framework for taking evidence in this way.

The intention of the Practice Note is to provide those protocols and structures that have been missing, to allow the appropriate examination and cross-examination of children to be recorded in advance; in particular, it borrows heavily from the English experience of the section 28 pilots, and from The Advocate's Gateway toolkits to introduce the idea of a Ground Rules Hearing to prepare these Commissions. It specifies what parties need to consider from the moment of making the application; directs them to the issues about which the court will wish to be informed; demands that they address the needs of the individual witness, including communication needs; gives significant case management powers to the judge; and, as I say, introduces the equivalent of a ground rules hearing. We have been able to do this without the need for legislation. However, there is also the possibility for legislation to help make the Commission process more streamlined, to bring it forward to an earlier stage in the process and to create a self-contained procedure with all the rules in the one place.

The second piece of work has been the development of new models to improve more fundamentally the quality of our treatment of vulnerable witnesses in Scotland. Over the past year or so, two working groups, with representatives of all the interest groups in the justice sector, have been examining how best to transform the experience of children and vulnerable people who have been the alleged victims of or witnesses to an offence. Each group has prepared a detailed report of its findings, with proposals for the way forward. The first of these, which will be published very shortly, contains a number of recommendations in relation to Joint Investigative Interviews, which are the Scottish equivalent of "Achieving Best Evidence" interviews. The recommendations are designed first, to improve the quality and consistency of Joint Investigative Interviews; and second, to make it easier to use those interviews as the evidence in chief in criminal proceedings.

The second report, due later this year, will set out our ambition for the long-term future – with a model that takes its inspiration from the Scandinavian Barnahus or Child's House model. Some of you may be familiar with the Child's House model, which brings together child protection, health care, social work and forensic interviewing services into a single facility for children who are the victims of or have witnessed violent or sexual abuse. It originated in Iceland about twenty years ago, and it is now in place throughout the Nordic countries, Baltic States and is being developed in many other European countries. There is, I understand, a pilot of this model in England too, led by the National Health Service. However, the English model may only be able to accommodate the Achieving Best Evidence interview, not the subsequent cross-examination.

In Scotland, we are exploring the extent to which the entirety of a child's evidence could take place in such a facility, with all questioning, favourable to the Crown or favourable to the defence, mediated through a trained forensic interviewer in circumstances where the child will not come to court at all. I do not wish to pre-empt the content of the report, which is still in development, so I cannot give any further detail. But I have every expectation that the report will set out an ambitious and far-reaching vision for the future, that could transform our legal system for the better. Because it is so far-reaching, it is not something that we will be able to achieve overnight. As we all know, proposals to change the way in which the courts operate can be slow to gain acceptance or approval. When dealing with highly complex and interconnected systems, it is essential to ensure that the full implications of any changes are properly and fully thought through. We are conscious that we may be revisiting some of the principles that have been at the heart of our legal system and our jurisprudence for decades, if not longer. It will be absolutely crucial to ensure that any changes proposed promote changes that improve the quality of justice, support the fairness of the trial for all concerned and maintain credibility in the system. That will take time.

But there is optimism because our vision is one that has been developed in collaboration with all those involved in the justice sector in Scotland. The working group includes members of the Faculty of Advocates and of the Law Society of Scotland, the judiciary, prosecutors, court staff, police, the Children's Commissioner, the Scottish Legal Aid Board and third sector groups representing the interests of victims and witnesses. This is indicative of the fact that there is a growing consensus behind the idea that change in this direction needs to happen. Although the initial impetus for change was judicially led, we are now at a point where the advocates for change can be found right across the legal system and further afield.

This includes the Scottish Government, which has promoted legislation in recent years that has substantially moved forward the treatment of complainers and witnesses. And the Government has indicated that it is still interested in new ideas in this area. The current Scottish Justice Secretary, Michael Matheson, has said that:

> "My view is that children should be spared the trauma of giving evidence in a formal court environment. Indeed, I want to eliminate the need for children to attend court at all during the trial...We have a duty to protect the best interests of each child and young person and, as such, the criminal justice process should adapt itself to their needs – not the other way around."[2]

[2]   Michael Matheson, Scottish Cabinet Secretary for Justice, speech to *Children 1st "Getting it Right for Child Witnesses"*, conference, Tulliallan Police College, October 12, 2016.

The emerging consensus I spoke of has not arisen by chance. It has arisen for a number of reasons, but I'd like to focus on one in particular. We have been able to get everyone around the table partly because of the effort that was put in at the outset into research – gathering all the evidence necessary to present a compelling case for change. That research encompassed both the need for change – the argument that to carry on as we were would be to continue to perpetrate an unacceptable injustice on the alleged victims of crime – and also the possible solutions. Our ability to point to good practice elsewhere in the world, and not just to rely on our own experience and intelligence, has been critical in shaping the way forward.

Most, if not all of us, in this room know and understand that the experience of giving evidence is, particularly for young or vulnerable witnesses, potentially traumatising. This is particularly the case where that evidence is given in a courtroom setting many months after the event, and traditional adversarial techniques are applied in questioning the witness. In short, the criminal justice system risks doing further damage to the very people that it should be designed to protect. But we also risk compromising the quality of the justice administered: traditional cross-examination is a poor way to get complete, reliable and accurate evidence. In the words of Dr Emily Henderson,

> "Thirty-odd years of empirical research have demonstrated that conventional cross-examination, with its preponderance of suggestive and confusing questioning tactics, is a veritable "how not to" guide for obtaining best—that is to say, full and accurate—evidence from vulnerable witnesses."[3]

But that view was not – and in some case is still not - common currency amongst the profession. They have spent their entire careers developing and honing their advocacy skills. It is asking a great deal of them to abandon the principles and practices and assumptions that have been the mainstay of their practice. And this applies equally to the judiciary, who would have had the same training and experience before their appointment to the Bench. It is quite hard to convince experienced practitioners that the way they have been taught to conduct themselves in court needs to change. But the research evidence is there, and in spades. There are academic studies into the short and long-term damage inflicted on vulnerable witness by the court process; and there is a wealth of material from organisations

[3] Dr Emily Henderson, "Communicative competence? Judges, advocates and intermediaries discuss communication issues in the crossexamination of vulnerable witnesses", *Crim L.R.* (2015) 9, 659 -678.

such as Victim Support, Children First and the NSPCC that highlights the real-life experiences of those who have gone through, and suffered from the system. It was extremely important for us to have that research at our disposal, to counter those who argued either that there was no real harm to address, or that experienced advocates are already sufficiently informed and skilled to adjust their questioning to mitigate that harm.

So, the research evidence about the effect on children was important; but perhaps even more important in developing the case for change, and in shaping what that change might look like, was the research we undertook into what was happening in other jurisdictions.

We either visited or studied by Skype, jurisdictions with an adversarial system such as England and Wales, Australia, Canada and the USA, and jurisdictions with more inquisitorial, continental systems such as the Netherlands and Norway. I can't emphasise enough how important that was. It was hugely valuable to see the section 28 pilots in practice in Liverpool and Leeds; these were practical demonstrations that a different approach could be taken, within the bounds of a comparable adversarial system. It meant that we could make the connections to the valuable work being undertaken by The Advocate's Gateway to provide advocates, and judges, with the tools that they need to be able to question vulnerable witnesses appropriately. The value of this was twofold. The first was that, again, we could counter any argument that introducing a new approach would not work or was inimical to justice.

On the publication of the first Evidence and Procedure Report in 2015, a senior representative of the Scottish Bar stated in the press that it was "inconceivable" for a witness to be subject to controlled cross-examination recorded in advance of the trial. But we could immediately point to the fact that it had already been conceived; that it was already happening; and that the tools were in place to make it happen, without detriment to the fairness of the trial. One of the issues we explored in some depth was how far the changes being suggested might be in breach of the accused's rights under Article 6 of the European Convention on Human Rights. It was again very useful to have to hand both decisions of the Court and examples of practice in other jurisdictions which went further in controlling cross-examination than we were at that stage proposing. Many of the questions raised by our working group as to the practicalities of pre-recording evidence could be answered by looking at how the section 28 pilots were operating in England.

This was reinforced by the fact that many of those involved in the section 28 pilots and the wider work on the treatment of vulnerable witnesses here in England were generously prepared to come to Scotland to share their experience and pass on their views. Inspired in part by the first Advocate's Gateway conference, our own Faculty of Advocates hosted a conference which brought together practitioners from North and South of the border to consider the measures that had been introduced. The conference, which was a great success, included contributions from former Lord Chief Justice Igor Judge, Angela Rafferty QC, Professor Penny Cooper, Dame Joyce Plotnikoff and others. The outcome from the conference was that there was a greater understanding not only that justice need not be compromised by measures to protect the vulnerable – but that in fact it is enhanced by such measures.

The second advantage the research into other systems brought was, of course, that there was a wealth of material that could be plundered to inform the design of our own model. I'm sure that you understand that it was never going to work for us to say to our colleagues in Scotland "Those clever English people have the answer – we'll do what they do". But the High Court Practice Note on Commissioner Evidence, for example, was quite deliberately designed to introduce the concept of a Ground Rules Hearing. Much of what is in the Practice Note is derived from or inspired by The Advocate's Gateway checklist[4] – and indeed the Note makes specific reference to the toolkits. But of course it was essential to incorporate the ground rules approach into our existing procedural framework, and to give a Scottish twist to the requirements, to ensure that we were not seen to be hauling an English system lock, stock and barrel over the Border, and to make absolutely sure that we respected our own traditions.

And, as I have already referred to, our longer-term ambitions have been inspired by the procedures in place in the Scandinavian Children's House, particularly those in Norway and Sweden. Again, we have been lucky both in being able to go and see these facilities in practice, but also in that those who run the Children's Houses have been very happy to come to Scotland to explain their methods and demonstrate the difference their approach has made. There is a great deal to be learnt from them, not least the value of having highly trained forensic interviewers to conduct all aspects of questioning vulnerable witnesses, and how the accused's article 6 rights are still provided for through the ability to propose lines of questioning to the interviewer. As I have said, we have had to think long and hard about how any of these more ambitious models might be applied within a Scottish context. But it is fair to say that the quality of our deliberations has

---

[4] Cooper, Penny. 2016. Ground Rules Hearing Checklist (London: Inns of Court College of Advocacy) Available at http://theadvocatesgateway.org/images/toolkits/ground-rules-hearings-checklist-2016.pdf (accessed October 10, 2017).

been greatly enhanced by our exposure to the many different procedures and practices that exist in other jurisdictions, and the willingness of practitioners from those jurisdictions to let us come and observe, question and challenge how they do things.

In conclusion then, I would say that in Scotland we have embarked upon a critically important journey to a better outcome for vulnerable witnesses. There is a widespread recognition that, in a civilised and modern society, all those who come into contact with the criminal justice system must be treated with respect, and be allowed to engage meaningfully with it. For children and other vulnerable witnesses, this means finding ways to take their evidence in an environment and in a manner that does not harm them further, that allows their evidence to be given fully yet tested appropriately. We have recognised that our current methods, while always improving, do not meet the highest mark, and we need to develop our own, Scottish, solutions to the challenge. In doing so, we have – and we will continue – to look beyond our boundaries to find inspiration, new ideas, new approaches and new partners. What we have learnt is the value of research, of collaboration and of leadership. And I would hope that, in time, those in other jurisdictions will seek to come to Scotland for their own inspiration.

CHAPTER 1

'Moving at a pace': Towards a new approach to vulnerability in courts and tribunals?

Professor Penny Cooper

Procedural requirements that decision-makers should listen to persons who have something relevant to say promote congruence between the actions of decision-makers and the law which should govern their actions...[1]

The second international conference of *The Advocate's Gateway* took place in London in June 2017 and focused on the theme of access to justice for vulnerable people. As the co-founder in 2012 and chair of The Advocate's Gateway ('TAG'), I am once again grateful to all those who helped organise the conference including my co-editor and the Inns of Court College of Advocacy at the Council of the Inns of Court. I am also grateful to the conference attendees, the presenters, Brian Hill at our publishers Wildy & Sons Ltd and those who wrote chapters for this post-conference publication. The easy part was having the idea for a TAG conference, it 'takes a village' to make it happen.

Procedural requirements for the treatment of witnesses change and develop over time. One does not have to look back very far to identify watershed moments. For example when Freud's theory 'that children tend to fantasise about sexual behaviour with their parents' became regarded as bad science.[2] In the 1980's high profile cases in the press reflected changing public attitudes to the treatment of children; paediatricians, lawyers, psychiatrists, psychologists, policemen, social workers and civil servants began to "think seriously" about children's evidence.[3] The introduction of intermediaries in 2004 has contributed to a 'paradigm shift' in the way we approach the participation of victims and witnesses in the criminal justice system in England and Wales.[4] We reached another key moment in 2013 when the pilot scheme for pre-recording children's cross-examination and re-examination began.[5] The law and practice in England and Wales

---

[1] Lord Reed in *Osborn v The Parole Board* [2013] UKSC 61, para 71, citing Fuller, *The Morality of Law*, revised ed. (1969), p 81, and Bingham, *The Rule of Law* (2010), chapter 6.
[2] Spencer, John, R. and Flin, Rhona, H. 1990. *The Evidence of Children. The Law and Psychology.* England: Blackstone Press. 7.
[3] Ibid. 12.
[4] Cooper, Penny and Hunting, Linda. 2016. (Eds.), *Addressing Vulnerability in Justice Systems.* London, England: Wildy & Sons.
[5] Cooper, Penny, and Mattison, Michelle. 2018. "Section 28" and the pre-recording of cross-examination. *Criminal Law and Justice Weekly.* 2018, 182(1).

for children and vulnerable adult witnesses has been "moving at a pace",[6] including during the last couple of years and since TAG held its inaugural conference in 2015 and publication of the first post-conference book.[7]

TAG and its supporters share an interest in improving the adversarial system of justice which must of course move with the times. There was no shortage of new material for this latest book about improving access to justice for vulnerable people. We know that 'vulnerable' is not capable of a single, once and for all definition. Each participant is different and will present with their own unique abilities and needs. There are many types of adjustments (also sometimes referred to as adaptations and accommodations) designed to enable the effective participation of vulnerable people in courts and tribunals.

For example, vulnerability might arise from physical, psychological or economic incapacity or it might be as a result of age. A witness might need a to give evidence remotely from a hospital, they might need an intermediary to help them understand the questions asked, they might need the support of an animal[8] or a combination of all three, to give just some examples. There is a need for scientific research about the impact of these and other adjustments. For example, though the court might direct that the witness is to be helped to communicate by an intermediary, what is the impact of the intermediary on the quality of the evidence given in court?[9]

Take two cases

I will now rely on two contrasting case examples to illustrate the treatment of two witnesses, 'Adam' (let us call him, it is not his real name) and Dr Sara Ryan. Adam was treated as vulnerable, Dr Ryan was not. Adam's case was reported to me by the witness intermediary;[10] this case went to trial in 2017:

> A teenage boy with a learning disability, Adam, gave evidence of sexual abuse by a close relative. The trial took place two years after Adam told his foster parent about the abuse and the subsequent police

[6] A phrase used by Lord Thomas, CJ, in reference to "the very significant improvements made in recent years to ensure vulnerable defendants participate effectively in the trial process and the wide range of special measures designed specifically to cater for the needs of the vulnerable", in *R v Grant-Murray & Anor* [2017] EWCA Crim 1228, para 225.

[7] n4.

[8] Cooper, Penny. 2018. Animals Supporting Effective Participation in Court: Some issues for England and Wales to consider (forthcoming).

[9] Cooper, Penny and Mattison, Michelle. 2017. Intermediaries, vulnerable people and the quality of evidence: An international comparison of three versions of the English intermediary model. *The International Journal of Evidence and Proof*. 21(4) 351–370.

[10] Trained by the author as a Registered Intermediary for the Ministry of Justice.

interview. In his video recorded interview, Adam gave a graphic and detailed account of sexual abuse. In the days preceding the trial, as is normal practice, he refreshed his memory, that is, he watched as his video interview was played back to him. The intermediary reported that there was a ground rules discussion involving her, the judge and counsel about how best to communicate with Adam. The defence advocate's cross-examination questions were written out and then vetted by the judge, with the assistance of the intermediary, and reduced to those which were relevant and could be understood by the witness. Adam's video interview was played to the jury and he was then cross-examined by defence counsel. Ultimately the jury found the defendant guilty on all counts.

The use of ground rules by the judge to set the parameters for the fair treatment, including questioning, of a vulnerable witness and the prior vetting of questions are both regarded as important elements of good practice in criminal cases in England and Wales when a witness is vulnerable.

The ground rules approach was written into the Criminal Procedure Rules in 2015.[11] Judicial vetting of questions for vulnerable witnesses has been commonplace since at least the introduction in December 2013 of a scheme for pre-recording of vulnerable witness cross-examination.[12] The Court of Appeal (Criminal Division) has endorsed both ground rules hearing and judicial pre-vetting of cross-examination questions:

> The court is required to take every reasonable step to encourage and facilitate the attendance of vulnerable witnesses and their participation in the trial process. To that end, judges are taught, in accordance with the Criminal Practice Directions, that it is best

---

[11] Writing the 'ground rules' approach into the rules occurred as a direct result of the author's research and recommendations. The ground rules approach and checklist were devised and refined over the course of a decade by the author. See Cooper, Penny (2016) Ground Rules Hearing Toolkit and the Ground Rules Hearing Checklist (London: Inns of Court College of Advocacy) both available at http://www.theadvocatesgateway.org/toolkits (accessed April 24, 2018). For the evolution of the ground rules approach, see Cooper, Penny, Backen, Paula, and Marchant, Ruth. 2015. Getting to grips with Ground Rules Hearings – a checklist for judges, advocates and intermediaries. *Criminal Law Review*, 6, 420-435. See also Cooper, Penny and Farrugia, Laura. 2017. Ground Rules Hearings, in Cooper, Penny and Norton, Heather. (Eds.), *Vulnerable People and the Criminal Justice System – A Guide to Law and Practice*. Oxford: OUP., Rule 3.9(6) and (7) of the Criminal Procedure Rules 2015 and Criminal Practice Direction 3E.1 to 3E.6, and 3D.7.

[12] The pilot scheme may be rolled out nationally. See Cooper, Penny, Mattison, Michelle, Norton, Heather. 2017. Looking Ahead. In Cooper, Penny and Norton, Heather. (Eds.), *Vulnerable People and the Criminal Justice System – A Guide to Law and Practice*. Oxford: OUP and n5.

practice to hold hearings in advance of the trial to ensure the smooth running of the trial, to give any special measures directions and to set the ground rules for the treatment of a vulnerable witness. We would expect a ground rules hearing in every case involving a vulnerable witness, save in very exceptional circumstances.[13]

...

So as to avoid any unfortunate misunderstanding at trial, it would be an entirely reasonable step for a judge at the ground rules hearing to invite defence advocates to reduce their questions to writing in advance.[14]

In *R. v Dinc* [2017], where the young witness was autistic, The Vice President of the Court of Appeal said in relation to a trial judge vetting cross-examination in advance:

[This] practice has been approved by this court on many occasions; it is the judge's duty to control questioning of any witness and to ensure it is fair both to the witness and the defendant. Far from prejudicing the defence, it is the experience of many trial judges that the practice ensures that defence advocates ask focussed and often more effective questions of a vulnerable child witness...[The trial judge] required the defence to submit their proposed questions in advance of cross-examination for approval, in this case, for good reason, given the complainant's age and level of difficulties. There can be no complaint about her direction in principle and there has been no complaint about any specific restrictions she imposed. [Defence counsel] failed to identify any issue about which he wished to cross examine and was prevented from doing so. Nothing arose during his cross examination that he had not foreseen. Had it done, he was perfectly entitled to seek the judge's consent to ask questions not previously authorised. Judges will accord an advocate, in this position, a degree of leeway provided, of course, their request is reasonable.[15]

In the second case example described below, unlike the child 'Adam' above or the teenager in *Dinc*, Dr Ryan would not be regarded as a 'vulnerable' witness in the criminal courts in that she is neither a child witness nor does she have a disability. But Dr Ryan was not giving evidence in a criminal case; she was a mere witness of fact at a tribunal.

[13] *R. v Lubemba; R. v JP* [2014] EWCA Crim 2064, para 42.
[14] Ibid., para 43.
[15] Lady Justice Hallett, VP, in *R. v Dinc* [2017] EWCA Crim 1206. Conclusions. Ground 1.

One might think in those circumstances, that she would be a long way from being vulnerable as a witness. However, this example illustrates that an unduly narrow approach to the notion of vulnerability in a witness can severely damage the chances of a court or tribunal hearing the best quality evidence, or hearing the relevant evidence at all.

Dr Sara Ryan's son was Connor Sparrowhawk, a young man diagnosed with autism, learning disabilities and epilepsy. Connor was admitted to hospital in March 2013 and 107 days later he drowned in the bath.[16] The tribunal of the General Medical Council (GMC) was investigating the fitness to practice of the psychiatrist (Dr Murphy) who was responsible for Connor's care. The hearing took place in Manchester. Connor's mother, Dr Ryan, travelled to Manchester, a substantial distance from her home in Oxford, to give evidence. What follows here is an extract from Dr Ryan's description of being cross-examined. Connor's is known as laughing-boy or LB for short.[17]

> The panel chair introduced the people around the table. The GMC barrister checked I'd signed and re-read my two statements which were in the front of the white file. Then it was over to Dr Murphy's barrister, Mr P.
>
> There was no apology. Our naive optimism was instantly crushed. Mr P asked me to turn to page x in the file and began a meticulous questioning that involved turning backwards and forwards between my *two statements in the front of the file and medical records 700 or so* pages towards the back of it.
>
> He had a skimpy pile of the relevant pages laid out in front of him. He didn't have to lob wedges of 1000+ pages backwards and forwards over a metal lever arch file bridge and leaf through numerous pages to find the relevant page, and section of text.
>
> Briefly scanning through pages of painful words about LB's horrific last few months.
>
> His lightness of documentation and organisation of the 'cross-examination' meant he effortlessly lined up question after question

[16] Ryan, Sara. 2017 *Justice for Laughing Boy Connor Sparrowhawk - A Death by Indifference.* Jessica Kingsley Publishing.
[17] Ryan, Sara. 2017. Mydaftlife blog, Writing Trauma, https://mydaftlife.com/2017/08/10/writing-trauma/ (accessed August 18, 2017).

after question. I felt I was being repeatedly sliced open with such a sharp knife there was no trace left on the blade.

"If you could turn to page x... Dr J is summarising his thoughts here, in this paragraph. Did he share them with you?"

"He made a phone call to Dr M. Can you remember how long that call lasted?"

"Turning back to page y. Do you recall Dr Murphy introducing herself in this meeting? In your statement on page j, you said..."

"If you could turn to page z of your statement. CTM meetings were held every Monday, you describe them as 10min meetings. Dr Murphy recalls the meetings being much longer..."

"Turning to page a, another meeting you did not attend, the notes state..."

A masterclass in something.

Over time, photos can become defining memories of particular events as the broader context fades away. Under Mr P's questioning, on the 7th floor of that imposing building on Oxford Street, Manchester, LB's medical notes became photo-like. It became impossible to think about and answer the questions that kept coming. To think beyond the words I was being directed to on different pages at different ends of the lever arch file. My heart started to thud so hard and erratically I thought it would knock me off the chair. Black edges creeping around my vision made it harder to find or read the notes. I became fearful of fainting and began to doubt my ability to answer questions truthfully.

"I don't remember." "I'm not sure." "I just don't know..."

Mr P continued asking questions. Apparently at ease with an approach that unsettles, distracts and confuses. Seemingly oblivious to my distress. No one intervened. I had no representation.

Dr Ryan is an articulate, intelligent woman yet she describes a horrible experience as a witness – a witness attending on a voluntary basis to assist the GMC panel. Her description of cross-examination reads as if it was a test of her ability to understand and remember questions, manually manipulate a file of papers and articulate answers whilst under extreme stress. Did cross-examination result in her giving the best quality evidence? Clearly not. As she gave evidence, Dr Ryan was a vulnerable (in the ordinary meaning of the word) witness and became unable to participate effectively. Yet, she was not a 'vulnerable' witness according to the only statutory definition in England and Wales, a definition derived from special measures eligibility criteria that only apply to criminal courts in any event.

A brief survey of the legal landscape across the courts in England and Wales reveals a hotchpotch of statutory and non-statutory provisions about 'vulnerable' participants. Who is regarded as 'vulnerable' and what adjustments are available for them depends heavily on which court or tribunal the person happens to be in; it is something akin to a procedural lottery for vulnerable participants.

A 'vulnerable' witness?

The legal concept of the 'vulnerable witness' arose from the 1998 United Kingdom Home Office report, *Speaking Up for Justice – Report of the Interdepartmental Working Group on the treatment of Vulnerable or Intimidated Witnesses in the Criminal Justice System.*[18] The report, concluded that if witnesses were to be classified as 'vulnerable',

> …any definition would need to identify first, which group or category of witnesses are eligible for consideration for special provisions to assist them to give best evidence, and secondly, to guide the court on how to exercise the discretion in selecting from that group those needing assistance. The definition should be clear and understandable and it should encompass those witnesses who are likely to require special provisions, while excluding the vast majority who do not need such assistance. (p.20)

The legislation which followed *Speaking Up For Justice* sought to address the needs of 'vulnerable' and 'intimidated' witnesses through a range of 'special measures'.[19] These accommodations were then defined in statute in order to enable the vulnerable or intimidated witness to give the best quality evidence. Sections 16 and 17 of the Youth Justice and Criminal Evidence Act 1999 (YJCEA 1999) contain the criteria which define 'Witnesses eligible for assistance on grounds of age or incapacity' and 'Witnesses eligible for assistance on grounds of fear or distress about testifying' respectively.

[18] The Home Office.1998. *Speaking Up for Justice. The Report of the Home Office Interdepartmental Working Group on the Treatment of Vulnerable or Intimidated Witnesses in the Criminal Justice System.* London, England: The Home Office.
[19] The Youth Justice and Criminal Evidence Act 1999, Part II, Chapter I.

If directed by the court, a vulnerable or intimated witness may be screened from the accused (section 23), they may give evidence by live-link, including with a supporter in the live link room with them if necessary, (section 24), the public gallery may be cleared so that they give evidence in private (section 25), the judge and advocates may remove their wigs and gowns whilst the witness gives evidence (section 26) and their video recorded interview with the police may be played in place of their evidence in chief (section 27). In addition, for section 16 witnesses, they may come to come court in advance, instead of coming to the trial, and give video recorded cross-examination and re-examination (section 28, implemented so far only in pilot areas), they may give evidence with the assistance of a communication facilitator called an intermediary (section 29) and they may give evidence using a communication aid/s (section 30).

A 'vulnerable' accused person

The accused is specifically excluded from eligibility for this range of special measures in sections 23 to 30 of the YJCEA 1999. Fairclough argues that:

> The exclusion of vulnerable and/or intimidated defendant witnesses from eligibility for special measures was not in keeping with [the principle of equality]. The reasons provided in the *Speaking up for Justice* Report were not sufficient to justify denying vulnerable and/ or intimidated defendant witnesses special measures assistance, thus treating all defendants the same.[20]

There is only one statutory special measure available for the accused and the eligibility criteria are different; if so directed, the vulnerable accused may use live link when giving evidence. Section 33A of the YJCEA 1999 making live link available to the vulnerable accused, was inserted by section 47 of the Police and Justice Act 2006. The conditions that must be met for eligibility are subtly different to those for a vulnerable witness.

Fairclough's 2016 study of criminal practitioners[21] revealed low levels of use of live-link for the accused and suggests that barriers to its use include a lack of awareness of its availability and poor levels of identification of vulnerability. It is also noteworthy that custody officers in police stations

---

[20] Fairclough, Samantha. 2018. Speaking up for Injustice: Reconsidering the provision of special measures through the lens of inequality. *Criminal Law Review* (1) 4-19.
[21] Fairclough, Samantha. 2016. 'It doesn't happen … and I've never thought it was necessary for it to happen: Barriers to vulnerable defendants giving evidence by live link in crown court trials', *The International Journal of Evidence and Proof, October*. 1-21.

are responsible for recognising vulnerability in suspects (as defined in Code C to the Police and Criminal Evidence Act 1984), however a recent study[22] recognized the definitional issues and called for greater clarity.

Confusion in practice in the criminal court as to who is 'vulnerable'?

In *R. v SG*[23] (later clarified by the Court of Appeal in *R. v Dinc* [2017]) the Court of Appeal considered the trial judge's response when an alleged victim of a sexual assault became distressed while being cross-examined. Though the alleged victim witness in *SG* was 'vulnerable' in the ordinary meaning of the word, she was testifying at a trial about sexual abuse by her brother, she was not a 'vulnerable' witness within section 16 of the YJCEA 1999.

> This was not a case of a witness who had difficulty in understanding the questions; and we consider that requiring an advocate to prepare a list of questions for the court's approval during the course of cross-examination in such a case should be regarded as an exceptional course. The present instance (where there was no impropriety nor any likely confusion as to the form of the questioning) was not such a case. (para 63)

In another recent case, *R. v Hamberger*,[24] the appeal centred on potential adjustments to facilitate a physically unwell defendant's attendance and participation. The defendant had a heart condition. Though the trial judge thought that the defendant was potentially eligible to give evidence by live link, in fact live link was not available as he did not satisfy the statutory test for eligibility; he did not fit the criteria for a vulnerable accused person as found in section 33A YJCEA 1999 eligibility criteria.

To further add to these already complex statutory definitions of 'vulnerable', a judge can direct non-statutory adjustments for an accused person (or a witness for that matter) when it is in the interests of a fair trial. The criminal court rules state:

> In order to prepare for the trial, the court must take every reasonable step— (a) to encourage and to facilitate the attendance of witnesses

---

[22] Dehaghani, Roxanna. 2017. Custody officers, Code C and constructing vulnerability: implications for policy and practice. *Policing,* 11(1). 74-86.
[23] [2017] EWCA Crim 617. See also Cooper, Penny. 2017. Case Comment Crim. L.R. 2017, 9, 733-737.
[24] [2017] EWCA Crim 273. See also Cooper, Penny. 2017. Case comment *R v Hamberger, Criminal Law Review.* 9, 708-711.

when they are needed; and (b) to facilitate the participation of any person, including the defendant.[25]

Thus, for example, a judge may use their inherent powers to order the use of an intermediary for a vulnerable defendant[26] or indeed order any reasonable adjustment in order to ensure a fair trial.[27]

In August 2017, the Court of Appeal (Criminal Division) delivered a long judgment concerning defendants who were vulnerable at their trials by virtue of their young age and/or mental condition. The then Lord Chief Justice, Lord Thomas, said,

> ...the changes [designed to cater for the needs of vulnerable people at trial] are moving at a pace that may not be readily discernible without detailed study of the changes and the development of the case law. They include the provision of intermediaries for defendants when necessary, the extensive training of judges and advocates (a national roll out of the training of advocates is currently underway), the provision of and repeated judicial endorsement of [The Advocate's Gateway] advocacy toolkits for questioning vulnerable witnesses and the holding of ground rules hearings designed to ensure the particular needs of individual witnesses and defendants are met.[28]

Currently the criminal justice system expects judges to adopt a very flexible approach to procedural fairness and the law is neither simple nor static. The Advocate's Gateway[29], which began in 2012, aims to provide

---

[25] Criminal Procedure Rules (2015), 3.9(3). See also Criminal Practice Directions (2015, as updated) which note at 3D.2 that 'many people other giving evidence' than those who meet the statutory criteria for special measures may require assistance.

[26] Cooper, Penny, and Wurtzel, David. 2013. A day late and a dollar short: in search of an intermediary scheme for vulnerable defendants in England and Wales, *Criminal Law Review*, 1, 4-22. See also Hoyano, Laura and Rafferty, Angela. 2017. Rationing defence intermediaries under the April 2016 Criminal Practice Direction. *Criminal Law Review*, 2, 93-105; Wurtzel, David. 2017. Intermediaries for defendants: recent Developments. Criminal Law Review. 2017. 6, 463-470.

[27] Wurtzel, David and Marchant, Ruth. 2017. Intermediaries. In Cooper, Penny and Norton, Heather (Eds.), *Vulnerable People and the Criminal Justice System – A Guide to Law and Practice*. Oxford. England: OUP. 2017 and Marchant, Ruth. 2017. Special Measures. In Cooper, Penny and Norton, Heather. (Eds.), *Vulnerable People and the Criminal Justice System – A Guide to Law and Practice*. Oxford. England: OUP. 2017.

[28] *R v Grant–Murray & Henry; R v McGill, Hewitt & Hewitt* [2017] EWCA Crim 1228, para 225.

[29] Originally TAG was a blog designed by the author and hosted on the web pages of the law school at City, University of London but now it is a website - theadvocatesgateway.org – run by a volunteer committee, chaired by the author and funded by the Council of the Inns of Court a charity registered in England and Wales.

knowledge and practice examples in short, accessible toolkits.[30] It is not only the criminal courts that must be flexible and adjust their traditional process to enable the participation of vulnerable people. The range of TAG toolkits has expanded to cover cases in other parts of the English legal system albeit that *beyond the criminal justice system* there are no statutory provisions for 'special measures' for vulnerable participants. Other parts of the justice system in England and Wales are making conspicuous attempts to promote access to justice for vulnerable witnesses and parties, none more so that the family justice system, but without extra resources for the family judges to draw upon we should not "expect fireworks".[31]

The Family Court playing catch-up

The Family Court, following the lead of the criminal courts, adopted the use of intermediaries and ground rules hearings to ensure the fair treatment of vulnerable people.[32] However progress in establishing a comprehensive set of rules and procedures has been painfully slow. In the summer of 2014 a working group[33] was tasked by the President of the Family Division, Sir James Munby, with making recommendations for reform for vulnerable witnesses and parties.[34] Though a report was produced the following year,[35] and a detailed practice direction on vulnerable witnesses was the subject of a consultation by the Ministry of Justice[36], the new rules did not come into force until November 2017.[37]

The practice direction represents progress, but there is only so much that the family judges can achieve without legislation to prevent vulnerable

---

[30] The first proto-type *toolkits* for advocates working with vulnerable people were published in 2011 by the Advocacy Training Council (which became the Inns of Court College of Advocacy) in appendices to the Raising the Bar Report of Charles Haddon-Cave QC and his working group. https://icca.ac.uk/advocacy-the-vulnerable/raising-the-bar (accessed September 15, 2017).
[31] Cooper, Penny. 2018. Participation of vulnerable people: don't expect fireworks. *Fam. Law*. 48 (Jan), 3
[32] Cooper, Penny. 2016. "Valuable Lessons and Poor Relations: Comparing the English Criminal and Family Justice Systems' Approaches to Vulnerable and Intimidated Witnesses," in *Addressing Vulnerability in Justice Systems*. Eds. Cooper, Penny and Hunting, Linda. (London, England: Wildy).
[33] The author was a member of that group.
[34] Munby, Sir James. 2014. '12th View from the President's Chamber: The process of reform: next steps'. *Fam Law* 978.
[35] Vulnerable Witnesses & Children Working Group. 2015. *Report of the Vulnerable Witnesses & Children Working Group*. London, England: Judiciary of England and Wales
[36] https://www.gov.uk/government/consultations/vulnerable-witnesses-practice-direction (accessed August 6, 2017).
[37] Cooper, Penny. 2017. New Family Procedure Rules on Participation of Vulnerable People: Enabling the Court of Protection to pick up the pace? *Mental Capacity Report: Practice and Procedure, November* 2017, 81, 6-9.

witness being cross-examined by their alleged abuser in person. The President of the Family Division said in December 2016:

> I would welcome a bar [on alleged perpetrators cross-examining their alleged victims]. But the judiciary cannot provide this because it requires primary legislation and would involve public expenditure. It is, therefore, a matter for ministers. I am disappointed by how slow the response to these issues has been and welcome the continuing efforts by Women's Aid to bring these important matters to wider public attention.

Mr Justice Hayden said a few months later,

> I understand that there is a real will to address this issue but it has taken too long. No victim of abuse should ever again be required to be cross examined by their abuser in any Court, let alone in a Family Court where protection of children and the vulnerable is central to its ethos.[38]

A plan for new legislation to stop this practice in the family courts[39] evaporated following the announcement of a General Election in June 2017.

The Court of Protection

The Court of Protection ('CoP') which exists to make decisions about the welfare and finances of vulnerable adults, has no legislation specifically aimed at supporting the effective participation of the people who are the subject of its proceedings.[40] There is much that could be learnt from the Family Court. Recently CoP guidance has been issued to 'provide helpful suggestions as to how practitioners might consider enhancing participation of [the vulnerable person] in proceedings in the Court of Protection'.[41]

> Surprisingly given it is a jurisdiction wholly devoted to matters concerning people with mental disabilities, the CoP has until recently given no systematic consideration to the special measures and reasonable adjustments that would be needed to facilitate the

---

[38]   *Re A (A Minor: Fact Finding; Unrepresented Party)* [2017] EWHC 1195 (Fam), para 63. See also Cooper, P. (2017). Vulnerable Witnesses. *Fam. Law* 2017, 47(Jul), 704-706.

[39]   Cooper, P. (2017). Cross-examination of vulnerable people by alleged abusers in person. Fam. Law 2017, 47 (Feb), 245-247.

[40]   Ruck Keene, Alex, Cooper, Penny and Hogg, Claire. 2016. "Special Measures" in the Court of Protection. *Elder Law Journal,* 6(1), 62-66.

[41]   Charles, Mr. Justice. 2016. "Facilitating participation of P and vulnerable persons in Court of Protection Proceedings".

participation of P. Recent (non-binding) guidance encourages judges and parties to consider these matters, but there is no provision in the [CoP Rules] or practice directions in relation to this matter, and questions remain as to how such measures would be funded.[42]

Researchers have recommended provision for special measures in the rules and practice directions and allocated resources to support access to justice in the CoP.[43]

The Employment Tribunal

The Employment Tribunal, is thought to be "well versed in being flexible and avoiding undue formality", and has on occasion adopted in all but name the ground rules approach.[44] In one appeal about the case of a claimant who had Asperger's Syndrome, the court acknowledged that the tribunal "has a duty as an organ of the state, as a public body, to make reasonable adjustments to accommodate the disabilities of Claimants".[45] However, the extent to which employment tribunals as a whole actually adjust for vulnerability is unclear as to date there is no published research on the topic.[46]

The Court of Appeal in Northern Ireland[47] issued a landmark judgment in 2016 that dealt with an employment tribunal's failure to make adjustments for the known disability of the applicant; the decision was quashed thus requiring the tribunal to hear the case afresh, and taking a fresh and proper approach.[48] Following a detailed analysis of this judgment, Clare Allely and I have suggested that the responsibility to ensure hearings are fair when a party is vulnerable lies not only lies with judges but also with lawyers in the case.[49] However not all potential claimants can get access lawyers and judges if there are financial barriers in their way.

---

[42] Series, Lucy. Fennel, Phil and Doughty, Julie. 2017. *The Participation of P in Welfare Cases in the Court of Protection.* England: Cardiff University and The Nuffield Foundation. 15.

[43] Ibid.

[44] Cooper, Penny and Arnold, James. (2017). Listening without prejudice? Procedural adjustments in the employment tribunal, *ELA Briefing*, March 2017, 5-7, 7.

[45] *J W Rackham v NHS Professionals Ltd* [2015] UKEAT 0110_15_1612 at para. 32.

[46] The first empirical research of this sort in the Employment Tribunal in England and Wales will be conducted in 2018/9 in a project funded by the Nuffield Foundation and led by the author.

[47] Northern Ireland and England and Wales have separate legal systems.

[48] *Galo v Bombardier Aerospace UK* [2016] NICA 25.

[49] As argued by Cooper, Penny and Allely, Clare. 2017. You can't judge a book by its cover: Evolving professional responsibilities, liabilities and 'judgecraft' when a party has Asperger's Syndrome. *Northern Ireland Legal Quarterly.* 68 (1), 35–58.

In the summer of 2017, as a result of action taken by the trade union UNISON, the Supreme Court quashed the order requiring applicants to pay fees in order to issue proceedings in the employment tribunal because it offended the 'constitutional right of access to the courts is inherent in the rule of law'.[50] This case is a reminder that vulnerability due to age or incapacity is just one aspect of access to justice, vulnerability arises when there is an unfair financial barrier. The nature of the vulnerability in the UNISON case was not age or incapacity, but economic.

> People and businesses need to know, on the one hand, that they will be able to enforce their rights if they have to do so, and, on the other hand, that if they fail to meet their obligations, there is likely to be a remedy against them.[51]

The Supreme Court concluded that charging fees to issue a claim in the Employment Tribunal was unlawful because the effect was to prevent access to justice for many applicants who could not afford the fee. Whilst this barrier has now been removed, other barriers may still exist for the vulnerable applicant because, as with the CoP discussed above, no systematic consideration has been given to access to justice for vulnerable people in the Employment Tribunal. The same could be said of the Tax Tribunal.

The Tax Tribunal

In one recent tax case, the court pointed to the duty of Her Majesty's Revenue and Customs (HMRC), to make all appropriate adjustments themselves and to inform the Tribunal of the other party's vulnerability. Since this had not happened, the approach taken by HMRC was described as "profoundly wrong".[52]

The Immigration Tribunal

In an immigration appeal case in 2017, the Senior President of Tribunals, Ryder LJ, issued guidance on the general approach to be adopted in law and practice by the First-tier Tribunal (Immigration and Asylum Chamber) and the Upper Tribunal (Immigration and Asylum Chamber) for "the fair determination of claims for asylum from children, young people and other

---

[50] *UNISON v Lord Chancellor* [2017] UKSC 51, para 66.
[51] Ibid, para 71.
[52] *E v Revenue and Customs (EXCISE DUTY – assessment to Tobacco Products Duty)* [2017] UKFTT 348 (TC).

incapacitated or vulnerable persons whose ability to effectively participate in proceedings may be limited."[53]

Cross-examining a 'vulnerable' witnesses and training for advocates

One issue common to all courts and tribunals in England and Wales which hold oral hearings is how advocates should be directed to approach the questioning of a vulnerable people, including challenging the accuracy and/or truthfulness of their account. There is a general rule that,

> …it will not do to impeach the credibility of a witness upon a matter on which he has not had any opportunity of giving an explanation by reason of there having been no suggestion whatever in the course of the case that his story is not accepted.[54]

It was argued before the Judicial Committee of the Privy Council ('the Board') in *Chen v Ng (British Virgin Islands)*[55] that a judge could not rely on grounds as reasons for disbelieving a witness when the ground had not been put to the witness in cross-examination. The Board stressed that there are no absolutes, and what must be put to the witness for there to be a fair hearing is a case-by-case decision.

> In a perfect world, any ground for doubting the evidence of a witness ought to be put to him, and a judge should only rely on a ground for disbelieving a witness which that witness has had an opportunity of explaining. However, the world is not perfect, and, while both points remain ideals which should always be in the minds of cross-examiners and trial judges, they cannot be absolute requirements in every case.[56]

As the Board has said in a previous case, "[t]he gravamen of it is fairness."[57] Court of Appeal (Criminal Division) judgments regarding cross-examination of vulnerable witnesses are in line with the approach of the Board. For example, the Court of Appeal has concluded that, on the facts in the particular cases under consideration, a judge may impose a time-limit on cross-examination,[58] cut short cross-examination,[59] and

---

[53] *AM (Afghanistan) v Secretary of State for the Home Department* [2017] EWCA Civ 1123.
[54] Lord Herschell LC in *Browne v Dunn* (1893) 6 R 67, 71. For a modern example of the rule being applied see *Markem Corpn v Zipher Ltd* [2005] RPC 31.
[55] [2017] UKPC 27.
[56] Ibid, para 52.
[57] *Director of Public Prosecutions v Nelson (Antigua and Barbuda)* [2015] UKPC, para 24.
[58] See for example, *R. v Butt* [2005] EWCA Crim 805.
[59] *R. v Pipe* [2014] EWCA Crim 2570.

require topics to be divided amongst co-defendants' counsel to avoid unnecessary repetition.[60]

Lady Justice Hallett VP encapsulated the position in relation to vulnerable witnesses in *R. v Lubemba*:

> It is now generally accepted that if justice is to be done to the vulnerable witness and also to the accused, a radical departure from the traditional style of advocacy will be necessary. Advocates must adapt to the witness, not the other way round. They cannot insist upon any supposed right "to put one's case" or previous inconsistent statements to a vulnerable witness. If there is a right to "put one's case" (about which we have our doubts) it must be modified for young or vulnerable witnesses. It is perfectly possible to ensure the jury are made aware of the defence case and of significant inconsistencies without intimidation or distressing a witness...[61]

The former Lord Chief Justice of England and Wales has impressed upon advocates the need to undertake specialist training [62] and the duty not to take cases involving the questioning of vulnerable witnesses unless they are competent to do this work:

> We would like to emphasise that it is, of course, generally misconduct to take on a case where an advocate is not competent. It would be difficult to conceive of an advocate being competent to act in a case involving young witnesses or defendants unless the advocate had undertaken specific training.[63]

Judges require training too; they receive lectures on case management and vulnerable witnesses on Judicial College courses.[64] However it is clear that there should be more:

> We continue to press the Ministry of Justice for further resources to extend the training of judges; it would, if resources permitted, be desirable to provide more extensive training in respect of evidence given by young defendants and witnesses.[65]

---

[60] *R. v Jonas* [2015] EWCA Crim 562.
[61] *R. v Lubemba; R. v JP* [2014] EWCA Crim 2064, para 45.
[62] See also Cooper, Penny. 2017. *R v Rashid, Criminal Law Review*, 5, 420 – 421.
[63] *R. v Grant–Murray & Henry; R. v McGill, Hewitt & Hewitt* [2017], para. 226.
[64] Including those delivered by the author at the Judicial College.
[65] *R. v Grant–Murray & Henry; R. v McGill, Hewitt & Hewitt* [2017], para. 226.

At the time of writing there is plan in place for justice system-wide training to promote the participation of vulnerable people in England and Wales.

Moving at a pace – but where to?

Dictionary definitions of vulnerable include being "able to be easily physically, emotionally, or mentally hurt, influenced, or attacked",[66] and being "open to attack or damage".[67] By these definitions every witness who gives evidence which is challenged is vulnerable. In 1998 the *Speaking Up For Justice* report called for a clear and understandable definition of vulnerable specifically to exclude what it felt was "the vast majority [of witnesses] who do not need such assistance". The result was that vulnerable took on a narrow legal meaning originating in the criminal courts of England and Wales in the YJCEA 1999. But recent appellate case law from England and Wales illustrates the difficulties judges and practitioners face when apply in the complex criteria of eligibility for special measures. It is perhaps no surprise that a qualitative study published in 2016,[68] found practitioners in the criminal justice system needed more 'clarity around when and what measures are appropriate under the YJCEA'.[69]

A drive towards flexibility to accommodate the needs of the individual vulnerable participate is typified by the ground rules hearing[70] approach which has spread beyond England and Wales to Scotland[71] as Lady Dorrian set out, as well as to Northern Ireland,[72] New South Wales, Australia and New Zealand.[73] I devised the ground rules approach to enable judges to proactively manage the treatment of vulnerable witnesses. The ground rules hearing is based on the simple principle that planning how to enable the vulnerable witness to give their best evidence requires an informed

---

[66] http://dictionary.cambridge.org/dictionary/english/vulnerable
[67] https://www.merriam-webster.com/dictionary/vulnerable
[68] Ewin, Robert. 2016. The vulnerable and intimidated witness: a study of the special measure practitioner. *Journal of Applied Psychology and Social Science*, 2, (1). 12-40.
[69] Ibid, 35.
[70] For a summary of the procedure and law in England and Wales see Cooper, Penny. 2016. Toolkit 1 Ground Rules Hearings and the fair treatment of vulnerable people in court, London, UK: Inns of Courts College of Advocacy. https://www.theadvocatesgateway.org/images/toolkits/1-ground-rules-hearings-and-the-fair-treatment-of-vulnerable-people-in-court-2016.pdf (accessed August 18, 2017).
[71] Scottish Government. 2017. Pre-recording Evidence of Child and other Vulnerable Witnesses: Consultation Analysis, available at http://www.gov.scot/Publications/2017/12/9674 (accessed December 17, 2017).
[72] The case of *Galo v Bombardier*, discussed above and see fns 48 and 49, was one example.
[73] Cooper, Penny and Mattison, Michelle. 2017. Intermediaries, vulnerable people and the quality of evidence: An international comparison of three versions of the English intermediary model. *The International Journal of Evidence and Proof.* 21(4) 351–370.

discussion in advance between the judges and the advocates following which, the advocates need to adhere to the Do's and Don'ts as directed by the judge. It is very encouraging to see 'ground rules go global' as I had hoped they would. Notwithstanding the widespread use of ground rules hearings, access to justice for vulnerable people in England and Wales is still work in progress. Subsequent chapters paint a picture of research and practice outside England and Wales, provide interesting comparisons and will inform ongoing research.[74]

In England and Wales novel practices relating to effective participation of vulnerable witnesses and parties have been developed in the criminal courts, the principles apply just as much to other courts and tribunals which generally lag far behind. The toolkits provided on The Advocate's Gateway website are designed to help advocates and judges approach ground rules hearings with clarity, confidence and flexibility. The TAG resources, provided on-line and free of charge, have been widely judicially endorsed; they are "designed to ensure the particular needs of individual witnesses and defendants are met."[75] In England and Wales, we are currently grappling with a confusing, hotchpotch of law and procedure and gaps in provision for vulnerable participants. Clearly it is not good enough.

For example, the system seems to assume that for an articulate and intelligent adult the task of giving evidence, is straightforward. It should be. It should never be needlessly harrowing as it was for Dr Ryan who was, in the end, unable to participate effectively as a witness. One positive shift would be the use of universal ground rules for questioning witnesses which promote more effective participation.[76] It is submitted that a narrow definition of 'vulnerable' is now an out of date approach to promoting participation; we must think more in terms of adjustments to meet the needs of all lay participants. Government investment in the justice system to remove barriers to participation of its citizens should be a priority. It is not.

In England and Wales procedural changes *have* been moving at a pace for vulnerable participants, now change needs to move at a pace to enable the effective participation of *all* participants. To that end, TAG conferences provide a unique opportunity for academics and practitioners to collaborate across continents and disciplines on access to justice issues so that we may

---

[74] http://www.nuffieldfoundation.org/vulnerability-courts-research-and-policy-project (accessed August 18, 2017).

[75] *R. v Grant–Murray & Henry; R. v McGill, Hewitt & Hewitt* [2017], para 225.

[76] Cooper, Penny. 2017. Moving the Bar: Is Cross-examination any good? *Mental Capacity Report: Practice and Procedure*, March 2017, 74, 3-6.

share best practice and put a spotlight on what needs to improve. These are pressing issues for policy and law makers. It is time to move on from twenty years ago and *Speaking Up for Justice* to *Speaking up for participants in the justice system.*

CHAPTER 2

Cartesian perfection: The route out of failure

The Rt Hon. Sir John Gillen[1]

As a student I first encountered the writings of Descartes. Pursuit of alcohol and rock'n roll in those days left little time to fully understand or appreciate him but the broad concept of Cartesian perfection broadly remained with me. Ideas are the most important item in Cartesian philosophy. The essence or nature of a mind is to think. He famously said "I am certain that I have no knowledge of what is outside me except by means of the ideas I have within me". Ideas are of course not the only modes of thought—for example doubting and judging are also modes of thought -- but the shape, efficiency and simplicity of ideas is really the endpoint of Cartesian perfection.

Hence as an unworthy disciple of Descartes I regard the 2017 conference of The Advocate's Gateway as a shining example of that model of perfection. That legal practitioners, policy makers, advocates, health and social care professionals and academics should meet today fuelled with a passion for justice, bent on sharing our ideas with the aim of shaping efficiently and simply the concept of access to justice for those with a disability is a jewel without price. This is the route out of past and present failure.

That is not to say that the court system unresponsive to the obligation to ensure fairness and true access to justice for those with a disability. Indeed the current shape of that system is developing apace with both those concepts in mind. However, it is my view that fresh approaches and renewed vigour are required if we are to make that system more efficient and simple --- if we are to offer meaningful justice to all. There are too many flaws and inadequacies in our present provision for justice for those with a disability – many of which, if not most, could be allayed with simplicity of thought and simple steps.

I should add at the outset that much of what I say has derived from a Civil and Family Justice review which I have chaired in Northern Ireland over the last two years and the privilege I had attending separate meetings with people with visual impairment or who are deaf and some with serious spinal injuries or a combination of all to hear first-hand accounts of their

---

[1]   This chapter is adapted from The Rt Hon. Sir John Gillen's keynote address delivered on Friday 2nd June 2017 at the Second International Conference of The Advocate's Gateway held at The Law Society, 133 Chancery Lane, London WC2A 1PL.

experiences and the barriers that they encounter when attempting to access court services.

The Current Shape

Justice is a wide concept. It includes justice viewed from the perspective of the system of which the courts are part in ensuring that the indulgence given to one party does not deprive another party of that justice to which they are also entitled. The scope of equality protection has evolved over the years. The existence of disability discrimination legislation is I am sure well known and I do not intend to make unnecessary reference to it.

It is right to say that for some years now the courts have recognised the need to ensure fairness in hearings where one or more parties has a disability. Courts have acted under the spur of:

- Articles 13 and 14 of the *UN Convention on the Rights of Persons with Disabilities*. To "ensure access to justice for persons with disabilities on an equal basis with others" and to "promote training".

- Article 6 of the *European Convention on Human Rights* to ensure a fair hearing and article 14 to ensure there is a benefit from antidiscrimination.

- Article 9(1) The *European Union Directive 2000/78/EC* of 27 November 2000 establishing a general framework for equal treatment in employment and occupation.

- Article 26 of The *European Union Charter on Fundamental Rights* which recognises the rights of persons with disabilities to benefit from measures designed to ensure their independence, social and occupational integration and participation in the life of the community.

The courts must comply with its duty to make reasonable adjustments in order to accommodate the needs of claimants. This is bound to be factor and case specific. Unlike other equality groups, it is recognised that in order to achieve fair participation for people with disabilities, positive action may need to be taken to remove barriers not only in the built environment but also for communication and information.

As a judge I have to recognise that disability can be difficult to assess and is a complex concept, partly because it can take many forms and partly because general awareness and standards in terms of what constitutes disability vary greatly from person to person and across societies. Thus, for example, autism is a spectrum condition (which includes Asperger's

Syndrome) and only around 45% of people with autism have a learning disability. Some people on the autism spectrum have high support needs whereas others do not regard themselves as having a disability at all, instead choosing to self-identify as "neurologically different".

In addition, the effects on the individual of some of the conditions encompassed by the definition of disability contained in the Disability Discrimination legislation, such as certain mental health conditions, can fluctuate over time or as a result of changing circumstances. The types of reasonable adjustments that might be required can, therefore, vary considerably, depending on the person, and may not be static. Consequently, there is no universally accepted definition of disability that meets the needs of all users at all times.

Current prevalence of disability

However, I fear that the first impediment to efficiency is that the prevalence of disability in the community in general and the court system in particular is underestimated and therefore overlooked. The Northern Ireland Survey of Activity Limitation and Disability (NISALD) was published in July 2007 and details the prevalence of disability among children and adults living in private households in Northern Ireland. Initial results published show:

- That 18% of the Northern Ireland population of all ages living in private households experience limitations in their daily living as a consequence of a disability or long term condition.

- Almost two out of every five households in Northern Ireland include at least one person with a limiting disability.

- More than one-fifth (21%) of the adults in Northern Ireland have at least one disability and amongst children 6% are affected by disability.

- There is a clear increase in disability with age, rising to 60% amongst those aged 75 and above. Amongst the very elderly, those aged 85 and above, two-thirds are living with a disability or disabilities.

- There is a higher prevalence of disability amongst females than males. Almost one- quarter (24%) of adult females living in Northern Ireland households indicated that they had some degree of disability, compared with approximately one-fifth (19%) of the adult males.

- The prevalence of disability amongst the very youngest within Northern Ireland households is higher amongst boys than girls. Around 8% of boys aged 15 and under were found to have a disability compared with 4% of girls of the same age.

- The most common types of disabilities reported by adults were associated with chronic illnesses, pain, and mobility and dexterity difficulties. Amongst children, the most common types of disabilities were linked with chronic illnesses, learning difficulties and social/behavioural difficulties.

There is no comprehensive register of people with disabilities. However, latest figures published for persons claiming disability benefits in Northern Ireland show a dramatic increase, with the number of recipients having increased by 45% in the last ten years. Figures show that there are approximately 125,000 (almost one in nine of the population in Northern Ireland) receiving Disability Living Allowance (DLA) Northern Ireland has consistently always had the highest proportion of claimants per head of population in the United Kingdom.

Current efficiency in the court system for those participating with a disability

A second problem we face in generating a momentum of change that will shape our endeavours is that the absence of empirical data makes it difficult to assess the extent to which persons with a disability are involved in the courts or wider justice system in Northern Ireland. That absence of statistics and data has been highlighted in a number of reports, most notably the recently published draft Report on the Implementation of the Convention on the Rights of Persons with Disabilities in Northern Ireland[2], which concludes, amongst other things, that the lack of relevant data is having an adverse impact on the formulation, implementation, monitoring and evaluation of policies and programmes designed to give effect to the Convention.

The only relevant data source available in relation to attendance at courts is the Northern Ireland Courts & Tribunals Service (NICTS) Customer Exit Survey, the most recent having been conducted by NISRA in 2011 at a number of court venues across Northern Ireland. A total of 2,145 customers responded to this survey.

---

[2] Disability Action. (2015) *DRAFT Report on the Implementation of the Convention on the Rights of Persons with Disabilities in Northern Ireland.* Available at http://www.disabilityaction.org/ fs/doc/publications/northern-ireland-draft-report-on-the-implementation-of-the-uncrpd-december-2015-2.doc (accessed July 29, 2017).

A summary of findings from this survey indicates that people with disabilities were also found to be more likely to be in attendance at court in relation to cases appearing in the civil and family courts, itself a troubling fact given the high priority given to assistance in the criminal courts. That survey found:

- When making an application for small claims, people with disabilities are much more likely to use the small claims online option.

- High proportions of people with disabilities felt that they did not have enough information before coming to court.

- While the information leaflets were useful, they did not provide enough detail.

- 70% of respondents were satisfied with venue access for people with physical needs.

- 54% of respondents were satisfied with venue access for people with learning needs.

- 58% of respondents were satisfied with venue access for people with hearing impairment.

- And 54% of respondents were satisfied with venue access for people with visual impairment.

Simple measures would help address this problem of lack of data at a stroke. Minor changes to initiating documentation and prescribed forms in civil and family proceedings – for example, small claims applications, C1 applications in the family court, writs, Certificate of Readiness in the county court, Notice of Setting Down, etc. - should be considered as a means of collating data and identifying at an early stage if either party to proceedings has additional requirements in terms of participating fully in proceedings or attending court.

While serving to promote the interests of disabled persons, it is felt that such a measure will also prompt legal representatives to consider their client's needs at the outset—something that may not be occurring at a sufficiently informed level currently, thereby affording sufficient time for liaison with the court and other organisations regarding any adjustments required.

Current programmes and provision for the disabled

A third problem impeding efficiency is the lack of prioritisation of the needs of the disabled in these straitened economic times. During 2009/10, the Northern Ireland Courts and Tribunal Service (NICTS) completed disability access audits to assess to what extent the estate was meeting its obligations under *The Disability Discrimination Act 1995 (DDA)*. A number of recommendations were made for work to be completed to further improve and enhance inclusive access throughout the estate for disabled users. As a result, a phased programme of work was commenced to upgrade the NICTS estate resulting in improvements to facilities across the court estate, to improve access into the buildings, to assist easier circulation throughout the corridors by re- locating the point of service to an accessible ground floor level or to a venue which had facilities which met the needs of the individuals, installation of induction hearing loops; automatic door openings; DDA compliant door handles and handrails; access ramps; wider witness boxes to accommodate wheelchairs; designated disabled toilets which are universally accessible; passenger lifts; additional signage and colour contrast in paint schemes to highlight doorways and stair treads.

Sadly, however plans to carry out further DDA works to the RCJ under Phase 4 had to be suspended in 2014 as a consequence of financial constraints across all Northern Ireland Civil Service (NICS) departments that resulted in manpower resource within Estates Branch having to be diverted to progress other measures targeted at delivering budgetary savings for the Agency.

A representative from Mindwise I met recently referred to a Court Defendant Support pilot scheme. While it was running, this scheme provided additional support to defendants with mental health issues, to help get them to court through initiatives such as court visits, talking to solicitors about an individual's mental health condition, avoidance behaviour and the difficulties this is likely to present in terms of securing their attendance at court hearings. Unfortunately this had to be suspended because of lack of funding.

In any event whilst it all sounded good if we ever gotten round to perfecting these changes, when I met groups of real people who were deaf, visually impaired and physically injured, one of the main complaints by both hearing and visually impaired people who attend courts is that they are not adequately supported through the court process and insufficient information is available on how to access the services available including interpreter services.

Moreover, little explanation is given to them in advance regarding the layout of the court, car parking spaces, entrances, toilet facilities, etc. In our climate, special disabled entrances and ramps need to be covered. Many premises do have internal steps and, therefore, individual lifts but there is often no-one present to operate these. The disabled person should have the facility to do a dry run in the facilities prior to the hearing. At the very least, lifts should be clearly labelled as regards to how they function as many people are too anxious on the day of the court to take these things on board easily. In addition hey need to be told in advance what persons are present in court, where they are positioned and who is speaking.

Disabled toilets are an absolute necessity and these toilets should not be used as storage rooms as they so often are. People have true access to justice only if adequate facilities are available. Signs on toilets in all court buildings should have Braille or Moon with elevated signage in large letters on a contrasting background to assist people who are visually impaired to be able to attend the proper toilet with minimal aid and embarrassment. There should be someone present in the court building with the specific task of assisting people with disability.

As regards entering the courtroom itself, people want to be able to enter inconspicuously with a pre-assigned space. Table heights should be such as to accommodate a wheelchair and the table should not have anything sticking out underneath the tabled surface which might impede a wheelchair. A straightforward plain table of the right height is needed. It is reassuring to people with disability to have some people with disability on the court staff. This would help them to realise that they were not being "syphoned off".

The use of technology to assist people with visual impairment to access documentary evidence and court documentation is crucial. The RNIB[3] and Sense[4] are two bodies both of whom have professional technical officers who are fully aware of current software and equipment which can be used to assist people who are visually impaired to participate fully in the court process.

It may well be that such equipment can be hired from time to time as and when it is required to avoid the cost of buying in such software, which can quickly go out of date or exist in many versions. Systems such as PenFriend[5] and software, which provides a voice- over for documents in the system with headphones, are but two examples of the kind of software which are vital for people with a visual impairment to be able to participate fully in the system. Similarly, large print should be made available and CDs should be provided of all judgments on request.

---

[3] Royal National Institute for the Blind.
[4] Sense is a national charity that supports people who are deafblind, have sensory impairments or complex needs, to enjoy more independent lives.
[5] Voice labeling system.

Problems of gaining access to courts could be met by virtual reality courts, where a blind person could more comfortably attend in their solicitor's offices with direct Skype or telephonic links to the courtroom. Some blind or deaf people, on the other hand, may wish to exercise their personal choice and avoid isolation and exclusion by actually attending the court venue. The availability of personal choice is vital.

Access to justice means having proper access to solicitors. Solicitors' premises are often not designed to allow easy access in old buildings nor are adequate arrangements in place to facilitate solicitors' initial consultations with hearing and visually impaired clients. There is no point having interpreter services available if you cannot get to use their services.

I found it a bewildering experience to discover that the simplest of steps to shape the idea of a court hearing are often cruelly overlooked in the court setting:

For the deaf or hard of hearing reasonable adjustments often denied include: allowing the person to sit where he or she can hear better; allowing a telecommunication system to communicate; providing a qualified sign interpreter appointed by the court; or providing an assistive listening system or computer-aided transcription device. In circumstances where a specialist communication aid is required, court staff fail to engage with sensory support organisations in relation to the provision of such equipment.

For those with visual impairment or blindness – depending on the needs of the individual and the nature of the disability, reasonable accommodation may involve: providing forms and instructions in Braille, large print or on audio tape; providing assistance at the counter in filling out necessary paperwork; having written materials read out loud in the courtroom, allowing the person to sit closer than usual if of limited vision, or to provide additional lighting. People who are blind or visually impaired can often be assisted by increasing the size of an object, by changing viewing distance, by improving illumination and contrast in written materials. The more words crowded on to a page and the more similar the ink and paper colour, the more difficult it is to discriminate.

For those with cognitive limitations reasonable adjustments often denied may include: having the court and witnesses speak less fast or write things down, when necessary, repeating information using different wording or a different communication approach, allowing time for information to be fully understood, taking periodic breaks;

scheduling court proceedings at a different time to meet the medical needs of the individual; providing a support person at the hearing; or allowing the use of video conferencing technology rather than requiring the individual to appear in person.

Current provision of interpreters

A fourth problem impeding efficiency is lack of joined up thinking across the legal fraternity and government piste. Generally, interpreter provision in Northern Ireland mirrors that already in place in England and Wales. NICTS also has arrangements in place to ensure interpreter provision for the courts in Northern Ireland in order to meet Article 6 of ECHR and DDA requirements. Any person charged with a criminal offence has the right to be informed promptly, in a language which they understand, and in detail, of the nature and cause of the accusation against them and to have the free assistance of an interpreter if they cannot speak the language used in the court If a deaf or hearing impaired defendant requires the assistance of a British Sign Language (BSL), Irish Sign Language (ISL) or other Language Service Professional (LSP), the same arrangements apply.

NICTS also arrange and pay for interpreters in all civil, family, coroners, tribunal hearings and Enforcement of Judgments interviews for people who are deaf and hearing impaired to ensure fullest compliance with the DDA and UN Convention on the Rights of Persons with

Disabilities. Where a person has multiple communication difficulties, such as deaf-blindness or speech and hearing disabilities, NICTS will work with them to ensure that their interpretation needs are met as effectively as possible. Telephone interpreting services are currently available at all public counters. In addition, if a document needs to be translated for the purposes of the court, procedures are in place to facilitate this.

Again, it all sounds good. However, a recent report on the Implementation of the Convention on the Rights of Persons with Disabilities in Northern Ireland published in December 2015[6] revealed that whilst there are two recognised sign languages, Irish Sign Language (ISL) and British Sign Language (BSL) there are currently only fifteen fully qualified interpreters in Northern Ireland serving a population of approximately 5,000 sign language users and thousands of people with whom they communicate.

Moreover, too many in the legal profession are themselves unaware of the obligations cast on them to arrange interpreter services for clients. Too few are aware that the Disability Discrimination Act, which came into effect

[6] Fn 2.

in 1995 and has been amended a number of times since by Regulations implemented in Northern Ireland, makes it unlawful for service providers to discriminate against people with disability in certain circumstances and asserts "those who are deaf are recognised under the DDA and therefore, solicitors/barristers are responsible for the booking and payment of sign language interpreters".

Current Information provision (including guidance materials)

A fifth problem is the failure to make truly informed decisions about what information needs to be provided to people with a disability. NICTS has produced a range of information leaflets covering court related activities and processes – for example, jury attendance, small claims, divorce and separation, youth courts, etc. These leaflets and links are available on the NICTS website and in hard copy from NICTS by post or at court office counters. In addition, the website also provides information, including access details for those with a disability, about each of the courthouses for people coming to a court building. It is worth recording that the Law Society, as part of the Connecting with our Community pilot initiative to promote greater access to information about the profession of solicitors, has to date produced 36 leaflets on a range of services provided by solicitors in Irish, Arabic, Portuguese, Chinese, French, German, Polish, Spanish and Czech.

Nonetheless during the course of discussions I have had with interested parties troubling issues were also raised in relation to access to information for persons with disabilities, in particular those with sensory impairments. The importance of ensuring inclusive provision of information about court proceedings and court hearings in a user friendly way, using appropriate language and format, were stressed alongside the need to consider additional supports for people who are deaf and blind and those with communication difficulties seeking to access information and services, including online alternatives.

The use of various media, including SMS/text messaging and social media sites such as Twitter, YouTube and Facebook, to communicate information to parties, groups and their representatives was also suggested as many disability groups already have a presence on these media sites.

It is not enough to simply make wheelchair access available in courts and believe that this is the job done. In my discussions with Disability groups I found that access to information for wheelchair users at some court venues soon emerged as a gap in our current provision alongside difficulties making contact with Disability Liaison Officers (DLOs) or Customers Service Officers (CSOs).

I suspect that in response to the concerns in this regard raised in our preliminary report a list of DLO/CSO telephone contact details has now been published on the NICTS website and shared with the NI Direct exchange. Individual courthouse information leaflets have also been updated to include these details. Information leaflets are provided in alternative fonts and formats on request and there are also a number of useful links included on the NICTS website to other key business areas which users can access for assistance in progressing business through the justice system. We have recommended that current website design and content could certainly benefit from review in terms of provision for visually and hearing impaired customers. Later this year, NICTS will request that the web development team in NI Direct re-develop its internet web site, not only to give it a 'fresh' appearance but also to comply with the WCAG (Web Content Accessibility Guidelines 4.0) which aims to make web content more accessible to people with disabilities.

In considering how information can be made more universally accessible, there is clearly much that voluntary sector support organisations such as the RNIB, the Royal National Institute for the Deaf (RNID) and the Royal College of Speech and Language Therapists (RCSLT) can offer by way of advice, practical support and best practice to promote effective communication with people with disabilities. We in the court system must embrace their help and expertise more readily. Regular and informed input from external organisations on what gaps or problems people with disabilities routinely encounter must become a hallmark of the justice system.

Current special measures provision

Piecemeal or partial recognition of the rights of people with a disability is a continuing frustration. It is the illogicality of the divisions that confounds me. Two examples will suffice. First, special measures. *The Criminal Evidence (Northern Ireland) Order 1999* specifies a range of measures that can be made available on application to children; witnesses with a mental disorder or a significant impairment of intelligence and social functioning, a physical disability or disorder; and those who are suffering fear and distress in connection with giving evidence in the criminal courts such as the use of screens, live link, removal of wigs and gowns, evidence in private, the use of intermediaries and aids to communication.

The Northern Ireland Law Commission (NILC), in its report entitled Vulnerable Witnesses in Civil Proceedings, published in 2011, considered the issue of the use of special measures in civil proceedings based on research which suggested that victims and witnesses in civil proceedings should be entitled to the same support as victims and witnesses in criminal proceedings. It recommended that a scheme of special measures be put in place on a statutory basis in relation to civil proceedings in Northern Ireland recommending, inter alia, that people with mental illness, personality disorder or physical disability should be eligible for similar special measures if the quality of their evidence is likely to be diminished because of that illness, disability or disorder. The special measures would include: the use of screening; the removal of gown and wigs in civil proceedings; video- recording of witnesses' evidence-in-chief in limited circumstances in relation to private and public law proceedings under *The Children (NI) Order 1995*; the use of intermediaries; the use of communication aids; that witnesses who give evidence by way of a live television link can avail of the services of a suitably trained supporter in the live television link room.

To date those simple protections have not yet been fully implemented in the Civil justice system. I can see no reason why the recommendations of the NILC in this regard should not be implemented if we are to comply with our domestic and international obligations to ensure that the disabled are not to be deprived of real access to justice.

Secondly registered intermediaries (RIs), who are communication specialists, were introduced into the criminal justice process in Northern Ireland in May 2013. RIs are professionals with specialist skills in communication, coming from backgrounds such as speech and language therapy and social work. They are required to pass accredited training, are bound by a Code of Practice and Code of Ethics and are subject to a complaints procedure. Taken together, this ensures that RIs have the necessary skills to assist those with communication difficulties to give their evidence. RIs are available in criminal cases for victims, witnesses, suspects and defendants, at police interview and court stages.

There is currently no funded scheme in Northern Ireland England and Wales or Scotland for the provision of registered intermediaries in the civil and family courts, although there is anecdotal evidence to suggest that registered intermediaries have been engaged to support people in a small number of civil and family justice matters. It was widely acknowledged by participants in discussions that I have had that the use of RIs in criminal proceedings was a positive intervention that has been successful in enabling those with communication difficulties to be interviewed and give evidence in a way that best suits their needs. It was strongly felt that intermediaries can also be of assistance to people who are deaf and blind and those with speech impairment and other communication difficulties as they could provide useful input in relation to early identification of individual requirements so that steps can be taken to ensure appropriate communication supports are in place. It was suggested that people who are deaf be afforded the opportunity to train and undertake the role of intermediary in the courts. Why are those who are disabled being denied this facility in civil and family cases?

Current disability awareness

A fundamental prerequisite of any fair and just system is disability awareness training and the need to tackle stereotypes. The draft Report on the Implementation of the Convention on the Rights of Persons with Disabilities in Northern Ireland (December 2015)[7] made this very point.

It is a strongly held view amongst those supporting people with disability that everyone coming into contact with people with disability attending court - most particularly the judiciary, legal practitioners, court staff and ancillary contractors - should receive disability awareness training. RNIB, RNID, RCSLT and other voluntary sector organisations supporting the disabled are keen to work with the Law Society and Bar Council on improving awareness/training for practitioners and would greatly welcome the opportunity to liaise with the Judicial Studies Board regarding the delivery of e-learning, audio/visual and interactive online training packages for the judiciary.

There is no doubt that some measure of training has been provided for the judiciary in Northern Ireland[8] and I am sure elsewhere. Further

---

[7] Fn 2.

[8] Much work has been done by the judiciary in the area of physical disability, mental disability and equality awareness to ensure that the judiciary is properly trained in and apprised of the relevant issues. Some recent examples include:

JSB workshop on equality awareness, 4 March 2016.

Dealing with litigants with mental health issues – 24 February 2016.

Dealing with litigants with mental health issues – 16 September 2015.

The Law Through Interpreters – A Presentation of Rights, Evidence and Procedure in Multilingual Courts – 17 June 2015.

Cybercrime workshop – 27 May 2015 and 24 February 2015.

Getting the Balance Right: Children and the Court – 24 January 2015.

Vulnerable Witnesses – Tuesday 18 November 2014.

Judicial Restrictions and Media Access to and Reporting of Court Proceedings – 21 October 2014.

The most recent training workshop took place in March 2016, delivered by Judge Hugh

refresher training is planned and consideration is also being given to the development of e-learning disability awareness training packages for judges.

The judiciary also have access to the Judicial College's Equal Treatment Bench Book, which provides detailed guidance for judges and judicial office holders on equal treatment in respect of such matters as race, belief systems, children, disability, women and sexual orientation.[9]

However have we in the legal profession more than a passing acquaintance with or a deep insight into the day-to-day issues that confront those with a disability? How many of my legal colleagues are aware of Report on the Implementation of the Convention on the Rights of Persons with Disabilities in Northern Ireland (December 2015) which found:

- The absence of any requirement for public bodies to monitor or evaluate Disability Action Plans which, amongst people with disabilities, means that these are often seen as little more than paper exercises that make no real impact on their lives.

- Persons with disabilities continue to experience issues with access to transport and physical access to premises and public spaces including courts.

- Accessible communication continues to be a barrier to disabled people accessing their right to freedom of expression and opinion, despite the Northern Ireland

- Disability Strategy having a strategic priority in relation to increasing accessibility/inclusiveness of communication so people with disabilities can access information as independently as possible and make informed choices.

- Signage, public address systems, the Internet, telephones and many other communication channels are generally designed for people who can hear, see and use their hands easily. Therefore making these media accessible to people with disabilities can require some ingenuity.

- While the strategy states that the Department of Finance (DoF) will produce a plan with specific actions to promote digital inclusion

---

Howard, a Regional Tribunal Judge in England who is also designated a Diversity and Community Relations Judge.

[9] The full text of the Bench Book, with 2015 amendments, is available on the NICTS Judiciary website and includes a general approach for judges to adopt when considering potential disability issues and guidance on how these might be overcome so that all parties in proceedings can participate as required.

for people with disabilities, there has been no progress in this area, notwithstanding that people with disabilities in Northern Ireland are less likely to access the Internet than their counterparts in the rest of the UK.

A recent case in the Court of Appeal in Northern Ireland called *Galo v Bombardier*[10] (Galo's case) involving an applicant with autism in a Fair Employment Tribunal observed that the contents of the Equal Treatment Bench Book must become part of the culture of all court hearings, with specific reference to the need to accommodate those with a disability. It emerged in that case that the ETBB was rarely consulted in that tier. That case sets out a number of guiding principles which a court should observe in such cases, including the invocation of an early "ground rules hearing" to ensure the proceedings are tailored to the disability in question.

Early Intervention

The importance of identifying the moment at which assistance is given to those with a disability has long been underestimated. It is essential that, where reasonable adjustments are required to support attendance at court or participation in court proceedings, these are identified at the earliest possible opportunity. It is important, therefore, that legal practitioners, frequently the first point of contact for people coming to court, play a proactive role in identifying the precise nature of the reasonable adjustment required and take steps to ensure that the DLO at the relevant court office is notified accordingly in advance of the case being listed for hearing. The changes proposed to court documentation above will prompt legal practitioners to consider individual requirements at an early stage. Lawyers need to be aware of indicators of disability and be proactive in seeking information from the clients.[11]

Judges need to be more interventionist at the earliest possible moment in cases where one party has a disability to ensure their effective participation. At an early stage, if unrepresented, they should be fully informed of the advantages of McKenzie friends or an independent mental health advocate.

"The Northern Ireland Court of Appeal decision in the case of Galo has placed a spotlight on procedural fairness when a party to legal proceedings has a disability and the stage at which it has to be addressed. Mr Galo has Asperger's Syndrome. He appealed

---

[10] *Galo v Bombardier Aerospace UK* [2016] NICA 45.
[11] Cooper, Penny and Allely, Clare. 2017. "You Can't Judge a Book by its Cover: evolving professional responsibilities and 'judgecraft' when a party has Asperger's Syndrome," *NILQ* 68(1) 35-58.

the decision of the Industrial Tribunal which dismissed his claim against his previous employers. He was suspended from work for alleged gross misconduct, namely throwing 'an item of work equipment behind him' and shouting at an occupational health doctor examining him. His employers investigated and dismissed his victimisation grievance and, after a disciplinary investigation and hearing, terminated his employment for gross misconduct. He made a claim in the industrial tribunal for, amongst other things, unfair dismissal and disability discrimination. Prior to Mr Galo launching his claim, his employers obtained a medical report from a clinical psychologist, which noted an earlier educational psychologist report concluding Mr Galo had Asperger's Syndrome. No attempt was made to engage with or address his disability of [Asperger's Syndrome]'. Despite the claimant furnishing the court and the parties with medical evidence that he was mentally unwell (in addition to having Asperger's Syndrome) and thus unable to comply with case management directions and unfit to attend on the date of the final hearing, the tribunal dismissed his claim in his absence. The Court of Appeal allowed the appeal, finding that Mr Galo had not benefited from fair case management or a fair [final] hearing."[12]

Importantly one of the steps the court advocated for future cases was the use of 'ground rule hearings' at the outset of proceedings. This would address such detailed matters of:

- The approach to questioning of the claimant and to the method of cross-examination by him/her. Adaptations to questioning may be necessary to facilitate the evidence of a vulnerable person.

- The manner, tenor, tone, language and duration of questioning appropriate to the witness's problems.

- Whether it is necessary for the Tribunal to obtain an expert report to identify what steps are required in order to ensure a fair procedure tailored to the needs of the particular applicant.

- The applicant under a disability, if a personal litigant, must have the procedures of the court fully explained to him and advised as to the availability of pro bono assistance/McKenzie Friends/ voluntary sector help available.

[12] Ibid., 37-38.

- Recognition must be given to the possibility that those with learning disabilities need extra time even if represented to ensure that matters are carefully understood by them.

- Great care should be taken with the language and vocabulary that is utilised to ensure that the directions given at the ground rules hearing are being fully understood.

- Consideration should be given to the need for respondent's counsel to offer cross- examination and questions in writing to assist the claimant with the claimant being allowed some time to consult, if represented, with his counsel.

Conclusion

I started with Descartes. Let me finish with Neitzsche. He said "Consider the cattle grazing as they pass you by; they do not know what is meant by yesterday or today. (They are) fettered to the moment and its pleasure or displeasure, and thus neither melancholy nor bored. The cow is content to be a cow for it is contained in the present, like a number without any awkward fraction left out".

As lawyers and judges we cannot chew the cud without an awareness of having done this before or that we will do it again in the future. Worse, we know that the future itself will at some point become the past. Do we as lawyers, clinicians and professionals in the field of disability forget this in an instant of bovine tranquillity and allow things to go on as they have been, consoled only by the dispiriting realisation that everything passes eventually or on the other hand do we frustrate ourselves by dwelling on the inadequacies of the system being wedded to the current malaise of perfection anxiety.

The truth of the matter is that the prejudice of being human is the requirement to cultivate ideas and reflect. If we follow Cartesian perfection in this field I am certain that we will reject the concept of bovine tranquillity and that changes will take place to ensure that true access to meaningful justice for those who are disabled will occur notwithstanding that we are well short of perfection.

CHAPTER 3

Bringing the court closer to the person with disability: Judicial exemption from the Equality Act and interference with reasonable adjustments for litigants with physical disabilities.

Dr. Anton van Dellen

In England and Wales the Equality Act 2010 is the key piece of legislation that is engaged in protecting the rights of litigants with disabilities in the court system. This is particularly relevant under section 4 of the Equality Act 2010 (EA 2010), as disability is a protected characteristic. Under section 6(1) of the EA 2010:

'A person (P) has a disability if (a) P has a physical ... impairment, and (b) the impairment has a substantial and long-term adverse effect on P's ability to carry out normal day-to-day activities.'

Under section 20 of the EA 2010, there is a duty imposed to make reasonable adjustments. There are two main requirements for litigants with physical disabilities.

The first, under section 20(3) of the EA 2010, is a requirement, where a provision, criterion or practice of A's puts a disabled person at a substantial disadvantage in relation to a relevant matter in comparison with persons who are not disabled, to take such steps as it is reasonable to have to take to avoid the disadvantage.

The second, under section 20(4) of the EA 2010, is a requirement, where a physical feature puts a disabled person at a substantial disadvantage in relation to a relevant matter in comparison with persons who are not disabled, to take such steps as it is reasonable to have to take to avoid the disadvantage.

Under section 20(9) of the EA 2010, a reference to avoiding a substantial disadvantage includes providing a reasonable means of avoiding it. There is a very broad definition to a physical feature which puts a disabled person at a substantial disadvantage as, under section 20(10), it includes any other physical element of quality.

Where a litigant with a physical disability is unable to travel to a more distant court, they appear to be able to request that the court system makes a reasonable adjustment and request a listing at a court centre which is closer to them. It is hard to imagine that this is particularly difficult or controversial, but as will become apparent below, the judicial exemption to the EA 2010 appears to have emptied this duty of any meaning in relation to such a request.

The judicial exemption to the EA 2010

Schedule 3 Part 1 of the EA 2010, provides an exemption for (a) a judicial function; and (b) anything done on behalf of, or on the instructions of a person exercising a judicial function. Deciding the venue of the hearing is considered to be listing function, which is consequently considered to be a judicial function and not an administrative function. Accordingly, the request for a reasonable adjustment for a closer court venue by a litigant with a physical disability would, somewhat surprisingly, appear to be exempt from the EA 2010 and not subject to the duty to make reasonable adjustments. Of course, as a general legal principle, an exception should be narrowly rather than broadly construed.

The Bench Book

The Equal Treatment Bench Book[1] (Bench Book) is the key guidance available to all courts and tribunals in England, Wales and Northern Ireland. The Bench Book, a very comprehensive set of guidance, gives practical guidance to judges about how they may comply with their duty under the EA 2010. It is also a document with which many practitioners and litigants are far less familiar; it not, for example, being included in the civil litigation module of the Bar Professional Training Course.

The Bench Book is rooted in the philosophy of combatting social exclusion, which refers to a situation of economic or social disadvantage which is broader than concepts like poverty or deprivation and includes disadvantage which arises from discrimination. The Bench Book explicitly recognises that many individuals drawn into all aspects of the justice system will come from socially excluded backgrounds.

However, despite being a very comprehensive document, the Bench Book is not clear in the guidance in the 'Physical Disability' section at [3] whether a request for a closer venue for a litigant with a physical disability is an administrative or judicial function:

> 3.   Steps should be taken at an early stage to ensure that suitable adjustments to the normal arrangements are made so as to avoid an adjournment when the impairment becomes apparent.   Not all of

---

[1]   Judicial College (2013), *Equal Treatment Bench Book 2013*. Available at www.judiciary.gov. uk/publications/equal-treatment-bench-book/ (accessed July 29, 2017).

these adjustments can be made by the administration and in some instances directions will be required from a judge.

However, the 'Disability' section of the Bench Book at [66] suggest that it is the judiciary's role to assist the administration to provide appropriate facilities suggesting that it is an administrative function that falls within the EA 2010 and is not exempted:

> 66. Whilst the *core* judicial functions are exempted[,] administration of Courts and Tribunal venues will … require compliance as to the provision of appropriate facilities, and legal action mat follow failure in that regard. However, it is the role of the judiciary to *assist the administration* to comply with its legal obligations. (emphases added)

The case law

There is very limited assistance from the case law, given that it simply refers parties to the Bench Book, rather than providing guidance as to the scope of the exception.

As per Brooke LJ in *R. (on the application of King) v Isleworth Crown Court* [2001] EWHC Admin 22 at [43-45]:

> 43. I wish to stress in this judgment that this [Bench Book] advice is important advice which every judge and every justice of the peace is under a duty to take into account when hearing a case involving people with one disability or another.

> 44. Article 6 of the European Convention of Human Rights and the jurisprudence of the Strasbourg Court underline the importance of fairness in court procedure. …

> 45. I know the difficulties the court have with their listing and the pressures which are on them to conduct their business economically and efficiently, but fairness is very important.

This approach was endorsed in *CPS v Fraser* [2014] Eq. L.R. 535; [2014] I.C.R. D18 (EAT), which held that judges should take account of the guidance in the Bench Book concerning litigants with a disability.

U v Butler & Wilson Ltd (2014) (unreported) (EAT) also referenced the Equal Treatment Bench Book at [65]. In this paragraph, the EAT held that a disability known to the tribunal is an important factor when making case management decisions:

65.   We do not, in this judgment, need to adjudicate upon the extent to which the specific statutory exemptions in the Equality Act 2010 are affected by what is said to be the incorporation of the [United Nations Convention on the Rights of People with Disabilities 2006 (UNCRPD)] into domestic UK law. It is sufficient that we agree and accept that *the fact of the appellant's disability, as known to the [Employment Judge],* was an important factor to which she *had to have regard* when *making case management decisions* in accordance with the overriding objective and reflecting good practice *as advised by the Equal Treatment Bench Book.*
(emphases added)

The most recent case to look at this issue was *Blacker v SRA* [2017] EWHC 892. An appeal to the Court of Appeal was dismissed on paper. The Appellant, who complained of a physical disability which he asserted placed him at risk of travelling long distances, requested a hearing in the North-West of England rather than in London. However, William Davis J held that the request for a closer venue was a listing function and was consequently exempt as a judicial function under the EA 2010. At [46], it was held that exemption was "likely to be limited to core adjudicative and listing functions" and further held at [47] that the venue of a hearing is a listing function which is a judicial function and the Equality Act did not apply to the decision about venue.

It is arguable that even if the exception in the EA 2010 does apply, the court should still have made reasonable adjustments as a result of the incorporation into UK law of the United Nations Convention on the Rights of People with Disabilities 2006 (UNCRPD) ratified by the UK on 7th August 2009 and by the European Union on 23rd December 2010.There are also arguments that failing to make reasonable adjustments is an infringement of the Appellant's Article 6 and 14 rights, by failing to ensure that parties are on an equal footing.

Conclusion

The judicial exemption from the EA 2010 in relation to deciding the venue of hearing is of great concern, as it appears to carve out an exception for the very type of reasonable adjustment that would be needed by a litigant with a physical disability who is unable to travel to a distant court or tribunal. The obvious solution is that the exception should be narrowly construed so that the choice of venue is an administrative function (and thus amenable to reasonable adjustments under the EA 2010) and not a judicial function. Alternatively, it may be that the solution is an amendment to the legislation to afford appropriate protection to litigants with physical disabilities, without risking them falling foul of the judicial exemption to the EA 2010.

CHAPTER 4

Judges and lawyers: Getting it wrong about the disabled for all these years?

John Horan

Discrimination is an insidious practice. Discriminatory law undermines the rule of law because it is the antithesis of fairness. It brings the law into disrepute. It breeds resentment. It fosters an inequality of outlook which is demeaning alike to those unfairly benefited and those unfairly prejudiced. Of course all law, civil and criminal, has to draw distinctions. ... Like cases should be treated alike, unlike cases should not be treated alike. ... But there are certain grounds of factual difference by which common accord are not acceptable, without more, as a basis for a different legal treatment. Differences of race or sex or religion are obviously examples. Sexual orientation is another. ... Unless some good reason can be shown, differences such as these do not justify differences in treatment. Unless good reason exists, differences in legal treatment based on grounds such as these are appropriately stigmatised as discriminatory.[1]

My Lords, it is not so very long ago in this country that people might be refused access to a so-called "public" because of their sex or the colour of their skin; that a women might automatically be paid three quarter of what a man was paid for doing exactly the same job; that a landlady offering rooms to let might lawfully put a "no blacks" notice in her window. We now realise that this was wrong.[2]

Introduction

The law relating to all Judges, magistrates or other judicial decision makers to make reasonable accommodation in accessing the court process to all disabled people is comparatively new. As co-counsel below the Employment Appeal Tribunal in *Rackham*[3] and co-author of the appellant's skeleton argument in *Galo*[4] the quality and quantity of articles has been breath-taking.[5] Here are my thoughts on the subject.

---

[1] Per Lord Nicholls of Birkenhead, *Ghairdan v. Godin-Mendoza* [2004] UKHL 30, paragraph 9.
[2] Per Baroness Hale of Richmond, *Ghairdan*, above, paragraph paragraph 130.
[3] *Rackham v. NHS Professionals Limited* [2015] UKEAT 0110/15/1612.
[4] *Galo v Bombardier Aerospace UK* [2016] NICA 25.
[5] Most recently in 2017, Penny Cooper and Clare Allely *"You can't judge a book by its cover"* NILQ 68(1): 35-58, which lays out in detail LJ Dillon judgement in *Galo*. Surely a "one spot shop" as to law in the area in Northern Ireland.

The law after the cases of Rackham and Galo
– England, Wales and Northern Ireland

Following *Rackham* and *Galo*, the law is, I think, as follows:

There is an obligation on every court to act fairly – an obligation which the common law requires and which is required of every court, tribunal and decision-making body – see *Galo* paragraph 47.[6]

The protection of human rights permeates our legal system. When domestic law fails to reflect fully a requirement of the European Convention on Human Rights it is open to Parliament to legislate in order to fulfil the UK's international obligations but also to courts to take into account these international obligations both in determining the common law and the interpretation of legislation – see *Galo* paragraph 49.

In considering whether fair procedures have been followed by a judicial decision-making body, the Court of Appeal is not merely to review the reasonableness of the decision-maker's judgment as to what fairness requires. The court must determine for itself whether a fair procedure was followed. The purpose of procedural fairness is to ensure that there would be better decisions as a result of the decision-maker receiving all relevant information and that such information is properly tested. Procedural requirements that decision-makers should listen to persons who have something to say promotes confidence between the actions of the decision-maker and the law by which their actions are judged – see *Galo* paragraph 50.

Cases concerning the common law and fairness in the disabled context will permeate with increasing emphasis on fairness arising out of the UN Convention of Rights of Persons with Disabilities (UNCRPD), Article 13 – see *Galo* paragraph 51.

To work out what an international convention means the court must determine, under Article 31 of the Geneva Convention, what the purpose of the Convention is and the purpose is to be found inter alia, in the preamble to the Convention. In the case of the UNCRPD, having read the preamble, the Convention must be read

---

[6] This is in addition to the duty on the Court and Tribunal Service to comply with the Equality Act 2010 in providing facilities and services.

with human, moral and realistic expectations in mind – see *Rackham* paragraph 35.

The same purposive approach is to be followed by courts and tribunals whenever domestic legislation, guidance or "rules" which are designed to bring the UNCRPD into force: human, moral, realistic expectations.[7]

The courts have general non-binding guidance and practical advice given to them by the Equal Treatment Bench Book ("ETBB"[8]) in considering how best to accommodate disabled litigants in the court process. It is clear therefore that the courts should pay particular attention to the ETBB in considering questions of disability and reasonable adjustment, including mental disability – see *Galo* paragraph 53(3).

Decisions concerning case management should address the needs of the individual concerned insofar as these are reasonable. Individuals should be given the opportunity to express their needs. Expert evidence may be required (see paragraph, chapter 7 of the ETBB and paragraph 23(4) of *Galo*).

An early ground rules hearing is indicated by the ETBB in almost all cases – see *Galo* paragraph 53(7).

Realism must be taken into account when assessing what sort of questions the judge must have in mind in order to deal with disability properly and how far the court or tribunal is to put itself in the position of having received all relevant information from the applicant or other sources before making the appropriate order or directions – see *Galo* paragraph 53(7).[9]

What are lawyers actually to do?

Lawyers should pause when they read *Galo* to think about what this actually means as a representative of a disabled client or, indeed, facing a

---

[7]   "Realistic" means realistic for brings about the articles of UNCRPD.

[8]   Published by the Judicial College in 2013.

[9]   And the judge should be realistic about what "realism" is. See, for a graphic demonstration *Galo* itself and LJ Gillen's comments on it at paragraph 53(7). A judge who hasn't been on a full training course would be at risk of not equipping himself with a picture of what the person's disability is and the reasonable adjustment on offer.

claim bought by a disabled person and actually addressing the social needs of the disabled community.

As is made plain from Article 13 of the UNCRPD, this is much wider than a "discrimination problem" which is dealt with by the court or tribunal. This applies for the litigant in criminal, family, employment and commercial proceedings as well, as well as the various tribunals and other bodies which have to have a person making judicial decisions over a person who is disabled. Incidentally, it is also clear that it applies to witnesses and other people who are disabled who have some connection to the court process. It is a culture of discrimination that we should all embrace and fight against: *Galo* paragraph 61.

When I am invited by barristers, solicitors and law centre workers to "cash out" what changes to their practice are appropriate, I advise as follows:

- Train all of their staff in the UN Convention and introduce them, if they do not already know it, to the ETBB and, in particular, chapters 1, 5, 6 and 7. You can't use it if you don't know it!

- Download from the internet a (free!) e-copy of the ETBB from www.judiciary.gov.uk/publications/equal-treatment/bench-book and have several hard copies around the office so that it becomes natural to look up the Bench Book during any material problem.

- Have a standard "conference procedure" and "client letter" writing process whereby the client's disability and any adverse effects that the likely court process may have are routinely discussed and early resolved with the court or tribunal.

- Have a paragraph in both interpartes correspondence and the court or tribunal letter raising the fact that the client is or may be disabled and may need the court to make reasonable adjustments. This should be done early in the process.

- Challenge both the other side and the court or tribunal service with the fact that people who are disabled have a right under Article 13 of the UN Convention to expect reasonable adjustments to be carried out by the court service and the judge. If appropriate, it should also be pointed out that the client with a disability must not be required to pay for any additional adjustments or that is very likely to involve a breach of Article 13 itself.

- In cases of complex disability, the court or tribunal should be asked for a *ground rules hearing*. Thought can be given as to whether a medical view needs to be obtained.

- Evidence is key to answering the question: What are the needs for *this particular person*? The lawyer should (respectfully!) remind the judge/person making the judicial decision that the way they dealt with other cases is not material.

Discrimination, judges and judgments

I think that the heart of *Galo* is this:

59. This case highlights perhaps the need for there to be better training of both the judiciary and the legal profession in the needs of the disabled.
...
61. We have formed the clear impression that the ETBB does not appear to be part of the culture of these hearings. That is a circumstance which must fundamentally change within a structure of a correction to ensure that this situation does not recur. Had there been proper cognisance of the content of the ETBB we are satisfied that a different approach would have been adopted in this case.

The two themes are:

Proper educational for judges and the legal profession about the needs of the disabled.

A "structure of correction" – surely a change in each court's procedures and (just as important) a change in courts' attitudes toward disabled people.

I see many people who come for advice on the court making reasonable adjustments to its procedure is cases which affect them. I know at first hand the effect the judgement in *Galo* has on those people: it re-established trust that the courts genuinely what to hear what people with disability have to say. It is judgecraft at its finest – recognition which, paradoxically, is a sign to the disabled community that the courts are willing to change.

The Equality and Human Rights Commission expressly raised *Galo* in its criticism of the UK Government and its record of compliance with the UNCRPD.[10] The International Commission, set up by the UN Convention had this clearly in mind when it asked the UK Government questions

---

[10] *Disability rights in the UK* page 34, footnote 145.

which relate to a speedy, effective and efficient procedure for people with disability and the training of the judiciary.[11] We await the UK governments response; however in response to a journalist question about this[12], the Justice Office stated:

> While reading their full conduct (i.e. the ETBB) is not mandatory, judges are expected to be aware of the protective characteristics in the ETBB and to seek and to be able to access the more detailed references, in particular areas, just as they do with all of the other bench books. ….The college is satisfied that the awareness of this resource is high and…is regularly promoted (with emphases).

As the disabled barrister I am forced to ask: Is this enough?

On two occasions leave to appeal has been refused by the Court of Appeal in cases remarkably similar to *Galo*.[13] In both cases *Galo* and arguments based upon it were rejected as unarguable. Surely the disabled community in England & Wales deserve at full judgement explain (if it is so) why they are not to be granted the same protection as the counterpart is Northern Ireland.

---

[11] *List of issues in relation to the intial report of the United Kingdom of Briatan and Northern Ireland* paragraph 8 a) and d).
[12] John Pring, disabilitynewsservice.com.
[13] Rackham v NHS Professional Trust (LJ Johnson) 14/12/16, Webb v Webber and Ors (LJ Maccombe) 15/03/17.

CHAPTER 5

Challenges in defining and identifying a suspect's vulnerability in criminal proceedings: What's in a name and who's to blame?

Lore Mergaerts, Professor Dirk Van Daele, Professor Geert Vervaeke[1]

Introduction

Both case law of the European Court of Human Rights (ECtHR) and recent EU legal instruments on the one hand, and academic literature on the other, recognise the specific needs of so-called vulnerable suspects. From that perspective, the important role of the criminal defence lawyer in compensating for a suspect's vulnerability is stressed, especially because vulnerable persons need special care to understand their legal rights and to improve the quality of their statements. Consequently, the defence lawyer has to identify early on whether his client can be qualified as vulnerable. There is, however, still a lack of theorization on the precise meaning of vulnerability in criminal proceedings. In that sense, it remains unclear who – and under what conditions – is to be considered as being vulnerable. In addition, the (early) identification of a suspect's vulnerability raises important challenges for the defence lawyer.

The issues raised in this chapter (and at the second international conference of The Advocate's Gateway in June 2017) result from the ongoing PhD project at the Faculty of Law of KU Leuven (Belgium) of the first author, under the supervision of the second and third author of this chapter. First, the different perspectives concerning the concept of vulnerability will be described, especially focusing on adult suspects in criminal proceedings. Next, the differences between and bottlenecks within these perspectives will be discussed, followed by a proposal for a new conceptual framework of a suspect's vulnerability in criminal proceedings. In addition, several challenges in the identification of a suspect's vulnerability by the defence lawyer will be outlined. Where considered relevant, legal and practical insights from the Belgian case will also be discussed throughout this chapter.

[1] *Department of Criminal Law and Criminology, Faculty of Law, KU Leuven Herbert Hooverplein 10 Box 3418, B-3000 Leuven, Belgium.* Corresponding author (lore. mergaerts@kuleuven.be).

Different perspectives regarding the conceptualization of a suspect's vulnerability

The attention given to a suspect's vulnerability at a European level: the cross-fertilization between the Council of Europe and the European Union[2]

The case law of the European Court of Human Rights

The case law of the European Court of Human Rights (ECtHR) with respect to a suspect's vulnerability seems to have developed along two pathways. On the one hand, it is stated that this vulnerability results from the mere involvement in a criminal procedure. In the leading case of *Salduz v. Turkey* – and in subsequent case law[3] – the ECtHR ruled that during the investigative stage:

> an accused often finds himself in a particularly vulnerable position [...], the effect of which is amplified by the fact that legislation on criminal procedure tends to become increasingly complex, notably with respect to the rules governing the gathering and use of evidence.[4]

It is furthermore explicitly stated that "in most cases, this particular vulnerability can only be properly compensated for by the assistance of a lawyer whose task it is, among other things, to help to ensure respect of the right of an accused not to incriminate himself".[5] On the other hand, however, it can also be delineated from the case law of the ECtHR that certain suspects are to be considered particularly vulnerable. In this regard, the ECtHR considers as relevant factors: the age and maturity of a suspect, chronic alcoholism, a physical disability and belonging to a socially disadvantaged group.[6]

The perspective taken in legal instruments of the European Union

Not only at the level of the Council of Europe, but also at the EU level, increased attention towards suspects' vulnerability can be observed. In

---

[2]   This part of the chapter is based on the following article (in Dutch): Lore Mergaerts, Dirk Van Daele and Geert Vervaeke, "Naar specifieke procedurele rechten voor kwetsbare verdachten en beklaagden: een nieuwe stap in de Europeanisering van de Belgische strafprocedure," *Nullum Crimen* 10 (2015): 459-472.

[3]   See for instance also *Panovits v. Cyprus* (2009), ECtHR; *Shabelnik v. Oekraïne* (2009), ECtHR; *Pishchalnikov v. Russia* (2009), ECtHR; *Dayanan v. Turkey* (2010), ECtHR.

[4]   *Salduz v Turkey* (2008), ECtHR para 54.

[5]   Ibid.

[6]   See for instance *T. v UK* (1999), ECtHR para 62, 84-89; *V. v UK* (1999), ECtHR para 86; *S.C. v UK* (2004), ECtHR para 28-29; *Panovits v Cyprus* (2008), ECtHR para 67; *Plonka v Poland* (2009), ECtHR para 38; *Bortnik v Ukraine* (2011), ECtHR para 43; *Blokhin v Russia* (2016), ECtHR para 194 and 199.

a Green Paper of 2003, the European Commission developed minimum procedural safeguards for suspects and defendants in criminal proceedings throughout the European Union.[7] In that context, it is emphasised that specific groups of persons cannot fully participate in criminal proceedings because of certain individual factors. More specifically, the Green Paper contains a non-exhaustive list proposing eight groups of potentially vulnerable suspects and defendants:

> (1) foreign nationals, (2) children, (3) persons suffering from a mental or emotional handicap, in the broadest sense, (4) the physically handicapped or ill, (5) mothers/ fathers of young children, (6) persons who cannot read or write, (7) refugees and asylum seekers, (8) alcoholics and drug addicts.[8]

In addition, the question was raised by the Green Paper whether this list should be extended with other potentially vulnerable groups and whether the authorities involved should assess this potential vulnerability.[9]

After a failed attempt in 2004 to establish a Council Framework Decision[10], in 2009 the next step was taken with regard to the protection of vulnerable suspects and defendants. On the 30th of November 2009 – one day before the implementation of the Treaty of Lisbon – the Council adopted a Resolution on a roadmap for strengthening procedural rights of suspected or accused persons in criminal proceedings.[11] The annex of this Resolution consists of a roadmap with six measures, inviting the Commission to submit proposals to strengthen the rights of suspected or accused persons in criminal proceedings. The fifth measure of this roadmap, Measure E, is specifically dedicated to special safeguards for suspected or accused persons who are vulnerable. It is stated that special attention is needed to suspected or accused persons "who cannot understand or follow the content or the meaning of the proceedings, for example because of their age, mental or physical condition".[12] Thus far, this aspect of the roadmap has been included in six European legal instruments.

---

[7]   Green Paper from the Commission on Procedural Safeguards for Suspects and Defendants in Criminal Proceedings throughout the European Union, Feb. 19, 2003, COM(2003) final, def.

[8]   Ibid., 32-34.

[9]   Ibid., 35.

[10]   European Commission Proposal for a Council Framework Decision on Certain Procedural Rights in Criminal Proceedings throughout the European Union, April 28, 2004, COM(2004) 328 final.

[11]   OJ 2009, C 295/1.

[12]   Annex, Measure E, Resolution Roadmap for Strengthening Procedural Rights.

Firstly, the Directive 2010/64/EU on the right to interpretation and translation[13] stipulates that the special needs of vulnerable persons have to be considered by the Member States when implementing this Directive.[14]

Secondly, the same goes for Directive 2012/13/EU[15], in which common minimum standards are established with regard to the information about the rights and accusation to be given to persons suspected or accused of having committed a criminal offence.[16] In this regard, Member States should ensure that the information is provided in simple and accessible language, considering any particular needs of vulnerable suspects or accused persons.[17] Competent authorities are in that sense expected to pay particular attention to persons "who cannot understand the content or meaning of the information, for example because of their youth or their mental or physical condition".[18]

Thirdly, article 13 of Directive 2013/48/EU[19] on the right of access to a lawyer in criminal proceedings explicitly states that Member States should consider the particular needs of vulnerable suspects and accused persons when implementing this Directive. This provision aims to enable these suspects and defendants to truly exercise their procedural rights in order to safeguard their right to a fair trial. On the one hand, the competent authorities need to take into account all factors that may jeopardize the ability to exercise the right of access to a lawyer or to have a third party informed upon deprivation of liberty. On the other hand, they have to provide for suitable measures to ensure the exercise of these rights.[20]

Fourthly, the Recommendation of 27 November 2013[21], in which the Commission encourages the Member States to strengthen the procedural rights of so-called vulnerable persons in criminal proceedings[22], is of particular importance. This Recommendation can be seen as an elaboration

[13] Directive 2010/64/EU of the European Parliament and of the Council on the Right to Interpretation and Translation in Criminal Proceedings, Oct. 22, 2010, OJ 2010, L 280/1.
[14] Recital 27 Directive on the Right to Interpretation and Translation.
[15] Directive 2012/13/EU of the European Parliament and of the Council on the Right to Information in Criminal Proceedings, May 22, 2012, OJ 2012, L 142/1.
[16] Ibid., art. 1.
[17] Ibid., art. 3.2.
[18] Ibid., recital no. 26.
[19] Directive 2013/48/EU of the European Parliament and of the Council on the Right of Access to a Lawyer in Criminal Proceedings and in European Arrest Warrant Proceedings, and on the Right to Have a Third Party Informed upon Deprivation of Liberty and to Communicate with Third Persons and with Consular Authorities while Deprived of Liberty, Oct. 22, 2013, OJ 2013, L 294/1.
[20] Ibid., recital no. 51.
[21] Recommendation of the Commission on Procedural Safeguards for Vulnerable Persons Suspected or Accused in Criminal Proceedings, Nov. 27, 2013 OJ 2013, C 378/8.
[22] Ibid., recital no. 1.

of article 13 of Directive 2013/48/EU and thus of the responsibility for the Member States to consider the specific needs of vulnerable suspects and defendants. It aims at strengthening the right to liberty, the right to a fair trial and the rights of defence by offering vulnerable persons appropriate assistance and support.[23] Whereas the three aforementioned instruments actually do not contain a description of what is to be understood by a vulnerable person, the Recommendation does provide a definition, stating that vulnerable persons are "all suspects or accused persons who are not able to understand and to effectively participate in criminal proceedings due to age, their mental or physical condition or disabilities".[24] Furthermore, the Recommendation indicates that Member States should adopt a presumption of vulnerability regarding suspects and defendants with serious psychological, intellectual, physical or sensory impairments, or mental illness or cognitive disorders. These persons are presumed to encounter difficulties in understanding and effectively participating in the proceedings.[25] In addition, there appear to be certain persons who are particularly vulnerable, who are unable to follow and understand the criminal proceedings and who should not be allowed to waive their right to a lawyer.[26]

However, it should be noted that this definition is not commonly accepted among Member States of the European Union. That is precisely the reason why the Commission opted for a non-binding Recommendation.[27] Nevertheless, there exists a consensus that minors are particularly vulnerable. From that perspective, the binding Directive of 11 May 2016 contains procedural safeguards for children suspected or accused in criminal proceedings.[28] Whereas children, by virtue of their age, are in general considered to be vulnerable and not always able to fully understand and follow criminal proceedings, it is also explicitly stated that children are in a particularly vulnerable position when they are deprived of liberty.[29] As such, it can be argued that there is an unequal level of attention given to the vulnerability of adult suspects and defendants compared to suspected or accused children.[30] Likewise, an unequal level of attention

---

[23] Ibid., recital no. 18.
[24] Ibid., recital no. 1.
[25] Ibid., art 7.
[26] Ibid, recital no. 11.
[27] European Commission Proposal for a Directive of the European Parliament and of the Council on Procedural Safeguards for Children Suspected or Accused in Criminal Proceedings, Nov. 27, 2013, COM(2013) 822 final, 3.
[28] Directive (EU) 2016/800 of European Parliament and the Council on Procedural Safeguards for Children Who are Suspects or Accused Persons in Criminal Proceedings, May 11, 2016, OJ 2016, L 132/1.
[29] Ibid., recital no. 25 and 45.
[30] See also Michaël Meysman, "Quo Vadis with Vulnerable Defendants in the EU?,"

can be observed when comparing the non-binding instrument for adult suspects and defendants who are considered vulnerable to (vulnerable) victims, whose minimum rights are also established in a Directive[31].[32]

Finally, in 2016 the European Parliament and Council also adopted a Directive on the strengthening of certain aspects of the presumption of innocence and of the right to be present at the trial in criminal proceedings[33], in which – by readopting the 'definition' of vulnerable persons mentioned in the Recommendation – it is again indicated that the particular needs of vulnerable persons need to be considered when implementing the Directive.[34]

The attention given to a suspect's vulnerability in Belgian legislation

The attention paid towards a suspect's vulnerability in Belgian legislation should be interpreted against this European background. Belgium was one of the last Member States of the Council of Europe to comply with the case law of the ECtHR on access to a lawyer during the pre-trial investigation.[35] It took until 2011 – three years after the case of *Salduz v. Turkey* – before the right of access to a lawyer prior to and during police interviews was regulated.[36] Initially Belgium, amongst the other continental Member States with a predominantly inquisitorial procedure, was rather resistant to the evolution within the case law of the ECtHR regarding access to a lawyer in the early stages of criminal proceedings.[37] This reserved attitude resulted in the restrictive manner in which the role

European Criminal Law Review 4 (2014): 179, 191-193.

[31] Directive 2012/29/EU of the European Parliament and of the Council Establishing Minimum Standards on the Rights, Support and Protection of Victims of Crime, and Replacing Council Framework Decision 2001/220/JHA, Oct. 25, 2012, OJ 2012, L 315/57.

[32] See also Suzan van der Aa, "Variable Vulnerabilities? Comparing the Rights of Adult Vulnerable Suspects and Vulnerable Victims under EU Law," *New Journal of European Criminal Law* 7 (2016): 41.

[33] Directive (EU) 2016/343 of the European Parliament and of the Council on the Strengthening of Certain Aspects of the Presumption of Innocence and of the Right to be Present at the Trial in Criminal Proceedings, March 9, 2016, OJ 2016, L 65/1.

[34] Ibid, recital no. 42.

[35] See Wetsvoorstel (Parliamentary Bill), *Parl.St.* Senaat 2010-11, no. 5-663/1, 2.

[36] This was regulated by the following law: Wet tot wijziging van het Wetboek van Strafvordering en de Wet van 20 juli 1990 betreffende de voorlopige hechtenis, om aan elkeen die wordt verhoord en aan elkeen wiens vrijheid wordt benomen rechten te verlenen, waaronder het recht om een advocaat te raadplegen en door hem te worden bijgestaan, August 13, 2011, *BS* 5 september 2011.

[37] Ilias Anagnostopoulos, "The Right of Access to a Lawyer in Europe: A long Road Ahead?," *European Criminal Law Review* 1 (2014): 4; Dimitrios Giannoulopoulos, "Strasbourg Jurisprudence, Law Reform and Comparative Law: a Tale of the Right to Custodial Legal Assistance in Five Countries," *Human Rights Law Review* 16 (2016): 104; John, D. Jackson, "Responses to *Salduz*: Procedural Tradition, Change and the Need for Effective Defence," *The Modern Law Review* 79 (2016): 99.

of the defence lawyer during police interviews was initially regulated.[38] Since it was argued that the suspect and not his lawyer is interviewed by the police, the lawyer was not allowed to communicate with the suspect or to give remarks about the questions asked. The lawyer was also obliged to be seated behind the suspect and to adopt a very cautious attitude.[39]

However, although the case law of the ECtHR does allow for some interpretation about the scope of the defence lawyer's role during police interviews, a new amendment of the Belgian legislation became inevitable under the influence of the aforementioned Directive 2013/48/EU, which was required to be implemented by the Member States by the 27th of November 2016.[40] Belgium managed to comply with this Directive just in time by adopting a law on certain rights of persons who are interviewed, which entered into force on precisely the 27th of November 2016.[41] Besides an expansion of the right of access to a lawyer to all police interviews and certain other investigative acts, the legislation now foresees a more active role for the defence lawyer, for instance implying that the lawyer is also allowed to communicate with and to take their place next to the suspect.[42]

Against this background, a rather limited level of attention given to a suspect's vulnerability can be observed in the Belgian legislation. The first legislation on access to a lawyer in 2011 did not even include any measures for vulnerable suspects. However, a Circular of the Board of Procurators General stipulated that the regulations for minors should be applied when an adult person is recognized as being vulnerable, for example because of an intellectual disability.[43] In addition, the so-called 'Salduz-code of conduct' for lawyers prescribes that, during the confidential consultation prior to a police interview, the lawyer should check whether his client is physically and/or mentally capable of being interviewed.[44] These provisions were retained after the amendment of 21 November 2016 to comply with Directive 2013/48/EU.[45] Since then, the Code of Criminal Procedure also explicitly states that the language used by the police to inform a person about

---

[38] See also Giannoulopoulos, "Strasbourg Jurisprudence, Law Reform and Comparative Law," 110.

[39] Tom Decaigny, "De Bijstand van een Advocaat bij het Verhoor," *Tijdschrift voor Strafrecht* 1 (2010): 4.

[40] Art. 15, first paragraph Directive 2013/48/EU.

[41] Wet van 21 november betreffende bepaalde rechten van personen die worden verhoord, *BS* 24 November 2016 (ed. 2).

[42] Omzendbrief no. COL 8/2011, Nov. 24, 2016 (second revised edition), 46.

[43] Omzendbrief no. COL 8/2011, June 13, 2013 (first revised edition), 75.

[44] Omzendbrief no. COL 8/2011, Nov 24, 2016 (second revised edition), 65; Flemish Bar Association (Orde Van Vlaamse Balies), *Salduz-Gedragscode na Afkondiging van de Wet Consultatie- en Bijstandsrecht van 13 Augustus 2011*, Dec. 7, 2011, 3.2.

[45] Orde Van Vlaamse Balies, *Salduz-Gedragscode* (revised edition), Jan. 18, 2017, 3.2.

his rights should be adapted to the person's age or potential vulnerability which hampers his ability to understand these rights.[46] Furthermore, it is recognized that assistance of an interpreter is required for persons who are vulnerable because of language barriers or a speech or hearing disability.[47] It should, however, be noted that these provisions remain rather vague, especially with regard to who is considered to be vulnerable and how this vulnerability should be identified.

The attention given to a suspect's vulnerability in academic research

Lastly, the concept 'vulnerable suspect' can be linked to academic research in the field of psychology and law, of which the three dominant research domains will be discussed below. Since a comprehensive review of this literature exceeds the aim and scope of this chapter, merely some key elements relevant to the conceptualization of a suspect's vulnerability will be discussed.

Academic research on false confessions

Based on the results of the large body of research on false confessions over the past decades, a suspect's vulnerability appears to be associated with three categories of risk factors for falsely confessing: individual factors, situational factors and innocence.[48] First, the concept 'vulnerable suspect' is explicitly used in relation to individual factors rendering a suspect prone to falsely confessing during police interviews. Kassin and colleagues, for instance, state that a suspect can be vulnerable "by virtue of his or her youth, naiveté, intellectual deficiency or acute emotional state".[49] Gudjonsson specifically refers to this category as 'psychological vulnerabilities' and, based on the description in Code of practice C[50] of the Police and Criminal Evidence Act of England and Wales, (the PACE

---

[46]   Art. 47*bis*, § 6, 2) Belgian Criminal Procedure Code. See also Omzendbrief no. COL 8/2011, Nov. 24, 2016 (second revised edition), 13 and 30.

[47]   Ibid., § 6, 4).

[48]   Saul M. Kassin, "On the Psychology of Confessions. Does Innocence put Innocents at Risk?," *American Psychologist* 60 (2005): 215-228; Saul M. Kassin, "False Confessions: Causes, Consequences, and Implications for Reform," *Policy Insights from the Behavioral and Brain Sciences* 1 (2014): 114-116; Saul M. Kassin and Gisli H. Gudjonsson, "The Psychology of Confessions. A Review of the Literature and Issues," *Psychological Science in the Public Interest* 5 (2004): 51-56; Saul M. Kassin, Steven A. Drizin, Thomas Grisso, Gisli H. Gudjonsson, Richard A. Leo and Allison D. Redlich, "Police-Induced Confessions: Risk Factors and Recommendations," *Law and Human Behavior* 34 (2010): 16-23; Guy A. Norfolk, "Fit to be Interviewed by the Police – an Aid to Assessment," *Medicine, Science and the Law* 41 (2001): 6-10.

[49]   Kassin et al., "Police-Induced Confessions," 29.

[50]   See Police and Criminal Evidence (PACE) Act, Codes of practice, Code C, 1984, 11.18 and 11C.

Act) defines these psychological vulnerabilities in the context of a police interview as "psychological characteristics or mental states which render a suspect prone, in certain circumstances, to providing information which is inaccurate, unreliable (or invalid) or misleading".[51] These individual factors constitute a wide-ranging category, including minors, certain personality traits (such as suggestibility and compliance) and mental disorders (such as an intellectual disability, ADHD and schizophrenia).[52]

Secondly, the results of this research domain show that certain situational factors, inherent to the pre-trial investigation, can also render a suspect prone to falsely confessing during a police interview. These factors refer to the isolation of family and friends; sleep deprivation and fatigue; lengthy interviews; and certain (coercive) interview techniques.[53]

Lastly, the innocence in itself of the suspect also appears to be a risk factor for false confessions. Assuming that they have nothing to hide, innocent suspects often are willing to cooperate with the police and to waive their rights to access to a lawyer and to remain silent.[54] Moreover, innocent suspects may falsely confess – with or without pressure exerted by the police – because of a (false) belief that innocent persons are not convicted and that their innocence eventually will become apparent to the judicial authorities.[55]

Vulnerability and fitness for interview

In addition to the academic research on false confessions, a suspect's vulnerability is also associated with the concept of fitness for interview.

---

[51] Gisli H. Gudjonsson, *The Psychology of Interrogations and Confessions. A Handbook* (Chichester: John Wiley & Sons, 2003), 316.

[52] For a review, see Kassin and Gudjonsson, "The Psychology of Confessions," 51-53 and Kassin et al., "Police-Induced Confessions," 19-22.

[53] See for instance Mark Blagrove, "Effects of Length of Sleep Deprivation on Interrogative Suggestibility," *Journal of Experimental Psychology: Applied* 2 (1996): 48-59; Richard, P. Conti, "The Psychology of False Confessions," *Journal of Credibility Assessment and Witness Psychology* 2 (1999): 14-36; Steven A. Drizin and Richard A. Leo, "The Problem of False Confessions in the Post-DNA World," *North Carolina Law Review* 82 (2004): 891-1007; Yvonne Harrison and James A. Horne, "The Impact of Sleep Deprivation on Decision Making: a Review," *Journal of Experimental Psychology: Applied* 6 (2000): 236-249; Kassin et al., "Police-Induced Confessions," 16-19; Christian A. Meissner, "Accusatorial and Information-Gathering Interrogation Methods and their Effects on True and False Confessions: a Meta-Analytic Review," *Journal of Experimental Criminology* 10 (2014): 459-486.

[54] Maria Hartwig, Pär Anders Granhag and Leif. A. Strömwall, "Guilty and Innocent Suspects' Strategies during Police Interrogations," *Psychology, Crime & Law* 13 (2007): 219-220; Saul M. Kassin and Rebecca J. Norwick, "Why People Waive their *Miranda* Rights: the Power of Innocence," *Law and Human Behavior* 28 (2004): 216; Kassin, "On the Psychology of Confessions," 224.

[55] Kassin, "On the Psychology of Confessions," 224. See also this publication for a full analysis of how innocence may induce suspects to falsely confess.

According to the legal definition of fitness for interview in Code of Practice C of the PACE Act, a detained suspect can be unfit for interview:

if it is considered that:

(a) conducting the interview could significantly harm the detainee's physical or mental state;

(b) anything the detainee says in the interview about their involvement or suspected involvement in the offence about which they are being interviewed might be considered unreliable in subsequent court proceedings because of their physical or mental state.[56]

Furthermore, three elements are listed that need to be evaluated when assessing fitness to be interviewed:

(a) how the detainee's physical or mental state might affect their ability to understand the nature and purpose of the interview, to comprehend what is being asked and to appreciate the significance of any answers given and make rational decisions about whether they want to say anything;

(b) the extent to which the detainee's replies may be affected by their physical or mental condition rather than representing a rational and accurate explanation of their involvement in the offence;

(c) how the nature of the interview, which could include particularly probing questions, might affect the detainee.[57]

The academic research on fitness for interview contributes to the understanding of what factors precisely should be considered when evaluating a suspect's fitness for interview.[58] In this regard, for instance the acronym 'PHIT' was proposed to represent the factors that are associated with unfitness for interview. PHIT includes factors that may render an individual 'vulnerable' to providing a false confession and refers to a suspect's personality; mental and physical health; the demands and characteristics of the police interview; and the totality of the circumstances of the custody.[59] Consequently, this body of literature is closely related to the research on false confessions, especially because these factors are used as 'criteria' to assess a suspect's fitness for interview.[60]

---

[56] PACE Act, Codes of practice, Code C, 1984, Annex G, 2.

[57] Ibid., 3.

[58] Gisli H. Gudjonsson, "'Fitness for Interview' during Police Detention: a Conceptual Framework for Forensic Assessment," *The Journal of Forensic Psychiatry* 6 (1995): 195; Norfolk, "Fitness to be Interviewed," 6; Keith J. B. Rix, "Fit to be interviewed by the police?," *Advances in Psychiatric Treatment* 3 (1997): 37-38.

[59] Norfolk, "Fitness to be Interviewed," 6.

[60] See also Gisli H. Gudjonsson, "Detention: Fitness to be Interviewed," in *Encyclopedia of*

Competence to stand trial

Finally, academic research on the competence to stand trial[61] is worth mentioning in relation to the conceptualization of a suspect's vulnerability. Although the terms 'vulnerable' suspect or defendant or 'vulnerability' are not explicitly used in this large body of research, the research domain is nevertheless relevant when it comes to defining these concepts. This especially becomes apparent when comparing the key features of competence to stand trial to the description of vulnerable suspects and defendants within the aforementioned EU legal instruments. The latter precisely link vulnerability to the inability to understand and to participate in the criminal proceedings. Interestingly, competence to stand trial significantly corresponds to that approach, because the extent to which a suspect is able to understand his rights and the criminal proceedings on the one hand, and the ability to contribute to his own defence on the other, are key elements of competence to stand trial across different jurisdictions.[62] In this large body of research, individual characteristics of the suspect are again studied in relation to a defendant's incompetence to stand trial. These can be categorized into sociodemographic (e.g. employment status), criminological (e.g. prior competency evaluation) and psychological factors (e.g. a psychiatric diagnosis).[63]

The lack of an unequivocal and comprehensive definition and the need for a conceptual framework

As the previous sections illustrate, the terms 'vulnerable suspect' and 'vulnerability' are used in both the legal and academic domain, albeit both perspectives mainly exist next to each other. As a consequence, the concept has a somewhat different meaning depending on the perspective taken. Although Gudjonsson and colleagues have already stated nearly twenty-

---

Forensic and Legal Medicine, 2nd edition, ed. Jason Payne-James and Roger W. Byard (Oxford: Elsevier, 2016), 218.

[61] This is, just as *"adjudicative competence"*, the term used in the United States. Whereas in Canada, New Zealand and Australia *"fitness to stand trial"* is used, *"fitness to plead"* is used in England and Wales. The different terms are, however, used interchangeably and, to some extent, they appear to be similar to each other. See: Gianni Pirelli, William H. Gottdiener and Patricia A. Zapf, "A Meta-Analytic Review of Competency to Stand Trial Research," *Psychology, Public Policy, and Law* 17 (2011): 2; Ronald Roesch, "Social Worker Assessments of Competency to Stand Trial," *Journal of Forensic Social Work* 5 (2015): 191; Tim P. Rogers, Nigel J. Blackwood, F. Farnham, G. J. Pickup and M. J. Watts, "Fitness to Plead and Competence to Stand Trial: a Systematic Review of the Constructs and their Application," *The Journal of Forensic Psychiatry and Psychology* 19 (2008): 576.

[62] Dusky v. United States, 362 U.S. 402 (1960); Criminal Code of Canada, section 2, *Unfitness to Stand Trial*, http://laws-lois.justice.gc.ca/eng/acts/C-46/page-1.html#h-2; R. v. Pritchard (1836) 7 C&P 303; R v. John M (2003) EWCA Crim 3452; Ron Roesch, Patricia A. Zapf and Stephen D. Hart, *Forensic Psychology and Law* (New Jersey: John Wiley & Sons: 2010), 31-32.

[63] See for instance Pirelli et al., "A Meta-Analytic Review of Competency to Stand Trial Research," 1-53 for a meta-analysis on the factors associated with (in)competence to stand trial.

five years ago that an operational definition of a suspect's vulnerability is 'urgently needed'[64], it is still lacking nowadays. This is also true for the EU legal instruments, wherein similar yet not identical nor exhaustive descriptions of vulnerability are used. In that sense, there is a lack of clarity as to what has to be understood by the vulnerability of a suspect or defendant.

On the one hand, several Directives stress that the specific needs of so-called vulnerable persons have to be considered, without, however, providing for an explanation of whom exactly is to be considered. On the other hand, the non-binding Recommendation of the European Commission on special safeguards for vulnerable suspects and defendants foresees some kind of a definition, but it remains rather vague and is to some extent even confusing, given the seeming distinction that is made between vulnerable persons, particularly vulnerable persons and persons for whom a presumption of vulnerability needs to be foreseen.[65] Likewise, while the case law of the ECtHR points to a number of factors that put a suspect in a 'vulnerable position' during a criminal procedure, it does not offer a specific description of vulnerability.

In addition, there appear to be both broad and strict interpretations of when a suspect's vulnerability is at stake. In light of this, it should first be questioned what persons are considered vulnerable. Whereas the (in) ability to understand the procedural rights and to effectively participate in criminal proceedings is the central element in the legal perspective, a suspect's vulnerability is predominantly linked to the risk of a false confession in the legal psychological literature. In this regard, the scope of a suspect's vulnerability is most restricted in the research on false confessions because it is limited to the context of a police interview. Moreover, linking a suspect's vulnerability to the risk of a false confession implies that this vulnerability is limited to innocent persons instead of all persons suspected of an offence. In contrast, the EU legal instruments are aimed at *all* suspected or accused persons in criminal proceedings. The same goes for the case law of the ECtHR, which focuses on the position of a suspect during the entire investigative stage of the proceedings.

The comprehensibility of the concepts is further hampered because of the plurality of risk factors related to a suspect's vulnerability. This might of course be partially explained by the mere fact that vulnerability appears

---

[64] Gisli, H. Gudjonsson, Isabel C.H. Clare, Sue Rutter and John Pearse, *Persons at Risk During Interviews in Police Custody: the Identification of Vulnerabilities. Royal Commission on Criminal Justice* (London: HMSO, 1993), 27.

[65] Recommendation on Procedural Safeguards for Vulnerable Persons, recital no. 1, recital no. 11 and art. 7.

to have different meanings across disciplines and that, as a consequence, different aspects are essentially being measured. Yet, it should be remarked that the EU legal instruments and the research on competence to stand trial focus merely on individual factors rendering a suspect or defendant unable to understand the procedural rights and to participate in criminal proceedings. This leads to the question of whether defining a 'vulnerable suspect' should be seen as a strictly personal or psychological matter.

The case law of the ECtHR, however, recognizes that both individual and situational factors may put a suspect in a particular vulnerable position. The scope of the concept therefore seems to be more restricted within the EU legal instruments compared to that case law of the ECtHR in which it is ruled that all suspects are essentially considered vulnerable merely because of their involvement in a criminal procedure, at least in addition to a number of categories that are considered 'particularly vulnerable'.[66] Likewise, the results of research on false confessions show that both individual and situational factors may render a suspect vulnerable, although it should be noted that the results of research on the influence of certain individual factors are inconsistent within this research domain.[67] In this regard, two 'trends' exist within the research on false confessions, either focusing on individual differences or situational factors rendering a suspect prone to a false confession.

Taking all the perspectives together, some 'degrees of vulnerability' can be observed ranging from a rather general vulnerability (stemming from the mere fact that one is involved in a criminal procedure), to a heightened vulnerability (when the suspect is detained and questioned), to a particular vulnerability (where personal or psychological factors are at stake). Consequently, a clear and unequivocal definition of a suspect's vulnerability is lacking.[68] It should be recognized though that a suspect's vulnerability is an elusive and abstract construct.[69] In addition, the lack

---

[66] See the part on the case law of the European Court of Human Rights in this chapter.

[67] See for instance Robert Horselenberg, Harald Merckelbach and Sarah Josephs, "Individual Differences and False Confessions: a Conceptual Replication of Kassin and Kiechel (1996)," *Psychology, Crime & Law* 9 (2003): 3-5; Jessica R. Klaver, Zina Lee and Gordon V. Rose, "Effects of Personality, Interrogation Techniques and Plausibility in an Experimental False Confession Paradigm," *Legal and Criminological Psychology* 13 (2008): 75 and 82. The same goes for the individual factors that are thought to contribute to a person's incompetence to stand trial (see Jeremy G. Gay, Laurie Ragatz and Michael Vitacco, "Mental Health Symptoms and their Relationship to Specific Deficits in Competency to Proceed to Trial Evaluations," *Psychiatry, Psychology and Law* 22 (2015): 781 and Pirelli et al., "A Meta-Analytic Review of Competency to Stand Trial Research," 1-53).

[68] See also Penny Cooper (2017), *Toolkit* 10, The Advocate's Gateway, 5.

[69] For a comparable view, applied to legal competency, see Thomas Grisso, *Evaluating Competencies: Forensic Assessments and Instruments. Second Edition* (New York: Kluwer Academic/Plenum Publishers, 2003), 22-23.

of theorization on the precise meaning of vulnerability might be partially explained by the predominant focus of academic research on mapping the causes of false confessions, whereas legal instruments mainly aim to provide special procedural safeguards for vulnerable suspects. Nevertheless, strengthening the procedural safeguards of (certain) suspects and defendants will only be meaningful when it is fully clear to whom they apply. An early identification of so-called vulnerable suspects and defendants will likewise only be possible if it is clear when a person should be considered as such and which factors might be indicative of such vulnerability.

Towards a conceptual framework of a suspect's vulnerability

In the interests of clarity, it should be underlined that the conceptual framework discussed below concerns adult suspects during the pre-trial investigation and that, as a consequence, the vulnerability of defendants at trial is disregarded.

First, it seems preferable to step away from the term 'vulnerable suspect' because it only emphasizes the individual characteristics of the suspect. This might give the impression that the causes of any problems that may occur always need to be attributed to (characteristics of) the suspect. The case law of the ECtHR and the results of research on false confessions, however, rightfully demonstrate that this is not the case. Therefore, the term 'vulnerable suspect' detracts from the complexity and dynamics of a suspect's vulnerability. External factors should indeed also be considered. Hence, the concept 'the vulnerability of a suspect' is preferred instead of the concept 'vulnerable suspect'. Although this adjustment might seem a minor linguistic distinction, it is more neutral as to the causes of the problems and allows for a broader interpretation of the concept, considering the interactive and dynamic nature of a suspect's vulnerability.

The (in)ability to exercise procedural rights as a common denominator

Based on an extensive analysis of the existing perspectives regarding the vulnerability of a suspect, it can be argued that vulnerability essentially comes down to a suspect's inability to exercise his procedural rights. The most relevant procedural rights in the context of a criminal procedure are the rights included in article 6 of the European Convention of Human Rights (ECHR) to safeguard a fair trial. It should be noted that some of these procedural rights are strengthened by the aforementioned EU legal instruments.

Although it cannot be neglected that the police interview is still key in criminal investigations, the vulnerability of a suspect is not restricted to that context. Instead, it can be at stake throughout the entire pre-trial investigation, both during other investigative acts (such as a reconstruction or confrontation) as, for instance, during conversations with a lawyer when preparing the defence strategy. Hence, vulnerability should be defined rather broadly. Moreover, procedural rights are exercised in a broader context. There are indeed a number of elements that are of importance throughout the entire pre-trial investigation, including the type of case and offence; the complexity of the proceedings; the evidence gathered; the potential detention of the suspect; but also whether or not the suspect is a foreigner. This broader context also determines the extent to which a suspect understands his rights and is able to exercise them.

Defining vulnerability in terms of the ability to exercise procedural rights further implies that this concept cannot be limited to innocent suspects nor to false confessions. The extent to which a person will be able to exercise his procedural rights does not depend on his innocence or guilt. Therefore, the risk of a false confession is not required to determine a suspect's vulnerability. Nevertheless, the inability to exercise, for instance, the right to remain silent or not to incriminate oneself may still result in an involuntary (and even false) confession. The risk factors associated with a false confession often seem to impair a suspect's ability to understand the procedural rights, which may subsequently jeopardize the exercise of those rights. In the United States the so-called *Miranda rights* were, from that perspective, introduced precisely to curb the number of false confessions.[70]

Providing a suspect with several procedural rights, however, does not suffice. Being able to exercise these rights requires three necessary conditions: 1) information about and knowledge of the procedural rights; 2) understanding of the procedural rights; and 3) rational decision-making regarding the exercise of those rights.[71] First, the police (and the defence

---

[70] Saul M. Kassin, "False Confessions: from Colonial Salem, through Central Park, and into the Twenty-First Century," in *The Witness Stand and Lawrence S. Wrightsman Jr.*, ed. Cynthia Willis-Esqueda and Brian H. Bornstein (New York: Springer, 2016) 55; Lawrence S. Wrightsman, "The Supreme Court on *Miranda* Rights and Interrogations: the Past, the Present, and the Future," in *Police Interrogations and False Confessions: Current Research, Practice, and Policy Recommendations*, ed. Daniel G. Lassiter and Christian A. Meissner (Washington DC: American Psychological Association, 2010), 164-165; Kassin et al., "Police-Induced Confessions," 7.

[71] This trichotomy is, *inter alia*, inspired by the criteria used for competency to waive the Miranda rights in the United States and the academic research in this area. In addition, it is inspired by the research on fitness for interview and competence to stand trial, in which the criteria a suspect or defendant needs to comply with to be fit for interview/competent to stand trial are concretized. The specific meaning that is given to these legal criteria within the psychological literature provided a frame of reference to further elaborate the own conceptual framework.

lawyer) need to inform the suspect of the charges and of his rights on time and properly. The words used to inform the suspect and the manner in which this occurs (written and/or orally) are also important, because suspects are usually unfamiliar with legal vocabulary.[72] Subsequently, the suspect needs to be able to understand the precise meaning and implications of his rights. Lastly, a suspect must be able to make a deliberate decision about whether or not he will exercise a particular right. The supportive and crucial role of the defence lawyer may not be neglected in this regard. Since a suspect cannot be obliged to consult a lawyer, however, it remains important that he is able to be informed of his rights, to understand them and to take a deliberate decision himself.

An interactive and dynamic approach to a suspect's vulnerability

Until now, a suspect's vulnerability has been mainly seen from the perspective of the individual, as a rather fixed and stable condition, instead of adopting a helicopter view in which it becomes clear that this vulnerability is also caused by characteristics inherent to the pre-trial investigation and the interactions with other persons involved. If that first viewpoint, which is especially adopted in the more legal perspectives – i.e. the EU instruments and the research on competence to stand trial – were to be followed, the conclusion would be that the extent to which a suspect is able to exercise his rights is exclusively determined by the individual characteristics of the suspect. The exercise of the procedural rights is, however, not a static concept. The situation wherein the suspect exercises these rights should indeed always be considered as well.[73]

The inability to exercise the procedural rights should therefore not be regarded as a matter that merely occurs within persons who are unable to do so because of individual characteristics (the 'classic vulnerable suspects', such as those persons who suffer from a mental disorder).[74] Restricting

---

[72] See for instance Anthony J. Domanico, Michael D. Cicchini and Lawrence T. White, "Overcoming *Miranda*: a Content Analysis of the *Miranda* Portion of Police Interrogations," *Idaho Law Review* 49 (2012): 1-22; Susanne Fenner, Gisli H. Gudjonsson and Isabel C.H. Clare, "Understanding of the Current Police Caution (England and Wales) Among Suspects in Police Detention," *Journal of Community & Applied Social Psychology* 12 (2002): 83-93.

[73] Alan M. Goldstein, Naomi, N.E. Goldstein and Heather Zelle, "Evaluation of Capacity to Waive Miranda Rights," in *Forensic Assessments in Criminal Law and Civil Law: a Handbook for Lawyers*, ed. Ronald Roesch and Patricia A. Zapf (New York: Oxford University Press, 2013), 51; Richard A. Leo and Steven A. Drizin, "The Three Errors: Pathways to False Confession and Wrongful Conviction," in *Police Interrogations and False Confessions: Current Research, Practice, and Policy Recommendations*, ed. Daniel G. Lassiter and Christian A. Meissner (Washington DC, American Psychological Association, 2010), 12.

[74] Joseph Eastwood and Brent Snook, "Comprehending Canadian Police Cautions: are the Rights to Silence and Legal Counsel Understandable?," *Behavioral Sciences and the Law* 28 (2010): 376.

the issue to these persons would result in 'labelling' certain groups of persons, while this would not *per se* be indicative of the inability to exercise the procedural rights. The presence of, for example, a particular mental disorder cannot be regarded as a definite marker of the inability to exercise procedural rights.[75] Assuming this may result in a false positive outcome, wrongfully concluding that the suspect is unable to exercise his procedural rights simply because of the presence of that mental disorder. A person with a mental disorder may well be able to exercise his rights if he receives an adapted and appropriate treatment, considering and remedying the difficulties the suspect encounters. Such a restrictive approach could also result in a false negative outcome – an underestimation of the issue – since the ability to exercise the procedural rights always needs to be evaluated in light of the specific situation.[76] The absence of a mental disorder in that sense neither automatically means that the suspect will be able to exercise his procedural rights.

Therefore, one cannot simply conclude that certain (groups of) persons per definition, in all circumstances, will or will not be able to exercise their procedural rights. Suspects cannot be assigned beforehand to predefined categories of vulnerable and invulnerable persons, merely because they possess or do not possess certain personality traits or suffer from certain mental disorders.[77]

The cognitive abilities of a suspect

Consequently, it can be argued that a suspect's vulnerability should not be determined based on the presence or absence of a certain personality trait or mental disorder. Instead of focusing on such 'fixed labels', the vulnerability of a suspect should be assessed on the basis of a number of functional cognitive abilities. Following the rationale put forward by Grisso to define legal competency, it can be argued that a suspect's actual functioning "is related to, but distinct from, psychiatric diagnoses or conclusions about general intellectual abilities and personality traits.

---

[75] Grisso, *Evaluating Competencies*, 20-21; Gisli H. Gudjonsson, "Confession Evidence, Psychological Vulnerability and Expert Testimony," *Journal of Community & Applied Social Psychology* 3 (1993): 126; Gisli H. Gudjonsson and Theresa Joyce, "Interviewing Adults with Intellectual Disabilities," *Advances in Mental Health and Intellectual Disabilities* 5 (2011): 18; Peter V. Verbeke, Gert Vermeulen, Michaël Meysman and Tom Vander Beken, "Protecting the Fair Trial Rights of Mentally Disordered Defendants in Criminal Proceedings: Exploring the Need for Further EU Action," *International Journal of Law and Psychiatry* 41 (2015): 71.

[76] A comparable view can be found in Richard J. Bonnie, "The Competency of Criminal Defendants: Beyond Dusky and Drope," *University of Miami Law Review* 47 (1993): 550.

[77] See also Penny Cooper (2014), *Toolkit* 10, The Advocate's Gateway, 2. In the updated version of this toolkit, this aspect is mentioned only regarding vulnerability in court. See also Penny Cooper (2017), *Toolkit* 10, 8.

Psychiatric and psychological conditions [...] are hypothetical constructs that are presumed to influence functioning".[78] In this regard, it is not the mental disorder or personality trait as such that renders a suspect 'vulnerable', but rather the distortions in a suspect's cognitive abilities that often, but not exclusively, go along with suffering from a mental disorder or having a certain personality trait.

In the context of a pre-trial investigation, these cognitive abilities are language skills; attention and concentration abilities; reasoning abilities and memory capacities. In addition, the physical condition and potential substance (ab)use (including alcohol, drugs and medication) need to be considered, because these in turn may affect the cognitive ability of a suspect. Accordingly, these cognitive abilities are not constant or unchangeable, as a result of which they need to be assessed in relation to the specific context and moment.[79] Moreover, the level of cognitive abilities required will be determined by the situation wherein the procedural rights are exercised. Not every police interview, for instance, will be equally demanding of the suspect. The actual cognitive abilities of a suspect therefore always need to be assessed in relation to the demands of the specific situation.[80]

The interaction between the suspect, the defence lawyer and the police and judicial authorities

As a result, the exercise of procedural rights should be seen on a continuum and approached in an interactive and dynamic way.[81] It is interactive because it is determined by the way in which the interaction occurs between the police and judicial authorities on the one hand and the suspect (and his lawyer) on the other.[82] The extent to which a suspect will be able to exercise his procedural rights is dependent on the attitude of the police and judicial authorities, but also on the interaction with police officers during an investigative interview and other investigative acts such

---

[78]   Grisso, *Evaluating Competencies*, 24.
[79]   Ibid., 33. See also Felicity Gerry QC, "Vulnerable Witnesses and Parties in all Civil Proceedings – Dignity, Respect and The Advocate's Gateway Toolkit 17," in *Addressing Vulnerability in Justice Systems*, ed. Penny Cooper and Linda Hunting (London: Wildy, Simmonds & Hill Publishing, 2016), 32.
[80]   Grisso, *Evaluating Competencies*, 32-34.
[81]   A similar approach, applied to the police interview, can be found in Gisli H. Gudjonsson, "Psychological Vulnerabilities during Police Interviews," *Legal and Criminological Psychology* 15 (2010): 166. See also: Gudjonsson and Joyce, "Interviewing Adults with Intellectual Disabilities," 18.
[82]   Nadine Deslauriers-Vatin, Eric Beauregard and Jennifer Wong, "Changing their Mind about Confessing to Police: the Role of Contextual Factors in Crime Confession," *Police Quarterly* 14 (2011): 7-8; Stephen Moston, Geoffrey M. Stephenson and Thomas M. Williamson, "The effects of Case Characteristics on Suspect Behaviour during Police Questioning," *British Journal of Criminology* 32 (1992): 25-29.

as a reconstruction or confrontation. For instance, during each of these investigative acts, pressure may be exerted on the suspect, inappropriate questions may be asked or the suspect may be exhausted. Likewise, the conduct of the defence lawyer at these moments is of importance, especially given his crucial role in supporting the suspect to exercise his rights.

The exercise of the procedural rights is furthermore dynamic because it is variable: the extent to which a suspect is able to exercise his rights may change during a criminal procedure and may even vary depending on the specific procedural right to be exercised.[83] The exercise of a procedural right is in that sense primarily steered by the immediate, specific situation and should be specifically assessed for each moment, implying that it cannot be assessed conclusively early in the pre-trial investigation.[84] This also enables the consideration of the variable ability to exercise the procedural rights across moments and situations. A suspect may be able to understand his rights and to take a decision about exercising them at one moment, while this might not be the case at another moment.

Challenges in the identification of a suspect's vulnerability by the defence lawyer

A complex but increased responsibility for the defence lawyer

Regardless of the different approaches taken to define a suspect's vulnerability, it is widely acknowledged that an early identification is crucial. Referring back to the attention given to a suspect's vulnerability at the European level, the aforementioned Recommendation of 27 November 2013 clearly states that "it is essential that the vulnerability of a person suspected or accused in criminal proceedings is promptly identified and recognised. For that purpose, an initial assessment should be carried out by police officers, law enforcement or judicial authorities".[85]. As has been mentioned earlier, in Belgium this responsibility is explicitly allocated to the defence lawyer, who during the confidential consultation prior to a police interview needs to check whether his client is physically and/or mentally

---

[83] Ed Cape, Zaza Namoradze, Roger Smith and Taru Spronken, "Effective Criminal Defence and Fair Trial," in *Effective Criminal Defence in Europe*, ed. Ed Cape, Zaza Namoradze, Roger Smith and Taru Spronken (Antwerp: Intersentia, 2010), 6; Cooper (2017), *Toolkit* 10, 5; Ministry of Justice, *Vulnerable and Intimidated Witnesses. A police Service Guide*, 2011, 2.2.2.

[84] Bonnie, "The Competency of Criminal Defendants," 561; Yueran Yang, Max Guyll and Stephanie Madon, "The Interrogation Decision-Making Model: a General Theoretical Framework for Confessions," *Law and Human Behaviour* 41 (2017): 81.

[85] See Recital no. 6 and article no. 4 Recommendation of the Commission, Nov. 27, 2013.

capable of being interviewed.[86] This is in line with the previously cited ECtHR case law stating that "in most cases, this particular vulnerability can only be properly compensated for by the assistance of a lawyer […]".[87]

Lawyers, but also police officers and magistrates, should thus be aware of the risk factors that may hamper a suspect's ability to exercise the procedural rights. The early identification of such factors is not only vital to safeguard the rights of defence and the right to a fair trial, but also contributes to the quality and fairness of criminal proceedings. Detrimental consequences, such as the risk of a breach of the right to a fair trial, involuntary confessions and miscarriages of justice may be prevented by an early identification, allowing to facilitate and safeguard the exercise of procedural rights in an early stage of the criminal proceedings.

It is, however, not evident that a lawyer (or a police officer or magistrate) must verify the necessary conditions for the suspect to exercise their procedural rights at a given moment during the criminal investigation. As has been argued, the vulnerability of a suspect is interactive and dynamic, determined by numerous elements which are rather complex to assess and not always easy to discern.[88] In addition, given its interactive and dynamic nature, the vulnerability of a suspect should be identified for each situation and moment separately, considering the influence on the exercise of the procedural rights and the extent to which an adapted treatment is necessary.[89] Consequently, the vulnerability of a suspect is often unnoticed or overlooked by police officers and lawyers, which is especially true for the more 'subtle' vulnerability that is not readily observable.[90] Besides these issues, one also needs to be vigilant of suspects who deliberately feign certain symptoms (such as memory loss or a physical condition) to deceive the lawyer and/or the judicial authorities, for instance aiming for a lower

---

[86] Omzendbrief no. COL 8/2011, Nov 24, 2016 (second revised edition), 65; Orde Van Vlaamse Balies, *Salduz-Gedragscode*, Jan. 18, 2017, 3.2.

[87] Salduz v Turkey (2008), ECtHR para 54.

[88] See also Meysman, "Quo Vadis with Vulnerable Defendants in the EU?," 189-190.

[89] Gudjonsson, "Confession evidence," 126.

[90] See for example Lynn Douglas and Monica Cuskelly, "A Focus Group Study of Police Officers' Recognition of Individuals with Intellectual Disability," *Psychiatry, Psychology and Law* 19 (2011): 35-44; Connor Gillespie, "The Best Interests of the Accused and the Adversarial System," in *Addressing Vulnerability in Justice Systems*, ed. Penny Cooper and Linda Hunting (London: Wildy, Simmonds & Hill Publishing, 2016), 110; Gudjonsson, *The Psychology of Interrogations and Confessions*, 57-74; Gudjonsson et al., *Persons at Risk During Interviews in Police Custody*, 26; Susan Young, Emily J. Goodwin, Ottilie Sedgwick and Gisli H. Gudjonsson, "The Effectiveness of Police Custody Assessments in Identifying Suspects with Intellectual Disabilities and Attention Deficit Hyperactivity Disorder," *BMC Medicine* 11 (2013): 1-11.

sentence.[91] Consequently, the identification of a suspect's vulnerability becomes even more complex.

Given the time pressure inherent in a criminal investigation, the lack of specific (psychological) knowledge and training and the fact that identifying a suspect's vulnerability is not their primary task, lawyers (and police officers) are not fully liable for not being able to identify all suspects' vulnerabilities. In addition, the existing legal framework does not provide for clear and specific guidance on the approach to be taken to identify a suspect's vulnerability.[92]

The added value and limitations of existing screening tools

To overcome the complexity of this identification and considering its importance, several instruments, of which some are validated,[93] have been developed to facilitate the identification of psychological characteristics in particular. Firstly, reference can be made to the DSM-5[94], a handbook for defining and classifying mental disorders. Secondly, psychological tests and instruments have been developed for the purpose of 1) evaluating fitness for interview;[95] 2) evaluating competence to stand trial;[96] 3) measuring personality traits relevant to police interviews, such as compliance (GCS)[97] and suggestibility (GSS)[98]; and 4) the detection of feigned symptoms (SIMS).[99] Yet, most of these instruments are not readily

---

[91] See for instance John F. Edens, Norman G. Poytress and Monica M. Watkins-Clay, "Detection of Malingering in Psychiatric Unit and General Population Prison Inmates: a Comparison of the PAI, SIMS and SIRS," *Journal of Personality Assessment* 88 (2007): 33; Peter Giger, Thomas Merten, Harald Merckelbach and Margit Oswald, "Detection of Feigned Crime Related Amnesia: a Multi-Method Approach," *Journal of Forensic Psychological Practice* 10 (2010): 440-463; Kim Van Oorsouw and Harald Merckelbach, "Detecting Malingered Memory Problems in the Civil and Criminal Arena," *Legal and Criminological Psychology* 15 (2010): 97-114.

[92] See also Meysman, "Quo Vadis with Vulnerable Defendants in the EU?," 188.

[93] Not all screening tools used in criminal proceedings are validated (see Salma Ali and Scott Galloway, "Developing a Screening Tool for Offenders with Intellectual Disabilities," *Journal of Intellectual Disabilities and Offending Behaviour* 7 (2016): 163).

[94] Diagnostic and Statistical Manual of Mental Disorders, American Psychological Association, *DSM-5* (Arlington: American Psychiatric Publishing, 2013).

[95] Gudjonsson, "'Fitness for Interview'," 185-197; Norfolk, "Fit to be Interviewed by the Police," 5-12; Rix, "Fit to be Interview by the Police?," 33-40.

[96] See for instance Patricia A. Zapf and Ronald Roesch, *Evaluation of Competence to Stand Trial* (New York: Oxford University Press, 2009).

[97] Gudjonsson Compliance Scale, Gisli H. Gudjonsson, "Compliance in an Interrogative Situation: a New Scale," *Personality and Individual Differences* 10 (1989): 535-540.

[98] Gudjonsson Suggestibility Scale (Gisli H. Gudjonsson, "A New Scale of Interrogative Suggestibility," *Personality and Individual Differences* 5 (1984): 303-314.

[99] Structured Inventory of Malingered Symptomatology, Harald Merckelbach and Glenn P. Smith, "Diagnostic Accuracy of the Structured Inventory of Malingered Symptomatology (SIMS) in Detecting Instructed malingering,", *Archives of Clinical Neuropsychology* 18 (2003): 145-152.

applicable in practice and primarily aimed at mental health experts, while mostly a psychological examination will only occur when demanded by the defence lawyer, the police or competent magistrate. A mental health expert will only be involved after the initial identification of the potential vulnerability of the suspect has been made by these primary actors. Thirdly, other instruments are designed for practitioners in criminal cases and aim to support such identification, for instance with regard to intellectual disabilities.[100]

Although some of these instruments are intended to be used within the criminal justice system, they are nevertheless aimed at screening for specific psychological traits and disorders, as a result of which the interactive nature of a suspect's vulnerability is not considered. In addition, none of these are specifically aimed at defence lawyers. In England and Wales, though, valuable initiatives have been taken to assist the defence lawyer in identifying a suspect's vulnerability.

First, some practical suggestions are offered by Cape with regard to defending suspects in general, but also in particular regarding minors and (the identification of) adults who are mentally disordered or otherwise vulnerable because of possible language difficulties.[101] Although the responsibility to identify the potential vulnerability of a suspect is in the first instance put on the police officers,[102] Cape stresses that the lawyer should remain vigilant as well.[103] In the second instance, a rather extensive guideline is in place, specifically developed to assist lawyers in assessing their 'client's vulnerability'.[104] In addition to common sense and intuition as the best guide to identify a suspect's vulnerability, several sources of information are listed that can be used by the defence lawyer, including information from third parties; manner of speech; behavioural signs of stress; consciousness and coordination levels; medication use; and the suspect's performance on quick and small tests (such as a memory

---

[100] For instance the RAPID (Rapid Assessment of Potential Intellectual Disability), Ali and Galloway, "Developing a Screening Tool," 161-170; HASI (Hayes Ability Screening Index), Susan Carol Hayes, "Early Identification or Early Incarceration? Using a Screening Test for Intellectual Disability in the Criminal Justice System," *Journal of Applied Research in Intellectual Disabilities* 15 (2002): 120-128; LDSQ (Learning Disability Screening Questionnaire), Karen McKenzie and Donna Paxton, *LDSQ. Screening for Intellectual Disabilities in Adults* (Edinburgh: GCM Records, 2012), https://gcmrecords.wordpress.com/about/the-learning-disability-screening-questionnaire-ldsq/.

[101] Ed Cape, *Defending Suspects at Police Stations. The Practitioner's Guide to Advice and Representation* (London: LAG, 2011).

[102] See Codes of Practice C to the PACE Act, para 1.4.

[103] Ibid., 426.

[104] Eric Shepherd, *Police Station Skills for Legal Advisers: Practical Reference* (London: Law Society, 2004), 306-320.

or literacy test).[105] Finally, the (updated) Toolkit 10 to support the early identification of vulnerability in witnesses and defendants, developed by The Advocate's Gateway, serves as a valuable instrument to identify a suspect's vulnerability.[106] Grounded in best practices and the expertise of numerous professionals, it provides, in addition to general insights on vulnerability, good practice examples, suggestions for questions and behavioural indications that may contribute to an early identification of the vulnerability of witnesses, suspects and defendants.[107] The tremendous added value of these tools cannot be neglected nor underestimated, but they are still rooted in practice, not validated (yet) and particularly focused on individual characteristics.

It is worth mentioning that, especially in Belgium, there is insufficient knowledge of the approach to be taken by the defence lawyer in identifying a suspect's vulnerability. This knowledge gap relates to both the legal framework and current practices of that identification. Based on our on-going research project, it appears that the legal framework in Belgium does provide legal possibilities to identify a suspect's vulnerability during the pre-trial investigation. Preliminary results from interviews with lawyers, however, suggest that there is insufficient knowledge of and training about the potential vulnerability of suspects. In this regard, similar to the aforementioned perspectives, there appear to be very divergent views on the scope of a suspect's vulnerability. In addition, readily observable indicators (such as manner of speech and behaviour), experience and human knowledge seem to be the 'tools' used to identify that vulnerability instead of standardized or targeted methods or questions to be asked.

Therefore, in general – but definitely in Belgium – more emphasis should be placed on (developing) useful tools for lawyers,[108] especially because the responsibility of identifying and compensating for a suspect's vulnerability is increasingly assigned to them. This identification fits within the defence lawyer's task to defend the suspect and to serve in his best interest. Given the conceptualization of vulnerability and the challenges in its identification put forward in this chapter, an 'all-inclusive' tool – also including the interactive and dynamic nature of vulnerability – is needed. This tool should be an easily applicable and validated screening tool that enables lawyers (but possibly also police officers and magistrates) to identify early indicators of vulnerability throughout the pre-trial investigation.

---

[105]   Ibid.

[106]   Cooper (2017), *Toolkit* 10, 2.

[107]   Ibid. Interestingly, it can be noted that, in comparison to the initial version of the Toolkit, the updated version is less aimed at suspects in particular.

[108]   See also Verbeke et al., "Protecting the Fair Trial Rights of Mentally Disordered Defendants in Criminal Proceedings," 71.

By developing and validating such a tool as part of our ongoing research project, we hope to contribute to reducing the number of suspects whose vulnerability remains undetected in Belgium.

Conclusion

The increased attention given to so-called vulnerable suspects and defendants cannot be neglected and, given the importance of access to justice for all persons, this increased attention can only be encouraged. In this regard, the initiatives taken at the European level are to be embraced, but concrete actions in each Member State should also be encouraged in order to achieve an effective implementation of procedural safeguards. In addition, there is a need for more clarity on which persons need to be considered as vulnerable. This chapter, to some extent, tried to fill the knowledge gap on the theorization of the vulnerability of a suspect by proposing a new conceptual framework. To fully capture all the aspects of a suspect's vulnerability, an interactive and dynamic approach was suggested. In this regard, a suspect's vulnerability should be detached from individual characteristics or the impression that it concerns a homogenous group of persons that can be labelled as such beforehand.[109] In light of this, it was also suggested that the term 'vulnerable suspect' should be avoided and the term 'the vulnerability of a suspect' used instead.

Whereas some ambiguity exists as to the scope of a suspect's vulnerability, it is widely and clearly recognized within both the legal and academic perspectives that the identification of a suspect's vulnerability is crucial, but complex. It remains a difficult task for defence lawyers, police officers and magistrates, as a result of which a considerable number of suspects are missed out. Given the proposed conceptual framework, this is especially true if the actual functioning of the suspect is to be assessed for each specific moment and situation during the pre-trial investigation. The existing instruments to support the early identification of suspects have already importantly contributed to improvements as to identifying the vulnerability of suspects, but major challenges remain. In this regard, there is still more to be gained in reducing the under identification of a suspect's vulnerability. Although there is probably still room for improvement in every country regarding this issue, it can be argued that some major steps are still needed in Belgium especially, both in regards to the legal framework concerning a suspect's vulnerability and in respect of its identification. This becomes apparent when comparing Belgium with, for instance, England and Wales, where the legal provisions appear to be more established and where some decent screening tools to support practitioners are already developed and used.

---

[109] See also Cooper (2017), *Toolkit* 10, 8.

CHAPTER SIX

Caught by language: The language competence of young offenders and the implications for the (Dutch) youth justice system

Mr. Mw. K.G.M. van Dijk – Fleetwood-Bird [*]

The presence of severe language problems in the majority of the indigenous and immigrant young offenders is an unknown phenomenon in the Netherlands. Once juveniles encounter Dutch law enforcement, elaborate profiles are being created where the possible risk factors are mentioned.[1] However, what is not happening in the Netherlands is that young offenders are screened (as early as possible) for language problems. Policymakers in England are aware that these juveniles are disadvantaged because of undiagnosed language problems and realize that their 'fair trial' rights may be violated. In the Netherlands, this realization has yet to come.

It seems rather obvious that youthful defendants with multiple social-emotional, cognitive and developmental problems may also have a language problem. Is the one a consequence of the other? Why is it so important for the Youth Justice System to identify the language problems of these young people? This article will formulate an answer to this question.

Where language problems are concerned, the knife cuts both ways. On the one hand, language difficulties will affect the juveniles *personally* and there is a relationship with delinquent behaviour, which has implications in terms of (early) screening, treatment and the interventions offered. On the other hand, juveniles with language problems – are *vulnerable* as a suspect in legal proceedings, especially when it comes to the 'fair trial' principles. This has implications for the guarantees, which ought to be present for the young accused. In recent years, the research of language skills of young offenders is in attendance. In the United States, research has been done

[*] Mr. K.G.M. van Dijk – Fleetwood-Bird is a lecturer/researcher at the Erasmus School of Law, department of Healthlaw at the Erasmus University in Rotterdam. She has been working as a Speech- and language therapist for 20 years in the Rotterdam area. She has worked with young people with speech- and language difficulties in the primary care. This article is based on the developing dissertation of van Dijk – Fleetwood-Bird: *'Caught by language', Oral language competence of young offenders and the implications for the Dutch Youth Justice System.* Promotores: Prof. M.J.A.M. Buijsen, Prof. P.C. Snow & mr. dr. J. uit Beijerse.

[1] For example in the Netherlands; *'Landelijk Instrumentarium Jeugdstrafrechtketen'* (LIJ). Accessed May 12, 2017.http://www.wegwijzerjeugdenveiligheid.nl/fileadmin/w/wegwijzerjeugdenveiligheid_nl/oudesite/doc/criminele_jongeren/LIJ-Leidraad-in-de-Keten.pdf.

by Sanger et al.,[2] in England by Bryan et al.[3] and by Snow and Powell in Australia.[4] Research shows that a large percentage (ranging from 50% to 73,3%) of the juveniles in the criminal justice system have a significant, and not previously diagnosed, severe language disorder. The question that is addressed in this chapter is how these severe language problems may affect the current practice of the juvenile justice system. One must then think of police interrogations, participation in the criminal hearing, appointments with the probation service, and interventions offered (which are verbally), but also the restorative justice conferencing where language is the primary means to get the message across. It appears that in the Netherlands, young offenders are suffering from such language problems to the same extent.

Below the relationship between linguistic skills and delinquent behaviour will be explained. In her capacity as speech- and language therapist, the author has conducted linguistic research at the Young Offenders Institution 'De Hartelborgt', in the Netherlands. The outcome of her findings are described. Problems occurring during interrogations of young offenders with language disorders are outlined. Subsequently this chapter discusses language difficulties and the right to effective

---

[2] D. D. Sanger et.al., "Cultural analysis of communication behaviours among juveniles in a correctional facility", *Journal of Communication Disorders* 33 (2000): 31–57; D. D. Sanger, K. Hux & M. Ritzman, "Female juvenile delinquents, pragmatic awareness of conversational interactions", *Journal of Communication Disorders* 32 (1999): 281–295; D. Sanger et.al.,, "Prevalence of language problems among adolescent delinquents", *Communication Disorders Quarterly* 33 (2001): 17–26; D.D. Sanger et.al., "Oral skills of female juvenile delinquents", *American Journal of Speech-Language Pathology*, 6-1 (1991): 70-76.

[3] K. Bryan, "Preliminary study of the prevalence of speech and language difficulties in young offenders", *International Journal of Language and Communication Disorders* 39-3 (2004): 391–400; K. Bryan, J. Freer & C. Furlong, "Language and communication difficulties in juvenile offenders", *International journal of language & communication disorders* 42-5 (2007): 505-520.

[4] P.C. Snow & M.B. Powell, "Australian Institute of Criminology. Youth (in)justice: Oral language competence in early life and risk for engagement in antisocial behaviour in adolescence", *Trends & issues in crime and criminal Justice* 3 (2012): 421; P. C. Snow, "Child maltreatment, mental health and oral language competence: Inviting speech language pathology to the prevention table", *International Journal of Speech Language Pathology* 11-12 (2009): 95–103; P. C. Snow & M. B. Powell, "Oral language competence in incarcerated young offenders: Links with offending severity", *International Journal of Speech Language Pathology* 13-6 (2011): 480-489;. P. C. Snow & M. B. Powell, "Oral Language Competence, Social Skills and High-risk Boys: What are Juvenile Offenders Trying to Tell us?", *Children & Society* 22-1 (2008): 16-28; P.C. Snow & M.B. Powell, "What's the story? An exploration of narrative language abilities in male juvenile offenders", *Psychology, Crime and Law* 11-3 (2005): 239–253; P. C. Snow & M.B. Powell, "Developmental language disorders and adolescent risk: A public-health advocacy role for speech pathologists?", *International Journal of Speech Language Pathology* 6-4 (2004a): 221–229; P.C. Snow & M.B. Powell, "Interviewing juvenile offenders: The importance of oral language competence", *Current Issues in Criminal Justice* 16-2 (2004b): 220–225; P.C. Snow et.al., "Language functioning, mental health and alexithymia in incarcerated young offenders", *International Journal of Speech- Language Pathology* 26-1 (2016): 111-136.

participation, as protected by the Convention of the Rights of the Child, the UN Convention on the rights of persons with disabilities as well as a number of European directives. Conclusions are followed by a short summary of recommendations.

Language skills and the relationship with delinquent behaviour

Language skills refer to a set of auditory/verbal (listening and speaking) skills which would normally be developed steadily from birth. One can differentiate receptive skills (language comprehension) and productive skills (speaking of language). The receptive skills are developed slightly earlier than the productive skills, this applies to language acquisition of the mother language but also when learning a second language. During the first five years of life most of the language is acquired. In infancy the language acquisition process develops at an explosively high rate. *"All hell breaks loose"* during this period, according to Pinker, an American linguist.[5] This means that when children go to school, they already have a comprehensive receptive and productive language use and are able to share their experiences with others through talking.

Under optimal conditions, speech- and language development takes place in the context of a secure attachment, and the development of conscience. These parallel developments show the crucial role of language development for the generation of social skills. There is also a relationship between problems of neglect and abuse of children and a speech- and language development disorder.[6]

Language skills of young children play a crucial role in the transition to literacy in the first school years. Learning to read is basically a linguistic skill.[7] The children who have mastered this skill early are usually the ones who start school with well developed speaking- and listening skills, particularly in the way of storytelling, phonemic awareness (the ability to connect sound- and letter characters) and the skill to divide words into syllables. Reading- and spelling-skills are an integral part of being successful throughout the school career, as it applies to most school subjects.[8] Success in school increases the chance that a young person

---

[5] S. Pinker, *The Language Instinct. How the Mind Creates Language* (Harmondsworth: Penguin 2015) in: A.M. Schaerlaekens, *De taalontwikkeling van het kind* (Groningen: Wolters-Noordhoff, 2016), 146.

[6] P. C. Snow, "Child maltreatment, mental health and oral language competence: Inviting speech language pathology to the prevention table", *International Journal of Speech Language Pathology* 11-12 (2009): 95–103.

[7] H. W. Catts & T. P. Hogan, "Language basis of reading disabilities and implications for early identification and remediation", *Reading Psychology* 24 (2003): 223–246.

[8] J.E. Dockrell, G. Lindsay & O. Palikara, "Explaining the academic achievement at school leaving for pupils with a history of language impairment: Previous academic achievement

continues with an education and eventually achieves enough skills to enter the employment market.

In Australia they only pay attention to 'learning to read' during the first three years of school. Subsequently the education is guided towards 'reading to learn'.[9] It is no different in the Netherlands, the first school years are used to master the reading skill, and thereafter reading is an indispensable tool to follow the other subjects. Children who have not mastered the first skill (learn to read) will subsequently have incredible difficulty in mastering the second skill (read to learn). For boys in particular this is often the period (approximately 8 years old) when these problems are showing up in class.[10] These boys, whose language disorders are not diagnosed and who are troublesome in the classroom are seen as children with behavioural problems (while they actually have a language problem).

Language acquisition is a multifactorial process: language input, congenital language learning ability, cognitive development, social emotional development and fine motor skills all play a role. This way language development is closely intertwined with the general development of the child.[11] One speaks of a *primary* language disorder when the language disorder stands on its own and cannot be explained by other problems. There is a delay in the language development with a primary language disorder, which can express itself in a delay in language comprehension, language production (the vocabulary and sentence structure) or in pronunciation (forming the sounds).

Secundary language problems may arise due to other problems such as attention and concentration disorders, or in relation to cognitive problems (such as intellectual disabilities), a hearing disorder or and mental disorder. Secundary language problems may also arise if there is multilingualism or when a second language is learned later in life. For professionals it is not always easy to figure out what is causing the language problem. With most young people the cause of the language impairment remains unknown.[12]

---

and literacy skills", *Child Language Teaching and Therapy* 27-2 (2011): 223–237 and A.M. Schaerlaekens, *De taalontwikkeling van het kind* (Groningen: Wolters-Noordhoff, 2016), 225.

[9]   P. J. Hines, B. Wible & M. McCartney, "Learning to read, reading to learn", *Science* 23-328 (2010): 447.

[10]   N.J. Cohen, R. Menna & D. Vallance, "Language, social cognitive processing, and behavioural characteristics of psychiatrically disturbed children with previously identified language and unsuspected language impairments", *Journal of Child Psychology and Psychiatry* 39 (1998): 853–864.

[11]   A.M. Schaerlaekens, *De taalontwikkeling van het kind* (Groningen: Wolters-Noordhoff, 2016), 252.

[12]   S. McLeod, F. Press & C. Phelan, "The (In)visibility of Children with Communication Impairment in Australian Health, Education, and Disability Legislation and Policies", *Asia Pacific Journal of Speech, Language and Hearing* 1 (2010): 68.

In English-language research primary language disorders are commonly referred to as 'Specific Language Impairment' (SLI), and both primary and secundary language disorders as 'Speech, Language and Communication Needs (SLCN).[13] In the Netherlands the term 'Taalontwikkelingsstoornis' is used for primary language disorders. In this article reference is made to 'language disorders' and 'language problems', by which both primary and secundary language disorders are meant.

Young offenders present a complex problem and a challenge for those who work professionally with them. Juveniles with language disorders have to deal with prejudice and stigmatization. This stigma often starts at a young age, in the classroom where they have difficulty with language, reading and writing assignments and the demands posed on them by interaction in the classroom. These skills are also called 'oral language competence', which is described as:

> ... the ability to engage successfully with a range of communication partners via the spoken word, in order to conduct a wide variety of personal, social, educational, commercial and professional relationships. Such engagement should be reciprocal at the level appropriate to the nature of the interpersonal relationship and should conform to a range of developmental, cultural, and socio-linguistic norms. Oral language competence also confers the ability to progress to reading and writing at an educationally and developmentally timely juncture, provided adequate and appropriate instruction is provided.[14]

And in short, "The ability to use and understand spoken language in a range of situations and social exchanges, in order to successfully negotiate the business of everyday life."[15]

A number of studies have shown a relationship between language- and behavioural problems in young children. Insufficient language skills constitute a risk factor with unfavorable outcomes.[16] Language

---

[13] J. Bercow, *A Review of Services for Children and Young People (0-19) with Speech, Language and Communication Needs* (London: Department for Children, Schools and Families (DfES), 2008), 13.

[14] P.C. Snow & D.D. Sanger, "Restorative justice conferencing and the youth offender: Exploring the role of oral language competence", *International Journal of Language and Communication Disorders* 46-3 (2011): 324-333.

[15] P.C. Snow & M.B. Powell, "Australian Institute of Criminology. Youth (in)justice: Oral language competence in early life and risk for engagement in antisocial behaviour in adolescence", *Trends & issues in crime and criminal Justice* 3 (2012): 421.

[16] N. Cohen, M. Davine & N. Horodeszky, "Unsuspected language impairment in psychiatrically disturbed children: Prevalence and language and behavorial characteristics", *Journal of the American Academy of Adolescent Psychiatry* 32 (1993): 595–603.

development disorders in five-year-old boys are a risk factor for antisocial- and delinquent behaviour by the time they are 19 years old.[17] English research shows that language problems in early childhood constitute a risk factor for other problems such as reading- and writing problems and stagnation in school, which in turn pose a risk for delinquent behaviour. Despite the fact that juveniles often are labelled 'vulnerable' (because of - for example - drug-use, mental health problems or out-of-home care), the language disorder is rarely acknowledged.[18]

Australian longitudinal study has shown that poor language skills in the early years will increase the chance of antisocial behaviour in 14 year olds.[19] They have therefore advocated that solving language problems in young children can be used as a preventive strategy, aimed at reducing antisocial and delinquent behaviour. If these preventive measures are absent, these high risk children can 'slip through the net' and end up in the judicial system. Therefore, in Australia, a preventive initiative has started on a large scale: The Pathways to Prevention project.[20] This project was aimed, amongst other things, at enlarging the communicative and social skills of young children (4-6 years) to prevent or reduce antisocial and delinquent behaviour, as the children grew older. The results of the program were positive, particularly the boys showed a reduction in problematic behaviour at school.[21]

Research shows that these preventive programs are most (and lastingly) successful if different risk factors – including language problems – are addressed simultaneously, for an extended period. There is not one primary cause for criminal behaviour, and there is not one solution.[22] In any

---

[17] J. H. Beitchman et.al., "Fourteen year follow-up of speech/language-impaired and control children: Psychiatric outcome", *Journal of the American Academy of Child and Adolescent Psychiatry* 40 (2001): 75–82; J. H. Beitchman et.al., "Adolescent substance use disorders: Findings from a 14-year follow-up of speech/language impaired and control children", *Journal of Clinical Child Psychology* 28-3 (1999): 312–321; E. B. Brownlie et.al., "Early language impairment and young adult delinquent and aggressive behaviour", *Journal of Abnormal Child Psychology* 32-4 (2004): 453–467.

[18] K. Bryan et.al., "Language difficulties and criminal justice: the need for earlier identification", *International Journal of Language & Communication disorders* 50-6 (2015): 763.

[19] W. Bor, T. R. McGee & A.A. Fagan, "Early risk factors for adolescent antisocial behaviour: An Australian longitudinal study", *Australian and New Zealand Journal of Psychiatry* 38-5 (2004): 365–372.

[20] R. Homel et.al., "The Pathways to Prevention project: doing developmental prevention in a disadvantaged community", *Trends & Issues in Crime and Criminal Justice* 323 (2006): 1-6.

[21] The project is called since 2011: *Creating Pathways to prevention*. Accessed May 12, 2017. http://www.griffith.edu.au/criminology-law/griffith-criminology-institute/our-programs-of-research.

[22] National Crime Prevention, '*Pathways to prevention: developmental and early intervention approaches to crime in Australia, Summary Volume*, National Crime Prevention Attorney-General Department (1999): 20.

case, these studies all show that language problems in juveniles constitute an independent risk factor for developing delinquent behaviour. Snow and Powell have shown that over 50% of young male offenders have significant problems with figurative and abstract language, repeating sentences and the ability to tell stories. Perhaps the most important conclusion is that these language problems cannot only be explained by a low non-verbal IQ.[23]

A systematic review of 16 recent studies of the language ability of young offenders has revealed that both indigenous juveniles and juveniles with an immigrant background who come into contact with the judicial system, are very likely to have unnoticed (previously undiagnosed) severe language problems.[24] In all 16 studies, evidence is found for a strong correlation between juvenile delinquent behaviour and language problems. The delinquent youths score significantly lower on the language tests than the non-delinquent youths in the control groups. In England, these findings have given the signal that there should be more awareness and more training for this problem.[25]

If a gathering of professionals is asked to name the risk factors for delinquent behaviour for juveniles (criminogenic factors), it is very likely that factors such as low socio-economic status, low academic skills, parenting style and mental problems will be named as most important variables. Over the years a pendulum motion can be observed in the different criminological approaches and explanations.[26] Delinquent behaviour can generally not be explained by one single factor. The experts will probably point out the benefit of improving social skills but they will probably not specifically mention language skills, and their importance as a risk factor. This way of looking at language skills is no different in the Netherlands.

Extensive research has been carried out on minor learning disabilities in the criminal justice chain, the so-called 'LVG youths' in the Netherlands.[27] This research also mentions the risk factors as a complex interplay of different elements within the various fields of life, which may contribute to criminal behaviour. The criminogenic- or risk factors mentioned

[23]   P. C. Snow & M. B. Powell, "Oral Language Competence, Social Skills and High-risk Boys: What are Juvenile Offenders Trying to Tell us?", *Children & Society* 22-1 (2008): 16-28.
[24]   The studies took place between 1982 and 2016 in the United States, England and Australia. See: A.S. Anderson, J. Hawes & P.C. Snow, "Language impairments among youth offenders: A systematic review", *Children and Youth Services Review* 65 (2016): 195.
[25]   Ibid., 200.
[26]   I. Weijers & C. Eliaerts, *Jeugdcriminologie, Achtergronden van jeugdcriminaliteit* (Den Haag: Boom Lemma uitgevers, 2015), 18.
[27]   M. Teeuwen, *Verraderlijk gewoon, Licht verstandelijk gehandicapte jongeren, hun wereld en hun plaats in het strafrecht*, (Amsterdam: SWP, 2012).

include mental or physical disability, illness, divorce or death of parents, delinquent friends, leaving school prematurely, moving away, and poor living environment. There will be a particularly increased risk of criminal behaviour when confronted with an accumulation of risk factors in several areas.[28] In the research of youths with a minor learning disability, language skills, and the role they play as (independent) risk factor, are not specifically discussed, and 'language and communication' are only mentioned to be 'less developed' as a cognitive characteristic.[29] And to think that there is increasing evidence available that language skills can be identified as a 'key competence'.[30] There has even been research done to establish a link between the type of language disorder and the type of offense. Danish research, for example, shows that adolescents with severe expressive language difficulties were significantly more often convicted for sexual offenses.[31]

Language competence in a Young Offenders Institution

The research of language competence of young offenders in the Netherlands was carried out in 2012 in the Young Offenders Institution 'The Hartelborgt', location Spijkenisse. (Hereafter: The Hartelborgt). The Hartelborgt is one of the three locations of the Governmental Judicial Youth Institutions (Rijks Justitiële Jeugdinrichting RJJI).[32]

Since 2005, the number of juveniles with a conviction has declined steadily in the Netherlands. In 2012 a total of 1869 criminally convicted juveniles were incarcerated in a Governmental Judicial Youth Institution, in 2015 this number dropped to 1437. The Hartelborgt can accommodate 105 juveniles aged between 14 and 24, and is a closed facility.[33] The Hartelborgt houses juveniles who have been incarcerated in a youth penitentiary institution because of criminal convictions. They have been remanded for reasons of preventive custody, night detention, youth detention or a custodial sentence in a Judicial Youth Institution. The Hartelborgt has a shelter section,

---

[28] M. Teeuwen, *Verraderlijk gewoon, Licht verstandelijk gehandicapte jongeren, hun wereld en hun plaats in het strafrecht* (Amsterdam: SWP, 2012), 16.
[29] Ibid., 23.
[30] P.C. Snow et.al., "Improving communication outcomes for young offenders: A proposed response to intervention framework", *International Journal of Language & Communication disorders* 50-1 (2015): 1-13.
[31] S.E. Mouridsen & K.M. Hauschild, "A long term study of offending in individuals diagnosed with a developmental language disorder as children", *International Journal of Speech and Language Pathology* 11 (2009): 171-179.
[32] Justitiële Jeugdinrichting de Hartelborgt. Accessed May 12, 2017. http://www.dji.nl/locaties/justitiele-jeugdinrichtingen/de-hartelborgt/.
[33] Ministerie van Veiligheid en Justitie: Dienst Justitiële Inrichtingen, *DJI in getal 2011-2015, de divisies GW/VB en ForZo/JJI nader belicht.* April 2016. Accessed May 12, 2017. https://www.dji.nl/binaries/dji-in-getal-2011-2015-definitief_tcm41-121762.pdf, 77-79.

a treatment section and a forensic observation and supervision (counselling) section, as well as a ward for severe psychiatric problems.

A random selection[34] of 30 boys aged 15 to 18 years participated in the tests. The Clinical Evaluation of Language Fundamentals (CELF-4[nl]) was used.[35] This research tool is identical to the instrument that has been used in the language research in, inter alia, the United Kingdom and Australia. The CELF-4[nl] is standardized for Dutch children and adolescents. The aim of the language study is to determine which percentage of juveniles can be diagnosed with language disorders and whether this percentage differs from non-delinquent youths. A control group of non-delinquent youths has not been included in the test. Estimates of the prevalence of language disorders in young people range from 1 to 19% depending on the criteria and definitions.[36] Researchers in the United States and Australia have tested a control group of non-delinquent youth (12-19 years). Of these young people, 0-4% had a language disorder.[37]

In addition to the CELF-4[nl], a questionnaire about communication has been used. This questionnaire gives an idea of how the young person thinks about his or her speaking- and communication skills. Questions are asked about the voice, language comprehension and interaction with others. This questionnaire has been used in previous research, including in the research of Burrows and Yiga Citro in England and in Italy.[38] The Dutch questionnaire had an added question, namely: *"Have you ever had*

[34] A random selection of 30 juveniles has been made. The juveniles were not older than 18 years, they had followed a Dutch education for over three years and they did not stay in the forensic observation and guidance section (FOBA). Both indigenous youths and youths with a migration background were tested.

[35] The Clinical Evaluation of Language Fundamentals 4 – Dutch version (CELF-4[nl]) is a tool to be used individually in order to diagnose language and communication problems in children and juveniles between 15 – 18 years old. The test may be conducted by speech- and language therapists, school psychologists, and remedial educationalists. The test is an edited version of the American CELF-4(2003) and may be used in any given situation where a researcher wishes to check the linguistic skills of a juvenile. See: E. Semel, E.H. Wilg & W.A. Secord, *CELF-4[nl] Clinical Evaluation of Language Fundamentals Nederlandse versie Handleiding*, (Amsterdam: Pearson, 2010), 17-23.

[36] F. Coster, "Behavioral Problems in Children with Specific Language Impairments", (PhD diss., Rijksuniversiteit Groningen, 2001); L. Leonard, *Children with Specific Language Impairment* (Cambridge Mass: MIT Press, 2000) in: A.M. Schaerlaekens, *De taalontwikkeling van het kind* (Groningen: Wolters-Noordhoff, 2016), 260.; J. Tomblin et.al., "The association of reading disability, behavioural disorders and language impairment among second grade children", *Journal of Child Psychology and Psychiatry* 41 (2000): 473-482.

[37] See Table 1 in: A.S. Anderson, J. Hawes & P.C. Snow, "Language impairments among youth offenders: A systematic review", *Children and Youth Services Review* 65 (2016): 198.

[38] S. Burrows & I. Yiga, *Youth Offending and Speech Language Therapy (a controlled study)* (London: Ealing Counsel, 2012); R. Citro, A.G. De Cagno & T. Rossettio, "Federazione Logopedisti Italiani, Prevalence of Speech-Language-Communication difficulties in Italian young offenders: a pilot study", CPLOL Conference May 2012.

speech- and language therapy?". This question is intended to identify how many juveniles have been in contact with speech- and language therapy.

The *Core-index*[39] is used in the Dutch research to determine whether there is a language problem in general. Of the juveniles, 90% were diagnosed with a language disorder, 76.7% of which suffered from a *severe* language disorder. The findings are consistent with linguistic research in delinquent youths in England, where the percentage of delinquent youths with language disorders was 73.3%.[40] More specific than de Core-index is the *Expressive Language-index*.[41] This is used to determine whether there is a problem in the *use* of language (language expression). 90% of the young boys had a disorder of the expressive function, and 76.7% of which were diagnosed with a *severe* disorder of the expressive function.

The Communication Questionnaire results are not consistent with the extent of identified language problems: three-quarters of the young offenders (76.7%) will indicate that there are little or no communication problems, while 90% of young offenders have, in fact, been diagnosed with a language problem. 70% of the offenders with language problems have never had speech- and language therapy. Of the group of young offenders who need it most, the category with a *severe* language disorder, 60% have not received speech- and language therapy.

We can conclude that the results of research in the Netherlands are consistent with the findings of similar research in other countries, namely that youth offenders often have language problems. 90% of juvenile detainees are diagnosed with a language disorder and from that 90%, 76.7% are diagnosed with a *severe* language disorder. Assuming a rate of language disorders in non-delinquent youngsters of 0-4%,[42] the percentage of language disorders in young offenders in the Netherlands is considerably higher.

---

[39] The *Core-index* is made up from the total number of norm scores of the various components 'Repeating Sentences', 'Formulating Sentences, 'Word Definitions' and 'Word Categories Total'. A score of up to 77 indicates the presence of a language disorder.

[40] K. Bryan, "Preliminary study of the prevalence of speech and language difficulties in young offenders", *International Journal of Language and Communication Disorders* 39-3 (2004): 391–400; K. Bryan, J. Freer & C. Furlong, "Language and communication difficulties in juvenile offenders", *International journal of language & communication disorders* 42-5 (2007): 505-520.

[41] The *Expressive Language* Index is used to define the possible existence of a disorder in language *use*, (as opposed to language *understanding*). The *Expressive Language Index* is made up from the total number of components 'Repeating Sentences', 'Formulating Sentences', 'Word Definitions' and 'Expressive Word Categories'. A score of up to 77 indicates the presence of an *expressive* language disorder.

[42] See Table 1 in: A.S. Anderson, J. Hawes & P.C. Snow, "Language impairments among youth offenders: A systematic review", *Children and Youth Services Review* 65 (2016): 198.

Below a case study will illustrate how a young person may be challenged in his functioning because of a previously undiagnosed and untreated language problem.

Linguistic competences are measurable, as is intelligence. In a heterogeneous group of delinquent juveniles linguistic problems may

---

Case A. *

A 17-year-old boy participated in the CELF-4[nl] test in The Hartelborgt. He has a bilingual background and was born in the Netherlands. He usually speaks Dutch. It is, according to him, his best language. At first glance, it seems as if he has no severe language problems because he talks a lot, and fast. In his spontaneous speech, he speaks in simple, short sentences. He regularly looks for words and then uses 'stop words' like *"uhm"*, *"yeah right"*, *"thing"* and *"you know"*. His comprehensibility is not optimal, sometimes he shows a rather casual and indifferent impression and he makes little eye contact. A. has repeated a class when he was 6 years old and his high school is (yet) unfinished. He entered The Hartelborgt because of a severe violence offence.

Result:

A. scored on Core-index and Expressive Language-index 'less than average'. (Standard deviation of -3 and below). He has a *severe* language disorder in all language modalities: language form, -content and -use.

Explanation:

A. had an overall weak score on the test. He worked diligently during the test and his concentration was rather good. When using the Communication Questionnaire he said that he only occasionally encountered problems with his communication, he had *"a bit of trouble with language "* at school and he sometimes gets stuck for words when he does not understand people. He never followed a special education, speech- and language therapy or extra language lessons given at school. He said that he finds it difficult to keep appointments because he does not always understand what is asked from him. Given his scores, this is not surprising. In the section 'Understanding spoken paragraphs' (comprehension of language), he answered 40% of the questions correctly. Establishing connections between words is difficult for him (section 'Word Classes'), he scored only 23% of the questions correctly. An example: in four words: book-photo-phone-newspaper the correct answer is that book and newspaper belong together because they can both be read. A. said that *"books and photo"* belong together and gave as explanation: *"picture you can keep in a book."* Defining words is difficult for him. A 'valley' is *"a kind of small field or something"* and 'population' *"a sort of town or something."* With this section he scored 20% correctly. In the section 'Formulate Sentences', he answered 0% of the questions correctly. He did not once succeed in formulating a correct sentence in accordance with the illustration. He tried very often, but always used the wrong words or conjugation. For example, when he had to make a sentence with the word 'smiling' in connection with an illustration of a relay race with children he said: *"These children are smile because they passing piece of wood to the other child."*

Advice for severe language problems

A. can remember a sentence up to 9 words, with longer phrases he misses too much information. He has a lot of trouble understanding a question, with his syntax and telling a chronological story. Given the large language comprehension- and formulation problems of A., the advice is to avoid figurative speech, and to use short, simple sentences when talking to him, to explain difficult words and to always ascertain whether he has understood them. By allowing him, for example, to repeat what has been agreed upon or to ask questions in different ways and observe whether the response is consistent. Try to visualize important appointments wherever possible, so he can better understand the agreements he made, remember them and keep his appointments.

* A. is one of the 76,7% of youngsters diagnosed with a severe language disorder. The Dutch expressions have been translated into English.

arise through various circumstances. The cause of the linguistic problem could primarily be due to a language disorder, but could also be caused by a secundary language problem, due to cognitive problems, social-emotional hardships, multi-lingual problems, or a combination of causes. Research shows the 76.7% of the juveniles examined in a Young Offenders Institution are suffering from severe language problems, regardless of cause or background complications. In a large number of these juveniles the linguistic problems will show predominantly, although in a large number the language problem will probably remain unnoticed, even for the professionals. For them these language problems will remain in the background as other problems take priority.

Interrogation of juveniles with language problems

In 2015, twenty three thousand juveniles under 18 in the Netherlands were interrogated by the police.[43] Since March 1st, 2016, suspects of a criminal offence and held in custody by the police have the right to legal assistance during questioning. Since March 1st, 2017, an act has been effectuated with the aim to implement Guideline 2013/48/EU, regarding the right to access to counsel during criminal proceedings. And as from March 1st, 2017, an implementing decree[44] has come into effect, formalizing the rules regarding the role and competences of a lawyer during police interrogations and the already existing right to legal assistance from a lawyer prior to the police interrogation. (Hereafter: Decree Police Interrogations). In accordance with article 489 of the Code of Criminal Procedure, youthful suspects will not be able to refrain from legal assistance prior to police questioning.

The interrogation of suspects, regulated in, amongst others, Title II of the Code of Criminal Procedure. Article 29a is of importance in this respect. Paragraph 2 formulates it as follows: "The statements of the suspect, in particular those containing an admission of guilt, shall, for as much as possible, be registered in his own words. The statement of the suspect shall be as complete as possible and registered in the manner of questions and answers."

The question concerning suspects with severe language problems is whether the police report will be accurate enough, and representative enough to do the story justice. To what extent have 'his own words' been used? Below is an account of the problems which may be encountered because of the severe (unnoticed) language problems of a suspect during interrogation.

A major risk of undiagnosed language problems[45] is that under pressure - for example when a young person is interrogated by a police officer – this person will probably give a 'one-word-sentence' answer, will not be

---

[43] De Kinderombudsman, *Kinderrechtenmonitor 2016*, Universiteit Leiden, 110, Accessed May 12, 2017. http://www.dekinderombudsman.nl/ul/cms/fck-uploaded/Kinderrechtenmonitor2016.pdf.

[44] See for the Decree: Besluit van 26 januari 2017, houdende regels voor de inrichting van en de orde tijdens het politieverhoor waaraan de raadsman deelneemt (Besluit inrichting en orde politieverhoor), *Stb.*2017, 29.

[45] These language difficulties express themselves in poor auditory skills, a small vocabulary and poor narrative skills. See: P. C. Snow & M. B. Powell, "Oral Language Competence, Social Skills and High-risk Boys: What are Juvenile Offenders Trying to Tell us?", *Children & Society* 22-1 (2008): 16-28.

accurate and will give vague answers. Juveniles develop (consciously or unconsciously) ways to cover up their language problems, for example, by repeating words or phrases used by the interviewer, by giving stereotyped answers, by affirmative answers to yes/no questions, even if they do not understand the question and by using short stop words like *"thing"*, *"uuum"*, *"dunno"*, *"maybe"*. This is accompanied by poor eye contact and an occasional shrug.[46]

One possible consequence of these language problems is that the interviewer wrongly assumes that this behaviour arises from social- or emotional factors (e.g., avoidance behaviour, rudeness, guilt or refusal to cooperate with the interviewer) and not from an underlying language problem. This misinterpretation may compel the interviewer to ask more lengthy, leading and persistent questions, with even less clear answers as a result.[47]

When it comes to storytelling, language research has detected more reasons for concern. Juveniles with a severe language problem are much less able to tell a *chronological* story, and it is striking that these stories often lack specific details. This means that juveniles with a severe language problem find themselves at a disadvantage when it comes to telling 'their story', a skill crucial during interrogation and during the interactions in the courtroom. These juveniles leave out important details and even if details are mentioned, there are significant deficiencies in the information provided. If the interviewer is unaware of the underlying language problem, parts of the story might possibly be misunderstood, not believed, or will never surface.

There is such a thing as a *'conversational repair'*, which is the ability of a person to recognize that the listener did not understand something and then 'fix' it. This causes problems for juveniles with a severe language problem because they are not very good at it. Moreover, the balance of power during such an interview or interrogation does not provide enough incentive for the juvenile to engage in a 'conversational repair'.[48]

---

[46] P.C. Snow & M. Powell, "Contemporary Comments, Interviewing juvenile offenders: The importance of oral language competence", *Current Issues in Criminal Justice* 16-2 (2004): 223.
[47] P.C. Snow & D.D. Sanger, "Restorative justice conferencing and the youth offender: Exploring the role of oral language competence", *International Journal of Language and Communication Disorders* 46-3 (2011): 324-333.
[48] P.C. Snow & M. Powell, "Contemporary Comments, Interviewing juvenile offenders: The importance of oral language competence", *Current Issues in Criminal Justice* 16-2 (2004): 223.

This knowledge is not only important to the police officer and the professionals in court but also to the counsel of the young suspect. After all, part of the defense strategy of the accused is based on the story provided. Over the past decade the responsibilities of the defense have increased in the Netherlands. Consequently, the importance of the abilities of the accused and counsel has also increased, according to Kempen. These abilities cannot be detached from each other, they are interconnected, the quality of the defense depends on the capabilities of the defense counsel as well as the accused, and their cooperation.[49]

When it comes to the understanding of- and waiver of certain procedural rights, such as the right to remain silent (*Miranda* warning in the United States), Goldstein et.al. have also concluded that there is reason for concern:

> (...) Overall, the linguistic difficulties of juveniles impair both their receptive and expressive language abilities. Therefore, juveniles are likely to have problems (1) understanding the information provided to them in Miranda warnings and (2) communicating their understanding of their rights (or lack thereof) to police, parents, or attorneys. Given the combination of juvenile offenders' poor linguistic abilities with the high linguistic demands of juvenile warnings, juvenile suspects are at risk for failing to provide knowing and intelligent right waivers.[50]

Juveniles with a severe language problem are at risk of not understanding procedural rights, such as the right to remain silent or the assistance of a lawyer prior to the first interrogation. And they are at risk of not being understood or misunderstood when telling 'their story' during interrogation, with all its consequences. This way the right to a fair trial can (unintentionally) be denied to the young accused with unidentified severe language problems.

Language problems and the right to effective participation

Language problems of juvenile suspects can be seen as an 'invisible disability', which causes juveniles with a severe language problem to be disadvantaged during a criminal trial. The language problems described above are currently undiagnosed in the Netherlands – and, therefore, are

---

[49] P.H.P.H.M.C. van Kempen, "Aandacht voor de slechts beperkt capabele verdachte in voor- en hoofdonderzoek – aanbevelingen voor de wetgever", *DD* 22-34 (2016): 3.

[50] N.E.S. Goldstein et.al., "Potential impact of juvenile suspects' linguistic abilities on Miranda understanding and appreciation", in: M. Tiersma & L. Solan, *The Oxford Handbook of Language and Law* (Oxford: Oxford University Press, 2016), 302.

not visible to the professionals - before, during or after criminal proceedings. When a minor is suspected of an offense, it is essential that he understands the criminal proceedings in which he becomes involved. If that is not the case, his right to a fair trial as protected by Article 6 of the ECHR is at stake.

Rap and Weijers identify three moments of active participation of young offenders during youth criminal proceedings. The first moment occurs after reading the indictment by the prosecution and dealing with facts and circumstances by the judge. Usually the suspect will have the opportunity to clarify his or her side of the story. The second moment occurs when the juvenile is invited to comment on the rapports and clarify his or her personal circumstances. The third moment occurs when the suspect is given the opportunity to give a final comment, 'the final say'.[51] Rap and Weijers have done extensive research into the youth criminal proceedings in a number of European countries, using two core concepts, *participation* and *understanding*. Their judgement for the Netherlands regarding *participation* was generally positive, although they noted a considerable difference in approach in interrogation techniques amongst the various Dutch juvenile judges. They have advised training courses. Their judgement about *understanding* was less positive, though: a rather poor motivation of the judge's rulings, and a rather worrying amount of judiciary terms and jargon. They have ascertained that the use of language in general, and the use of judiciary jargon in particular will result in the juvenile feeling disconnected with a large part of the judicial process and cause a sense of disassociation.[52]

Young people should be able to participate effectively and that is not possible if they do not fully understand the process or when they cannot make themselves understood. With regard to effective participation, the European Court ruled in *SC v. United Kingdom*[53] that the accused has the right to participate effectively, which means not merely the right to attend and follow the proceedings. However, not every detail needs to be understood by the young person, a trial is already complicated enough to follow for adults with normal intelligence. The Court does, in fact, clarify this as follows:

> (…) However, "effective participation" in this context presupposes that the accused has a broad understanding of the nature of the trial process and of what is at stake for him or her, including the

---

[51] S. Rap & I. Weijers, *De jeugdstrafrechtzitting: een pedagogisch perspectief, De communicatie tussen jeugdrechter en jeugdige verdachte, Raad voor de rechtspraak* (Den Haag: Sdu Uitgevers, 2011), 99.
[52] Ibid., 142-143.
[53] ECHR 15 June 2004, nr. 60958/00, *(SC/United Kingdom)*, par. 28-29.

significance of any penalty which may be imposed. It means that he or she, if necessary with the assistance of, for example, an interpreter, lawyer, social worker or friend, should be able to understand the general thrust of what is said in court. The defendant should be able to follow what is said by the prosecution witnesses and, if represented, to explain to his own lawyers his version of events, point out any statements with which he disagrees and make them aware of any facts which should be put forward in his defense.

The question is whether juveniles with a severe language problem can participate effectively in a manner as described above by the Court. These young people run the risk of not understanding their procedural rights, including the right to remain silent or the right of access to a lawyer prior to the first interrogation, and the risk of not being understood, or their story mispresented during interrogation and this at their peril. In the context of a fair trial, one might also wonder whether the rights of juveniles with a severe language problem are sufficiently secured in connection with the rights derived from Article 12 of the International Convention on the Rights of the Child (CRC), 'the right to be heard' and article 13 'access to justice' from the UN Convention on the rights of persons with disabilities (which came into force in the Netherlands in January 2016), the rights deriving from European legislation. This summary is obviously not exhaustive, there are many treaties, laws and regulations that can be identified which may prove to be bottlenecks for juveniles with a severe language problem. For this article I shall confine myself to the ICRC, the UN Convention on the rights of persons with disabilities (hereafter: UN Disability Convention) and the implementation of three European directives in the Netherlands.

Convention on the Rights of the Child

The United Nations General Assembly declared 1985 to be the year of the child. The United Nations have developed various Child rights guidelines in recent years to shape the rights of juveniles in the juvenile justice system. In 1985, the Beijing Rules for the administration of juvenile justice[54] were adopted and, in 1990, so were the UN guidelines for the prevention of juvenile delinquency (Riyadh Guidelines 1990)[55] and the UN Minimum Rules for the protection of juveniles deprived of Their Liberty (Havana Rules 1990). [56] [57] The Beijing Rules and the Havana Rules are

---

[54] UN GA A/resolution 40/33, 1985.
[55] UN GA A/resolution 45/112, 1990.
[56] UN GA A/resolution 45/113, 1990.
[57] I. Mijnarends & T. Liefaard, "Het internationale kader", in: I. Weijers (red.), *Jeugdrecht in internationaal perspectief* (Den Haag: Boom Juridische uitgevers, 2014), 73.

both UN resolutions and therefore not legally binding as such. The UN Committee on the Rights of the Child, recommended in 2017 in General Comment No. 10 (Children's Rights in Juvenile Justice)[58] to incorporate both instruments into national legislation in order to fulfil the treaty obligations under the International Convention on the Rights Child (hereafter: the CRC).[59] Paragraph 4 of General Comment No. 10 advises States to implement a comprehensive juvenile justice policy to include and safeguard in particular the general principles of Article 2, 3 and 12 CRC and the specific juvenile justice principles of Article 37 and 40.[60]

The acceptance by the General Assembly of the CRC was an important step towards the protection of the rights of the child. With this treaty, legally binding frameworks were issued at international level for the treatment of juvenile suspects, as well as the manner of prosecution and trial. Towards the end of the last century the awareness grew that juvenile suspects should not only substantively, but also procedurally be treated differently from adult suspects. When dealing with juvenile suspects with severe language problems, Article 12 (Right to be heard) and Article 40, paragraph 2, under b VI (Free assistance of an interpreter) of the CRC, and recommendations 43-45 (Right to be heard), and 62-63 (Free assistance of an interpreter) of General Comment no. 10 will be important. According to the authors of the CRC, all treaty rights are necessary for optimal development of the child and all rights must be implemented to safeguard this development. For this reason treaty rights do not follow a specific hierarchy, which means that each specific treaty right must always be considered in relation to other rights.[61]

CRC Article 12 - the right to be heard – is essential for the juvenile who comes into contact with criminal law and this right extends throughout the trial to all professionals in the chain.[62] For the police, this means that the defendant has, in addition to the right to remain silent, an important right to give his or her perspective on what happened. Juvenile suspects,

---

[58] VN Kinderrechtencomité, *General Comment nr. 10* (CRC/C/GC/10), 25 April 2007.
[59] Y.N. van den Brink & T. Liefaard, "Voorlopige hechtenis van jeugdige verdachten in Nederland, naar rechterlijke besluitvorming conform internationale kinderrechten", *Strafblad* 3 (2014): 44-55.
[60] S. Rap & I. Weijers, *The Effective Youth Court, Juvenile Justice Procedures in Europe* (Den Haag: Eleven International Publishing, 2014), 36.
[61] I. Mijnarends & T. Liefaard, "Het internationale kader", in: I. Weijers (red.), *Jeugdrecht in internationaal perspectief* (Den Haag: Boom Juridische uitgevers, 2014), 76-78.
[62] *Art. 12 CRC, 1: States Parties shall assure to the child who is capable of forming his or her own views the right to express those views freely in all matters affecting the child, the views of the child being given due weight in accordance with the age and maturity of the child. 2: For this purpose, the child shall in particular be provided the opportunity to be heard in any judicial and administrative proceedings affecting the child, either directly, or through a representative or an appropriate body, in a manner consistent with the procedural rules of national law.*

therefore, should know from the beginning what their rights are and what they imply. An addition to the text formulates that the opinion of the child is related to the age and level of development of the child. Not merely for the sake of not burdening the child with the responsibility for the consequences of his opinion, but also to link the value and impact of his story to the juvenile's age phase.[63] Liefaard speaks in this context of 'Child-Friendly Justice': "The concept of Child-Friendly Justice has emerged under the European human rights system but is rooted in international children's rights, in particular in the child's right to be heard and participate as laid down in the UN Convention on the Rights of the Child." [64] Liefaard refers to the Guidelines on Child-friendly Justice and in particular, to Guideline 28: [65]

> (…) Whenever a child is apprehended by the police, the child should be informed in a manner and in language that is appropriate to his or her age and level of understanding of the reason for which he or she has been taken into custody. Children should be provided with access to a lawyer and be given the opportunity to contact their parents or a person whom they trust.

Using 'Child-Friendly *language*' is essential in Child-Friendly Justice and is mentioned as a recommendation, which appears several times in the Guidelines. 'Child-friendly *language*' is first and foremost language tailored to the child's level, in such a way that it is really understood.[66] Also, General Comment no. 10 is of interest in this context. Recommendation 44 emphasizes that the right to be heard must be guaranteed during all stages of the process. This means that a child must be well informed to be able to participate effectively, not only about the indictment but also about the process itself.[67] Moreover, the recommendations also apply to adolescents, according to the General Comment No. 20 (2016).[68] The effects of the severe language problems do not cease to exist when young people turn adolescent.[69]

---

[63] I. Mijnarends & T. Liefaard, "Het internationale kader", in: I. Weijers (red.), *Jeugdrecht in internationaal perspectief* (Den Haag: Boom Juridische uitgevers, 2014), 84-85.
[64] T. Liefaard, "Child-friendly justice: protection and participation of children in the justice system", *Temple Law Review* 88-4 (2016): 905.
[65] Comm. Of Ministers of the Counsel of Eur., Guidelines of the Committee of Ministers of the Counsel of Europe on Child-Friendly Justice 1, 13 (2010).
[66] Ibid., par. 28.
[67] VN Kinderrechtencomité, *General Comment nr. 10* (CRC/C/GC/10), 25 April 2007, par. 43-45.
[68] VN Kinderrechtencomité, *General Comment nr. 20* (CRC/C/GC/20), 6 December 2016, par. 23-25 (Right to be heard), par. 31-32 (Children with disabilities) en par. 87-88 (Justice for adolescents).
[69] K. Bryan et.al., "Language difficulties and criminal justice: the need for earlier identification", *International Journal of Language & Communication disorders* 50-6 (2015): 766.

According to Rap there are 4 conditions to facilitate understanding in juvenile suspects during the criminal proceedings.1) to explain the aim and procedure, as well as the role of all participants. 2) to avoid judicial jargon, 3) to explain the verdict and sentence, 4) to actually contribute in helping the suspect understand the implications of the criminal offence.[70] A number of implications will occur when dealing with juveniles with severe language problems.

How can those conditions be met when there is uncertainty about the existence of a severe language problem? Earlier research has shown that (all) juveniles under the age of 14 are experiencing difficulty in understanding the judicial process.[71] Linguistic research has made clear that even adolescents are having trouble with this. How does one explain adequately to juveniles what their rights are, if one is not certain whether understanding this explanation will pose a problem? How to make absolutely sure that the youngster has in fact understood the impact of his or her statement?

Consequently, when dealing with juvenile suspects with severe language problems, Article 12 CRC may prove to be a bottleneck. Juveniles with a severe language problem find themselves at a disadvantage when it comes to telling 'their story', a skill that is crucial during the interrogation and during interactions in the courtroom. Without understanding the language problems of these juveniles, the right to a fair trial could (unintentionally) be compromised or even denied.

The UN Convention on the rights of persons with disabilities

Language problems can be seen as a communication handicap. According to the World Health Organisation (WHO) and the International Classification of Functioning, Disability and Health for Children and Youth (ICF-CY) language problems fall under cognitive impairment and disability. In addition, language (developmental) problems originated from youth fall under this category.[72] Juveniles with a severe language problem can be seen as young people with a language *disability*. However, judging from the content of the recently ratified (in the Netherlands) UN Convention on the rights of persons with disabilities[73] it is doubtful

---

[70] S. Rap, "A Children's Rights Perspective on the Participation of Juvenile Defendants in the Youth Court", *International Journal of Children's Rights* 24 (2016): 103.

[71] Ibid., 100.

[72] Classification. Accessed May 12, 2017. http://www.who.int/classifications/icf/en/.

[73] 33 992 (R2034) Rijkswet houdende goedkeuring van het op 13 december 2006 te New York tot stand gekomen Verdrag inzake de rechten van personen met een handicap (Trb. 2007, 169 en Trb. 2014, 113).

whether the right deriving from Article 13 (access to justice)[74] is sufficiently secured for these young people.

The Dutch Explanatory Memorandum of the UN Disability Convention states that the possible effect of treaty provisions, as such, has not been discussed when establishing the Convention. Most treaty provisions are programmed to instruct the State to take the necessary measures to secure the rights of persons with disabilities.[75] The Court, in their assessment of the direct effect of provisions of the UN Disability Convention might find it helpful to determine whether those provisions correspond with provisions of other conventions such as the International Covenant on Civil and Political Rights (ICCPR) and the Convention on Human Rights and fundamental freedoms (ECHR). A less drastic way international law can 'work through' in Dutch law, is by non-direct application. The Dutch court has already more than once ruled a non-direct application of Article 13 of the UN Disability Convention. [76] [77] The Optional Protocol to the UN Disability Convention[78] has currently not yet been signed by the Netherlands.[79] If the Netherlands would join the Optional Protocol in the future, a special individual complaint right will then be created - as well as an investigative competence of the Committee.[80]

The first paragraph of Article 13 of the UN Disability Convention determines that persons with disabilities will be able to participate and

---

[74] *Article 13 UN Convention on the rights of persons with disabilities, 1: States Parties shall ensure effective access to justice for persons with disabilities on an equal basis with others, including through the provision of procedural and age-appropriate accommodations, in order to facilitate their effective role as direct and indirect participants, including as witnesses, in all legal proceedings, including at investigative and other preliminary stages. 2. In order to help to ensure effective access to justice for persons with disabilities, States Parties shall promote appropriate training for those working in the field of administration of justice, including police and prison staff.*

[75] *Kamerstukken II* 2013/14, R2034, 3, (MvT), 9.

[76] G.J. Pulles, *VN Gehandicaptenverdrag, Tekst en Toelichting* (Den Haag: Boom juridisch, 2016), 19.

[77] Gerechtshof Leeuwarden, 13 April 2010, ECLI:NL:GHLEE:2010:BM1464 and HR 17 December 2010, ECLI:NL:HR:2010:BO1801 (concl. Langemeijer).

[78] The Optional Protocol to the Convention on the Rights of Persons with Disabilities, Accessed May 12, 2017. https://zoek.officielebekendmakingen.nl/trb-2009-194.HTML

[79] State Secretary van Rijn (Ministry of Health, Wellbeing and Sports) recently sent a letter to the Senate announcing that they will start with the Optional Protocol to the International Covenant on Economic, Social and Cultural Rights (ICESCR). The State Council will be asked to consider the potential impact the Optional Protocol for the national legal system. On the basis of that decision, the Cabinet will make a judgment about the other protocols (including The Optional Protocol to the Convention on the Rights of Persons with Disabilities). See: *Kamerstukken I* 2016/17 33 992 (R2034), F, 3.

[80] G.J. Pulles, *VN Gehandicaptenverdrag, Tekst en Toelichting* (Den Haag: Boom juridisch, 2016), 11.

have effective access to justice.[81] According to the Dutch Explanatory Memorandum, persons with disabilities can always ask employees of the Court for additional help and guidance, but as it is, the staff receives no extra training for this.[82] However, in the Convention the importance of language and communication is emphasized and the definition of communication is explained very extensively.[83]

In General Comment no. 1 to the UN Disability Convention it is highlighted in recommendation 39, that professionals should be trained to recognize (and interact with) people with disabilities. And a person with a disability should be able to rely on additional support to make statements or give evidence, in order to enable them to follow and understand all legal proceedings. The shape of this extra support is not compulsory, for example, it may consist of the use of alternative communication methods, the use of video recordings, or a special sign language interpreter.[84] In the Netherlands, Kempen has recently asked for attention to be given to the limited capabilities of vulnerable suspects at the preliminary hearing. He also indicates that under Article 13 of the UN Disability Convention, there is an obligation for the authorities to take positive measures to ensure the right to effective participation. States should ensure and facilitate that persons with disabilities can play an effective role as direct and indirect participants, in all legal proceedings.[85]

European directives

Defence for Children [86] has researched whether the procedural rights of minors, who do not have the Dutch nationality and come into contact with criminal law, are adequately secured. The outcomes and recommendations of this study are also important for indigenous youths and youths with a migration background with a severe language problem. The implementation of three European Directives have been looked at: Directive 2010/64 / EU

---

[81] Regarding the information given to suspects, the starting point for the information material of the Court authorities is language level B1 of the internationally recognized guideline for language level index (Common European Framework of Reference).

[82] *Kamerstukken II* 2013/14, 33 993 (R2034), 3, (MvT), 48.

[83] Ibid., 23. Communication has been broadly defined. It includes languages, text presentation, braille, tactile communication, capital letter printing, written texts, audio texts, simplified language, spoken language, and alternative methods, means and ways of communication. Language includes speech, sign language and other ways of non-spoken language.

[84] VN Kinderrechtencomité, *General Comment nr. 1* (CRC/C/GC/1), 19 May 2014, par. 39.

[85] P.H.P.H.M.C. van Kempen, "Aandacht voor de slechts beperkt capabele verdachte in voor- en hoofdonderzoek – aanbevelingen voor de wetgever", *DD* 22-34 (2016): 3.

[86] Defence for Children International The Netherlands – ECPAT The Netherlands: *Procedural Rights of Juveniles Suspected or Accused in the European Union,* Terres des Hommes: 14 November 2016.

on the right to interpretation and translation in criminal proceedings; Directive 2012/13 / EU on the right to information in criminal proceedings and Council; Directive 2013/48 / EU The Right of Access to a Lawyer, the Right to have a Third Party Informed upon Deprivation of Liberty and the Right to Communicate with Third Persons and with Consular Authorities. Since March 1st, 2017, an act has been effectuated with the aim to implement Guideline 2013/48/EU, regarding the right of access to counsel during criminal proceedings. As from March 1st, 2017, the Decree Police Interrogations has come into effect, formalizing the rules regarding the role and competences of a lawyer during police interrogations.[87]

One of the most important conclusions of the study is that a language barrier renders the child *vulnerable* during criminal proceedings. However, it is not true that every child who does not have the Dutch nationality has insufficient command of the Dutch language by definition, nor that every Dutch child has sufficient command.[88] No distinction is made between the granting of rights for Dutch and non-Dutch minors, according to the researchers. They still issue a number of recommendations regarding the three European directives. A relevant recommendation for this subject is Recommendation II of the Right to interpretation and translation (Directive 2010/64 /):

> ... ensure that more attention is given to the implementation of a specialized sign language interpreter for children, who are deaf or have a hearing impediment. For this purpose, it is important that officers conducting interrogations have more knowledge of the language development of these groups of children.

Also with respect to the right to information (Directive 2012/13 / EU), the distinction is made in Recommendation VI for children who are deaf or have a hearing impediment:

> Verify whether sufficient appropriate information material is available. (...) Moreover, it was pointed out that, with regard to deaf children or children with a hearing impediment, the available information material is not adapted to their limitations and that they

---

[87] See for Decree: Besluit van 26 januari 2017, houdende regels voor de inrichting van en de orde tijdens het politieverhoor waaraan de raadsman deelneemt (Besluit inrichting en orde politieverhoor), *Stb.*2017, 29.

[88] Defence for Children International The Netherlands – ECPAT The Netherlands: *Procedural Rights of Juveniles Suspected or Accused in the European Union,* Terres des Hommes: 14 November 2016, 50.

are generally completely deprived of information material that is.[89]

Both recommendations acknowledge the needs of a specific group of children who are deaf or have a hearing impediment. It is the author's view that these recommendations for special training of professionals and customized information for juveniles should also apply to *all* young suspects with severe language disorders and communication problems. Regardless of the cause or the underlying problems of the youths.

According to the ECHR, one of the skills important for effective participation is language competence.[90] Suspects who do not speak the (necessary) language, must have at least an interpreter present and States have a positive obligation to provide additional protection for vulnerable suspects who are (functionally) illiterate.[91] For certain crimes[92] in the Netherlands the protection currently offered to suspects under 16 years of age or suspects with an (apparent) intellectual disability or cognitive dysfunction, consists of the mandatory audio-visual recording of the interrogation. With the help of these recordings a trial judge can form his or her own opinion whether a defense (made on behalf of the suspect) has been carried out under too much pressure or exertion by the police during questioning.[93] [94] Whether this protection is sufficient for young suspects with a severe language problem is still questionable.

---

[89] Defence for Children International The Netherlands – ECPAT The Netherlands: *Procedural Rights of Juveniles Suspected or Accused in the European Union,* Terres des Hommes: 14 November 2016, 50-51.

[90] For example: ECHR 14 Oktober 2014, nr. 45440/04 *(Baytar/Turkey),* par. 46-59 (violation due to absence interpreter during police interview), ECHR 19 December 1989, nr. 10964/84 *(Brozicek/Italy),* par. 38-42 (information should be given in a language that is understood), ECHR 5 April 2011, nr. 35292/05 *(Saman/Turkey),* par. 27-37 (violation due to absence interpreter during police interview).

[91] ECHR 5 April 2011, nr. 35292/05 *(Saman/Turkey),* par. 27-37 (violation due to absence interpreter during police interview).

[92] Direction auditory and audiovisual recording of interviews of complainants, witnesses and suspects.
Accessed May 12, 2017. http://wetten.overheid.nl/BWBR0032552/2013-01-01. Translated from Dutch: *Under A: Audio registration of interrogations is mandatory when dealing with suspects of crimes punishable under the Criminal Code and which include a victim fatality, or which offence will result in a conviction of 12 years or more, or when evident severe bodily harm has been established, or with respect to a sexual offence in a dependency relationship.*

[93] Ibid., *Under B: Audio visual registration is mandatory: 1. during all interrogations of suspects and intended interrogations of witnesses and informants when the interrogating officer during interrogations has the support of a behavioural expert, or when the interrogated suspect is vulnerable and dealing with a misdemeanor as mentioned under A. Vulnerable are those minors under 16, and persons with an evident mental disability or cognitive disorder. If the minor is under 12 years of age, the interrogation will be conducted in a child-friendly studio. 2. When a witness is being interrogated by a behavioural expert.*

[94] J. uit Beijerse, *Jeugdstrafrecht, Beginselen, wetgeving en praktijk* (Apeldoorn: Maklu, 2013), 113.

The counsellor plays an important role during questioning. The Decree Police Interrogations enables counsel to start making observations or ask questions at the very beginning of the interrogation, or just before closure.[95] It would also enable counsel to alert the officer of the suspect's possible language problems and any ensuing problems this might cause during questioning.

Based on the Decree Police Interrogations counsel is also entitled to point out to the officer that a suspect has not understood a question.[96] However, the Explanatory Memorandum signals a bottleneck in this article: how does counsel determine whether the suspect has understood a question without being able to ascertain this for himself? The counsellor, based on article 5 of the Decree, will not be granted permission to ask questions during interrogation. Which makes this entitlement a mere *'dead letter'*.

According to the Explanatory Memorandum, most suspects are perfectly capable of indicating whether they have understood a question and that the interrogating officers are also able to make their own assessment. Therefore, the police have suggested cancellation of this item.[97] Luckily, for the suspect - this has not happened. It is questionable whether the suspect is indeed capable of indicating whether he, or she, has understood a question, and whether all interrogation officers are sufficiently experienced to make such an assessment. Moreover, it is not likely that counsel would be able to notice this without conferring with the suspect.

In England, there is a 'special measure' included in the Youth Justice and Criminal Evidence Act 1999[98] which can help juvenile witnesses before and during trial to use so-called "Intermediaries". The judge will determine whether this special provision is needed. All young witnesses under 18 with a communication problem may qualify for this special provision, but also (adult) witnesses and suspects with a severe language problem, with deafness or a hearing impediment, a learning disability or a mental problem. Unfortunately, in England and Wales the statutory provision does not apply to suspects and defendants in England and Wales thus there

---

[95] Artikel 5, lid 2. Besluit van 26 januari 2017, houdende regels voor de inrichting van en de orde tijdens het politieverhoor waaraan de raadsman deelneemt (Besluit inrichting en orde politieverhoor), *Stb.*2017, 29.

[96] Artikel 6, onder a. Besluit van 26 januari 2017, houdende regels voor de inrichting van en de orde tijdens het politieverhoor waaraan de raadsman deelneemt (Besluit inrichting en orde politieverhoor), *Stb.*2017, 29.

[97] Besluit van 26 januari 2017, houdende regels voor de inrichting van en de orde tijdens het politieverhoor waaraan de raadsman deelneemt (Besluit inrichting en orde politieverhoor), *Stb.*2017, 29. (NvT), 14.

[98] Youth Justice and Criminal Evidence Act 1999, section 29. Accessed May 12, 2017. http://www.legislation.gov.uk/ukpga/1999/23/contents.

is no accredited scheme[99] though Registered Intermediaries are uniquely available for vulnerable suspects in the police interview and vulnerable defendants (if they choose to give evidence at trial) in Northern Ireland.[100] A judge's power to direct an intermediary for a defendant in England and Wales is severely limited.[101] In England and Wales and Northern Ireland a vulnerable suspect should have an 'appropriate adult' at the police station however this person's role is different from that of a communication facilitator;[102] the appropriate adult is not likely to be an expert in speech and language.

In the Netherlands, it is now common practice at the police station that 'third parties' join the interrogation once the interviewers believe that the nature of the offence or the physical or mental condition of the accused warrants this.[103] Dealing with a suspect with severe language problems would, in my view, be sufficient reason to do the same. A 'third party' should in this case be an expert, such as a forensic speech- and language therapist, or an Intermediary (like the English model). Speech- and language therapists in the Netherlands are mainly engaged in primary and secondary healthcare and education. In the Netherlands, speech- and language therapists do not play a role in the criminal justice system, unlike other countries such as Australia, England and Scotland, where evidence-based practice of speech- and language therapists in the judiciary is much more common.[104]

---

[99]   Penny Cooper & David Wurtzel, "A day late and a dollar short: in search of an intermediary scheme for vulnerable defendants in England and Wales," *Crim. L.R,* 2013, 1, 4-22.

[100]   Penny Cooper & David Wurtzel, "Better the second time around? Department of Justice Registered Intermediaries Schemes and lessons from England and Wales," (2014) 65(1) *NILQ,* 39. Penny Cooper & M. Mattison, "Intermediaries, vulnerable people and the quality of evidence: An international comparison of three versions of the English intermediary model," *International Journal of Evidence and Proof* (2017) (in press).

[101]   L. Hoyano and A. Rafferty, "Rationing defence intermediaries under the April 2016 Criminal Practice Direction," *Crim. L.R.* 2017, 2, 93-105 and Cooper P. "Case comment *R v Rashid,*" *Crim. L.R,* 2017, 5, 420 – 421.

[102]   Fn 101.

[103]   G.J. Pulles, *VN Gehandicaptenverdrag, Tekst en Toelichting* (Den Haag: Boom juridisch, 2016), 57.

[104]   A. Clark, E. Barrow & K. Hartley, "Unmet need in Scotland's criminal justice system", *Feature Criminal Justice* 2 (2012): 20-21; J. Clegg et.al., "Language abilities of secondary age pupils at risk of school exclusion: A preliminary report", *Child Language Teaching and Therapy* 25-1 (2009): 123–139; R. Homel et.al., "Canberra: Australian Institute of Criminology. The pathways to prevention project: Doing developmental prevention in a disadvantaged community", *Trends & Issues in Crime and Criminal Justice* 323 (2006): 1-6.

> An English example of a young person with language problems in court, without the assistance of an Intermediary.[*]
>
> A judge says in a loud, deep voice to a young suspect: *"Are you remorseful?!"* The young suspect does not understand the word 'remorseful' but the word sounds like a 'serious' offence. With a wavering voice the suspect answers: *"No."* The judge then imposes a measure restricting his freedom instead of a community service.
>
> [*] Interview with D. Minnitt. Operational Manager, Milton Keynes Youth Offending Team, People Directorate, Milton Keynes Council.

Conclusion

Research in recent years in the United States, England and Australia of language skills of young offenders has demonstrated that a large percentage of juveniles in the criminal justice system have a significant, and earlier undiagnosed (severe) language disorder. Evidence is accumulating that language competences are being identified as a 'key-competence'.[105]

Research in the Netherlands has brought to light that 90% of the juveniles have a language disorder, and 76.7%, have a severe language disorder. These findings are consistent with linguistic research of delinquent youth in England, where the percentage of language disorders was 73.3%.[106]

The language problems of these young people can be seen as an 'invisible disability' within the juvenile justice system. The fact that a young person who comes into contact with criminal law, may have undetected severe language problems has wide implications for the juvenile justice system, particularly when fair trial principles are at stake, such as the right to remain silent, access to justice and the right to be heard. These problems should be taken into account during all the criminal proceedings, when arrangements are made with probation, for (verbal) interventions or therapies, or in victim-offender meetings where sufficient language skills are essential for an effective and satisfying conversation.

[105] P.C. Snow et.al., "Improving communication outcomes for young offenders: A proposed response to intervention framework", *International Journal of Language & Communication disorders* 50-1 (2015): 1-13.

[106] K. Bryan, "Preliminary study of the prevalence of speech and language difficulties in young offenders", *International Journal of Language and Communication Disorders* 39-3 (2004): 391–400; K. Bryan, J. Freer & C. Furlong, "Language and communication difficulties in juvenile offenders", *International journal of language & communication disorders* 42-5 (2007): 505-520.

Where language problems and the right to effective participation are concerned, Article 12 CRC, the right to be heard, has been examined. This right is essential for the juvenile who has come into contact with the judicial system and extends to every professional in the chain during the entire proceedings. For the police this means that the suspect, besides the right to be silent, is by rights entitled to express his vision of what has occurred. The juvenile suspect must, therefore, be informed from the start of the proceedings what his rights are, and what they contain.

Interrogations might become strenuous when a juvenile suspect with severe language problems shows signs of inattentiveness and has developed ways to cover up, or hide any language problems. His aptitude to tell a chronological story is less developed, and specific and accurate details are left out. In addition, the absent, or diminished, ability of the suspect to engage in *'conversational repair'* might lead to misunderstandings. These language problems may result in a disadvantageous position for the juvenile when telling 'his or her story' during interrogation. Parts of the story might be misunderstood, not believed, or might simply never surface.

With regard to three European directives (on the right to interpretation and translation in criminal proceedings, the right to information in criminal proceedings and the right of access to a lawyer) and Article 13 of the UN Disability Convention and Article 12 of the UNCRC, it has been explained why there are bottlenecks when it comes to juveniles with a severe language problem. The problems are centered in particular around the supply of information, understanding the procedural rights and their consequences, and the ability to tell 'one's story' during all criminal proceedings.

As from March 1st, 2017, the Decree Police Interrogations has been effectuated, formalizing the rules regarding the role and competences of a lawyer during police interrogations as well as the existing right to consultation with counsel prior to questioning. The Decree gives counsel the possibility to ask questions immediately after the start of the interrogation, and give comments or ask questions just before closure. It would also give counsel the opportunity to alert the questioning officer to the fact that the suspect may have language problems and the possible ensuing problems during questioning. Based on the Decree counsel is also entitled to inform the interrogating officer when the suspect does not understand the question put to him. However, it is hard for counsel to judge whether the suspect has understood a question without conferring with him. This rather diminishes the effectivity of such an entitlement.

The first recommendation which can be made, has, in fact, been made before: to organize proper training for anyone dealing with these vulnerable suspects.[107] And specifically a training to recognize and acknowledge severe language problems in young offenders and to apply communication techniques to ensure and facilitate *accurate* communication. Rap and Weijers have already made a recommendation in 2011 to juvenile court judges to follow a course in the field of communication with young vulnerable people.[108] Van den Brink too stresses the importance of these training sessions and, in his opinion, the judge has an *'active duty'* to ensure that the accused understands what is being said, in order to participate as fully as possible.[109]

Another recommendation which can be made is to set up a system in the Netherlands – following the Northern Ireland example - of intermediaries for vulnerable suspects and defendants. In Northern Ireland (and in England albeit not as a statutory scheme for suspects and defendants), many professionals have already gained years of experience with this system of intermediaries and the results seem positive so far. Moreover, England has introduced 'The Advocates Gateway', a platform which brings together both judges and lawyers with the aim to protect the rights of vulnerable suspects and witnesses.[110] The goal of The Advocate's Gateway is to provide free access to practical, evidence-based information, to organize continuing education for professionals and they offer a dozen 'Toolkits' to facilitate questioning of vulnerable suspects (including suspects with cognitive - and language problems) and ensure the fair trial rights. The idea is to launch an international scientific debate on vulnerable suspects. Despite the fact that the legal system in England has a fundamentally different (adversarial) character compared to some other countries, this problem knows no boundaries.[111] Another useful organization in England, called 'The Communication Trust', shares information via a website[112] and focuses on professionals working with delinquent youths with language- and communication problems.

---

[107] Defence for Children International The Netherlands – ECPAT The Netherlands: *Procedural Rights of Juveniles Suspected or Accused in the European Union*, Terres des Hommes: 14 November 2016, 50-52.;VN Kinderrechtencomité, *General Comment nr. 10* (CRC/C/GC/10), 25 April 2007, par. 63., VN Kinderrechtencomité, *General Comment nr. 20* (CRC/C/GC/20), 6 December 2016, par. 23 and VN Kinderrechtencomité, *General Comment nr. 1* (CRC/C/GC/1), 19 May 2014, par. 39.
[108] S. Rap & I. Weijers, *De jeugdstrafrechtzitting: een pedagogisch perspectief, De communicatie tussen jeugdrechter en jeugdige verdachte, Raad voor de rechtspraak* (Den Haag: Sdu Uitgevers, 2011), 142.
[109] Y.N. van den Brink, "De onschuld voorbij? Over de toepassing van de voorlopige hechtenis ten aanzien van minderjarige verdachten in Nederland", *FJR* 1 (2012): 11.
[110] The Advocates Gateway. Accessed May 12, 2017. http://www.theadvocatesgateway.org/.
[111] P. Cooper & L. Hunting, *Addressing Vulnerability in Justice Systems* (London: Wildy, Simmonds & Hill Publishing, 2016), xvii.
[112] Sentence Trouble. Accessed May 12, 2017. http://www.sentencetrouble.com.

The last recommendation is the development of an accessible, validated language screening that can be carried out by multiple professionals, for example a police officer.[113] The problem of 'invisible disability' can be overcome to a great extent if a short, simple language screening is carried out as early as possible (Similar to the SCIL instrument developed in the Netherlands, to identify slightly mentally disabled young people, including young offenders).[114] If police officers were to conduct this language screening prior to a preliminary hearing, timely expert advice (as described above) could be invoked if necessary and it will be clear during the criminal proceedings whether or not a young suspect has a severe language problem. If appropriate, the suspect may undergo a more thorough examination by an expert at a later stage. By organizing early identification one has taken account of the fact that a young suspect might have a severe language problem and this knowledge can be extended to all relevant professionals throughout the criminal proceedings. This way the State will honour the positive obligations and the *special protection measures'* resulting from international, European and national regulations, and the rights of the juvenile suspects with severe language problems will be optimally secured.

---

[113] The use of a universal language screening for juveniles who come into contact with the justice system is also recommended by Snow and others in: P.C. Snow et.al., "Improving communication outcomes for young offenders: A proposed response to intervention framework", *International Journal of Language & Communication disorders* 50-1 (2015): 1-13.

[114] See: SCIL 14-17 and SCIL 18+ from: H. Kaal et. al., "Identifying offenders with an intellectual disability in detention in The Netherlands", *Journal of Intellectual Disabilities and Offending Behaviour* 6-2 (2015): 94-101.

CHAPTER SEVEN

Justice denied? The experience of unrepresented defendants in the criminal courts

Penelope Gibbs

"I have prosecuted trials against unrepresented defendants. It is a complete sham and a pale imitation of justice." (prosecutor)[1]

Executive summary

What price justice? There have always been defendants in the magistrates' courts who have appeared without a lawyer, particularly in traffic cases. But research suggests that there has been a significant increase in the number of people representing themselves who are not choosing to do so. The main reasons are:

- ineligibility for legal aid due to income or type of offence,

- lack of awareness of rights to legal aid, and

- lack of organisation.

How vulnerable are unrepresented defendants? We have no data on the proportion with mental health problems, learning difficulties, English as a second language etc, but everyone who does not have a lawyer is potentially vulnerable. All unrepresented defendants are actors in a drama for which they have no script, stage directions or prompts, and in which the stakes are very high.

The judges and lawyers we interviewed are all concerned that unrepresented defendants are at a disadvantage, and only differed in their views of how significant that disadvantage was. As one Magistrate pointed out, luck plays its part. If an unrepresented defendant appears in front of a very empathetic bench, an experienced legal advisor and a prosecutor who is also used to defending, they are likely to be patiently coached through the process. But they may instead face a busy court, with no legal advisor, where inexperienced and/or impatient advocates and judges are under pressure to deal with cases speedily. It takes time, skill and confidence to deal with unrepresented defendants well, and involves treading a fine line between providing support, and maintaining the neutrality of the court process. Unfortunately, many lawyers felt that some colleagues and court

---

[1] Quotations throughout this paper are extracts from "Justice denied? The experience of unrepresented defendants in the criminal courts," London: Transform Justice, 2016.

staff do not go the extra mile and, even when they do, cannot make up for the lack of a defence advocate.

There are no official figures for the number of unrepresented defendants in the Magistrates' Courts, though all interviewees felt numbers had recently increased. 7% of defendants in the Crown Court are unrepresented. The lack of data means unrepresented defendants in the Magistrates' Courts are invisible in policy terms. Many advocates doubt there are genuine savings to the state in denying legal representation to defendants, but the absence of a cost benefit analysis means we don't know for certain.

What is clear is the cost to justice – interviewees had witnessed unrepresented defendants not understanding what they were charged with, pleading guilty when they would have been advised not to, and vice versa, messing up cross examination of witnesses, and getting tougher sentences because they didn't know how to mitigate. Most advocates felt more and better access to legally aided lawyers was the only answer.

Certainly, that is one potential remedy, but we should also look at the whole system. Lawyers and judges themselves find it hard to keep up with criminal law and procedure, and are under constant pressure to speed up cases. If we are to deliver justice, we essentially have two options - to fund lawyers for all defendants who want or need them, or to change the whole system so that the needs of unrepresented defendants are integral.

Research sources and methods

This has been a difficult area to research since there is very limited academic research or data on the subject. We have used qualitative evidence, the data that exists, and articles from mainstream and social media to reach our conclusions.

Data: We used a survey conducted by the Magistrates' Association (MA)[2], and data generated by the Ministry of Justice (MoJ) and the Legal Aid Agency. Some of the latter has been obtained via FOI[3] requests.

Transform Justice worked with the Institute for Criminal Policy Research[4] (ICPR) to gather evidence. Dr. Gillian Hunter and Dr. Jessica Jacobson designed a survey for prosecutors in December 2015/January 2016, to which 42 responded. This was promoted on Twitter and via email.

---

[2] Magistrates Association. *Survey on litigants in person and unrepresented defendants (2015)*. Magistrates' Association members in certain areas agreed to report on numbers of unrepresented defendants and type of case each time they sat. We have excluded Family Court cases in our analysis.

[3] Freedom of Information Act 2000.

[4] Part of Birkbeck, University of London.

An earlier survey was promoted on Twitter in February 2015 to which 54, mainly solicitors, responded. Lastly Transform Justice posted a poll on Twitter. The identities of the respondents are unknown but Transform Justice's following is dominated by lawyers and legal experts.

Interviews: ICPR interviewed ten prosecutors from the independent Bar, four District Judges and seven Magistrates. We are very grateful to the Judicial Office for permission to interview the judges[5] involved. We did not have permission from the relevant bodies to interview CPS staff or legal advisers. We also made ultimately unsuccessful efforts to interview unrepresented defendants themselves.

Observations: we commissioned four post-graduate students (Niall Williams, May Deegan, Amanda Clough and Claire Kershaw) to observe unrepresented defendants in court proceedings in the Magistrates' Courts in the East, South-East, North-East and West of England. They observed courts over 34 whole days in December 2015 and January 2016 focussing on hearings involving unrepresented defendants.

In the main, we have focussed our work on unrepresented defendants in the Magistrates' Courts. Our evidence on unrepresented defendants in the Crown Court comes from the prosecutors we interviewed and surveyed, most of whom worked in both Magistrates and Crown Courts.

How many people are unrepresented?

There are few people prosecuted in court who have no help from a lawyer at any point. Some people use the same trusted lawyer (or solicitor plus barrister) at every stage, from police station interview, throughout every court hearing. Others may use a lawyer for some stages but not others.

In the magistrates' courts, the MA survey and all our interviewees indicate that the numbers who are unrepresented for at least one hearing make up a significant minority. Magistrates in the MA survey reported that 26% of defendants who came before them in 2014 were unrepresented. The number unrepresented in different types of hearings varied immensely from nearly half in private prosecutions, to one in five at first hearings. The magistrates said that defendants were unrepresented in over a fifth of (non-traffic) trials and sentencing hearings.

The Magistrates and District Judges we interviewed had very differing estimates of the proportion of unrepresented defendants, ranging from 15% to 40% of non-traffic cases - the differences may be due to individual

---

[5]   Any reference in this paper to judges encompasses both Magistrates and District Judges.

experiences or to regional differences. Cases ranged from first hearings, to trials and remand hearings, and the offences included assault, theft and public order. As mentioned previously, there are no official statistics on the number of unrepresented defendants in the magistrates' courts. Although all legal advisers and court associates fill in court forms which ask whether the defendant is represented and whether they applied for legal aid, this data is not systematically collected or collated.

MoJ have published figures showing that 6985 (7% of all) Crown Court defendants were unrepresented at first hearing in 2015.[6] There is also a significant number of people who are unrepresented at appeal. 5% (where representation was noted) of those appealing conviction or sentence from the magistrates' court were unrepresented in 2014 and 2015[7]. And in the annual report of the Court of Appeal the registrar wrote; "applications for leave to appeal lodged by applicants acting in person have increased by 25.3% this year: a significant proportion"[8]. In 2014/15, 6% of applications to appeal were from unrepresented people – the same proportion as in the crown court.

Has there been a change in the number of unrepresented defendants?

Of 143 responses to a Transform Justice poll on Twitter,[9] 90% of respondents felt that there had been an increase in unrepresented defendants in the criminal courts in the last two years, while 8% felt that there had been a decrease. There has definitely been a small but significant increase of 2% in the proportion of unrepresented defendants in the Crown Court 2013-2015.

The Magistrates Association survey (which has a relatively small sample size) indicated a small increase in numbers of unrepresented defendants in the magistrates' courts from 23% in February 2014 to 27% in November 2014. Numbers of unrepresented defendants increased across all criminal hearings except remand and traffic trials.

Who has a right to a legally aided lawyer?

Legal Aid in Magistrates' and Crown Court criminal cases is granted if the defendant's income meets the prescribed criteria, and it is in the interests of justice to provide representation[10]. The right to a legally aided lawyer has not changed since 2010. Means testing for Magistrates' Court

---

[6]   Ministry of Justice Criminal Courts Statistics Quarterly (Jan-March 2016).
[7]   Ministry of Justice Freedom of Information request 103857.
[8]   Court of Appeal Criminal Division Annual Report (2014-15).
[9]   https://twitter.com/PenelopeGibbs2/status/706444378127073280.
[10]   Ministry of Justice guidance: Criminal Legal Aid Testing accessed online May 2017.

cases was re-introduced in 2006, and for Crown Court cases in 2010. In practice you usually cannot get legal aid in the Magistrates' Court if you are accused of a non-imprisonable offence. This includes nearly all traffic offences.[11]

In the case of imprisonable offences, people who have a disposable household income of less than £22,325 can get legal aid for a case in the magistrates' court. Those who are accused of more serious crimes, which are heard in the Crown Court, will be granted legal aid if their disposable household income is less than £37,500 a year.[12] Some Crown Court defendants get a proportion of their costs met by legal aid, and also pay a contribution themselves. Those who qualify for legal aid can choose their own solicitor, as long as their firm is registered with the Legal Aid Agency.

Some people who turn up at court without a lawyer, can still consult one, whatever their means. All those who are accused of an imprisonable offence (and those already in custody) are entitled to consult the duty solicitor in the Magistrates' Court, if it is their first appearance, they are pleading not guilty and they have not already contacted or contracted an alternative solicitor. Most Magistrates' Courts have a duty solicitor to whom court staff and judges will refer eligible defendants with a court hearing that day. Duty solicitors are only permitted to give advice to a client for one hearings; all subsequent hearings will be covered by a non-duty lawyer, or the individual may be unrepresented.

If a judge suspects that an unrepresented defendant is entitled to legal aid, or to see the duty solicitor, they can and often do delay or adjourn the case.

Why do defendants represent themselves?

"When I first started, the unrepresented ones were the mad ones who you couldn't talk to. Now it's because they can't afford to pay the legal aid contributions" (prosecutor Crown Court).[13]

There are have always been unrepresented defendants, but our interviewees felt that changes to the way legal aid has been managed in recent years have prompted an overall increase. There is neither routine

---

[11] The interests of justice test determines whether a client is entitled to legal aid based on merits. As part of the test,the assessor must consider the 'Widgery criteria' which include whether someone is likely to lose their livelihood or suffer serious damage to their reputation. All cases involving under 18 year olds meet the Widgery criteria.

[12] Thresholds for legal aid have not been adjusted for inflation since their re-introduction.

[13] Ibid n1.

data nor research on why people are unrepresented, so our conclusions are based on our interviews, survey, and court observations.

Our findings appear to suggest that the growing barriers to accessing legal representation mean that it is this group which may be increasing in number.

Noone can be compelled to use a lawyer. There have always been people who refuse a lawyer because they feel they can advocate for themselves as well as, or better than, a lawyer. All our interviewees had come across members of what some called the "awkward squad". One interviewee was prosecuting an unrepresented defendant in the Crown Court in a major money laundering case. The defendant had sacked one set of lawyers and was determined to defend himself, even in this complex case. One prosecutor described such people as being on "a self-destruct collision course", another thought the decision was more tactical, "I have prosecuted two unrepresented defendants who had clearly worked out they could cause more disruption that way". One District Judge felt that such unrepresented defendants tended to be male, middle class and middle aged. Some judges mentioned Freemen on the Land[14] as examples of those who refuse to have a lawyer on principle. A significant minority of the "awkward squad" were perceived to have mental health problems which clouded their understanding of the value of legal advice. Prosecutors felt that a greater proportion had chosen to represent themselves in the Crown Court than in the Magistrates' Courts. But our findings suggest that the growing barriers to accessing legal representation mean that it is the group of "reluctant unrepresented" which may be increasing in number.

Why do people end up representing themselves but not by choice? Most of the prosecutors who responded to our survey felt financial considerations were the dominant factor why people represented themselves but not by choice.

These are the main reasons why defendants represent themselves suggested by those we interviewed:

- Legally aided defendants become dissatisfied with the lawyers they have been using and prevented from seeking another. Some defendants dismiss their lawyers because they feel they are not defending them well enough. They are usually allowed to seek new lawyers once, but judges' patience may run out if they want to change lawyer a second or third time. Some lawyers and judges

---

[14] Freemen on the Land do not believe they are bound by our laws, and therefore do not consent to any part of the legal process.

see such defendants as part of the "awkward squad". But refusal to let a defendant seek another lawyer can leave defendants feeling they have no choice but to conduct long and complex Crown Court trials themselves (see the case of Roger Khan[15]).

- Some people of middle income cannot afford to employ a lawyer. Many people earn too much to qualify for legal aid, but not enough to afford to employ a lawyer privately. Others feel the contributions demanded by the Legal Aid Agency (LAA) are too high. Private lawyers are likely to charge at least twice legal aid rates (which all advocates say are not adequate, particularly after recent cuts), and a defendant will not get back all their private fees even if their case collapses or they are acquitted.[16]. This prompts many, who would prefer to have a lawyer, to defend themselves.

- Some defendants appear to be eligible for legal aid on income grounds, but their applications are rejected. People who are self-employed, do casual work or rely on the charity of friends and family, often have very low or no income, but find it hard to prove their financial situation to the LAA.

- If an LAA form is filled out incorrectly in any way, it can be rejected. A delay may occur while this is resolved, which leads to the defendant not being represented by a lawyer for at least one hearing.

- Anyone who has already contracted or contacted a solicitor may be prevented from using the duty solicitor at the court. So if a legal aid application has not been approved, or a solicitor does not turn up, defendants can find themselves unrepresented.[17] One defendant who was observed at court was accused of assaulting a police officer. His solicitor had not turned up and he was about to represent himself in court: "It doesn't matter if I go in on my own or not. It won't change anything. They said I punched that copper so I'm going to prison". Another problem is that some defendants feel the duty solicitor is working for the state and so can't be trusted.

---

[15] https://www.theguardian.com/law/2016/jun/10/defendant-represented-himself-case-review-roger-khan (accessed July 31, 2017).
[16] Transform Justice. Innocent but broke (2015).
[17] The duty solicitor can act as in these circumstances if it is a non-business day (i.e. Saturday) or the own client solicitor cannot be contacted prior to the hearing or the court is unable to determine whether there is a own client solicitor already acting for the client.

- Many first time defendants simply don't understand the system, and arrive at court not knowing their rights to legal aid, or the importance of having legal advice. They may have been unrepresented at the police station.

- Those with chaotic lives may not be organised enough to arrange a lawyer. "For some people with learning needs, or drink and drug issues, even though they have been through the system many times, they lack knowledge about how to find a solicitor and tend to just come to court and hope to get the duty solicitor" (District Judge).[18]

- Some interviewees felt that access to the duty solicitor had become more limited in recent years, and thus they had less time to help unrepresented defendants.

- Courts are under huge pressure to reduce delays and avoid adjourning cases. Some advocates felt judges had become less likely to stop a case to allow a defendant to seek legal aid or to see the duty solicitor.

Understanding the charge and whether to plead guilty or not

"I could count on the fingers of one hand how many have actually understood the charges. I have had one who was facing a GBH s18 charge, believing he is in court for common assault and being shocked when I had to tell him the serious nature of the charge" (prosecutor).[19]

Many prosecutors were concerned that people would accept the charge against them without understanding the implications of the charge, or that alternative, lesser, charges might be more appropriate. Lawyers will ask for a charge to be "downgraded" if the evidence supports this.

Prosecutors also said that unrepresented defendants found it hard to understand whether the case against them was strong or weak. As a result, it was felt they could not make an informed decision about whether they should plead guilty or not. Unrepresented defendants are often not clear what counts as a viable defence. This leads them to plead not guilty when they have no real chance of being acquitted. A lawyer would have been able to advise them of their situation, and of the risk of losing credit for a guilty plea in going to trial.

[18] Ibid n1.
[19] Ibid.

"There are more not guilty pleas, definitely because people don't understand the difference between a defence and mitigation. They might accept the conduct...but plead not guilty because they had a good reason to do it. But this is not a reason to plead not guilty" (prosecutor).[20]

The opposite also occurs, with one prosecutor suggesting that sometimes unrepresented defendants do not realise the strength of their case and "are bullied by the clerks and bench into pleading guilty." A magistrate was also concerned:

> ...they are told by the clerk if you plead guilty at the earliest opportunity the court will be more lenient than if you plead not guilty and are found guilty in the long run, so it's a bit of a game of poker in this respect, and I think...that's wrong. If someone believes they are innocent, then they should hold their nerve but a lot of them will cave in.[21]

Trials

Our research suggests that those who find themselves forced to go to trial without representation are subject to multiple disadvantages. Some of these are practical - one usher told us that unrepresented defendants usually end up at the bottom of the court list, sometimes even having their case adjourned to the next day, despite arriving first. Lacking proper understanding of the court system, they were unable to prevent this happening.

One barrister was also concerned that the court experience could be very stressful for someone not familiar with it:

> the court can be a scary place, people can be incredibly nervous and distressed by the experience of going to court - they might fear they are going to be sent to prison for a basic road traffic offence when the most they are going to get is a fine...So the anxiety and stress of the court process, and ignorance of it, can be worse for [an unrepresented defendant].[22]

Waiting many hours in court for their case to be called can exacerbate the anxiety. For many, this is just the start of their problems.

[20] Ibid.
[21] Ibid.
[22] Ibid.

Preparatory paperwork and the digital system

"You have to make sure they have the correct papers – they will often lose the papers that have been sent to them, or not bring them to court, or bring the wrong bundle" (prosecutor).[23]

Unrepresented defendants are at an immediate disadvantage in preparing for their cases. The CPS are required to send all the relevant files by post to the defendant before their trial. However, our evidence suggests that this is not a reliable system. Examples were given of files being sent to a solicitor the defendant had met but did not engage. Other times, the defendant may not have a fixed address at which to receive post. One prosecutor felt this in itself could lead to miscarriages of justice:

"... a defendant does not know what documents to expect and by when. CPS will often dump loads of evidence on the defendant on the day of trial. I recently did a case ... where there was simply no evidence of the first count. Having listed the matter for an application to dismiss, the CPS denied receiving the Skeleton (court had it and defence had proof of sending); it was put over to the day of trial to argue. The trial had started when the evidence was provided to the defence."

Court observation: unrepresented defendant does not have paperwork

A Polish man was accused of the theft of a bankcard and possession of a knife. He had an interpreter but no lawyer, despite wanting to be represented. The CPS said they served papers on the solicitors they thought were acting for him, but the defendant had not received them. In court the documents were emailed to the legal assistant and then given to the defendant. He was given time to read them but came back into court, and said he thought there were a number of discrepancies in the documents he was given. The defendant said he didn't want to represent himself, "I don't really know the law enough. I'd like to have a fair trial". In the end the chair of the bench conceded that the documents had not been served on the accused or they had been served a month late, and that the current trial had been compromised and needed to be adjourned.

---

23 Ibid.

Unrepresented defendants are excluded from the new digital case file system being rolled out across England and Wales. This can put an individual at a significant disadvantage, as they must work from paper copies of the files. The police, prosecutors, defence, judges and court staff will all have access to the same digital case files. As a result, unrepresented defendants are likely to see the files later than others (if they get them at all), and in a form which is potentially much less convenient for them. If the defendant has not received the case files in advance, the court should adjourn to a different day. However, there is pressure on courts to avoid delay, and unrepresented defendants may be unaware of their rights. So far, unrepresented defendants are also excluded from using the new court wi-fi systems which are being introduced throughout England and Wales.

Evidence and disclosure

Our research suggests that unrepresented defendants do not have an effective understanding of evidence and the rules of disclosure:

> "...very few (even those who have been through it before) understand how the process works. They also have difficulties when evidence/ disclosure is not done, in knowing they are entitled to it, and can force the crown's hand at this point. I have prosecuted some who have simply no idea what was happening." (prosecutor).[24]

Another prosecutor pointed out that, "their clumsy approach to the laws of evidence and admissibility mean that sometimes evidence is introduced that would not normally feature in a trial, thus requiring further discussion and remedy".

Unrepresented defendants also struggle to challenge evidence. As one prosecutor explained, "some of these issues or challenges will not come to light, no-one analyses it, no-one picks holes in it and it's just unfair. The state is paying people to prosecute and it's got to pay someone, if you can't afford it, to defend."

Perhaps the biggest problem is that unrepresented defendants don't understand the procedures in relation to evidence. Experienced advocates will focus only on particular points of disputed evidence as opposed to the agreed facts. One prosecutor suggested that, "people on the outside forget how much the system depends on people co-operating really." Our research suggests that unrepresented defendants struggle to navigate the legal processes and procedure and to coherently present their case.

---

[24] Ibid.

Calling witnesses and cross-examination

"Justice isn't served simply because they can't do a thorough cross-examination" (Magistrate).[25]

There was consensus amongst interviewees that the unrepresented defendant often flounders in preparing for and conducting cross-examination. Interviewees reported that they often do not call the right witnesses to back up their defence, or fail to call a prosecution witness when they don't agree with their evidence. Interviewees suggested that the normal procedure of court can be upset when unrepresented defendants force the prosecution to call witnesses whose evidence could have been agreed in advance: "An unrepresented defendant will "fully bind" more witnesses than a competent lawyer" (prosecutor). [26]

We were told of a witness to a minor car park accident who travelled from Slough to St Albans to give evidence, only to discover that noone actually disputed his testimony.

Prosecutors and judges said most unrepresented defendants did not understand the basic rules of cross-examination. One prosecutor told us: "[u]nrepresented defendants don't understand the question and answer process, and they tend to try and put their [whole] case to the witness".

Concern among interviewees arose in relation to a range of things they had witnessed in court. Unrepresented defendants wanted to make statements to witnesses rather than ask questions, and when they did, often asked irrelevant or "illegal" questions. Above all, it was felt they often did not understand how to challenge prosecution witnesses: "…they don't make the right points, they don't ask the right questions. They can actually undermine their own case" (prosecutor). In seeking to make cross-examination as fair as possible, judges and prosecutors explained that they may step in where an unrepresented defendant is struggling. This raised concerns in itself, as one prosecutor outlined:

> "The judge has to do all of the work for them, and is in a tricky position because he is meant to be impartial, but may have to take over cross-examination. I have, in all my years of prosecution, never met a layperson who can [cross-examine] on their case. They choose to give statements and expect an answer. I often seek to have a

---

[25] Ibid.
[26] Ibid.

court appointed defence advocate to aid through this minefield." (prosecutor)[27]

Unrepresented defendants and vulnerability

"It's defence solicitors...who realise [their client] has difficulty understanding or certain vulnerabilities...They are the ones who flag up that there should perhaps be a psychiatric report or some change to the court process – an intermediary to help the defendant understand the questions...If you don't have a solicitor flagging those things up...nobody knows, they remain hidden." (prosecutor)[28]

A full assessment by a mental health practitioner may pick up issues, while experienced advocates may be able to spot signs too. However, vulnerable unrepresented defendants may slip through the net. As one prosecutor described, there are a,

"... number of defendants who suffer either from undiagnosed mental health conditions, or serious mental health conditions, which mean that they have no insight into their disorder. And it is wrong to imagine that it is obvious when someone suffers from serious mental health problems, often it really is not."

Judges and Magistrates we interviewed stressed they would deal with disabled defendants with the same care and compassion, whether unrepresented or not. Where vulnerabilities are clear, judges adapt the process or seek legal help, but advocates, and the evidence of our observations, suggested vulnerabilities may be missed or even ignored. If this happens, unrepresented defendants miss out on the support available – assessments, expert reports, access to intermediaries, input into mitigation, ability to argue that they are not fit to plead.

One issue highlighted by a Magistrate was that only some of her colleagues have enough training to recognise hidden vulnerability:

"What you need are very highly trained, specialist Magistrates, which in that sense we don't have ... So you may have someone who really doesn't understand the questions they are being asked... and you may have a very good legal adviser who can [re-phrase them], but it's pot luck and I don't think a court process should be pot luck."

[27] Ibid.
[28] Ibid

Court observation: unrepresented defendant with mental health problems

A man in his late 20s was on remand for the theft of a mobile phone. He had mental health issues and had seen a mental health practitioner but was refusing to see a solicitor. He gave evidence to the court via video-link. When the legal adviser to the Magistrates asked the unrepresented defendant for his plea, he asked if he would be allowed home again. He then said it was a "not guilty plea due to a psychotic episode". The adviser accepted the plea but said, if he was relying on a defence of psychosis, he would need medical evidence covering the period of the offence. The unrepresented defendant was not granted bail. The CPS had very little on file about the offence, but said the unrepresented defendant was remanded in custody as he had failed to attend court after being charged with the offence.

Sentencing

"On balance a person who is unrepresented stands a 15% chance of getting a longer sentence or a worse outcome than if he was represented, even by a not very competent advocate." (prosecutor)[29]

"Sentencing requires access to the guidelines, an understanding of what they are reading and then how to apply them...I have watched a bench give a community penalty when a skilled advocate would have got a Conditional Discharge for the same offence and facts." (prosecutor)[30]

A few respondents had seen unrepresented defendants get relatively lenient sentences, in their view because judges or juries felt sorry for them: "Sometimes you get cases where the jury think that it is obviously unfair that the defendant hasn't got a lawyer, and I've seen cases where somebody has been acquitted because the jury didn't like the imbalance" (prosecutor).[31]

However, most advocates thought unrepresented defendants got tougher sentences - not because judges were tougher on them, but because unrepresented defendants had no idea how to mitigate. A lawyer will find out as much as possible about their client's personal circumstances,

[29] Ibid.
[30] Ibid.
[31] Ibid.

and the circumstances of the crime, and knows what mitigating factors fit the sentencing guidelines. Unrepresented defendants have no idea what is, and isn't relevant. We heard from one prosecutor that, "I have not yet heard a good plea in mitigation from a self-representing defendant. The mitigation usually turns out to be a rehearsing of the facts...or a simple "I don't know what to say"".[32]

If judges do not have information to mitigate the sentence, they can't act on it. A District Judge admitted that mitigation was, "particularly important. An advocate can make all the difference to a conditional discharge instead of a fine - they tell you a bit more that a defendant might not think to tell you themselves". One prosecutor said unrepresented defendants could even confuse aggravating and mitigating features of an offence, and end up getting themselves a longer sentence: "Most people for instance, think it's mitigation to say they were drunk at the time. The sentencing guidelines say that's an aggravating feature!"[33]

Pre-sentence reports (PSRs) help judges understand what mitigation might be relevant for an unrepresented defendant. PSRs are completed by probation officers, either in full or in a shortened version, but only for some offences and offenders. Interviewees felt that full PSRs were particularly helpful in sentencing unrepresented defendants, but that they were disadvantaged because they did not understand the role of the PSR in the sentencing process, nor how to encourage a judge to order a full one.

One District Judge was also concerned that unrepresented defendants may not actually understand their sentence. Normally she would ask the advocate to explain the sentence, but an unrepresented defendant may, "go away not fully understanding no matter how hard you try...and it must be such a scary experience that a lot of it can go over your head". A prosecutor with experience of representing defendants, also worried that unrepresented defendants may walk away from court in a fog of ignorance: "The court is an intimidating place for most people and it is not unusual that I will have to sit down and explain what happened following a hearing where the client was present but simply didn't understand what was happening". Another prosecutor said, "I would think that approximately 25% do not have a clue what has just happened. I often find that the ushers in court are having to explain what has just happened...Most ushers are good, but there are some who are as clueless as the defendant".[34]

---

32 Ibid.
33 Ibid.
34 Ibid.

> *Court observation: not understanding mitigation*
>
> A man in his 30s has pleaded guilty to speeding. He is faced with a six month driving ban, since he had too many points on his licence. He is a delivery driver and is in danger of losing his job. When he turned up at court unrepresented he seemed to have no idea of what to do. He had not told his employer that he is in court. The judge told him, "this could be very significant for you as you are in danger of losing your job, it would be fairer to you to allow you time to speak to your employer". The legal adviser to the Magistrates told him to get a letter from his employer to say he could lose his job, "as the court has to ban you unless you can prove to the court reasons why not". The case was adjourned to allow the defendant to try to mitigate his sentence.

The complexity of criminal law and procedure

"Given the fundamental changes in the court procedures in recent years, culminating in better case management,[35] it can be tricky enough for lawyers to know the details of current procedure. Unrepresented individuals have little chance of fair process" (prosecutor).[36]

The Government has added thousands of new criminal offences in the last ten years to an already complex system. Most lawyers and judges would find it hard to keep up with new laws, rules on procedure and sentencing guidelines, let alone case law. None of these developments are written in layman's language and the evidence suggests that many people find it very hard to understand what is going on in court. Additional challenges of limited literacy, and English as a second language are not uncommon. All this makes it difficult for an unrepresented defendant to understand the law and how it can be used. They are likely to be at a huge disadvantage in trying to defend themselves against trained lawyers.

It is submitted that if the numbers of unrepresented defendants remain high, justice will only be achieved if the system itself is simplified - both in terms of legislation and legal process.

---

[35] Programme of reforms to criminal procedure in the crown court introduced to develop speedier justice.
[36] Ibid n1.

Do unrepresented defendants get a different outcome?

"I worry about the outcomes for [unrepresented defendants] more than anything else. In the twenty-four years I've been practising now, the culture has changed...I think we have a victim court culture now...there are so many ways to catch a defendant out now that weren't there five years ago. ...There are so many things that a defendant wouldn't know, nor be expected to know...I just think they are at a massive disadvantage, but they don't know it." (prosecutor)[37]

"There are technical, legal issues which, if done badly, will result in an adverse result for the defendant. As to the running of a trial, I think it borders on the unethical for a person who wants representation, or needs it, to be asked to run their own trial; especially in magistrates' courts, where the bench is heavily led by the CPS." (prosecutor)[38]

The question of whether unrepresented defendants receive worse outcomes is at the heart of this enquiry. Our findings suggest that there are many ways in which lack of representation impacts individuals' experience of court, and how the case unfolds. But there is also evidence that being unrepresented can affect the sentence received.

Judges were more confident than prosecutors that the outcomes of trials and sentencing were the same, whether or not someone had a lawyer. Prosecutors felt that unrepresented defendants were more likely to be disadvantaged in terms of sentence than verdict.

Whether someone pleads guilty or not, and to what charge, greatly affects any court outcome. Prosecutors (many of whom also act for the defence) were concerned that unrepresented defendants pleaded not guilty when they had no good defence, and pleaded guilty when they did. They were also concerned that an unrepresented defendant may not even understand what they are charged with.

Without a rigorous quantitative study of cases and their outcomes, it is difficult to draw concrete conclusions. However, the qualitative data that we have gathered for this report raises sufficient concern to warrant further examination.

[37]   Ibid.
[38]   Ibid.

Policy on unrepresented defendants in the criminal courts

Unrepresented defendants are almost a policy free zone. There is little guidance for judges, prosecutors and court staff on how to deal with them, and what there is may not be up to date. The Equal Treatment Bench Book has a section on unrepresented defendants which suggests, erroneously, that most have actively refused a lawyer: "Those who dispense with legal assistance do so usually because they decline to accept the advice which they have been given, whether as to plea or the conduct of the trial."[39]

The criminal procedure rules make little reference to unrepresented defendants except to clarify that: "The legal adviser is under a duty to assist unrepresented parties, whether defendants or not, to present their case, but must do so without appearing to become an advocate for the party concerned."[40]

The rules do not explain who should fulfil this role in the absence of a legal adviser.

While unrepresented litigants in civil courts have been the subject of five years intense work by the Civil Justice Council, unrepresented defendants are not mentioned in Government policy in recent years. The Leveson "Review of Efficiency in Criminal Proceedings" (January 2015) is the template for court reform, but barely mentions them. The almost complete invisibility, in policy terms, of unrepresented defendants in the criminal courts could be to blame for their exclusion from thinking on criminal case digitisation.

The Civil Courts

It is unlikely that anyone in the civil and family courts and tribunals would say that unrepresented litigants get all the help they need. However, more is available than in the criminal courts. There are advisers in Law Centres and CAB's, pro bono legal advice from charities like the Free Representation Unit (FRU) and clinics run by universities, and practical help from the Personal Support Unit (PSU). Over five hundred PSU volunteers based in courts support unrepresented litigants through the process, give non-legal advice and referrals to pro bono assistance.

There are many guides online for unrepresented litigants in the civil courts including a handbook published by the judiciary in 2015.[41] Meanwhile

---

[39] Judicial Office. *Equal Treatment Benchbook 2013*.
[40] Criminal Procedure Rules 24A.16, Neutral Citation Number: [2015] *EWCA Crim* 1567, https://www.judiciary.uk/wp-content/uploads/2015/09/crim-pd-2015.pdf.
[41] Judicial Office. *A handbook for litigants in person 2013*.

lawyers can consult guidelines[42] published by the Law Society, CILEX, and the Bar Standards Board.

Conclusion

Unrepresented defendants face considerable difficulties at every turn, from knowing how to prepare for court, to understanding what they are charged with, to countering the evidence against them. Incomplete data makes it difficult to draw firm conclusions about the numbers involved and the scale of any changes. However, the strong perception among those that were involved with this study was that the situation is deteriorating.

All our interviewees, including judges, felt that unrepresented defendants were at a disadvantage. They only differed in their views of how great that disadvantage was. Their biggest concern was that unrepresented defendants were getting more punitive sentences as a result of not understanding what they have been charged with, entering the wrong plea and not understanding how to mitigate. This raises concern about whether cases involving unrepresented defendants meet the criteria of Article 6 of the ECHR – the right to a fair hearing. As yet, no strategic litigation has tested this.

Dealing with unrepresented defendants is certainly causing huge stress in the courts, particularly for unrepresented defendants themselves, and costing time and money. It would be worth at least investing resources in increasing the take up of legal advice and supporting those who are representing themselves. Few groups get so little help in complying with the demands of the state. Unfortunately, because they are a desperate and often vulnerable group of people, they have no co-ordinated voice, nor a channel for effectively raising collective concerns. Criminal courts have muddled along for years, dealing with unrepresented defendants as best they can. Increasing numbers, and recent reforms mean that muddle is turning into what some of our interviewees perceive to be daily miscarriages of justice.

Recommendations

We have a criminal court system designed to be operated by lawyers. Most of the problems encountered by unrepresented defendants arise from the fact that the system itself has only made slight adjustments to their needs. If we are to properly serve unrepresented defendants, and have a justice system that operates effectively, we should either provide legal representation, or completely redesign the system to meet the needs of unrepresented defendants. The following recommendations are made:

---

[42] *Litigants in person. Guidelines for lawyers.* (June 2015).

Research

1. Conduct further research to understand why there are unrepresented defendants, why numbers appear to have increased in the magistrates' courts and what they perceive to be their greatest barriers to accessing justice.

2. Research the psychology of those who choose to represent themselves and explore whether there is value in investing more resources in persuading them to access and maintain legal representation.

3. Analyse the extra time taken by cases involving unrepresented defendants and undertake a full cost benefit analysis.

Increase uptake of legal aid and legal advice

1. Update the income thresholds for legal aid in line with the rise in inflation.

2. Increase the recompense offered to those who pay privately and are acquitted – to disincentivise self-representation.

3. Grant legal aid to all defendants in cases where an advocate is currently appointed to cross-examine.

4. Improve communication about the availability of legal aid and how to access it, particularly for those unfamiliar with the system.

5. Ensure applications getting stuck in the LAA system do not lead to defendants missing out on representation.

6. Expand the role of the duty solicitor so they have more flexibility to deal with unrepresented defendants who have already contacted a solicitor, and with other hearings such as trials to prevent people being imprisoned on remand or sentence without access to legal advice.

Help and support unrepresented defendants

1. Ensure that the new digital courts programme does not disadvantage unrepresented defendants.

2. Ensure effective means for identifying mental health and other vulnerabilities in defendants, including the unrepresented.

3. Provide better online and printed information for unrepresented defendants on how they can prepare for and conduct their case.

4. Give prosecutors, legal advisers, court associates, ushers and judges specific training in dealing with unrepresented defendants, and appraise their performance in doing so.

5. Pilot the provision in criminal courts of practical help similar to that provided by the Personal Support Unit in Civil Courts.

Overall

1. Simplify the law and the legal process.

2. Factor the impact on unrepresented defendants into policy making in criminal justice.

CHAPTER 8

Anunga 40 years on – Rights remain limited for indigenous suspects in the Northern Territory of Australia

Felicity Gerry QC[*] and David Woodroffe[**][***]

The work of The Advocate's Gateway ('TAG') in the UK to improve access to justice for vulnerable persons in criminal proceedings is gradually being followed in Australia.[1] The TAG open access, research-based, toolkits provide guidance for recognising vulnerabilities in witnesses and suspects, for effective communication and procedural adaptation throughout the criminal justice process from arrest to sentence.[2] They complement a statutory *Code of Practice in the Police and Criminal Evidence Act 1984* (PACE)[3] in relation to the detention, treatment and questioning of suspects and EU Directives on child suspects, vulnerable adult suspects and human trafficking victims who commit crime. The modern approach to effective participation of accused persons is rights based, prioritising access to justice through communication and adjusted procedures through judicial case management in relation to any necessary procedural adaptations and decisions to exclude evidence where suspect's rights have not been respected.

In Australia, this research-based approach to effective participation in justice systems is being increasingly discussed in the context of therapeutic jurisprudence, restorative justice, collaborative law and procedural justice through a range of contemporary practices which take a non-adversarial approach.[4] Such an approach would be a long way from common law roots of the Australian system but has long been recognised in the context of communication with Indigenous people who come into contact with

---

[*] QC Carmelite Chambers, London, UK and Crockett Chambers, Melbourne, Australia. Professor of Legal Practice, Deakin University and PhD candidate, Charles Darwin University (CDU), Darwin and Adjunct Fellow, University of Western Sydney, Australia.

[**] NAAJA Principal Legal Officer, Darwin.

[***] The authors were assisted in the writing of this paper by barrister and project coordinator Julia Kretzenbacher, and students Yasmin Osborne, Lucy Zhao and Errol Chua, from the NAAJA / CDU clinical program with additional research from students in The Indigenous Justice and Exoneration Project: Phillip Carroll, Emma Fuller, Mark Munnich, Gabrielle Hill, Ferg Ferguson and Rebecca Rosser.

[1] Gerry, F., Cooper, P., Effective Participation of Vulnerable Accused Persons: Case Management, Court Adaptation and Rethinking Criminal Responsibility. *Journal of Judicial Administration* 26, no 1, (2017): 265-275.

[2] The Advocate's Gateway Toolkits < https://www.theadvocatesgateway.org/>.

[3] *Code of Practice in the Police and Criminal Evidence Act 1984* (UK), code C.

[4] Warren Brookbanks, "Non-Adversarial Justice: An Evolving Paradigm" *Australian Journal of Judicial Administration* 26, no 4 (2017).

the justice system. It is worth remembering that adjusting the system, particularly for Indigenous people is not new: It is now four decades since the decision in *R v Anunga*[5] where Forster J sitting in the Northern Territory of Australia ('NT') set out some minimum guidance with respect to the conduct of police officers when interrogating Indigenous Australians ('the *Anunga* Guidelines').

Forster's guidance was 'designed simply to remove or obviate some of the disadvantages from which Indigenous people suffer in their dealings with police'.[6] Forty years on this chapter reflects on the progress since that ground-breaking decision, not just in police questioning but the ongoing development of reasonable adjustments for effective participation of Indigenous people in the criminal justice system in this unique part of Australia.

Some protections are statutory such as video recording of interviews, others remain discretionary. It has been recognised that language and cultural differences affect communication and understanding of the trial process as can vulnerability, trauma or a disability or a combination of such factors.[7] Various tools are now available to assist investigators and advocates including judicial guidance from Riley CJ in advocacy handbooks.[8] However, as Victoria has recently legislated to use intermediaries for witness communication[9], concern remains that not enough is being done to truly engage the Aboriginal community and ensure that suspects are fairly treated.

Whilst the ability of the courts to regulate questioning[10] or admissibility of evidence[11] by virtue of the *Evidence (National Uniform Legislation) Act 2012* (NT) ('the *ENULA*') may arguably put the *Anunga* Guidelines on a statutory footing, this chapter suggests that procedural adaptations in court are not enough to protect basic human rights. Using the EU Roadmap for vulnerable suspects, the work of The Advocate's Gateway in the UK[12] and the requirements of the *Convention on the Rights of Persons with*

---

[5]   *R v Anunga.* 1976. 11 ALR 412.
[6]   Id.
[7]   See various papers, Criminal Lawyers Association of The Northern Territory, (CLANT) 1997 to 2017, The Bali Conference: CLANT's Biennial Conferences. < http://clant.org.au/index.php/the-bali-conference>
[8]   Little Red Book of Advocacy, Volumes 1 and 2 <http://territorystories.nt.gov.au/handle/10070/265353>.
[9]   Victorian Intermediaries program < http://www.justice.vic.gov.au/home/justice+system/courts+and+tribunals/victorian+intermediaries+program>.
[10] *Evidence (National Uniform Legislation) Act* 2011 (Northern Territory), § 41.
[11] Id. § 135 to 139.
[12] Victoria Disability Access Bench Book < http://www.judicialcollege.vic.edu.au/disability-access-bench-book>.

Disabilities ('CPRD'), this chapter suggests that the NT still has a long way to go and, given its high rates of incarceration of Indigenous Australians, it is disappointing that it is taking so long to change its approach to effective participation for Indigenous people in the criminal justice system.

In particular, there are three simple changes that could be made almost immediately to improve access to justice. These are to allow for a right to a lawyer trained in Indigenous Protocols on arrest and throughout the process, require a comprehensive expert health and welfare assessment before interview and to ensure there is a ground rules hearing[13] in any case where there is a vulnerable suspect. These, as a minimum, would help ensure proper provision is made for support and participation but, overall, the NT, in our view, needs to address wholesale systemic failure in the participation of vulnerable people as suspects in the system.

Indigenous Australians and the Criminal Justice System

It is important to remember that not all Indigenous Australian people are vulnerable, but the research is clear that those in contact with the criminal justice system can and do have multiple vulnerabilities.[14] In the NT it is estimated that Indigenous people account for over 30% of the population.[15] Indigenous Australians have the highest birth rate, highest death rate, the worst health and housing and the lowest educational, occupational, economic, social and legal status across all groups in Australia.[16] These factors greatly impact the health and well-being of the Indigenous population which contributes to ongoing disadvantage.[17] It is well documented that disadvantage leads to high rates of incarceration.[18] This is supported by data that whilst Indigenous people make up approximately 2.5% of the overall population of Australia, they also account for 26% of the

---

[13]   The Advocate's Gateway. 2016. *TAG's Toolkits on Ground Rules Hearings.* The Council of the Inns of Court. <https://www.theadvocatesgateway.org/images/toolkits/1-ground-rules-hearings-and-the-fair-treatment-of-vulnerable-people-in-court-2016.pdf.> See also: Cooper, P., Backen, P., Marchant, P., 'Getting to Grips With Ground Rules Hearings – A Checklist for Judges, Advocates and Intermediaries'. 6 *Criminal Law Review*, (2015): 420-435.
[14]   North Australian Aboriginal Justice Agency. 2013. *Access to Justice in the Criminal Justice System for People with Disability: Response to the Australian Human Rights Commission.* <http://www.naaja.org.au/wp-content/uploads/2014/05/Access-to-justice-in-the-criminal-justice-system-for-people-with-disability.pdf>.
[15]   Australian Bureau of Statistics. 2016. *Regional Statistics of Northern Territory.*
[16]   National Population Inquiry. 1975. *Population & Australia, A Demographic Analysis and Projection.* Canberra: Australian Government Publishing Service, 455.
[17]   Zhao, Y., et al, "Health inequity in the Northern Territory, Australia" *International Journal Equity Health* 12, no 4 (2013).
[18]   Walker, J., McDonald, D., *The Over-Representation of Indigenous people in Custody in Australia* (Canberra: Australian Institute of Criminology, 1995).

population currently incarcerated.[19] It is particularly notable in the NT that the proportion of adult prisoners identifying as Indigenous is over 84%, with the rate reaching some 96% for youths.[20] The primary contributing factor for the high rates of incarceration is disadvantage.[21] In addition, a problematic relationship still exists between police officers and Indigenous people which stem from cultural, socio-economic, historical and linguistic factors.[22] An interim report by the *Royal Commission into the Protection and Detention of Children* indicates that evidence received by the Commission to date:

> ... overwhelmingly demonstrates that community safety and the well-being of all who live within the community – children and adults – is best achieved by a comprehensive, multifaceted approach based on crime prevention, early intervention where there is a risk of offending by children and young people, diversion of children and young people away from the courts, and community engagement and involvement at all levels.[23]

Despite the obvious potential for vulnerability there is no right to access to a lawyer meaning that Indigenous people often face questioning on serious criminal matters without the automatic assistance of legal advice, no protection by way of legal professional privilege nor the benefit of early assessment by a defence lawyer trained to use the available Indigenous protocols.[24]

The North Australian Aboriginal Justice Agency ('NAAJA') is a Legal Service for Indigenous Australians operating in the NT. NAAJA provides a culturally appropriate, legal and justice-related service that supports Indigenous people who access their services throughout their interaction with the criminal justice system. In addition to day to day lawyering, their policy work and resources, including video and musical tools assist in communicating legal issues to Indigenous communities and assist lawyers

[19] Australian Bureau of Statistics. 2016. *Indigenous Australians and Torres Strait Islander Prisoner Characteristics.*
[20] Ibid.
[21] Cunneen, C., Racism, Discrimination and the Over-representation of Indigenous People in the Criminal Justice System: Some Conceptual and Explanatory Issues; *Current Issues in Criminal Justice* 17, no. 4 (2006).
[22] McKay, G., Language Issues in Training Programs for Northern Territory Police. *Australian Review of Applied Linguistics* 2, no.1 (1985) 2.1, 32-43.
[23] White M., Gooda, M., 2017. *Royal Commission into the Protection and Detention of Children in the Northern Territory Interim Report.* < https://childdetentionnt.royalcommission.gov.au/about-us/Documents/RCNT-Interim-report.pdf>.
[24] Indigenous Protocols for Lawyers (Law Society Northern Territory, 2nd ed, 2015). <https://lawsocietynt.asn.au/for-the-profession/publications-7/indigenous-protocols-for-lawyers.html>.

and the judiciary to understand the perspective of Indigenous people.[25] More recently, for example, NAAJA was involved in the development of an iPad application which allows for the communication of the caution in the most common Indigenous languages, which is a significant development.[26]

However, these developments are set against a backdrop of high Indigenous incarceration and without any statutory police Code of Practice, only guidance, on the detention, treatment and questioning of anyone taken into custody and no statutory requirement to take into account Aboriginality. In the NT, the right to a fair trial in the International Covenant on Civil and Political Rights (*ICCPR*) is preserved in the context of improperly or illegally obtained evidence in section 138(3)(f) of the *ENULA* but there is no Constitutional human rights mechanism,[27] no implementation of the *United Nations Declaration on the Rights of Indigenous Peoples*[28] which focusses on participation, no acknowledgement in the criminal justice system of the access to justice requirements in the *Convention on the Rights of Persons with Disabilities* ('CRPD')[29] and no adoption of the ground rules hearing process pioneered by Professor Penny Cooper who leads TAG.

The work being done by the NAAJA in the NT on providing representation, recognising vulnerability and improving communication is valuable but in the absence of systemic change through an improved rights-based statutory framework, there remains a risk to full access to justice for Indigenous people. In Australia more broadly, alternative summary courts operate where the purpose of these courts is to accommodate Indigenous accused. Their proceedings are usually less formal and relevant cultural needs are taken into account when sentencing offenders.[30] This does not necessarily apply in the same way in senior courts. There is nothing similar available for Indigenous accused in the NT.

---

[25] NAAJA You Tube Channel <https://www.youtube.com/channel/UCdh6RXUBqg-B2abOMWGhGZdQ>.

[26] Caution translated into 18 Indigenous Languages < http://www.pfes.nt.gov.au/Media-Centre/Media-releases/2015/December/21/Caution-App-Wins-Award.aspx>.

[27] ABC: Proposal for a Bill of Rights delayed < http://www.abc.net.au/news/2017-10-19/northern-territory-parliament-throws-out-bill-of-rights-motion/9067490>.

[28] UNDRIP < https://www.un.org/development/desa/indigenouspeoples/declaration-on-the-rights-of-indigenous-peoples.html>.

[29] CRPD < https://www.un.org/development/desa/disabilities/convention-on-the-rights-of-persons-with-disabilities.html>.

[30] See Koori courts in Victoria < https://www.magistratescourt.vic.gov.au/koori-court>.

Detention, Treatment and Questioning

The decision in *R v Anunga* (*'Anunga'*) in the Supreme Court of the Northern Territory of Australia was not a decision by a senior court but it began the discussion on procedural adaptation of the common law process.[31] The basic guidance given by Forster J can be summarised as follows:

- an interpreter should be present if the suspect is not fluent in English;

- consideration should be given to the presence of a 'prisoner's friend';

- great care in administering the caution (right to silence) and ensuring that it is understood should be taken;

- reasonable steps should be taken to obtain legal assistance, albeit this was limited to when it was requested;

- there should be provision of substitute clothing and basic refreshments if needed; and

- there should be no questioning while the suspect is unwell, intoxicated or tired.

Similar guidance now exists in most Australian jurisdictions. The Anunga guidelines "were enunciated because the court recognised the very real disadvantages of so many Aboriginal people in this territory when confronted with an authority figure such as a policeman. It recognised also the difficulties the police experienced in satisfying the courts that confessional material obtained was voluntary which involved proof that the defendant truly and fully comprehended his right to speak or remain silent".[32]

Since the decision in *Anunga*, the NT Police General Orders ('PGOs') have integrated the general position into police internal instructions.[33] The PGOs aim to ensure that material obtained during an interview or interrogation was provided voluntarily, was fairly acquired and is an accurate reflection of what the parties have said to each other.[34] Unfortunately, what was not

---

[31] 1976. 11 ALR 412.

[32] Pauling, T., *Revisiting Anunga* 2009 < https://clant.org.au/the_bali_conference/2009-2/attachment-pauling-tom-_qc_-revisiting-anunga/>.

[33] Police General Orders cited in *R v Weston* [2005] NTSC 49. (NT Police 1998a. General order Q1 Questioning and investigations. Darwin: NT Police; NT Police 1998b. General order Q2—Questioning people who have difficulties with the English language - The 'Anunga' guidelines. Darwin: NT Police. (NT Police 1998a: 3)).

[34] Ivory scales: black Australia and the law / edited by Kayleen M. Hazlehurst: New South Wales University Press, 1987.

incorporated were the final words of Forster J where he explained that his guidance was based on his personal and professional experience and were not to be taken as finite suggestions on how to communicate with Indigenous people:

> It may be thought by some that these guidelines are unduly paternal and therefore offensive to Indigenous Australians people. It may be thought by others that they are unduly favourable to Indigenous Australians people. The truth of the matter is that they are designed simply to remove or obviate some of the disadvantages from which Indigenous Australians people suffer in their dealings with police. These guidelines are not absolute rules, departure from which will necessarily lead to statements being excluded, but police officers who depart from them without reason may find statements are excluded. The judges of this court do not consider the effectiveness of police investigation will be set back by compliance with these recommendations. It is basic that persons in custody should be treated with courtesy and patience.[35]

The requirement for 'courtesy and patience' has not been included in the police guidance. Instead, the *Anunga* list is included and the approach is set out as a question of fairness:

> [w]here a person who is apparently a vulnerable suspect, that is, they may have limited mental capacity or by reason of age, education or ethnicity are disadvantaged, measures must be taken to ensure a fair interrogation.[36]

The result is that the *Anunga* Guidelines remain as an important principle for judges to sustain the accused's right to a fair trial, as well as incorporating the right against self-incrimination and procedural fairness.[37] However, whilst the Guidelines and the PGOs together must be considered by police dealing when with Indigenous suspects[38] there remains a level of flexibility[39] for the courts to consider the lengths in which the police have taken.[40] This has resulted in admissible interviews despite the guidance not

---

[35] 1976. 11 ALR 412.
[36] NT Police 1998b. General order Q2—Questioning People Who Have Difficulties with the English Language- The 'Anunga' Guidelines.
[37] Douglas, H., The Cultural Specificity of Evidence: The Current Scope and Relevance of the *Anunga* Guidelines," *UNSW Law Journal* 21, no.1 (1998): 30.
[38] Id.
[39] *R v McKenzie.* 2015. NTSC 85 at 34.
[40] *Evidence (National Uniform Legislation) Act* 2011 (Northern Territory), § 85 (2).

being followed.[41] More importantly, neither the *Anunga* Guidelines nor the PGO's focus on basic rights for access to justice nor do they prioritise effective participation. The primary focus is on the reliability of police interviews. Since *Anunga*, there have been additional developments including a statutory requirement to warn a suspect that they have a right to silence and may inform a friend or relative of their whereabouts[42] and that police interviews must be conducted on video[43] but, there is no right to free and independent legal advice and no right to have a person present. Health or communication assessments pre interview are left to police discretion as to whether they take the view the suspect needs assistance. Whilst this gives the police choice, in the particular context of the NT, without a basic rights based framework, the system remains lacking for Indigenous Australians who, given the known situation that Indigenous Australians, are rarely in a position to make meaningful informed choices on arrest, in our view, compromises their right to a fair trial.

Since *Anunga*, judges have expressed concern that communication with Indigenous Australians must be effective.[44] However, there has been very little formal progress for defendants: There is no statutory duty to inform a lawyer that an Indigenous person is in custody[45] or to ensure a lawyer is present, there is no automatic assessment for additional health issues such as hearing impairment, Foetal Alcohol Spectrum Disorder ('FASD') or learning disability and no intermediary system to ensure effective communication. Although some difficulties may be obvious, the risk is that conduct is put down to alcohol abuse rather than ill health. There are some relatively good tools in the NT including Indigenous protocols for lawyers[46] and a plain language dictionary written by peak Indigenous legal service bodies to define NT criminal legal terms using language that closely matches the words, grammar, genre and structure of Indigenous languages.[47] There is also an interpreter system, although resources are limited. This includes a sign language interpreter although there is only one for the whole of the NT, with a population suffering significant hearing problems. These tools are not as comprehensive as recommended by the

---

[41] *R v Gaykamanu*. 2010. NTSC 12.
[42] *Police Administration Act* 2017 (Northern Territory) § 140.
[43] Id. § 142.
[44] Id. n11
[45] Cf *Crimes Act 1958* (Vic) s 464C, which requires an investigating official to inform a suspect of the right to communicate with a friend, relative and/or a legal practitioner.
[46] Id. n27.
[47] *The Plain English Legal Dictionary - Northern Territory Criminal Law* (Indigenous Australians Resource and Development Services, North Australian Indigenous Australians Justice Agency, Indigenous Australians Interpreter Service, Northern Territory Government, 1st ed, 2015).

toolkits produced by TAG in the UK although, at the time of writing, it is understood that Community Legal Education is in the process of producing a website to host all tools available. This is being produced informally and not as part of a State centred, statutory-based approach to ensure the justice system is accessible and rights enforceable.

In the NT, the lack of balance is exemplified in the statutory requirements for pre-recorded video interviews with witnesses and other special measures enabling the courts to control questioning of vulnerable witnesses, whereas in relation to suspects, in the NT, the court process is still very much an adversarial one. Whilst courts do exclude poorly conducted police interviews, it is usually only in limited circumstances, such as where an interpreter was not used, or a suspect has expressed that through a lawyer they do not wish to participate in an interview, but police forge ahead anyway. Rarely is the vulnerability of a suspect considered more broadly when it comes to the way in which the process should be conducted or the admissibility of evidence. It is a sorry state of affairs reliant on dedicated lawyers rather than governed by comprehensive statutory procedures in circumstances where the suspect may also be a victim of the types of disadvantages that beset Indigenous people in the NT.

England and Wales

In England and Wales, the Police and Criminal Evidence Act 1984 provides similar evidential provisions[48] to the UNELA enabling judges to exclude evidence but there the two jurisdictions diverge. In England and Wales, the work of TAG has been endorsed in the Criminal Procedure Rules 3D to G[49] ('CPR') providing a structured approach to children and vulnerable adult accused persons appearing in the Crown Court. The CPR require that the particular vulnerability of an accused be recognised and is intended to enable the accused person to effectively participate in the proceedings. The age, maturity, identified conditions and development of the accused person concerned and all other circumstances of the case ought to be taken into account to give effect to the CPR.[50]

The purpose of the CPR is that the approach to be taken by criminal courts and advocates is to ensure that the welfare of a child or otherwise vulnerable accused is considered where necessary,[51] and that the process is adapted to ensure the accused can comprehend the proceedings and

---

[48] *Police and Criminal Evidence Act 1984* (UK).
[49] Criminal Procedure Rules < https://www.justice.gov.uk/courts/procedure-rules/criminal>.
[50] *R v H.* 2006. EWCA Crim 853.
[51] *Children and Young Persons Act* 1933. § 44.

engage fully in their defence.[52] In relation to the evidence of an accused, the procedural expectation is that an application should be made pursuant to CPR Rule 18 for a 'defendant's evidence direction'. That direction will be given to ensure the appropriate court adaptations are made and that the treatment and questioning of the accused is approached in a suitable way to facilitate effective participation. The presumption is that adult accused will be in court and, if they choose to give evidence, would do so in person. But measures such as clearing the public gallery or regular breaks, the presence of a supporting person or the use of communication aids can be considered to ensure the process is fair. Courts have inherent powers to ensure that an accused person receives a fair trial. These have been successfully deployed in the context of facilitating the participation of a vulnerable accused including by directing that the accused have the assistance of an intermediary to assist with communication.[53] All of these issues are raised at an early stage in a ground rules hearing[54] so best efforts are made to ensure that the appropriate adaptations are made for any individual.

These developments in relation to court procedure did not begin with the common law system but were driven by the decision of the European Court of Human Rights in *Venables and Thompson*[55] where it was held that very young children should not have been tried in an adult court and subsequent domestic cases in relation to trials for children and then in relation to vulnerable adults[56]. The developments in UK are now embedded in a wider formal framework focusing on access to justice: EU Directive (EU) 2016/800 of the European Parliament and of the Council of 11th May 2011 ('the Directive') provides procedural safeguards for children who are suspects or accused persons in criminal proceedings or subject to a European arrest warrant. The purpose of the Directive is to ensure that children, meaning persons under the age of 18, who are suspects or accused persons in criminal proceedings, are able to understand and follow those proceedings, and to exercise their right to a fair trial, and to prevent children from reoffending and foster their social integration.

---

[52]   *R(TP) v West London Youth Court.* 2005. EWHC 2583; *SC v UK.* 2004. EHRR 10.
[53]   *R(c) v Sevenoaks Youth Court.* 2010.1 All ER 735; *R (TP) West London Youth Court.* 2006.1 All ER 735.
[54]   Id. n16.
[55]   The judgment in full <http://news.bbc.co.uk/1/hi/uk/567631.stm>.
[56]   Penny Cooper and Heather Norton, *Vulnerable People and the Criminal Justice System* (OUP, 2017).

The Directive establishes minimum rules on the protection of procedural rights of children who are suspects or accused persons which include the following:[57]

- Rights to information;

- Right to have the holder of parental responsibility informed;

- Assistance by a lawyer;

- Right to an individual assessment concerning protection, education, training and social integration;

- Right to a medical examination;

- Audiovisual recording of questioning;

- Limitation on deprivation of liberty;

- Alternative measures to detention;

- Separate detention from adults;

- Timely and diligent treatment of cases;

- Right to protection of privacy;

- Right to be accompanied by the holder of parental responsibility during the proceedings;

- Right to appear in person and participate in their trial;

- Right to legal aid;

- Effective remedies for breach of rights; and

- Specific training for law enforcement authorities and detention facility staff who handle cases involving children to a level appropriate to their contact with children with regard to children's rights, appropriate questioning techniques, child psychology, and communication in a language adapted to the child. This includes the judiciary, the legal profession and child support organisations.

The Directive does not apply to vulnerable adults, but on the 30 November 2009, the Council of the European Union adopted a *Resolution on a Roadmap for Strengthening the Procedural Rights of all Suspected or Accused Persons in Criminal Proceedings*. Taking a step-by-step approach the road map calls for the adoption of measures regarding the right to translation

---

[57] Directive (EU) 2016/800 of the European Parliament and of the Council of 11th May 2011 provides procedural safeguards for children who are suspects or accused persons in criminal proceedings <http://eur-lex.europa.eu/legal-content/EN/TXT/?uri=CELEX%3A32016L0800>.

and interpretation, the right to information on rights and information about the charges, the right to legal advice and legal aid, the right to communicate with relatives, employers and consular authorities, and special safeguards for suspected or accused persons who are vulnerable.[58] Some procedural rights have been adopted through Directive 2010/64/EU[59] on interpretation and translation, Directive 2012/13/EU[60] on the right to information, Directive 2013/48/ EU[61] on access to a lawyer and having persons informed of arrest, and Directive 2016/343/ EU[62] on strengthening the presumption of innocence and the right to be present at trial.

There is still some work to be done, even where there is a road map for the treatment of vulnerable suspects. A survey of 100 defence practitioners in the EU in respect of the treatment of vulnerable suspects unearthed a number of issues. The most common responses were that vulnerable suspects are often mistreated by the police and the police often lack awareness and therefore fail to identify vulnerabilities. In addition, recurring problems were highlighted, such as inconsistent approaches to vulnerable suspects, the exclusion of some groups, lack of training, disrespect and the fact that treatment of vulnerable suspects is worse at the pre-trial stage than the trial. The survey also found that whilst there are some safeguards for vulnerable suspects, their application varies widely from case to case.[63] These concerns are often reflected in the submissions made by advocates in cases where interviews have been excluded. However, the fact that the application of the current processes continues to lead to unfair proceedings, where such submissions have to be made, remains confined to the courtroom rather than considered as part of systemic reform.[64]

[58] Resolution of the Council of 30 November 2009 on a Roadmap for strengthening procedural rights of suspected or accused persons in criminal proceedings (Text with EEA relevance).
[59] DIRECTIVE 2010/64/EU OF THE EUROPEAN PARLIAMENT AND OF THE COUNCIL of 20 October 2010 on the right to interpretation and translation in criminal proceedings.
[60] DIRECTIVE 2012/13/EU OF THE EUROPEAN PARLIAMENT AND OF THE COUNCIL of 22 May 2012 on the right to information in criminal proceedings.
[61] DIRECTIVE 2013/48/EU OF THE EUROPEAN PARLIAMENT AND OF THE COUNCILof 22 October 2013 on the right of access to a lawyer in criminal proceedings and in European arrest warrant proceedings, and on the right to have a third party informed upon deprivation of liberty and to communicate with third persons and with consular authorities while deprived of liberty.
[62] DIRECTIVE (EU) 2016/343 OF THE EUROPEAN PARLIAMENT AND OF THE COUNCIL of 9 March 2016 on the strengthening of certain aspects of the presumption of innocence and of the right to be present at the trial in criminal proceedings.
[63] Ibid.
[64] *Queen v Gaykamanu.* [2010] NTSC 12.

The Northern Territory

In the NT there are statutory arrangements for vulnerable witnesses but these do not yet extend to suspects. The approach for accused persons is left to court discretion. Research is limited but a major concern in the NT is that Indigenous people exercise their right to silence not as a free choice after legal advice but out of fear, lack of comprehension or reluctance to engage in the system at all.[65] There is no definition of a vulnerable defendant[66] in Australian law. The definition of a vulnerable witness in the *Evidence Act* s 21A[67] could just as easily describe a vulnerable defendant. Limiting vulnerability consideration to witnesses does not appear to reflect the European approach to the primary question of vulnerability,[68] nor the access to justice requirements of the CRPD,[69] which would envisage the same treatment for a vulnerable witness to be extended to a vulnerable defendant.[70] Vulnerability tends to come to light, not in a whole of justice approach but in pre-trial arguments about the admissibility of evidence. For example, over the years, the NT courts have excluded evidence on the basis of non-compliance in relation to the confession being involuntary,[71] or a breach of common law directions relating to fairness.[72] However, the move away from the *Anunga* Guidelines to police guidance has not been complemented by legislative reform placing vulnerable defendants as a recognised category.

Research maintains that the most important factor when dealing with vulnerable individuals is effective communication.[73] This is recognised in

---

[65] See various papers, Criminal Lawyers Association of The Northern Territory, (CLANT) 1997 to 2017, The Bali Conference: CLANT's Biennial Conferences. < http://clant.org.au/index.php/the-bali-conference.

[66] For the purpose of this essay, accused, defendant and suspect are used interchangeably and refer to defence matters. When referring to vulnerable groups it includes all parties such as the accused, witness or victims.

[67] *Evidence Act* 2017 (Northern Territory), § 21A.

[68] 'Resolution of the Council on a Roadmap for Strengthening Procedural Rights Of Suspected Or Accused Persons In Criminal Proceedings' (2009) 295/1 *Official Journal of the European Union.*

[69] UN CRPD infographic>.

[70] 'Resolution of the Council on a Roadmap for Strengthening Procedural Rights Of Suspected Or Accused Persons In Criminal Proceedings' (2009) 295/1 *Official Journal of the European Union.*

[71] McCrimmon, L., The Uniform Evidence Act and the Anunga Guidelines: Accommodation or Annihilation? *Northern Territory Law Journal* 2, no. 2 (2011): 91. *R v Riley.* 1994. NTSC 62; *DB v the Queen.* 2010. NTSC 65.

[72] McCrimmon, L., The Uniform Evidence Act and the Anunga Guidelines: Accommodation or Annihilation? *Northern Territory Law Journal* 2, no. 2 (2011): 91; R *v Nagawallli.* 2009. NTSC 25.

[73] Agnew, S., Powell, M., Snow, P., 'An Examination of the Questioning Styles of Police Officers and Caregivers When Interviewing Children With Intellectual Disabilities.' *Legal and Criminological Psychology* 11, no.1 (2006): 35-53.

some ways through the protections which exist in the NT for vulnerable witnesses,[74] which allows courts to have regard to any relevant condition or characteristic of the witness, including age, education, ethnic and cultural background, gender, language background and skills, level of maturity and understanding and personality, which could render them as vulnerable.[75] Provisions from the *Evidence Act 2017* (NT) ('the *Evidence Act*') are intended to protect vulnerable witnesses by increasing the number of modes of delivery of evidence and limiting the amount of time they are required to give evidence.[76] Some of these protections that are available to vulnerable witnesses include giving evidence by way of closed circuit television outside of the court room,[77] giving evidence behind partitions so the accused cannot see the witness,[78] giving evidence in the company of a support person,[79] or closing the court session whilst giving evidence.[80] For investigators, interviews with Indigenous people should be 'interviewee centred', meaning the interviewee is to determine the level of vocabulary and content.[81] It is recognised that gratuitous concurrence can be an issue but measures should go further. In addition, it should be a requirement that physical and environmental factors (e.g. does the person suffer hearing loss?), language/ cultural factors (e.g. too much direct eye contact) and psychological environment (e.g. is the person fearful of the consequences of the interview?) are considered before an interview is commenced.[82] Other considerations should include the use of non-leading questions, as well as using meaningful labels for concepts related to time, distance and number that the Indigenous person can comprehend.[83] Culturally-specific training for police by Indigenous Australians Legal Services, Indigenous Australians English experts, and by the interpreter service should be regular, in-depth and compulsory.

However, the wording of s 21B restricts the application of the legislative protections to the Supreme Court, as the Act explicitly mentions 'trial' and

---

[74]   *Evidence Act 2017* (Northern Territory), *Sexual Offences (Evidence and Procedure) Act* 2016 (Northern Territory, *Domestic and Family Violence Act 2017* (Northern Territory).
[75]   *Evidence Act 2017* (Northern Territory), § s 1 (a).
[76]   Id.
[77]   Id §21A (2) (a).
[78]   Id §21A (2) (b).
[79]   Id §21A (2) (c).
[80]   Id §21E (2) (d).
[81]   Bull, R., The Investigative Interviewing of Children and Other Vulnerable Witnesses: Psychological Research and Working/ Professional Practice *Legal and Criminological Psychology* 15, no.1 (2010): 5–23.
[82]   Agnew, S., Powell M., Snow, P., An Examination of the Questioning Styles of Police Officers and Caregivers When Interviewing Children with Intellectual Disabilities. *Legal and Criminological Psychology* 11, no.1 (2006): 35-53.
[83]   Id.

'jury'. Thus, in the lower courts, many vulnerable people will not have procedural protections. In addition, there are no specific provisions in the *Police Administration Act 1996* (NT)[84] focussing on Indigenous suspects, which relate to the recording of confessions and admissions. Indigenous suspects in the NT are not treated adequately as a vulnerable group, despite research signifying they experience language and comprehension difficulties, cultural differences and health issues thus risking injustice during criminal proceedings.

Although research is scant, worryingly it appears that few Indigenous accused choose to give evidence and diversity amongst jurors seems limited. Perhaps the greatest signal to a lack of diversity is the Oaths Act allows for one religious oath (Christian) otherwise the option is to affirm. There are few Indigenous lawyers, and no Indigenous judges or lay assistants are present. The lack of adaptation for disabled persons is perhaps exemplified by the fact that the witness box in the Darwin Supreme Court has a step up which, on one occasion involved manually lifting a vulnerable elderly witness into place. Special adaptations for those with disabilities, whether mental or physical, remain at the discretion of a judge and can only be dealt with if brought to the attention of the court.

In comparison, TAG guidance on ground rules hearings is a simple approach that allows for an assessment of vulnerabilities at an early stage which could be easily adopted as could the comprehensive guidance in the CRPD in relation to disabled people who come into contact with the criminal justice system. The CRPD recognises the need to reframe the needs and concerns of persons with disabilities in terms of human rights, moving away from the medical model of disability and towards a social model of disability which regards people with disabilities as subjects of the full range of human rights on an equal basis with others, and where people's capacity to make decisions is presumed. The Convention requires practical measures and is enforced through reporting and complaints mechanisms. It is a valuable tool for persons with vulnerabilities to use to argue for better case management and special adaptations to court processes. Although, since Forster's decision in *Anunga*, judges will also give some guidance to juries when an Indigenous person is accused but, again, this is informal and if a suspect is physically disabled discretionary approaches will follow from the judiciary. The difficulties largely arise where mental disabilities interact with cognitive function which in turn is an issue in relation to

---

[84]   *Police Administration Act* 2017 (Northern Territory) div. 6A.

substantive offences. The development of procedural adaptations is often hindered by old fashioned processes related to fitness to plead.[85]

When deciding who is covered by the *Anunga* Guidelines, the Australian Law Reform Commissions suggested that their application to Indigenous people is best dealt with on a case-by-case basis.[86] This means that evidence is not excluded simply because the *Anunga* Guidelines are not followed, and the suspect is Indigenous.[87] Exclusion of interviews is still at the discretion of the courts. This is not unusual, but what is important here is that the process does not put the focus on the wider issues of vulnerability in the same way as the statutory provisions do in relation to vulnerable witnesses.[88] Differentiating between vulnerable witnesses and vulnerable suspects, in our view, goes a long way to the continued examples of poor interviewing.[89] Recognising vulnerability is not just a question of language[90] or understanding abstract concepts such as the right to silence or the caution. It is about access to justice through effective communication and appropriate procedural adjustments. The abiding legacy is that for 40 years the justice system has failed to sufficiently change and the inevitable conclusion is that this contributes to the high levels of Indigenous people in prison. It is remarkable that in such a unique jurisdiction where such major disadvantage is recognised there is no apparent will to ensure a suspect has access to a lawyer trained on issues of vulnerability and Indigenous disadvantage from the outset and to ensure full and effective participation throughout the process.

Importantly, there has been a shift in how important the *Anunga* Guidelines are now considered in the NT, with the introduction of the *ENULA* in 2012 but not necessarily in a way that prioritises the rights of the suspect. Issues of voluntariness have now largely been replaced by the requirement to primarily focus on the reliability and probative value of the evidence. The *Anunga* Guidelines are 'no longer a binding authority on the admissibility of evidence'.[91] An example of this shift away from the *Anunga*

---

[85] See CLANT submissions to the Senate Inquiry on Indefinite detention of people with cognitive and psychiatric impairment in Australia <http://clant.org.au/images/images/Indefinite_detention_inquiry_oral_submission.pdf>.

[86] Australian Law Reform Commission, *Recognition of Indigenous Australians Customary Laws*, Report no 31 (1986).

[87] 17 SASR 304.

[88] *Gudabi v R*. 1984. 1 FCR 187 at 70-8.

[89] *The Queen v BM*. 2015. NTSC 73.

[90] *The Queen v BL*. 2015. NTSC 85.

[91] McCrimmon, L., "The Uniform Evidence Act and the Anunga Guidelines: Accommodation or Annihilation?" *Northern Territory Law Journal* 2, no. 2 (2011): 91. See also, *R v GP*. 2015. NTSC 53 at 25 (Barr J).

Guidelines is *R v Lawrence*[92] where two electronic records of interview were held to be inadmissible pursuant to ss 85(2), 90, 138 and 139 of the *ENULA*.

Section 138(1) *ENULA* in particular is a provision which, broadly, states that evidence is not to be admitted if it has been obtained improperly or in contravention of an Australian law, unless the desirability of the admission of the evidence outweighs the undesirability of admitting evidence that has been obtained improperly or unlawfully. It is here that s138(3)(f) refers to the right to a fair trial preserved in the ICCPR. Grant CJ stated that:

> [i]n the context of s 138 of the *ENULA*, the ultimate focus on the enquiry concerning impropriety is not whether there was a breach of the *Anunga* Guidelines or [PGO 2], but whether the conduct in question was inconsistent with the minimum standards which a society such as ours should expect and require of those entrusted with powers of law enforcement.[93]

With that statement, Grant CJ in *Lawrence* moved away from the primacy and importance of the *Anunga* Guidelines to the approach to Indigenous suspects and to consider the impact on fairness of proceedings by the investigators conduct. To further cement this move away from Forster's recognition of the particular disadvantages of Indigenous people in contact with the criminal justice system, Grant CJ held that the *Anunga* Guidelines, as incorporated into the PGOs, are not an 'Australian law', for the purposes of s 138 of the *ENULA* and that therefore a breach of the *Anunga* Guidelines does not necessarily establish that evidence was obtained improperly or unlawfully. ENULA, as a statutory framework for the admissibility of evidence does nothing to further the rights of Indigenous people to effective participation. The loss of the 'courtesy and patience' envisaged by Forster risks reducing the necessary protections for vulnerable Indigenous suspects making a statutory framework addressing vulnerability, including Indigenous vulnerability more urgent. If what he meant was 'dignity and respect', the language of the Universal Declaration of Human Rights, then his legacy is in danger of being completely lost.

Despite the legalistic approach of the NT courts, there has at least been a growing recognition that young defendants should have access to effective communication arrangements to enable them to fully participate in order to receive a fair trial.[94] The ARLC joint report on the *ENULA* states that all Australian jurisdictions should work towards harmonisation of

---

[92]   2016 NTSC 65.
[93]   Id. at 99.
[94]   *Camberwell Green Youth Court, ex parte D* [2005] 1 All ER 999.

provisions in relation to issues such as evidence from vulnerable groups.[95] A report from the NT Department of Justice reviewed the vulnerable witnesses legislation to establish if any amendments should be made.[96] The review concluded that the vulnerable witness protections in the NT are comprehensive and are in line with other Australian jurisdictions. However, this appears to have totally ignored the groups who may come into contact with the system in ways other than as victims or witnesses, or the fact that those accused may also have been victims themselves at one time or another. It is remarkable, for example, that use of an interpreter remains a matter of guidance rather than being mandated[97] and that judicial and lawyer training on Indigenous Protocols is not compulsory. The situation is exacerbated by the lack of a statutory obligation for the police to contact an Indigenous Australians Legal Service following arrest. Often when some notification does come, it is after the vulnerable person has already been interrogated and charged.[98] There is, in our view, an urgent need to re-evaluate the current legislation and include protection for all vulnerable groups including both witnesses and suspects at all court levels given the step backwards in respect of how the *Anunga* Guidelines are now considered by the courts in the NT, since the introduction of the *ENULA*. Without political will to recognise that the vulnerability of Indigenous people is recognised at all stages of the criminal justice process through a rights-based mechanism similar to the EU road map, the chances of a fair criminal justice process are much reduced.

Status of Children in the Northern Territory

With specific regard to children as a vulnerable group, the NT currently lags behind our European counterparts. As previously mentioned, the European Parliament reached an accord on the Children's Directive[99] in 2015 implementing a European Union-wide minimum standard protocol

---

[95] Australian Law Reform Commission Human Rights, and Equal Opportunity Commission, *Seen and Heard: Priority for Children in the Legal Process*, Report no 84 (1997).

[96] Department of Justice, Review of Vulnerable Witness Legislation (Northern Territory Government, 2011).

[97] *Crimes Act* 1914 (Commonwealth) §23N and § 23A(6); *Crimes Act* 1958 (Victoria) §464D; *Criminal Investigation Act* 2006 (Western Australia) §10; §138(2)(d); *Criminal Law Detention and Interrogation Act 1995* (Tasmania) §5; *Law Enforcement (Powers and Responsibilities) Act* 2002 (New South Wale) §128; *Police Powers and Responsibilities Act* 2000 (Queensland), §433; *Summary Offences Act* 1953 (SA), §79A(1)(b)(ii)).

[98] Australian Law Reform Commission, *Criminal Investigation and Police Interrogation*, Report no 31 (1986).

[99] European Council, 'Procedural Safeguards for Children in Criminal Proceedings: Council Confirms Deal with EP' (Press Release, 941/15, 16 December 2015) < http://www.consilium. europa.eu/en/press/press-releases/2015/12/16-procedural-safeguards-for-children-in-criminal-proceedings/>.

addressing the legislative need to arrest inadequacy and inconsistency in procedural protections to ensure that the 1 million children estimated to be facing criminal justice proceedings in the EU each year[100] are able to understand, be aware of and exercise their rights as well as to prevent reoffending and promote social reintegration. Following the Directive's implementation of uniform legislation to protect the rights of children undergoing criminal proceedings, the inexorable questions then become firstly, "under the *Youth Justice Act* ("*YJA*"),[101] what procedural rights do children subject to criminal charges in the NT have?" and secondly, "whether said rights exist or not in the NT, what specific areas should we be paying attention to?" Addressing these concerns, the Legal Experts Advisory Panel ("LEAP"), a network of 150 criminal justice and human rights NGOs and academics across 28 EU Member States, in their expansive report raising support for the Directive provisions judiciously identified three main areas:

1. The practical realities of the provisions on access to a lawyer;

2. the need for audio-visual recording (with additional safeguards); and

3. ensuring that individual assessments cannot be derogated from in ways which void them of purpose.[102]

Regarding the first concern, it is apparent that in a concerted effort to ensure procedural fairness for the child, the Directive calls for a mandatory right of access to a lawyer.[103] Conversely, the *YJA* does not impose any absolute right and even permits a child to self-represent under s 62.[104] Further, while a "support person" is to be available during certain

---

[100] Legal Experts Advisory Panel, *Defence Rights in Europe: The Road Ahead*, Report (2016) ("LEAP") 14 [25]; see also The Council of the European Union, 'Resolution of the Council on a Roadmap for Strengthening Procedural Rights Of Suspected Or Accused Persons In Criminal Proceedings' (2009) 295/1 *Official Journal of the European Union* ("European Council"), where the interest of fairness, the same treatment afforded to child and vulnerable witnesses was held to apply to child defendants as well.

[101] *Youth Justice Act 2005* (NT) ("*YJA*"), s 6: Meaning of Youth; Note: For the purpose of consistency, a "child" under the Directive, and defined by the United Nations *Convention on the Rights of a Child*, has the same meaning as a "youth" under the *YJA*, namely, a person under 18 years of age at the time of the alleged offence.

[102] LEAP, above n 4, 89 [46].

[103] Consistent with *Directive (EU) No 2013/48 of the European Parliament and the Council of 22nd October 2013 on the Right of Access to a Lawyer in Criminal Proceedings and in European Arrest Warrant Proceedings, and on the Right to have a Third Party Informed upon Deprivation of Liberty and to Communicate with Third Persons and with Consular Authorities while Deprived of Liberty* [2013] OJ.

[104] *Youth Justice Act 2005* (Northern Territory) § 62 (YJA) whether or not the self-representing child will require legal representation is subject to the discretion by the Court.

procedures and situations under the *YJA*,[105] such support persons are defined under s 35 as being one of the following: a) a responsible adult; b) a nominated person; c) a legal practitioner acting for the youth; or d) a person under the support person registry.[106] Thus, a lawyer is available only in the capacity of a nominal support person and depending on the circumstances a child may not even be privy to legal advice.[107] The problem created by this array is twofold. Firstly, how many children in custody, when presented with such an option in such circumstances would opt to have a lawyer present over a family member or any other support person given a choice? Secondly, the child would have to be prodigally aware of their legal rights and the role of a lawyer from the first point of custody.

Even supposing the Court's discretion (under § 62) to appoint legal representation for a child who has none, the child at this stage would have already been greatly disadvantaged by not having the guidance of legal advice from the time of the indictment to the day of the hearing.[108] The ALRC states that '[l]egal advice early in the process is critical to ensure young people are not pleading guilty simply because of environmental pressures. It is common for young people to agree with police allegations simply to get out of police custody.'[109] Further, despite this power imbalance between adults and child suspects, the ALRC notes that 'there is no common law right [for children] to have a lawyer present during police interrogation'[110] and submitted in Recommendation 226 that:

> The national standards for juvenile justice should provide that *a child suspected of committing an offence should have a statutory right to access legal advice* prior to police interview and that police must inform young people of this right at the time of apprehension. Duty solicitor schemes should be appropriately resourced to enable *practitioners to meet with their child clients before the first court appearance*. [Emphasis added]

---

[105] §18(2), interview of youth; §19, search of youth; §29, restriction on carrying out procedure; §30(11): Intimate procedure & §34, youth to be provided with a copy of report.
[106] §14, register of appropriate support persons.
[107] Arguably, this offends Article 37(d) of the *Convention on the Rights of the Child*, above n 8, which states that, '[e]very child deprived of his or her liberty shall have the right to prompt access to legal and other appropriate assistance…', in that even though the YJA does not explicitly remove this right making it optional places the onus on the child to both know their right and to exercise it accordingly.
[108] *Queen v Gaykamanu* 2010 NTSC 12, in the interest of fairness, it is imperative that safeguards are provided to vulnerable suspects, including children suspects, at the earliest stages of criminal proceedings.
[109] Australian Law Reform Commission, *Seen and Heard: Priority for Children in the Legal Process*, Report No 84 (1997) ("ALRC") [18.147].
[110] ALRC, above n 16, [18.148].

Although there is no obvious barrier to prevent a child from seeing a lawyer there seems to be no active encouragement either. Evidence presented to the ALRC by focus groups around Australia suggests that police may not always forthcoming or helpful in assisting children in custody to get legal advice, with one remarkable report from Alice Springs even claiming that police attempted to intimidate children from requesting a lawyer during interrogation.[111] With regard to the EU where this right is absolute, obstacles that plague the fulfilment of this provision are generally brought about by the vast disparity between the Member States. Some States voice concerns that the Directive is 'adding obligations where there was no legal aid system in place to realise them in practice'- the alternative would be that the child may be required to have a lawyer that they are unable to afford.[112]

Arguably, the abovementioned issues do not present that same level of challenge in the NT which already has a functioning legal aid system with regard to children[113] and so there is no reason why a child should not receive mandatory legal aid. In any event, should the tide turn and threaten to overwhelm the legal aid system, there are always pro bono services, as is a practice in Germany where the majority of children that do not qualify for legal aid are represented pro bono so as not to be disadvantaged by not being able to afford representation.[114]

The second concern, in the context of interrogations, is that 'audio-visual recording is not itself sufficient: it is important to have additional safeguards- such as the presence of a social worker- to ensure the testimony of the child is not the result of undue pressure or intimidation.'[115] This raises two issues: first, the need for the presence of a specialised person in addition to a lawyer; and secondly, in the event that the specialised person or lawyer is not required to be present (as in the NT)[116] additional safeguards to ensure that the testimony of the child is not influenced must be established.[117] The significance of the presence of a specialised person is

---

[111] ALRC, above n 16, [18.151].

[112] LEAP, above n 4, 89 [47].

[113] Evidenced by National Legal Aid Statistics Report, *Child Representations* (August 2017) National Legal Aid <http://lacextra.legalaid.nsw.gov.au/NLAReports/reportviewer. aspx?reportname=ChildRepresentation> where in August 2017 only one request was refused in ACT and all other requests were approved nationally.

[114] LEAP, above n 4, 89 [47].

[115] LEAP, above n 4, 89 [48].

[116] Australian Law Reform Commission, *Criminal Investigation and Police Interrogation*, Report no 31 (1986) reported that in the NT, there is no requirement for the police to contact legal services, specifically with regard to Indigenous persons, and often suspects only get see a legal representative after they have already been interrogated and charged.

[117] However, notwithstanding the ALRC report, above n 23, s 18(2) of the *YJA* states that a support person (not explicitly a lawyer) *must* be present while the police officer interviews

to address the concern that 'a lawyer is not necessarily able to provide the emotional support necessary in these situations'[118] which is vital given the child's vulnerability. For example, in situations dealing with Indigenous children a "prisoner's friend" would be a more appropriate first support person than a lawyer.[119] This lack of specialised skills is further highlighted by limitations in child protection service policy in sending only either a social worker or a lawyer to assist a child as social workers have their own specific skillset and lawyers have their own specific skillset.[120] This sentiment is echoed by the ALRC in Recommendation 206 which calls for more specialised training for police officers in accordance with the *Beijing Rules* which states that:

> In order to best fulfil their functions, police officers who frequently or exclusively deal with juveniles or who are primarily engaged in the prevention of juvenile crime shall be *specifically instructed and trained*. In large cities, special police units should be established for that purpose.[121] [Emphasis added]

The ALRC further acknowledges that "contact between [children] and police can have serious consequences for [the child] if it is adverse' and praised the role of dedicated 'youth officers' (citing the Victorian Police example) in encouraging a 'better informed approach to policing [children] and a greater rapport between the police service and the [children] in the local area."[122]   In any event, the role of the YJA "support person", as required by s 35, in interviews should not be filled by a police officer[123] which follows that this role should also not be thrust onto a lawyer who lacks the requisite expertise and skill but rather to a specialised person with training.

---

the child [Emphasis added].

[118]   LEAP, above n 4, 89 [48].

[119]   Douglas, H., The Cultural Specificity of Evidence: The Current Scope and Relevance of the *Anunga* Guidelines. *UNSW Law Journal* 21, no.1 (1998): 30; see also *R v Anunga*. 1976. 11 ALR 412 where generally the guidelines are 'designed simply to remove or obviate some of the disadvantages from which Aboriginal people suffer in their dealings with police' per Foster J.

[120]   Herke, C., Herke-Fabos, B., The Preventive Patronage and the Criminal Procedure against Juveniles in Hungary *Journal of Eastern-European Criminal Law* 2, no. 2 (2016): 214 - This is even more alarming given that at times the child welfare service is the only department allowed contact with the child.

[121]   *Standard Minimum Rules for the Administration of Juvenile Justice*, UN General Assembly, A/RES/40/33 (resolution/adopted 29 November 1985), Rule 12.1 ("Beijing Rules").

[122]   ALRC, above n 15, [18.82]; In a related note, see AGGC, below 40, 42, which reports that 'there have been some issues about all [NT Youth Detention workers] receiving [the appropriate] training and staff being current on that training'; for example, PART training involves de-escalation techniques but not all staff have received this training and it does not seem to be currently mandatory as there is no legislation for this requirement.

[123]   ALRC, above n 16, [18.105].

Arguably, the ideal situation would always have a lawyer present, with other support persons, during the interview process to safeguard against police interviews that violate the child's rights resulting in improperly obtained admissions. Such a policy in the interest of fairness and justice to the child should arguably trump any manpower or budgetary concerns.[124]

Thirdly, individual assessments that relate to the child's specific contextual needs and risks are recognised as an effective mechanism with which to address children's specific needs in proceedings. Department of Human Services (Victoria) instructs child workers that each "assessment is a cycle, rather than a static process" and that each child will have a unique profile (even compared to siblings in the same household).[125] The LEAP report concurs that "ensuring each child has an individual assessment, taking into account the child's personality as well as social and economic background, is a key safeguard for the interests of the child in criminal proceedings".[126] This policy is further supported by the ALRC, which states that "children's matters should deal with the contexts of children's lives and the variety of social, cultural and economic factors that contribute to juvenile offending", [127] as well as various advocacy groups that specialise in vulnerable and child witnesses such as TAG.[128]

The Australian Children's Commissioners and Guardians adds that the individual factors which lead a child into state care, and subsequently the justice system, are usually similar (namely, dysfunction at home or the community, alcohol and drugs, violence, disadvantage and poverty) and should always be considered during individual assessment and to weigh the risks when determining the appropriate level of intervention required.[129] The significance of the individual assessment relates to Articles

---

[124] McCrimmon, L., "The Uniform Evidence Act and the Anunga Guidelines: Accommodation or Annihilation?" *Northern Territory Law Journal* 2, no. 2 (2011): 91 see also Hitch, G., NT Royal Commission: Judge Criticises Widespread "Lack of Expertise" in Youth Justice System, *ABC News* (online) 8 May 2017 ("Hitch") <http://www.abc.net.au/news/2017-05-08/nt-royal-commission-hears-lack-of-expertise-youth-justice-system/8505796>: where Hannam J stated that under-funding by the NT Government of the relevant mechanisms undermined the effectiveness of the YJA.

[125] Victorian Government Department of Human Services, *Assessing Children and Yong People Experiencing Family Violence: A Practice Guide for Family Violence Practitioners* (State of Vitoria, 2013) 21; see also ACCG, below 31, which cites the Victorian model as 'overall best practice in providing youth justice services' at 20.

[126] LEAP, above n 4, 90 [51].

[127] ALRC, above n 16, [18.83].

[128] The Advocate's Gateway, *"Ground Rules Hearings and the fair treatment of Vulnerable People in Court Toolkit 1'* (The Advocacy's Gateway, 2017).

[129] Australian Children's Commissioners and Guardians, *Human Rights Standards in Youth Detention Facilities in Australia: the use of Restraint, Disciplinary Regimes and Other Specified Practices*, Report (2016) ("ACCG") 47.

6 and 6.1 of the *European Convention on Human Rights*[130] which states that the child has a right to a fair trial and a fair hearing respectively. The European Court of Human Rights has since held that this means the right to fully understand and participate in the trial and further calls for the flexibility of the proceedings to be tailored to the specific needs of the child subject to professional assessment.[131] However, the issue may not be so much the actual assessment of the child but the reluctance of the Courts to adapt criminal proceedings accordingly.[132] The LEAP Report cites experiences in the UK where 'even when the child was diagnosed with a mental illness, the authorities would make little effort to accommodate their needs' and in the Czech Republic, despite mandatory assessments at the start of proceedings, no "significant adjustments" were made.[133] In the context of the NT, there is no provision for individual assessment in the *YJA* which might explain the disproportionate representation of Indigenous children within the criminal justice system.[134] These children are consistently alienated by a system that seemingly 'ignores, rather than actively engages, with their socio-cultural identity and reality'.[135]

Citing the "community-up" approach,[136] NAAJA recommends that any practice involving indigenous children should be culturally relevant and 'any attempt by the youth justice system to better meet the needs of Aboriginal [children] must start from a position of trying to understand the world view of Aboriginal [children].' However, in considering the specific factors that affect a youth, special care must be taken not to cause "normalisation of the abnormal" such as the situation in some communities where children not going to school was so widespread that this practice had subsequently become normalised.[137] Such situations should arguably

---

[130] *Convention for the Protection of Human Rights and Fundamental Freedoms*, open for signature 4 November 1950, 213 UNTS 221 (entered into force 3 September 1953) (*"European Convention on Human Rights"*), Article 6: Right to a fair trial.

[131] *S.C. v. the United Kingdom* (60958/00).

[132] *R v Anthony Cox*. 2012. EWCA Crim 549.

[133] LEAP [51].

[134] Anthony, T., "Why Are So Many Indigenous Kids in Detention in the NT in the First Place?" The Conversation (online) 4 August 2016; Cunneen, C., Racism, Discrimination and the Over-representation of Indigenous People in the Criminal Justice System: Some Conceptual and Explanatory Issues; *Current Issues in Criminal Justice* 17, no. 4 (2006).

[135] North Australian Aboriginal Justice Agency, *A Review of the Northern Territory Youth Justice System*, Submission (2011) ("NAAJA") 22; see also John Walker and David Neil McDonald 'The Over-Representation of Indigenous people in Custody in Australia' (Report No 47 Australian Institute of Criminology, August 1995).

[136] Credited to Magistrate Deen Potter, Children's Court (WA) by NAAJA, above n 46, who calls for the design, delivery and integration of holistic approaches incorporating specific community considerations approach; see also Kelly Richards, *What Makes Juvenile Offenders Different from Adult Offenders?* (February 2011) Australian Institute of Criminology 2.

[137] Hitch, above n 28.

result in swift intervention based on the interests of child protection and the belief in the importance of education in reducing offending.[138]

Conclusion

Best practice procedures for advocacy with vulnerable people, Indigenous Australians or otherwise are now well known. In England and Wales this includes the Codes of Practice on Detention, Treatment and Questioning of Suspects,[139] and the requirements of the CPR and Practice Direction which have adopted the toolkits developed by TAG. Research and practice developments around judicial case management are slowly shifting the criminal justice process in relation to vulnerable accused. In addition, the effective participation of vulnerable suspects has some significant impetus through the access to justice and reasonable accommodation requirements of the CRPD. Attention to how an accused person's vulnerability is relevant to investigatory interviews, decisions to prosecute, fitness to participate in the trial, some currently available defences and the accused's presentation in court is now relatively routine. ground rules hearings[140] to determine the approach in a case involving a vulnerable person are also quite common.[141] Australia has adopted some guidance from various tools developed by the courts of England and Wales. For example, in the NT it has been judicially noted that failure to make use of tools for good communication taints the reliability of the evidence.[142] However, a formal substantive or procedural framework which takes a rights-based approach for the purposes of access to justice still seems a long way off.

The aim of the *Anunga* Guidelines was to ensure there is a fair and a reliable system for investigations and numerous cases are based on these principles.[143] However, 40 years later there are still examples of poor police procedures. Leaving these issues to the discretion of a court does not begin to accommodate vulnerable people into the common law system, especially when they are Indigenous. Further, since the introduction of

---

[138] Hitch n 28: 'that attending school is a very important protective factor for children both in terms of offending and child protection' per Hannam J; Bull, above n 84, who states that as Indigenous people are unable to comprehend concepts (eg. time, distance and numeracy) the same way as we do unless exposed to such concepts early on in school.

[139] PACE Ref.

[140] 'Ground Rules Hearings and the fair treatment of Vulnerable People in Court Toolkit 1' (The Advocacy's Gateway, 2016).

[141] Ibid n16.

[142] *The Queen v BM*. 2015. NTSC 73 at 22.

[143] Douglas, H., "The Cultural Specificity of Evidence: The Current Scope and Relevance of the *Anunga* Guidelines," *UNSW Law Journal* 21, no.1 (1998): 30.

the *ENULA*, the courts in the NT seemed to have moved away from the protection afforded to Indigenous accused by the *Anunga* Guidelines.

The implementation of the *ENULA* has meant that *Anunga* will no longer be binding authority in relation to the admissibility of evidence which, at the very least signals a relaxation in the requirements for 'courtesy and patience' towards Indigenous people. To ensure fairness, it should be imperative that special safeguards are provided to vulnerable suspects at all stages of criminal proceedings. This is to ensure access to justice and reasonable accommodation where necessary and appropriate from the perspective of the person's vulnerability, not their role in a trial. It follows that a Statutory Code of Practice for the detention, treatment, questioning and court appearance with a specific focus on vulnerable Indigenous people, in a Territory known for its high levels of vulnerability, is very long overdue. Duty holders such as police, lawyers and judges must find effective ways to manage vulnerable people by adapting procedures and increasing consistency and fairness. Having something similar to ground rules hearings in all courts would be a simple start which could be implemented immediately. Investigators should not proceed without a suspect having spoken to a lawyer and a health assessment having been completed for any vulnerable Indigenous suspect.

Vulnerability ought to be determined by the suitably trained. The EU 'Roadmap for Strengthening Procedural Rights of Suspected or Accused Persons in Criminal Proceedings' already provides a basic framework. A similar rights-based approach adapted to account for the very unique situation of Indigenous people and any further adaptations required for those with disabilities would allowing the NT to look forward to comprehensive and systemic change, which could result in a fairer criminal justice process for all.

CHAPTER 9

The effects of intersectionality: Women with learning disabilities, difficulties and autism in the criminal justice system

Dr. Hugh Asher

Abstract: This paper will explore the evidence underpinning the need for greater research into the experiences of women with learning disabilities in the criminal justice system. Often the needs of minority groups in the criminal justice system, such as women or people with learning disabilities, are viewed in isolation, for example the experiences of women are explored **or** the experiences of people with learning disabilities. This paper is going to describe why there is a need to address the 'intersectional' effects experienced by women with learning disabilities criminal justice system. Intersectionality is a way of looking at the interconnected nature of social categories such as age, gender, ethnicity, sexuality, or in this instance disability, that may lead to oppression or additional disadvantage for an individual (McCarthy et al., 2017). Commonly, such social categories are perceived as distinct spheres of experience, however theories of intersectionality explore how these spheres of experience can overlay one another creating more complex intersections. Such theories also seek to demonstrate how existing policy and practice can result in further discrimination or inequality of service provision (McCarthy et al. 2017). This paper proposes that the 'intersectional' nature of gender and disability means that the needs and experiences of this small, but significant minority within the criminal justice system are often overlooked and remain unacknowledged within policy and practice.

Introduction

Women's offending is more likely to be connected to their relationships than men's, such as acquisitive crime to purchase drugs for their partner; they are more likely to have committed non-violent offences than men; and are more likely than men to be sentenced to prison for a first offence (Earle, 2014). Their offending is more likely to be linked to drug or alcohol problems, itself often a response to previous abuse and trauma; to underlying mental health difficulties; and to coercive or abusive relationships (Prison Reform Trust, 2017). Evidence also suggests that women with learning disabilities are more likely than those without cognitive impairments to experience domestic violence, and that they are less likely to know where they can seek help and support for this (McCarthy *et al.*, 2017). Previous research has concluded that 20-30% of offenders have learning difficulties or learning disabilities that interfere with their ability to cope within the criminal justice system (Loucks, 2007). Whilst this has not been broken down by gender, in prisons the incidence of learning difficulties and difficulties in women is perceived to be higher than it is for men (Mottram, 2007). Guiney and Earle (2017) reported that whilst women make up approximately 15% of adult arrestees in police custody, they account for 22% of those referred to Liaison and Diversion services. Liaison and Diversion is a service providing support in custody and courts to adults who are perceived as vulnerable due to factors such as mental health issues and learning disabilities NHS England, 2014). Thus, it would appear that learning disabilities and related issues are also more prevalent in women in the criminal justice system than they are amongst men.

The Equality Act 2010 provides legal protection from discrimination to people with one or more of nine 'protected characteristics' including age, ethnicity, gender, sexual orientation and disability, including learning disabilities. It is important here, to recognise that equality does not mean treating everyone the same. Baroness Corston noted that, within the criminal justice system, women and men are different, they have differing needs and equal treatment of them does not result in equal outcomes (Corston, 2007). Duties under the Equality Act mean women and men *"should be treated with equivalent respect, according to need"* and *"equality must embrace not just fairness but inclusivity"* (Corston, 2007: 3). Whilst women are a minority group within the criminal justice system, making up about 23% (Ministry of Justice, 2012), they are not all the same. There are other smaller minority groups within this group with different needs and different problems, and a disproportionate number of them have learning disabilities and difficulties (Corston, 2007, Talbot, 2007), although these additional and more complex needs are often undiagnosed (Ministry of Justice, 2012). As such, and in terms of the Equality Act, women with learning disabilities or difficulties represent a 'protected characteristic within a protected characteristic'. Not only do they have different needs to men, they also have different needs to other women. The Public Sector Equality Duty requires public bodies including the police, prisons, probation services and courts to make reasonable attempts to eliminate discrimination and ensure equality of opportunity during the course of their activities. Thus, across the criminal justice system it is imperative, both at a legal and moral level, that the needs of both women and those with learning disabilities are addressed. Further, in relation to women with learning disabilities, it is therefore important to identify how the implications of gender and learning disabilities overlap and create further inequality and disadvantage.

Despite this, there is very little research to date that specifically looks at women with learning disabilities in the criminal justice system and a review of the wider literature highlights that the intersectionality of gender and learning disability does not receive in-depth attention compared to mental health. For example, the United Nations Rules for the Treatment of Women Prisoners and Non-Custodial Measures for Women Offenders ('the Bangkok Rules') do refer to 'mental disability' relating to wider mental health issues but do not specifically discuss 'learning disability', 'intellectual' disability' or 'cognitive impairments'. Similarly, the Women's Custodial Estate Review (Robinson, 2013) published by the National Offender Management Service acknowledges the complex needs of women prisoners, including personality disorder and mental-health related issues, but does not mention learning disabilities or difficulties.

However, the necessity for a better understanding of such intersectional issues within the criminal justice system has previously been identified. According to Her Majesty's Prison Service, learning disability has commonly been under diagnosed in women prisoners, leading to concerns that where it is not identified, women may not receive appropriate support (HMPS, 2008). An NHS survey conducted at HMP Styal in 2007 (Mottram, 2007) reported that 8.3% of the sample had an IQ below 70 (considered to be a learning disability), and a further 31.7% were classed as having a borderline learning disability. This compared to 7.1% and 23.6% in the adult male prisoners sampled. It is recognised though, that minority groups with learning disabilities, such as women, may have additional needs (Betts, 2015), though these often go unmet. Good practice guidance from Her Majesty's Inspectorate of Prisons (HMIP, 2014) propose that women's needs are accurately and effectively assessed on arrival at prison, including formal assessment of learning disabilities and difficulties, and that timely action is taken to address these needs. This approach is described as essential in promoting equitable outcomes, allowing reasonable adjustments to be made to ensure that women with disabilities have equitable access to programmes and services within prison, and within the wider criminal justice system (Ministry of Justice, 2012, HMIP, 2014). However, it is also recognised that the smaller number of female offenders, particularly in prisons, can make this more difficult. As the Prison Service Order relating to women (PSO 4800) identifies,

> In the male estate if a particular prison is unable to make "reasonable adjustments" to enable a prisoner with disabilities to benefit from a particular service or programme, it is possible another nearby prison will be able to do so. This is less likely in the women's estate where with fewer prisons it is quite likely that a particular service or programme will only be available in one prison. (HMPS, 2008)

HMIP inspection reports indicate that such proactive identification of need and appropriate responses vary between establishments. Some screening tools utilised are described as lacking a sufficiently sophisticated approach to the identification of learning disability, and many examples are given of individuals whose needs were not identified on reception into prison. In one establishment, there was a specialist learning disability nurse who attended the prison one day a week, but they did not have any women on their case load. This is surprising given the reported prevalence of learning disabilities amongst this population. None-the-less areas of good practice have been also been identified in Inspector's reports. One prison had a specific wellbeing group for women with learning disabilities that had been established following consultation with prisoners and another had two learning disability nurses who assessed social care needs and capacity, with a clinical psychologist who provided structured support for them. Other prisons were noted for conducting reception interviews in private, a strategy to increase self-disclosure and minimise the risks of appearing different or vulnerable to other prisoners.

The biggest change to the support offered to people with learning disabilities in the earlier stages of the criminal justice system is the introduction of Liaison and Diversion services into police custody suites and courts. A key recommendation of the Bradley Report (Department of Health, 2009), 'Liaison and Diversion' is a process intended to ensure that young people and adults with vulnerabilities such as mental health problems, substance use problems or learning disabilities are identified at the earliest opportunity in the criminal justice system (NHS England, 2014). Effective assessment and appropriate sharing of the results is intended to allow reasonable adjustments and informed decisions to be made relating to diversion out of the criminal justice system, charging individuals, their case management and sentencing (ibid). The aims of the service are to:

- Improve access to healthcare and support services for vulnerable individuals and a reduction in health inequalities

- Divert individuals, where appropriate, out of the youth and criminal justice systems into health, social care or other supportive services

- Deliver efficiencies within the youth and criminal justice systems

- Reduce reoffending or escalation of offending behaviours

(Disley *et al.*, 2016, p. xiii)

Women make up approximately 15% of adult arrestees in police custody, but account for 22% of those referred to Liaison and Diversion services, highlighting the greater prevalence of such complex needs, but also providing an important opportunity to 'make every contact count' (Guiney and Earle, 2017). The benefits of using of women's centres as an alternative to custody, where women can receive person-centred and individualised support, have often be highlighted (see for example the Corston Report (Corston, 2007) and the Scottish 'Commission on Women Offenders'). The development of such services would also provide further resources for Liaison and Diversion services to divert women to. These may prove more appropriate for women with learning disabilities or difficulties whose needs may not be met in prison, and for whom community penalties may be inappropriate or harder to complete or comply with.

This paper has begun to address the paucity of information about the experiences of women with learning disabilities in the criminal justice system. This group has been shown to be over-represented but under identified within the system. It has highlighted that such women may be the most vulnerable of an already vulnerable group, but that very little is understood about the ways in which being female and having a learning disability combine to affect the experiences of women in the criminal justice system. Consequently, further research into their experiences may inform policy and practice that would better meet their needs and also help public services including the police, prisons, probation services and courts to meet their obligations under The Public Sector Equality Duty.

References

Betts, Nisha. *Equal Access, Equal Care; Guidance for Prison Healthcare Staff treating Patients with Learning Disabilities*. London: NHS England, 2015.

Corston, Baroness Jean. *The Corston Report: a review of women with particular vulnerabilities in the criminal justice system*. London: Home Office, 2007.

The Rt. Hon. Lord Bradley. *The Bradley Report: Lord Bradley's review of people with mental health problems or learning disabilities in the criminal justice system*. London: Department of Health, 2009.

Disley, Emma., Taylor, Celia., Kruithof, Kristy., Winpenny, Eleanor., Liddle, Mark., Sutherland, Alex., Lilford, Richard., Wright, Sam., McAteer, Lyndsay. and Francis, Viv. *Evaluation of the Offender Liaison and Diversion Trial Schemes*. Cambridge: RAND Europe, 2016.

Earle, Jenny., Nadine, Rebecca. and Jacobson, Jessica. *Brighter Futures - Working together to reduce women's offending.* London: The Prison Reform Trust and The Pilgrim Trust, 2014.

Guiney, Thomas. and Earle, Jenny. *Fair Cop? Improving outcomes for women at the point of arrest.* London: Prison Reform Trust, 2017.

Her Majesty's Inspectorate of Prisons. *Expectations – Criteria for assessing the treatment of and conditions for women in prison.* London: HMIP, 2014.

Her Majesty's Prison Service. *PSO 4800 Women Prisoners.* London: Ministry of Justice, 2008.

Loucks, Dr. Nancy. *No One Knows - offenders with learning difficulties and learning disabilities - review of prevalence and associated needs.* London: Prison Reform Trust, 2007.

Loucks, Dr. Nancy and Talbot, Jenny. *No One Knows – Identifying and supporting prisoners with learning difficulties and learning disabilities: the views of prison staff.* London: Prison Reform Trust, 2007.

McCarthy, Michelle., Hunt, Siobhan., and Milne-Skillman, Karen. "I Know it was Every Week, but I Can't be Sure it was Every Day: Domestic Violence and Women with Learning Disabilities." *Journal of Applied Research in Intellectual Disabilities* 30 (2) (2017): 269-282.

Ministry of Justice. *A Distinct Approach: A guide to working with women offenders.* London: NOMS Women and Equalities Group, 2012.

Mottram, Dr. Pat. G. *HMP Liverpool, Styal and Hindley Study Report.* Liverpool: University of Liverpool, 2007.

NHS England. *Liaison and Diversion Operating Model 2013/14.* London: NHS England Online (2014): https://www.england.nhs.uk/commissioning/wp-content/uploads/sites/12/2014/04/ld-ser-spec-1314.pdf. Accessed 31st March 2017.

Prison Reform Trust (2016) (*Transforming Lives Leaflet*).

Prison Reform Trust. *Why focus on reducing women's imprisonment?* Online (2017) http://www.prisonreformtrust.org.uk/Portals/0/Documents/Women/why%20women_final.pdf. Accessed 29th May 2017.

Robinson, Cathy. *Women's Custodial Estate Review.* London: NOMS, 2013.

Talbot, Jenny. *No One Knows-Identifying and supporting prisoners with learning difficulties and learning disabilities: the views of prison staff.* London: Prison Reform Trust, 2007.

Talbot, J. *No One Knows-Report and Final Recommendations*. London: Prison Reform Trust, 2008.

CHAPTER 10

The importance of identifying vulnerable females and males with autism in the prison environment

Dr. Clare S. Allely, Dr. Toni Wood, & Professor Christopher Gillberg *

Autism is a neurodevelopmental disorder that is characterised by impairments in social reciprocal interactions and communication and by restricted, repetitive pattern of interests and behaviour (American Psychiatric Association (APA), 2000, 2013). There has been little investigation into the difficulties experienced by individuals with autism when they enter prison. The few studies that have been published suggest the existence of additional difficulties faced by this population within the prison environment. In a recent review of the literature, Allely (2015) identified only four studies that investigated the experience of individuals with autism in the prison environment. All four found that prisoners with autism face a number of difficulties within the prison environment such as poor relationships with prison staff and other inmates. However, to date, these studies have involved case studies or small samples and are predominantly comprising of males with autism.

Adult males with autism in the prison environment

Recognising the importance of research in this field, lecturers at the University of Salford, Dr Clare Allely and Dr Toni Wood, have combined their expertise and started a unique prison project of males with autism. In it, they will use questionnaires and semi-structured interviews with a broad section of prison staff as well as with inmates with autism with the aim of increasing our understanding of what areas could be improved on and, crucially, to assist in the development of a toolkit for prison staff in order to try and increase the identification, recognition and understanding of autism within the prison environment. The urgency of further research and recognition of autism in the criminal justice process is emphasised by studies that have found that the severity of autistic traits is a risk factor for suicidality and common mental health issues in prisoners (McCarthy, Underwood, Hayward, Chaplin, Forrester, Mills, & Murphy, 2015).

* Dr. Clare S Allely. Lecturer in Psychology, School of Health Sciences, University of Salford, Manchester, England and affiliate member of the Gillberg Neuropsychiatry Centre, Sahlgrenska Academy, University of Gothenburg, Gothenburg, Sweden.
Dr. Toni Wood. Lecturer in Criminology, School of Nursing Midwifery Social Work and Social Science, University of Salford, Manchester, England.
Professor Christopher Gillberg, Gillberg Neuropsychiatry Centre, Sahlgrenska Academy, University of Gothenburg, Gothenburg, Sweden.

Adult females with autism in the prison environment

As mentioned, there has been a paucity of research looking at the experience of males with autism in prisons. However, there is even less research and clinical reports of the experience of females with autism in the prison environment. Morris (2009) conducted qualitative interviews with five inmates (four male and one female, all Caucasian), from the Oregon Department of Corrections. The one female participant in the study differed from the four men with respect to her assessment of relationships. For instance, she reported that gossip was "scary", a reference to relational aggression, something not reported by any of the four men in the sample (Morris, 2009). There is a need to focus research on autism in prison inmates, and perhaps particularly in females. Females with autism are more vulnerable and at-risk of engaging in antisocial behaviour compared to females without autism (Hare, 1999; Mouridsen, 2008). One group of authors reported that in a high secure unit over 10% (6 out of 51 females) were found to meet diagnostic criteria for autism, using the ICD–10 (Crocombe, Mills, & Wing, 2006).

The male:female autism ratio that has been widely quoted as being 4 to 5:1 and it has therefore long been considered to be predominantly a male condition (Fombonne, Quirke, & Hagen, 2011). However, Jensen and colleagues have recently highlighted that this male predominance has been on a decreasing trend of the past 20 years (Jensen, Steinhausen, & Lauritsen, 2014). Recent large-scale population/community-based epidemiological studies indicate a ratio of 2 to 3:1 (Lai, Lombardo, Auyeung, Chakrabarti, & Baron-Cohen, 2015), raising a number of implications (Lai, Baron-Cohen, & Buxbaum, 2015).

Females with autism are frequently identified and diagnosed much later compared to males (Begeer, Mandell, Wijnker-Holmes, Venderbosch, Rem, Stekelenburg et al., 2013; Giarelli, Wiggins, Rice, Levy, Kirby, Pinto Martin et al., 2010; Shattuck, Durkin, Maenner, Newschaffer, Mandell, Wiggins, et al., 2009). Further, females tend to receive a diagnosis only in cases where the autistic symptomology is more severe and/or have more co-existing behavioural and/or cognitive problems (Dworzynski, Ronald, Bolton, & Happé, 2012; Russell, Steer, & Golding, 2011; Russell, Steer, & Golding, 2011). Given that females with autism go unidentified, this has significant implications on our clinical and scientific understanding of autism in terms of how male-biased it is (Lai, Baron-Cohen, & Buxbaum, 2015). There is also the possibility of 'gender-based interpretation bias' (Kreiser & White, 2014) in that those who can highlight the need for a referral for further assessment and evaluation are misappropriating the social impairments which present in females with autism as being due to behaviours that are stereotyped as female-typical and therefore considered to be expressions of "just" shyness (Goldman, 2013). The possibility of greater 'diagnostic overshadowing or substitution in females' as a result of co-morbid secondary neurodevelopmental and psychiatric conditions (e.g., attention-deficit/hyperactivity disorder and mood disorders such as anxiety and depression) or misdiagnoses (e.g., borderline personality disorder) has also been suggested (Kopp & Gillberg, 1992; Trubanova, Donlon, Kreiser, Ollendick, & White, 2014).

Females "Meet the Criteria" in Different Ways than Males

Another important issue to consider is that females with autism tend to camouflage their symptomology which may also be a significant contributor to the under-identification of the condition in females leading to our current male-biased understanding of autism (e.g., Rynkiewicz, Schuller, Marchi, Piana, Camurri, Lassalle, & Baron-Cohen, 2016). Generally, females with autism frequently take more steps to camouflage their impairments given that they tend to have more self-awareness and better expressive behaviours (e.g., reciprocal conversation, sharing interests) and exhibit less repetitive use of objects and different types of restricted interests compared to males with autism (Rynkiewicz & Łucka, 2015; Head, McGillivray, & Stokes, 2014). This camouflaging in many females with autism can occur irrespective of the presence of similar social understanding impairments exhibited in males with autism (Head, McGillivray, & Stokes, 2014). Additional features have also been suggested in a relatively small number of important studies to be more associated with females as opposed to males (e.g., demand avoidance) (Kopp & Gillberg, 2011; O'Nions, Viding, Greven, Ronald, & Happé, 2014; Lai, Lombardo, Auyeung, Chakrabarti, & Baron-Cohen, 2015). Lastly, it has also been suggested that there may exist different subgroups in females with autism. Specifically, there may exist one subgroup who present clinically the more "classical" (male-typical) and/or cognitive delay. Given the similar clinical presentation to that found in males with autism, this subgroup may be more easily identified and at a younger age. On the other hand, the other subgroup may not be identified until much later or are misdiagnosed because they are higher-functioning and have atypical symptomology or are able to compensate or camouflage their autism impairments (Lai, Lombardo, Auyeung, Chakrabarti, & Baron-Cohen, 2015). It is imperative that we take these notions seriously and take appropriate and necessary action to prevent females with autism from being overlooked and to ensure that they are integrated into our understanding of autism (Shefcyk, 2015; Lai, Baron-Cohen, & Buxbaum, 2015).

Need for the development of a screening tool for autism for females in prison

The observed differences found in the diagnosis of males and females with autism outlined above may simply be due to the lack of sensitivity that the current tools have in identifying female clinical characteristic of autism (Lai, Lombardo, Auyeung, Chakrabarti, & Baron-Cohen, 2015). The tools include items which contribute to score which is likely to have been ascertain based on the 'male predominance in case identification' (Rutter, Caspi, & Moffitt, 2003; Kreiser & White, 2014). The existence of "female phenotypes" of autism is indicated by anecdotal clinical/autobiographical reports (Gould & Ashton-Smith, 2011; Attwood, 2007). A recent meta-analysis suggested that, on average, females with autism exhibit less restricted, repetitive behaviours and interests (RRBI) compared to males with the disorder (e.g., on the Autism Diagnostic Interview–Revised [ADI-R] and/or the Autism Diagnostic Observation Schedule [ADOS]). This is consistent with a relatively small number of other studies (e.g., Van Wijngaarden-Cremers, van Eeten, Groen, Van Deurzen, Oosterling, & Van der Gaag, 2014). If RRBIs are used as key diagnostic criteria, females with AUTISM may not be recognised (Rynkiewicz et al., 2016).

Therefore, there is a need to collect a wide range of behaviours which go beyond those that are included in the potentially male-biased autism screening tools and diagnostic assessments currently widely used (Lai, Lombardo, Auyeung, Chakrabarti, & Baron-Cohen, 2015). For instance, the Autism Diagnostic Observation Schedule Second Edition (ADOS-2, Lord, Rutter, DiLavorne, Risi, Gotham, & Bishop, 2012); the Autism Spectrum Quotient (AQ, Baron-Cohen, Wheelwright, Skinner, Martin, & Clubley, 2001) and Social Communication Questionnaire (SCQ, Rutter, Bailey, & Lord, 2010) are developed based on the phenotype which is presented by most boys with autism and are failing to include many of the clinical features exhibited by many girls with autism (Rynkiewicz & Łucka, 2015). The SCQ specifically assesses the social and communication domains. However, no study has been conducted to evaluate whether there are gender differences in its scores (Rynkiewicz et al., 2016).

The need to raise awareness amongst criminal justice professionals that autism is not only a male disorder

The need for greater awareness and recognition of how autism symptomology can present in females with autism and a tool to assist in the identification of possible autism in females is clearly of great importance. St Giles Trust's Autism Spectrum Disorder (autism) project provided support to prison leavers from HMP Holloway with autistic and personality disorder traits from 2014 – 2016 (Network Autism, 2016; Clinks Case Study, 2016). To the authors knowledge, this is the only project which included the support of female offenders with autism. The specific characteristics of female offenders with autism, the prevalence of autism in female offenders and the types of crimes they commit and the factors contributing to their possible over-representation in the criminal justice system clearly highlights the need for further research in this area (Dein & Woodbury-Smith, 2010). There is also the need to address the welfare of transgender women and men in prison (e.g., Whitman, 2016; Sevelius, Sevelius, Jenness, & Jenness, 2017). Studies have also indicated that there may be an association between gender identity disorder/gender dysphoria and autism (e.g., Baker & Shweikh, 2016). Particularly within the last decade, gender identity clinics have observed an overrepresentation of individuals with autism in their referrals for gender identity disorder (GID) or gender dysphoria (GD) (Robinow & Knudson, 2005; Lemaire, Thomazeau, & Bonnet-Brilhault, 2014). Bejerot and colleagues (2012) posit that rather than being characterised by masculinisation in both genders, autism may instead constitute a gender defiant disorder (Bejerot, Eriksson, Bonde, Carlström, Humble, & Eriksson, 2012). This notion is supported by Strang and colleagues (2014) who observed an over-representation of individuals with autism referred for GID. However, it remains controversial and not well understood as to whether GID and autism are associated or not. The only prospective systematic study of sexuality in autism (Asperger syndrome) did not suggest a high rate of GID (Davidsson et al 2017). However, it could be that some behaviours found in individuals with GID are atypical manifestations of restricted, repetitive and stereotypical behaviours and interests (RRBI).

In sum, there is a need for (1) prison populations to be screened for autism, (2) the development of screening and assessment tools, (3) finding appropriate screening and assessment tools for females, and (4) addressing the welfare of transgender individuals in prison populations.

References

Allely, C. S. (2015a). Autism spectrum disorders in the criminal justice system: police interviewing, the courtroom and the prison environment. *Recent Advances in Autism*, 1-13.

Allely, C. S. (2015b). Experiences of prison inmates with autism spectrum disorders and the knowledge and understanding of the spectrum amongst prison staff: a review. *Journal of Intellectual Disabilities and Offending Behaviour*, 6(2), 55-67.

Allen, D., Evans, C., Hider, A., Hawkins, S., Peckett, H., & Morgan, H. (2008). Offending behaviour in adults with Asperger syndrome. *Journal of Autism and Developmental Disorders*, 38(4), 748-58.

American Psychiatric Association (APA) (2000), Diagnostic and Statistical Manual of Mental Disorders, 4th rev. ed., American Psychiatric Association, Washington, DC.

American Psychiatric Association (APA) (2013), *Diagnostic and Statistical Manual of Mental Disorders, 5th rev. ed.*, American Psychiatric Association, Washington, DC.

Attwood, T. (2007). *The complete guide to Aspergers syndrome*. London: Jessica Kingsley Publishers.

Baker, P., & Shweikh, E. (2016). Autistic spectrum disorders, personality disorder and offending in a transgender patient: clinical considerations, diagnostic challenges and treatment responses. *Advances in Autism*, 2(3), 140-146.

Baron-Cohen, S., Wheelwright, S., Skinner, R., Martin, J., & Clubley, E. (2001). The autism-spectrum quotient (AQ): Evidence from asperger syndrome/high-functioning autism, males and females, scientists and mathematicians. *Journal of Autism and Developmental Disorders*, 31(1), 5-17.

Begeer, S., Mandell, D., Wijnker-Holmes, B., Venderbosch, S., Rem, D., Stekelenburg, F., & Koot, H. M. (2013). Sex differences in the timing of identification among children and adults with autism spectrum disorders. *Journal of Autism and Developmental Disorders*, 43(5), 1151-1156.

Bejerot, S., Eriksson, J. M., Bonde, S., Carlström, K., Humble, M. B., & Eriksson, E. (2012). The extreme male brain revisited: gender coherence in adults with autism spectrum disorder. *The British Journal of Psychiatry*, 201(2), 116-123.

Clinks Care Study (2016). St Giles Trust I Supporting Ex-Offenders With 'Hidden Disabilities'. Case study of a Clinks member. Accessed on

18th February 2017. http://www.clinks.org/sites/default/files/basic/files-downloads/st_giles_trust_final150816.pdf

Crocombe, J., Mills, R., & Wing, L. (2006). *Autism spectrum disorders in the high security hospitals of the United Kingdom. A summary of two studies*. The National Autistic Society, London.

Dein, K., & Woodbury-Smith, M. (2010). Asperger syndrome and criminal behaviour. *Advances in Psychiatric Treatment*, 16(1), 37-43.

Dworzynski, K., Ronald, A., Bolton, P., & Happé, F. (2012). How different are girls and boys above and below the diagnostic threshold for autism spectrum disorders?. *Journal of the American Academy of Child and Adolescent Psychiatry*, 51(8), 788-797.

Fombonne, E., Quirke, S., & Hagen, A. (2011). Epidemiology of pervasive developmental disorders. In: Amaral DG, Dawson G, Geschwind DH, editors. *Autism spectrum disorders*. New York, NY: Oxford University Press; 2011. p. 90–111.

Ghaziuddin, M., Tsai, L., & Ghaziuddin, N. (1991). Brief report: Violence in Asperger syndrome—A critique. *Journal of Autism and Developmental Disorders*, 21, 349–354.

Giarelli, E., Wiggins, L. D., Rice, C. E., Levy, S. E., Kirby, R. S., Pinto-Martin, J., & Mandell, D. (2010). Sex differences in the evaluation and diagnosis of autism spectrum disorders among children. *Disability and Health Journal*, 3(2), 107-116.

Goldman, S. (2013). Opinion: Sex, gender and the diagnosis of autism—A biosocial view of the male preponderance. *Research in Autism Spectrum Disorders*, 7(6), 675-679.

Gordon, R. (2002). Asperger syndrome: one prisoner's experience. *Prison Service Journal*, 143, 2-4.

Gould, J., & Ashton-Smith, J. (2011). Missed diagnosis or misdiagnosis? Girls and women on the autism spectrum. *Good Autism Practice* (GAP), 12(1), 34-41.

Hare, D. J., Gould, J., Mills, R., & Wing, L. (1999). *A preliminary study of individuals with autistic spectrum disorders in three special hospitals in England*. London: National Autistic Society.

Hayes, S.C. (2002). Early Intervention or Early Incarceration? Using a Screening Test for Intellectual Disability in the Criminal Justice System. *Journal of Applied Research in Intellectual Disabilities* 15(2), 120-128.

Head, A. M., McGillivray, J. A., & Stokes, M. A. (2014). Gender differences in emotionality and sociability in children with autism spectrum disorders. *Molecular autism*, 5(1), 19.

Jensen, C. M., Steinhausen, H. C., & Lauritsen, M. B. (2014). Time trends over 16 years in incidence-rates of autism spectrum disorders across the lifespan based on nationwide Danish register data. *Journal of Autism and Developmental Disorders*, 44(8), 1808-1818.

Kopp, S., & Gillberg, C. (2011). The Autism Spectrum Screening Questionnaire (ASSQ)-Revised Extended Version (ASSQ-REV): An instrument for better capturing the autism phenotype in girls? A preliminary study involving 191 clinical cases and community controls. *Research in Developmental Disabilities*, 32(6), 2875-2888.

Kopp, S., & Gillberg, C. (1992). Girls with social deficits and learning problems: Autism, atypical Asperger syndrome or a variant of these conditions. *European Child and Adolescent Psychiatry*, 1(2), 89-99.

Kreiser, N. L., & White, S. W. (2014). AUTISM in females: are we overstating the gender difference in diagnosis?. *Clinical Child and Family Psychology Review*, 17(1), 67-84.

Paterson, P. (2008). How well do young offenders with Asperger syndrome cope in custody?", *British Journal of Learning Disabilities, 36*(1), 54-58.

Lai, M. C., Lombardo, M. V., Auyeung, B., Chakrabarti, B., & Baron-Cohen, S. (2015). Sex/gender differences and autism: setting the scene for future research. *Journal of the American Academy of Child and Adolescent Psychiatry*, 54(1), 11-24.

Lai, M. C., Baron-Cohen, S., & Buxbaum, J. D. (2015). Understanding autism in the light of sex/gender. *Molecular Autism*, 6(1), 24.

Lemaire, M., Thomazeau, B., & Bonnet-Brilhault, F. (2014). Gender Identity Disorder and Autism Spectrum Disorder in a 23-Year-Old Female. *Archives of Sexual Behavior, 43*(2), 395-398.

Lewis, A., Foster, M., Hughes, C., & Turner, K. (2016). Management of prisoners with autism is not perfect but is improving. *British Medical Journal, 354.*

Lewis, A., Pritchett, R., Hughes, C., & Turner, K. (2015). Development and implementation of autism standards for prisons. *Journal of Intellectual Disabilities and Offending Behaviour, 6*(2), 68-80.

Lord, C., Rutter, M., DiLavorne, P. C., Risi, S., Gotham, K., & Bishop, S. L. (2012). *Autism Diagnostic Observation Schedule, Second Edition (ADOS-2) Manual (Part I): Modules 1-4.* Torrance, CA: Western Psychological Services.

Loucks, N. (2007). *No One Knows: offenders with learning difficulties and learning disabilities - review of prevalence and associated needs.* London.

Lugnegård, T., Hallerbäck, M. U., & Gillberg, C. (2011). Psychiatric comorbidity in young adults with a clinical diagnosis of Asperger syndrome. *Research in Developmental Disabilities*, 32(5), 1910-1917.

May, T. (2017) *Mental health problems are everyone's problem.* London: Huffington Post.

Ministry of Justice. (2016) *Prison Safety and Reform.* London: Ministry of Justice.

McAdam, P. (2009), "Knowledge and understanding of the autism spectrum amongst prison staff", *Good Autism Practice* (GAP), Vol. 10 No. 1, pp. 19-25.

McAdam, P. (2012), "Knowledge and understanding of the autism spectrum amongst prison staff", *Prison Service Journal*, Vol. 202, pp. 26-30.

McCarthy, J., Underwood, L. I. S. A., Hayward, H., Chaplin, E., Forrester, A., Mills, R., & Murphy, D. (2015). Autism spectrum disorder and mental health problems among prisoners. *European Psychiatry*, 30, 864.

Morris, A. (2009), "Offenders with Asperger's syndrome: experiences from within prison", doctoral dissertation, Pacific University, available at: http://commons.pacificu.edu/spp/525

Mouridsen, S. E. (2012). Current status of research on autism spectrum disorders and offending. *Research in Autism Spectrum Disorders*, 6(1), 79-86.

Mouridsen, S. E., Rich, B., Isager, T., & Nedergaard, N. J. (2008). Pervasive developmental disorders and criminal behaviour. A case control study. *International Journal of Offender Therapy and Comparative Criminology*, 52(2), 196–205.

Network Autism. (2016). Supporting autistic women in the criminal justice system. Network Autism. Accessed on 18th February 2017: http://network. autism.org.uk/good-practice/case-studies/supporting-autistic-women-criminal-justice-system

Newman, C., Cashin, A., & Waters, C. (2015). A hermeneutic phenomenological examination of the lived experience of incarceration for those with autism. *Issues in mental health nursing*, 36(8), 632-640.

O'Nions, E., Viding, E., Greven, C. U., Ronald, A., & Happé, F. (2014). Pathological demand avoidance: Exploring the behavioural profile. *Autism*, 18(5), 538-544.

Prison Reform Trust, the Association of Directors of Adult Social Services, the Centre for Mental Health, and the Education Policy Institute, (2016). *Leading change: the role of local authorities in supporting women with multiple needs*. London: Conquest Litho.

Robertson, C. E., & McGillivray, J. A. (2015). Autism behind bars: a review of the research literature and discussion of key issues. *The Journal of Forensic Psychiatry & Psychology*, 26(6), 719-736.

Robinow, O., & Knudson, G. A. (2005). Asperger's disorder and GID. Paper presented at the XIX Biennial symposium of the Harry Benjamin International Gender Dysphoria Association.

Robinson, L., Spencer, M.D., Thomson, L.D.G., Stanfield, A.C., Owens, D.G.C., Hall, J. & Johnstone, E.C. (2012). *Evaluation of a screening instrument for autism spectrum disorders in prisoners*. PLoS One, 7, 1-8.

Russell, G., Steer, C., & Golding, J. (2011). Social and demographic factors that influence the diagnosis of autistic spectrum disorders. *Social Psychiatry and Psychiatric Epidemiology*, 46(12), 1283-1293.

Rutter, M., Caspi, A., & Moffitt, T. E. (2003). Using sex differences in psychopathology to study causal mechanisms: unifying issues and research strategies. *Journal of Child Psychology and Psychiatry*, 44(8), 1092-1115.

Rutter, M., Bailey, A., & Lord, C. (2010). *SCQ: Social Communication Questionnaire. Manual*. Los Angeles, CA: Western Psychological Services.

Rynkiewicz, A., Schuller, B., Marchi, E., Piana, S., Camurri, A., Lassalle, A., & Baron-Cohen, S. (2016). An investigation of the 'female camouflage effect' in autism using a computerized ADOS-2 and a test of sex/gender differences. *Molecular Autism*, 7(1), 10.

Rynkiewicz, A., & Łucka, I. (2015). Autism spectrum disorder (AUTISM) in girls. Co-occurring psychopathology. Sex differences in clinical manifestation. *Psychiatry*. Pol. ONLINE FIRST, (31).

Sevelius, J., Sevelius, J., Jenness, V., & Jenness, V. (2017). Challenges and opportunities for gender-affirming healthcare for transgender women in prison. *International Journal of Prisoner Health, 13*(1), 32-40.

Shattuck, P. T., Durkin, M., Maenner, M., Newschaffer, C., Mandell, D. S., Wiggins, L., ... & Baio, J. (2009). Timing of identification among children with an autism spectrum disorder: findings from a population-based surveillance study. *Journal of the American Academy of Child & Adolescent Psychiatry*, 48(5), 474-483.

Shefcyk, A. (2015). Count us in: addressing gender disparities in autism research. *Autism*, 19(2), 131–132.

Strang, J. F., Kenworthy, L., Dominska, A., Sokoloff, J., Kenealy, L. E., Berl, M., ... & Wallace, G. L. (2014). Increased gender variance in autism spectrum disorders and attention deficit hyperactivity disorder. *Archives of Sexual Behavior*, 43(8), 1525-1533.

Trubanova, A., Donlon, K., Kreiser, N. L., Ollendick, T. H., & White, S. W. (2014). Under-identification of AUTISM in females: a case series illustrating the unique presentation of AUTISM in young adult females. *Scandinavian Journal of Child and Adolescent Psychiatry and Psychology*, 2(2), 66-76.

Van Wijngaarden-Cremers, P. J., van Eeten, E., Groen, W. B., Van Deurzen, P. A., Oosterling, I. J., & Van der Gaag, R. J. (2014). Gender and age differences in the core triad of impairments in autism spectrum disorders: a systematic review and meta-analysis. *Journal of Autism and Developmental Disorders*, 44(3), 627-635.

Whitman, C. N. (2016). Transgender Criminal Justice: Ethical and Constitutional Perspectives. *Ethics and Behavior*, 1-13.

CHAPTER 11

Confusion and communication in deaf cases:
Towards a model of best practice

Dr. Sue O'Rourke, Chantelle de la Croix, Noel Traynor and Robert Grieve

Introduction

The difficulties faced by Deaf sign language users in legal proceedings has received some prominence in recent years and are considered in relation to Special Measures, for example in the Advocacy Training Councils Toolkit 11 *Planning to Question Someone who is Deaf*.[1] However, for individual lawyers, a Deaf case is a rarity and most come to this with no more knowledge and expertise than the general public, with the resulting risk the assumptions are made and appropriate accommodation to the needs of the Deaf person are not. In the important case of Re: C (A child) [2014] EWCA Civ 128, the Court of Appeal handed down guidance regarding fair treatment in family cases involving Deaf parents, including the need to instruct appropriate experts to carry out assessments and an acknowledgement that accommodation is not simply a matter of employing suitable interpreters.

For the uninitiated, a Deaf case can involve a bewildering array of newly encountered professionals, all waving their arms about with an apparent lack of clarity of role. What is being said (signed) is not always accessible to the Court and there can be a worrying lack of transparency. We therefore argue in this article that clarity of role and best practice in accommodating the needs of the Deaf person is also in the interests of the Court.

Definitions

British Sign Language (BSL) is the natural language of the Deaf Community and was recognised as a language in the UK in 2003, and legally recognized as an official language in Scotland in 2015 (BSL Scotland Act). It has developed over the centuries, much like spoken language. It is not an 'invented' language and is not just a visual representation of English. BSL is not a 'limited' or 'concrete' language but is as full and rich as any language, able to express abstract concepts, use metaphor and be studied by linguists[2]. It is the first or preferred language of many deaf people in the UK. In the UK, there is BSL, in France, French Sign Language and so forth.

[1] "Toolkit 11: Planning to Question Someone who is Deaf" www.theadvocatesgateway.org/tookits (Accessed 23 April, 2018).
[2] Rachel Sutton-Spence and Bencie Woll, *The Linguistics of British Sign Language* (Cambridge: Cambridge University Press, 1999).

Sign Language Interpreters are qualified professionals who are skilled in the interpretation of English into BSL and vice versa and are accountable to their registration body, the NRCPD. All SLIs working in legal settings must be qualified and registered (RSLI) and should also have experience and/or specific training in working in legal settings.

A Deaf Relay is a deaf person who functions in a relay capacity between the deaf person and a hearing SLI and has a high level of skill in adapting sign language to meet the needs of those with communication difficulties This role is also sometimes known as a deaf interpreter. The SLI will interpret the English into BSL to the deaf relay, who will then relay the message to the deaf person in an appropriate form, or register. This can include interpreting into a different sign language, or working intralingually within BSL but employing additional strategies, such as, tactile signing, adding information or examples. Deaf Relays can be registered with the NRCPD as translators or interpreters. However, as this is a relatively new profession, many deaf people working in this capacity are not registered with a professional body.

Deaf Registered Intermediaries are provided by the Ministry of Justice. They work with vulnerable witnesses throughout proceedings, for example from the police interview onwards. They carry out an assessment of communication and bring a range of tools and aids to assist the person and the court with communication.

The goal of 'independent interpreting'

The notion of interpreters in Court having no prior knowledge of the case is well established and commonplace, reflecting the position of spoken language interpreters. The underlying model of interpreting espoused by this model is the conduit model, which sees the interpreter as a passive conveyor of information, much like a translation machine. This model is widely criticised within the interpreting community[3] (eg Wilcox & Shaffer (2004) yet persists as the ideal within the court setting, probably as a backlash to when it was not uncommon for family members or carers to be asked to 'interpret', and an acknowledgement of the professionalism of interpreters. The alternative model, known as the Practice Professional Model, acknowledges the complexity of the role and the need to work with other professionals in a team approach, in order to deliver the most accurate interpretation. The Practice Professional Model highlights the importance

[3] Sherman Wilcox and Barbara Shaffer, "Towards a Cognitive Model of Interpreting" in *Topics in Sign Language Interpreting: Theory and Practice*, ed. Terry Janzen (Amsterdam/ Philadelphia: John Benjamin's Publishing Company, 2004) 27-50.

of preparation and the need for prior knowledge of communication without which communication professionals cannot properly do their job.

We propose that complete lack of prior knowledge is neither realistic nor desirable. We will argue that spoken language and sign language interpreting is not equivalent and there needs to be separation between having no or little prior knowledge of the case and having no prior knowledge of the person and their communication. Clinging to the idea of 'independence' equating to having no information acts a hindrance to justice in deaf cases and is in nobody's interest.

However, this is not to propose a return to the 'bad old days', when frequently the social worker for the Deaf person or even a family member was asked to 'interpret'. These people were almost always not qualified for the task and not impartial, leading to confusion and arguably miscarriages of justice.

The aim of this paper is explore alternative models of practice in the Court room and to suggest a professional, accountable alternative to complete independence which takes account of the linguistic and cultural needs of the deaf person and the need of the Court for maximum clarity of communication.

The Deaf community is extremely small. In a particular area or region it is highly likely that local interpreters will have prior knowledge of most deaf people and possibly of the case also. In order to achieve the requirement of 'no prior knowledge' the court often must employ interpreters from a different geographical area. Even this is no guarantee, as both deaf people and interpreters tend to travel widely for social events and work respectively.

Difficult to achieve, we would argue that complete lack of prior knowledge is also not desirable. Sign Language is regionalised to some extent, with accents and dialect; interpreters from a different geographical area are not always easy to understand, particularly for vulnerable deaf people with limited BSL themselves. In addition, the interpreter struggling to understand the deaf client may do them a disservice by giving the impression that they are incompetent when they are merely signing in a strong local dialect.

More important than this is the fact that the reliability of interpreting is improved when the interpreter is aware of the nature of the deaf person's signing and has some context to the case. This has many dimensions; to what extent do they use pure BSL or SSE[4] – this relates to their education and history. Do they have limited BSL? Is this linked to deprivation or learning disability? What are their particular signs in relation to the case? A lack of awareness of signs used for names and places, or a particular way of signing something case greatly hinder interpretation. There appears no reason for keeping such matters in the dark, other than it perhaps suiting one party to do so.

Example: because things in BSL have to have, by necessity a shape in space, general terms can lead to confusion. Buildings and locations, if not familiar to the interpreter will have to be guessed at, in terms of shape and placement. Simple matters such as 'you went back to your place' can lead the questioning astray when the interpreter signs <house> when in fact the person lives in a flat; how much simpler to have sufficient preparation to know the person lives in a flat not a house?

Many deaf people do not know or cannot spell the names of people unless they know them well, for example referring to their social worker by their sign name e.g. <really curly hair> known to everyone in the local deaf community. If the interpreter does not know this person (although they may well) they can be fingerspelling the name repeatedly, with the deaf person not knowing who they are referring to or claiming no knowledge of that person. Prior knowledge would have assisted greatly in this case and simplified matters considerably.

Such confusion, which can make the deaf person look untruthful or incompetent and delay proceedings considerably, can be easily resolved by allowing prior knowledge of the person's communication and the case.

Given the anxieties about using interpreters that are familiar to the deaf person, one means of achieving this balance between preserving independence and maximising communication, is the use of a Deaf Intermediary to brief the interpreting team prior to the case and to support during the hearing.

The role of the Deaf Intermediary is quite different to that of the interpreter or relay, with a requirement to assess the person's communication and provide a report to the Court, be present to advise at the Ground Rules Hearing and with the ability to advise during proceedings. The DRI can use visual aids and is encouraged to do so, for example developing a pictorial timeline of events in the case or using photographs of key people. The DRI may have been present at the police interview and/or expert assessments

---

[4]   SSE is Sign Supported English – when BSL signs are used in English word order.

and carries a wealth of background information or 'prior knowledge'. This information can be used to great effect in assisting the interpreting team.

Models of Practice

SLI's only

The use of SLI's only in court cases is the default option. The current situation is that the SLI's in court have no prior knowledge of the case or the person, in the interests of 'independence'. They may meet the deaf person just prior to the case for a 'chat' to orientate them to the person's style of communication, but lack much information which would assist in court. This lack of background knowledge hinders the interpretation, introducing unnecessary error as in the examples above.

SLI plus Deaf Relay

The Deaf relay suffers from the same lack of preparation as the court interpreter, meeting the Deaf person for the first time in court; s/he is still going to sign <house> until told the person lives in a flat. If he or she does not know the way in which the person signs, his or her role is diminished. What tends to occur is familiarisation throughout the course of the hearing, with the relay alerting the court to areas of confusion and clarifying these as the hearing goes along. This is disruptive to the proceedings and often arouses the suspicion of the court that the deaf people present are having a 'chat' and 'tidying up' the evidence, when in fact they are clarifying meaning. The relay's role is also limited to the use of sign language and adaptation of register only; it is outwith his or her remit to employ other visual aids or methods to assist understanding or to advise the court how this may be done.

Deaf Intermediary and SLI

The DI has a role prior to the hearing in briefing the interpreters about the Deaf person's communication and in assisting during the hearing in monitoring and contributing when necessary, for example, clarifying that X lives in a flat not a house that <really curly hair> refers to a support worker named Jane and so forth. At times the DRI takes on the role of a relay; reinterpreting everything signed for the Deaf person and perhaps offering some additional explanation. Whilst this is feasible in short bursts, the slide into the DRI becoming a relay throughout proceedings is problematic.

Firstly, it is widely accepted that the quality of interpreting diminishes after about 30 minutes due to the cognitive demands of the task; hence the use of 2 or 3 interpreters to rotate. Although the task of the relay is arguably less demanding; from BSL to adapted BSL and in his or her first language, it is often the case that the relay works alone in this role over an entire day/ case, constantly concentrating with the eyes which is very tiring. Although research into error rate has not been conducted, it seems self-evident that fatigue will play a part when either a relay or DRI takes on this role alone.

Secondly, part of the role of the Intermediary is to monitor communication and alert the Court to any difficulties. We would argue that it is simply not possible to do this optimally when the Intermediary, in effect, becomes part of the interpreting team.

Interpreters, Relay and Intermediary.

The interpreters, relay and Intermediary all have separate roles, albeit that these are overlapping. In cases where the Deaf person is required in Court over a prolonged period, and particularly when this person has additional needs such as cognitive impairment or mental health issues, the role of Intermediary cannot subsume that of the relay, without compromising his or her own role, due to the amount of relaying that is required.

In two recent family cases both a relay and intermediary were booked, as well as the team of interpreters. The intermediary and relay agreed to work together and in doing so, found that the case ran more smoothly, the relay felt supported and the intermediary assisted with vital background information, relevant to communication, enabling the relay to do a better job. In both cases the Deaf parents, although not learning disabled, had limited and complex sign language due to issues of impoverished development. In both cases the Deaf parent had been assessed by an expert Clinical Psychologist in Deafness, as well as undergoing specialist assessments by a child and family psychologist in deafness, with an Independent Social Worker, carrying out a parenting assessment in BSL. In one case the Deaf parent did not give evidence, while in the other the Intermediary took over the role of relay for cross-examination. The importance of this is that she was able to use her extensive knowledge of his background and way of communicating to work with the barristers prior to cross-examination, advising on the feasibility of certain questions. Then during cross examination, this understanding was enhanced, using a range of visual aids and adaptations to augment communication; methods that are not permitted by the relay.

Various perspectives in relation to proceedings are outlined below:

Relay: working as a relay I generally arrive with no prior information about the client, their language issues or particular signs. My role is to adapt communication to suit the particular client's needs; that is really difficult with such limited knowledge of the person, as I need additional information in order to modify language. On this occasion the intermediary could 'feed' me with useful information about the client's signs which really helped. For example, the client had a particular name sign for an independent social worker, which I didn't know; the Intermediary clarified this easily. Sometimes issues for clarification were not urgent and the intermediary would write things down and we would talk about them in the break. The intermediary had read the reports and knew the client well so could really assist with my role. Also, when I am struggling I can inform the Court, but the Intermediary can do more than this; she could ask for a break and prepare some visual material to assist – she then took control of communication for a short while to explain a certain point, then back to me. One big benefit of having the intermediary as well as a relay is that I could have short breaks; she could take over for 10-15 minutes which was really helpful as relaying all day is extremely tiring.

Intermediary: when I arrived and saw there was a relay as well as the interpreters, at first I thought that was too much and a duplication of roles. But it worked really well. I was able to brief the interpreters and the relay prior to the hearing, in terms of the person's communication, particular signs, her background and issues that were likely to come up. I also helped prepare questions for cross examination; adapting these to be more accessible. This reduced the workload for the interpreters and relay and assisted communication. When I could see the relay struggling to understand a particular sign I could assist, and in terms of complex concepts I was able to step in and suggest alternative, such as the use of pictures. The fact that the relay was there meant I was more able to do my job, could monitor communication and step in when necessary. My view is that working as a team with the interpreters and relay led to the case proceeding more quickly, without interruptions due to interpreting issues and misunderstandings. In lengthy cases I would definitely recommend an intermediary and a relay to assist the interpreting team and the Court.

Interpreter: The case involved a Deaf client with minimal BSL and little understanding of court protocols, court personnel and legal language. Though the court had no Deaf awareness or understanding of the unique challenges this situation poses to Deaf people in general, let alone to the sort of Deaf client we had been asked to support, nevertheless they took care to follow the intermediary's advice and allowed time for translations to be made as well as time for the Intermediary to reinforce or aid the client's understanding (which proved necessary on a number of occasions).

I noted in doing so that the intermediary, as the result of having spent time getting to know the client and establishing their requirements, had developed a variety of strategies and tools to help support their understanding including for example pictorial references jointly agreed on prior to attending at court.

The Intermediary also supported the translations we gave, most particularly those given by the Relay Interpreter, by way of occasional prompts relating to her prior knowledge of how the client understood certain concepts; and/ or how they had *come* to understand certain concepts a result of her much needed preparation with the client proceeding the case.

Thus, each specialised role; that of Interpreter, Relay Interpreter and Intermediary; proved crucial to the court process and the Deaf client's understanding.

Judge: For the final hearing we had expected three BSL interpreters to attend booked by the court but in fact the court had seemingly booked two interpreters and a Deaf relay. The solicitors had with them one BSL interpreter for outside court and the intermediary.

I was told at the outset of the hearing that the plan was the court appointed interpreters would interpret direct to the mother but if there were any problems with her understanding the mother would alert her advocate and the court and at that point the intermediary would step in. Once we got going we realised how problematic it would be and how much we had to slow down. Quite quickly the relay from the court was brought in to assist and thereafter it seemed things went rather better. I felt it did go well, with the court booked team and the intermediary working well together.

Clinical Psychologist: Whilst giving quite complex evidence I was aware that the Deaf parent would struggle to understand, and I think this would remain the case whatever assistance was given. However, being in the line of sight of the communication team, I was struck by the ease of communication between the relay and the Deaf parent, with little involvement from the Intermediary. It was clear to me that the relay was aware of the Deaf parents style of signing and had been fully briefed by the Intermediary to match his level of signing. Compared with other cases I have observed, I felt confident that everything that could be done to enhance communication, had been done.

Conclusion

Both relays and intermediaries are relatively new professions and there has been some understandable confusion regarding their roles and to what extent they are interchangeable. The benefits of employing native BSL users, whether relays or intermediaries, is becoming more widely recognised and cannot be overstated. SLI's, Deaf Relays and Intermediaries are becoming more accustomed to working together in the interests of Deaf people in legal settings. Deaf professionals have a lifetime of communicating in BSL in a range of settings and with a huge variety of Deaf people, all of which informs their work. However, clarity is required and we would argue that the roles are and should be distinct. In long or complex cases, family cases in which Deaf parents remain in Court for long periods, or where there is a Deaf defendant, the value of the Deaf Intermediary should not be diminished by expecting him or her to subsume the role of relay, if this is a substantial requirement. Although it may be that the cost of the interpreters and an Intermediary appears prohibitive, this needs to be balanced with the likely saving in time that clear and safely monitored communication will provide.

References

Re: C (A Child) [2014] EWCA Civ 128.

Sutton-Spence, Rachel and Woll, Bencie *The Linguistics of British Sign Language*. Cambridge: Cambridge University Press, 1999.

The Advocate's Gateway "Toolkit 11: Planning to Question Someone who is Deaf." www.theadvocatesgateway.org/toolkits.

Wilcox, Sherman and Shaffer, Barbara "Towards a Cognitive Model of Interpreting". in *Topics in Sign Language Interpreting: Theory and Practice*. Edited by Terry Janzen (Amsterdam/Philadelphia: John Benjamin's Publishing Company, 2004)27-35.

Acknowledgement

We are grateful to HHJ Lynch for her comments and support in relation to this paper.

CHAPTER 12

Trauma and victim participation in the criminal process

Professor Louise Ellison,

Professor Vanessa E Munro

Abstract: Traumatic stress is one of several potentially serious mental health difficulties victims of crime may present with. Despite this, the likely prevalence of trauma amongst the victim population has barely been acknowledged, let alone addressed, by criminal justice policy-makers and criminal justice agencies in England and Wales. In this paper we highlight the barriers that experiences of trauma can present to effective victim participation and the extent to which current trial processes are often liable to exacerbate trauma amongst a broad constituency of victims.

Introduction

It is widely accepted that crime can have a devastating impact on victims. The psychological effects of victimisation can include traumatic stress – the effects of which can be severe and disabling. Trauma research informs us that it is common for those who experience a severe traumatic reaction to events to report intrusive 'flashbacks', for instance, during which the traumatic experience – including emotional and physical sensations - is vividly relived (Yule, 1999). Individuals can experience persistent negative thoughts about themselves or the world, leading to intense feelings of shame, guilt, fear and despair (Wilson et al, 2006). They will often remain hyper-vigilant and alert for danger; sleep disturbance, poor concentration and increased irritability are common. Individuals may seek to avoid people, places and situations which bring back memories of the traumatic incident, and this can have a profoundly detrimental effect on employment, and familial / social relationships (Van der Volk et al, 1996). There is also research evidence linking trauma with the development of major depression and anxiety disorders (Breslau et al, 2000).

While these effects are widely documented within the trauma literature, the prevalence and significance of trauma amongst the victim population has barely been acknowledged by criminal justice policy-makers or criminal justice agencies in England and Wales to date. Despite a raft of initiatives introduced with the declared aim of improving the treatment of victims within the criminal process, the specific effects of trauma and its implications for victims' engagement with the criminal process have largely escaped critical scrutiny. In this paper, drawing upon a broader examination of the significance of trauma within the criminal justice process

(Ellison & Munro, 2017), we argue that this failure to take due account of the extent and effect of traumatic stress within the victim population helps explain recognised shortcomings of the criminal justice process when it comes to helping victims recover in the aftermath of a crime or supporting them through the stresses of an investigation and trial. We highlight the barriers that experiences of trauma can present to effective victim participation and the extent to which current trial processes are often liable to exacerbate trauma amongst a broad constituency of victims.

Before embarking on this discussion, it is appropriate to first outline what the existing evidence base tells us about the prevalence of traumatic stress amongst victims of crime.

Prevalence of trauma amongst victims of crime

Empirical studies of the psychological impact of criminal victimisation have tended to focus upon the most severe stress reactions, documenting the link between criminal victimisation and the development of symptoms consistent with a diagnosis of post-traumatic stress disorder ('PTSD') (American Psychiatric Association, 1980). The offence of rape has attracted most attention within the literature. Rothbaum and colleagues (1992), for example, found that within the first few weeks after an assault, 94% of the female rape victims met symptomatic criteria for PTSD, and approximately 50% continued to do so 3 months later. Post-trauma reactions associated with sexual violence have also been shown to be enduring. A study by Kilpatrick and colleagues (established that 17% of rape victims displayed PTSD symptoms some 17 years post-assault (Kilpatrick et al, 1987). Alongside sexual violence, physical injury and threatened violence involving a perceived threat to life are important risk factors in the later development of severe trauma reactions. Thus, PTSD has also been shown to be common among victims of intimate partner violence (Jones et al, 2001), and violent offences more broadly (Johansen, et al, 2007). In a study of victims of street robbery, for example, a third of those surveyed were found to be experiencing PTSD symptoms 3 weeks after victimisation, with 15% of victims still severely affected 9 months later (Gale & Coupe, 2005). High rates of PTSD have been reported in victims of trafficking (Pathé & Mullen, 1997) and there is evidence that victims of persistent harassment are also at risk of developing the condition (Zimmerman et al, 2006).

There are various ways in which it may be anticipated that a victim's experience of trauma could negatively impact his or her engagement with the criminal justice process. Herein we focus on two areas of challenge: (i) the potential credibility barriers that those affected by traumatic stress face when they assume the role of witness; and (ii) the ability of victims to engage actively and effectively in the investigation and trial process without substantial cost to their psychological recovery.

(i) Trauma, memory and credibility

When victims engage with the criminal process, they assume the role of witness and are required to provide accounts of their experiences to police, prosecutors and, in the event that a case reaches court, to judges and to jurors. Research suggests that this is likely to prove a significant challenge for those severely affected by traumatic stress. Scientific research on the impact of trauma on memory indicates, for example, that trauma can produce memories that are fragmented, lacking in specific detail and difficult to position within a linear narrative (Conway & Holmes, 2010). Several explanations have been provided for this, ranging from the release of elevated levels of stress hormones which disrupt memory storage and retrieval processes, to a psychological tendency to dissociate during trauma which affects observation and recall of peripheral detail, or subsequent strategies of avoidance which lead to impaired memory performance (Brewin, 2001; Van der Volk & Fisler, 1995). Victims coping with trauma symptoms may thus provide accounts of experiences that contain omissions and inconsistencies – accounts which shift over time as different trauma memories are triggered or as dissociative symptoms subside. At the same time, a separate body of research indicates that those charged with evaluating witness accounts are liable to attach significance to the ability of witnesses to provide a detailed and consistent account (Bell & Loftus, 1989; Borckardt et al, 2003) and to consider witnesses less reliable when these 'credibility markers' are absent. This arguably places victims affected by traumatic stress at a disadvantaged position from the outset as they are less likely to conform to common notions of what constitutes a 'good' witness. More specifically and troublingly, there is a real risk that some traumatised victims will see their allegations unfairly dismissed or met with undue suspicion because common reactions associated with trauma are misinterpreted as indicia of unreliability or a lack of credibility. This risk is currently exacerbated by the lack of training provision within criminal justice agencies that specifically addresses the relationship between trauma and memory and its bearing on credibility assessment.

At the trial stage, in the wake of the Court of Appeal's decision in *R v Doody* [2008] EWCA Crim 2394, there is now precedent for giving jurors information about aspects of trauma where false or misguided beliefs may otherwise distort their decision-making. The Judicial College directions crafted in the wake of *Doody* specifically extend to a broad range of 'counter-intuitive' behaviours and include a recognition of the effect that trauma can have on memory and recall (Judicial Studies Board, 2010). This guidance has, however, been restricted to sexual offence trials to date. Such a restriction is illustrative, we suggest, of the failure of the courts and criminal justice policy-makers to take due account of the prevalence of traumatic stress and its significant ramifications for the criminal justice process and ought to be revisited.

(ii) Participation and re-traumatisation

It is not only in relation to the evaluation of credibility that victims affected by trauma are potentially disadvantaged. Recounting the detail of a traumatic event at trial goes against characteristic effects of avoidance and is likely to occasion an intense negative emotional reaction in victims falling within this category. Post-traumatic shame or guilt may render a witness particularly sensitive to negative insinuations made during questioning about her character, motivation or behaviour. More generally, as the Advocates' Gateway Toolkit 18 (currently under review) has recently acknowledged, the very design and ambience of the adversarial hearing itself "can and frequently does replicate non-specific cues such as the trauma dynamics of powerlessness, betrayal and stigmatisation" (Advocate's Gateway, 2015). Giving evidence is thus likely to be an acutely stressful – potentially re-traumatising – experience for many victims dealing with the effects of traumatic stress.

There are mechanisms through which the re-traumatising propensities of the trial could be mitigated. Initiatives under the Youth Justice and Criminal Evidence Act 1999 have already made a significant contribution by allowing 'vulnerable or intimated witnesses' access to a range of special measures for giving testimony. Though these have been broadly well-received when offered, concern about appropriate identification remains. Police and prosecutors reportedly receive limited training on mental health issues and the types of trauma-related symptoms experienced may be so pervasiveness as to become normalised (and undetected). Moreover, even where a witness is appropriately recognised as eligible for such protections, concern about their impact upon jurors' evaluation of evidence may make some police officers reluctant to recommend them, and where they are used, research suggests that police and prosecutors often fail to explain how specific measures operate or to consult properly with complainants about their individual requirements, undermining the potential utility of special measures protection (Burton et al, 2006).

Though special measures can reduce the stress associated with the mechanics of testimony-giving, moreover, they may do little to ameliorate witness' anxieties regarding the broader trial process, including, in particular the prospect of undergoing cross-examination. This is an area in which there has been blossoming acknowledgment of the need for improvement. The Bar Council have emphasised the duty of barristers to treat vulnerable witnesses with due consideration (Advocacy Training Council, 2011), whilst the CPS has issued guidance in which the prosecutor is acknowledged as having a legitimate role to play in reducing a witness' apprehension about going to court, familiarising them with procedures, managing their expectations on what will happen in the courtroom and informing them about any disclosure of third party material that has been made to the defence, for example medical records (CPS, 2015). The Court of Appeal has also placed a renewed emphasis on judicial responsibility for protecting witnesses from unduly distressing cross-examination (R v.B [2010] EWCA Crim 4, R v W [2010] EWCA Crim 1926, R v Wills [2011] EWCA Crim 1938), directing in Lubemba [2014] EWCA Crim 2064 that 'ground rules hearings' should be held as a matter of course in cases involving a vulnerable witness, and that these could cover arrangements for the general care of the witness, in particular when, where and how the parties (and the judge if identified) intend to introduce themselves, as well as the length of questioning and the nature of the questions to be asked. While these are promising developments, their potential utility in relation to those affected by severe trauma will crucially hinge upon the extent to which those charged with their implementation are sensitive to the effects of trauma and the ways in which the adversarial trial process - and cross-examination in particular - can replicate victims' experiences of acute stress and powerlessness. Such awareness could be usefully promoted, we submit, by revising current guidance on the use of ground rules hearings to specifically address their application in cases involving traumatised victims and witnesses.

Even if these initiatives were to be implemented fully and enthusiastically, moreover, there are other dimensions of the trial process that remain unaffected, but which can have a profoundly negative impact upon participants experiencing the effects of trauma. The average time from offence to completion for cases heard in the Crown Court in England and Wales stands at over 10 and a half months; and the most serious (indictable) offences where a defendant pleads not guilty typically take more than a year from offence to completion. The associated sense of one's life being 'on hold' is liable to have a detrimental impact upon psychological and emotional well-being. For those who enter the process experiencing trauma related symptoms, these delays have additional ramifications, entailing that they must postpone enlistment in therapies that involve talking about the offence for fear of evidence contamination. In line with guidance produced by the Home Office, CPS and Department of Health, victims may enlist support that focuses on improving their self-esteem or that aims to reduce the distress associated with legal proceedings, but any discussion of the evidence that the individual or other witnesses will give, or the specific substance of the alleged offence itself, is off-limits. Indeed, the guidance states that any such therapeutic intervention will render the criminal case "almost certain to fail" (CPS, 2001). Yet this can be juxtaposed against National Institute for Clinical Excellence guidelines which specifically identify 'trauma-focused' therapy, which involves helping a person come to terms with what has happened to them by working through the traumatic memory and discussing its personal meaning, as the most effective treatment to assist the recovery of those diagnosed with PTSD; and which recommend that this commence within 3 months of the initial stress event for those presenting with trauma symptoms, and within one month for those with severe PTSD (NICE, 2005).

Taking trauma seriously thus compels fresh consideration of how proceedings – or at least a victim's involvement therein – might be expedited so victims do not face the impossible dilemma of pursuing justice or recovery. One possibility, recently piloted in England and Wales, involves the introduction of pre-recorded cross-examination, which would allow those most severely affected by trauma to give their evidence several months ahead of trial via video (Ministry of Justice, 2016). While the pilot has focussed primarily upon child witnesses, subject to adequate investment, this could be made available to witnesses who are vulnerable on account trauma, facilitating timely access to effective therapeutic support for a wider witness population. However, at the time of writing, there seems little prospect of pre-recorded cross-examination being made available on such a scale.

Concluding remarks

In conclusion, then, we maintain that any criminal justice process which claims to be responsive to the needs of victims of crime must first acknowledge the extent of crime's emotional and psychological impact and, then, as far as possible, develop procedures that facilitate the participation of traumatised victims, ensure informed evaluations of their credibility, and support, or at least do not undermine, their recovery. Though there have been steps in the right direction, we submit that the criminal justice process in England and Wales currently fails on both measures and has yet to grasp the nettle of taking trauma seriously.

References

Advocacy Training Council, *Raising the Bar: The Handling of Vulnerable Victims, Witnesses and Defendants in Court,* London: Advocacy Training Council, 2011.

American Psychiatric Association, *Diagnostic and Statistical Manual of Mental Disorders* 3rd ed. Washington: American Psychiatric Association, 1980.

Bell, Brad., Loftus, Elizabeth. "Trivial Persuasion in the Courtroom: The Power of (a Few) Minor Details." *Journal of Personality and Social Psychology* 56 (1989): 669-679.

Borckard, Jeffry, Spronhge, Erik., Nash, Michael. "Effects of the inclusion and refutation of peripheral details on eyewitness credibility." *J App Soc Psychol* 33 (2003): 2187-2197.

Breslau, Naomi., Davis, Glenn., Petersen, Edward., Schultz, Lonni. "A Second look at comorbidity in victims of trauma: the posttraumatic stress disorder-major depression connection." *Biological Psychiatry* 48 (9) (2009): 902-09.

Brewin, Chris R. "Memory Processes in Post-traumatic Stress Disorder." *International Review of Psychiatry* 13 (2001): 159-163.

Burton, Mandy, Evans, Richard., Sanders, Andrew. *Are Special Measures for Vulnerable and Intimidated Witnesses Working? Evidence from the Criminal Justice Agencies* London: Home Office, 2006.

Conway, Martin., Holmes, Emily. *Guidelines on Memory and the Law Recommendations from the Scientific Study of the Human Mind* London: British Psychological Society, 2010.

Crown Prosecution Service, Department of Health, Home Office, *Provision of Therapy for Vulnerable or Intimidated Adult Witnesses Prior to a Criminal trial – Practice Guidance.* London: CPS, 2001.

Crown Prosecution Service, *Consultation on Draft Guidance Speaking to Witnesses at Court* London: Crown Prosecution Service, 2015.

Ellison, Louise, Munro, Vanessa E. "Taking Trauma Seriously: Critical Reflections on the Criminal Justice Process." *International Journal of Evidence & Proof* (2016) 21 (3) 2017: 183-208.

Gale, Julie-Ann., Coupe, Timothy. "The Behavioural, Emotional and Psychological Effects of Street Robbery on Victims." *International Review of Victimology* 12 (2005): 1-22.

Johansen, Venke A, Wahl, Astrid K, Eilertsen, Dag Erik, Weisaeth, Lars, "Prevalence and Predictors of Post-traumatic Stress Disorder (PTSD) in Physically Injured Victims of Non-Domestic Violence: A Longitudinal Study." *Social Psychiatry and Psychiatric Epidemiology* 42 (2007): 583-593.

Jones L, Hughes M, Unterstaller U, "Posttraumatic Stress Disorder (PTSD) in Victims of Domestic Violence: A Review of the Research *Trauma, Violence and Abuse.*" 2 (2001): 99-119.

Judicial Studies Board. *Crown Court Bench Book, Directing the Jury*. London: Judicial Studies Board, 2010.

Kilpatrick D, Saunders B, Veronen L, Best C, Von J, Criminal Victimisation: Lifetime Prevalence, Reporting to the Police and Psychological Impact *Crime and Delinquency* 1987; 33: 479-489.

Ministry of Justice. *Getting it Right for Victims and Witnesses*. London: Ministry of Justice, 2012.

Home Office. *Justice for All*. Cm. 5563, London: Home Office, 2002.

Ministry of Justice. *Process Evaluation of Pre-recorded Cross-examination Pilot* (section 28) London: Ministry of Justice, 2016.

National Institute of Clinical Excellence, Post-*traumatic Stress Disorder: The Management of PTSD in Adults and Children and Primary and Secondary Care, National Clinical Practice Guideline Number 26*. London: Gaskell and the British Psychological Society, 2005.

Pathé, Michele, Mullen, Paul E. "The impact of stalkers on their victims." *British Journal of Psychiatry 170* (1997): 12-17.

Payne, Sara. "Redefining Justice, Addressing the Individual Needs of Victims and Witnesses", London: Ministry of Justice, 2009.

Rothbaum, B, Foa, E, Riggs, D, Murdock, T, Walsh, W, *"A Prospective Examination of Posttraumatic Stress Disorder in Rape Victims." Journal of Traumatic Stress* 5 (1992): 455-475.

The Advocate's Gateway, Toolkit 18 Working with Traumatised Witnesses, Defendants and Parties http://www.theadvocatesgateway.org/ (currently under review), 2015.

Van der Kolk B, Fisler R, *"Dissociation and the Fragmentary Nature of Traumatic Memories: Overview and Exploratory Study." Journal of Traumatic Stress* 8 (1995): 505-525.

Van der Kolk B, McFarlane A, Weisaeth L, *Traumatic Stress: The Effects of Overwhelming Experience of Mind, Body and Society,* New York: The Guilford Press, 1996.

Wilson J, Drozdek B, Turkovic S, *"Posttraumatic Shame and Guilt Trauma." Violence and Abuse* 7 (2006): 122-141.

Yule W. *Post-Traumatic Stress Disorders, Concepts and Therapy.* Chichester: Wiley, 1999.

Zimmerman, C, Hossain, M, Yun, K, Roche, B, Morison, L, Watts, C. *Stolen smiles: A summary report on the physical and psychological health consequences of women and adolescents trafficked in Europe.* London: London School of Hygiene & Tropical Medicine, 2006.

CHAPTER 13

The pre-trial position of vulnerable victims of crime in Ireland

Dr. Alan Cusack

Abstract: This paper considers the interactions which shape a vulnerable crime victim's initial encounter with the Irish legal process. It will be shown that a politics of neglect, conceived at a legislative level, has permeated the professional attitudes and procedural practices of Ireland's criminal justice agencies. Consequently, in dealing with vulnerable crime victims, members of the An Garda Síochána fail to consistently follow appropriate interview techniques and Irish prosecutors have been known to entertain dismissive competency assumptions. This has, in turn, concretised the invisible status of vulnerable crime victims in Ireland who are disincentivised from reporting crimes owing to a scepticism about what the process entails.

Introduction

It is easy when critiquing adversarial systems of justice to overlook the significance of pre-trial proceedings. Given the theatricality with which stories are constructed through the processes of examination in chief and cross-examination, the influential role which judicial directions play in shaping the deliberative process and the unpredictable reaction of jurors to live testimony, there is a natural temptation to view the adversarial legal contest as an affair which commences and concludes almost exclusively within the formal surroundings of the courthouse. However, as Burton et al. point out, "What happens...in the pre-trial process may be just as important as what happens in the courtroom".[1] It is at the pre-trial stage of Ireland's criminal process, for instance, that complainants first report their experiences of victimisation, that the police carry out their preliminary investigations, that corroborating witnesses are identified and interviewed, that determinations about competency and credibility are made by the police and the DPP and that suitable testimonial supports are singled out and assembled for the anticipated court appearance of child witnesses or those with a learning disability. As gatekeepers of Ireland's criminal justice system then, members of An Garda Síochána (Ireland's police force) and prosecutors within the office of the DPP, hold great sway not only in determining whether a particular complaint proceeds to a formal trial,

---

[1] Mandy Burton, Roger Evans and Andrew Sanders, "Vulnerable and Intimidated Witnesses and the Adversarial Process in England and Wales" *The International Journal of Evidence and Proof* 11 (2007): 1, 8.

but also in determining the style and order by which the complaint will ultimately be relayed to the jury in court.

Accordingly, in order then to gain a holistic understanding of how persons with learning disabilities experience crime in Ireland and, perhaps more importantly, how they experience the Irish criminal justice process, it is imperative that appropriate consideration is given to the formative impact which pre-trial formalities exert over the outcome of their cases. With this in mind, this chapter takes as its starting point the preliminary interactions which shape a learning disabled victim's first encounter with the formal limbs of Ireland's criminal justice process. It will be shown that for some members of this victim constituency, an absence of awareness about their eligibility to seek formal redress through the criminal law means that certain incidents of victimisation remain unreported, while other victims simply choose not to make a formal report out of anxiety at the prospect of being formally interviewed at a police station and cross-examined in court. The prevalence of this elevated under-reporting culture operates, in turn, to heighten the vulnerability of these victims to incidents of crime as perpetrators come to realise that they can victimize them without fear of reprisal.[2]

High Victimisation and Under-Reporting

A discussion of how persons with a learning disability encounter the pre-trial formalities of Ireland's adversarial model of justice cannot be set in context without first referring to the unique way in which they experience crime. On a global scale, it is now widely recognised that persons with a learning disability are at an increased risk of having a criminal offence committed against them.[3] In McCarthy and Thompson's well-known study of the prevalence of sexual abuse amongst persons with a learning disability, for instance, it was found that 65% of all women and 25% of all men who attended a sex education course had been sexually abused at some point in the past.[4] Recent evidence, however, suggests that this

[2] Joan Petersilia, 'Crime Victims with Developmental Disabilities: A Review Essay' *Criminal Justice and Behaviour* 28 (2001): 655, 672.

[3] Chih Hoong Sin, Annie Hedges, Chloe Cook, Nina Mguni and Natasha Comber, *Disabled People's Experiences of Targeted Violence and Hostility* (Manchester: Equality and Human Rights Commission 2009); Barbro Lewin, "Who Cares About Disabled Victims of Crime? Barriers and Facilitators for Redress" *Journal of Policy and Practice in Intellectual Disabilities* 4(3) (2007): 170; Dick Sobsey, *Violence and Abuse in the Lives of People with Disabilities: The End of Silent Acceptance?* (Baltimore: Paul H. Brookes 1994); Christopher Williams, *Invisible Victims: Crime and Abuse Against People with Learning Difficulties* (London: Jessica Kingsley Publishers 1995).

[4] Michelle McCarthy and David Thompson, 'A Prevalence Study of Sexual Abuse of Adults with Intellectual Disabilities Referred for Sex Education' *Journal of Applied Research in Intellectual Disabilities* 10(2) (1997) 105.

figure might, in fact, under-represent the true rate of victimisation which vulnerable persons experience across the full spectrum of criminal offences. In a study carried out in 2007 on access to justice for people with mental health problems in England and Wales, it was found that a staggering 71% of respondents had been victimised within the preceding two-year period.[5] According to the study, nearly one in every five respondents (18%) rarely felt safe in their community and fewer than half felt safe most or all of the time (46%).[6]

While this research admittedly focused on the experience of mentally disordered crime victims as opposed to those with learning disabilities, the findings are nevertheless of significant heuristic value given the shared vulnerability of both constituencies in terms of failing to meet the exacting communicative and cognitive standards required by the adversarial legal tradition. As one support worker explained, the specific aetiology which gives rise to a complainant's vulnerability is relevant, it is his or her failure to correspond to conventional social behavioural or physical norms which ultimately contributes to their heightened risk of victimisation: "The more 'different' someone looks and the less 'conventional' their manner, the higher the level of problems experienced in the community".[7] In an Irish context, Jim Winters, the Policy Officer with Inclusion Ireland, recently remarked upon the prevalence of a similar fear of criminal victimisation amongst members of Ireland's learning disabled community: "Fear is the common word used with a learning disability or to explain their experience of abuse or assault or indeed to explain their fear of participating in mainstream events... They are afraid of being targeted. They're afraid of being robbed. They're afraid of being assaulted".[8]

---

[5] MIND, *Another Assault: MIND's Campaign for Equal Access to Justice for People with Mental Health Problems* (London: MIND 2007) 4. A more recent study which focused specifically on the rate of victimisation experienced by persons with severe mental illness concluded that 45% of persons with such a condition were the victims of crime in 2012. The study concluded that "People with [severe mental illness] were around three times more likely to be a victim of any crime, and five times more likely to be victims of an assault than the general population. The risks were particularly high for women with [severe mental illness], who were 10 times more likely to be victims of an assault than general population women". See MIND, *At Risk, Yet Dismissed: The Criminal Victimisation of People with Mental Health Problems* (London: Victim Support / MIND 2013) 18.

[6] MIND (2007) 4.

[7] MIND (2007) 4.

[8] See Amanda Haynes and Jennifer Schweppe, *'Out of the Shadows' Legislating for Hate Crime in Ireland: Preliminary Findings* (Dublin: Irish Council for Civil Liberties 2015) 32.

International research suggests that many of these targeted offences are violent in nature.[9] In Wilson and Brewer's survey of complainants in South Australia, for instance, it was found that persons with a learning disability were 12.8 times more likely to be robbed, 10.7 times more likely to be sexually assaulted and 2.8 times more likely to be physically assaulted than the rest of the population.[10] These figures are supported by more recent research conducted in England and Wales which revealed that 34% of respondents with mental health problems had been the victim of theft, 27% had been the victim of sexual harassment and 22% had been the victim of physical assault within the two-year period which preceded the report.[11] The uniquely high incidence rate of violent crimes committed against these victims has been attributed to a range of physical and social factors. In bio-physical terms, very often persons with learning disabilities lack the adaptive social skills which are required to identify and mitigate the risks of victimisation which arise in daily life.[12] They are frequently emotionally deprived, socially insecure and psychologically vulnerable to coercion and acquiescence.[13] These intrinsic vulnerabilities are in turn compounded by the social frameworks of society which reinforce ties of powerlessness and dependence. One key factor which appears to contribute significantly to their increased risk of victimisation in this regard is the paucity of education which is available to persons with learning disabilities about their legal rights, thereby rendering them entirely dependent on caregivers to engage with the formal limbs of the criminal justice process on their behalf.[14]

Notwithstanding the significantly high levels of victimisation experienced by persons with learning disabilities, international research

[9] Statistics from the United States National Crime Victimization Study in 2014 indicate that the rate of violent crime perpetrated against people with disabilities was 2.5 times that experienced by the general population. See Erika Harrell, *Crimes Against Persons with Disabilities 2009- 2014 Statistical Tables* (Washington D.C.: US Department of Justice 2016).
[10] Carlene Wilson and Neil Brewer, "The Incidence of Criminal Victimisation of Individuals with an Intellectual Disability" *Australian Psychologist* 27(2) (1997): 114.
[11] MIND (2007) 6.
[12] Dick Sobsey and Connie Varnhagen, "Sexual Abuse and Exploitation of Disabled Individuals" in Christopher Bagley and Ray J. Thomlinson (eds.) *Child Sexual Abuse: Critical Perspectives on Prevention, Intervention and Treatment* (Toronto: Wall and Emerson 1991): 203.
[13] Deborah Tharinger, Connie Horton and Susan Millea, "Sexual Abuse and Exploitation of Children and Adults with Mental Retardation and Other Handicaps" *Child Abuse and Neglect* 14 (1990) 301. See also Moira Carmody, *Sexual Assault of People with an Intellectual Disability* (Parramatta: Women's Co-ordination Unit 1990).
[14] In the sample surveyed by Wilson and Brewer, for instance, 56% of personal crimes and 63% of property crimes were reported to police by a third party, usually a caregiver, relative or neighbour. See Wilson and Brewer (1992) 116. In a separate study by Sanders et al., this phenomenon was found to be true of 78% of personal crimes and 66% of property crimes. See Andrew Sanders, Jane Creaton, Sophia Bird and Leanne Weber, *Victims with Learning Disabilities: Negotiating the Criminal Justice System* (Oxford: University of Oxford Centre for Criminological Research 1997): 10.

indicates that the number of incidents formally reported to the police by these victims is disproportionately low.[15] In one study it was found that up to 40% of crimes committed against persons with a mild learning disability went unreported whereas the figure was as high as 71% for crimes committed against persons with a severe learning disability.[16] Similarly, Sobsey and Varnhagen, in their study of the rate of sexual abuse perpetrated against persons with disabilities, found that almost 75% of incidents were not formally reported to the police.[17] Arguably, however the most staggering statistic to have emerged in connection with this phenomenon to date is to be found in Mencap's 1999 study where it was found that only 17% of respondents with learning disabilities who had been abused or victimised in the United Kingdom reported the incident to police.[18] In Ireland, the limited information which exists in this area appears to suggest that, while not quite reaching the highs witnessed in the United Kingdom, the under-reporting of offences is nevertheless a significant problem.[19] In a recent study carried out by Bartlett and Mears, for instance, it was found that 66% of persons with disabilities who suffered sexual violence and attended Rape Crisis Centres in Ireland between 2008 and 2010 did not report the abuse to a formal authority.[20] This figure is significantly higher than the level of under-reporting which is prevalent amongst Ireland's general victim population. Indeed, in a recent survey conducted for Ireland's Commission for the Support of Victims of Crime, it was found that "slightly more than one in five respondents did not report the crime to the Gardaí"[21] and the most recent edition of the Garda Public

---

[15] Cheryl Guidry Tyiska, *Working with Victims of Crime with Disabilities* (Alexandria, VA: US Department of Justice 1998); Hannah Sharp, "Steps Towards Justice for People with Learning Disabilities as Victims of Crime: The Important Role of the Police' *British Journal of Learning Disabilities* 29(3) (2001): 88; Peter M. Van Den Bergh and Joop Hoekman, "Sexual Offences in Police Reports and Court Dossiers: A Case File Study" *Journal of Applied Research in Intellectual Disabilities* 19(2006): 37.

[16] Wilson and Brewer (1992).

[17] Dick Sobsey and Connie Varnhagen, 'Sexual Abuse and Exploitation of People with Disabilities: Towards Prevention and Treatment' in Marg Csapo and Leonard Gougen (eds.), *Special Education Across Canada* (Vancouver: Centre for Human Development and Research 1989).

[18] Mencap, *Living in Fear: The Need to Combat Bullying of People with a Learning Disability* (London: Mencap 1999).

[19] The severity of this issue came to the fore following the publication of the Ryan, Murphy and Cloyne reports. In responding to the findings of these reports, the Irish legislature introduced the positive obligation on third parties to report certain offences against vulnerable persons, namely section 3 of the Criminal Justice (Withholding Information on Offences Against Children and Vulnerable Persons) Act 2012.

[20] Helen Bartlett and Elaine Mears, *Sexual Violence Against People with Disabilities: Data Collection and Barriers to Disclosure* (Dublin: Rape Crisis Network Ireland 2011) 44.

[21] Shane Kilcommins, Maire Leane, Fiona Donson, Caroline Fennell and A Kingston, *The Needs and Concerns of Victims of Crime in Ireland* (Dublin: Commission for the Support of Victims of Crime 2010) 32.

Attitudes Survey suggested that 75% of the Irish population were satisfied with the practice of An Garda Síochána.[22]

This non-reporting ethos, it is submitted, is not so much a reflection of positive civil disengagement by learning disabled crime victims or their carers, but rather it is a reflection of the exclusionary, mainstream values which underpin adversarial criminal justice systems. Victims, it must be appreciated, will be influenced in making their decision about whether or not to report an offence by their expectations about the likely response of the criminal justice system. In this context, the inverse relationship which exists between the elevated level of victimisation experienced by this vulnerable constituency on the one hand and the disproportionately low rate of crime reporting which they engage in on the other, raises serious questions about the accessibility of adversarial legal systems across the common law. In particular, this polarity begs the question, what is so fundamentally wrong with the formalities of adversarial justice that persons with a learning disability are willing to endure experiences of victimisation, sometimes repetitively, rather than formally seeking redress by reporting the incident to the appropriate authorities?

In answering this question, the remainder of this chapter will analyse, not only the epistemic assumptions which underpin the pre-trial formalities of Ireland's criminal justice process, but also the wider political wisdom which shapes them. Through the course of this analysis, it will become apparent that a range of factors conspire to discourage and inhibit learning disabled crime victims and their carers from taking formal legal action. These factors range from their own limited understanding of the criminal justice system (attributable to a culture of *political neglect*), to their fear of being dismissed by criminal justice agencies as being unpredictable or too insecure for the rigours of the adversarial contest (attributable to a culture of *professional neglect*), to ultimately their personal anxiety at the prospect of interacting with a burdensome series of evidentiary practices which ignore the lived experience of learning disability (attributable to a culture of *procedural neglect*).

Political Neglect of Persons with Disabilities as Victims of Crime

1. Neglect at a Legislative Level

In the leading Irish study to consider the treatment of non-able-bodied crime victims, Edwards et al. concluded that people with disabilities "are not being strategically identified as a victim group, either by victim

---

[22]   An Garda Síochána, *Public Attitudes Survey* (2016) 12.

support organisations, or those engaged at a central government policy level in dealing with victims' issues".[23] In other words, the interests of crime victims with disabilities in Ireland are in a state of neglect both at an operational level and at a central legislative level. As one interviewee in the study explained, the priority for Irish lawmakers and criminal justice agencies has been to address the needs of mainstream crime victims in the first instance at the expense of engaging in a more nuanced holistic consideration of the individuated concerns of those with a learning disability:

> I think the issue at the moment is to get all victims treated consistently according to the Victims Charter... That's what's using our energy and that we're focusing on and the victim is marginalised in the criminal justice system... To look at the 'marginalised within the marginalised' is difficult because even to get the victim's agenda on the table at all requires a lot of efforts.[24]

That is not to say, however, that all aspects of Irish legal policy have been immune to the inclusionary rhetoric of the disability rights movement. Indeed, as Edwards has pointed out elsewhere, "since the wide ranging 1996 Commission on the Status of People with Disabilities, there has been a growing move to institutionalise and mainstream the rights of people with disabilities in different areas of 'public' life in Ireland".[25] Importantly, however, these developments have, for the most part, taken hold in the field of Ireland's civil, as opposed to criminal, law. The Equal Status Acts 2000-2015, for instance, put in place a highly sophisticated anti-discrimination framework with regard to the provision of services to the public in Ireland.[26] These Acts specifically enumerate 'disability' as one of the nine prohibited grounds for discrimination and they oblige all public service providers operating within this jurisdiction to make 'reasonable accommodation' for the needs of persons with disabilities.[27]

This momentum towards securing the identity of persons with disabilities as equal citizens under Irish law was consolidated by the promulgation of the Disability Act 2005, which established firm requirements on public

---

[23] Claire Edwards, Gillian Harold and Shane Kilcommins, in *Access to Justice for People with Disabilities as Victims of Crime in Ireland* (Cork: University College Cork 2012): 100.
[24] Edwards, Harold and Kilcommins (Cork: 2012): 100.
[25] Claire Edwards, 'Pathologizing the Victim: Law and the Construction of People with Disabilities as Victims of Crime in Ireland' *Disability and Society* 29(5) (2014): 685, 695.
[26] Section 5(1) of the Equal Status Act 2000 provides that: "A person shall not discriminate in disposing of goods to the public generally or a section of the public or in providing a service, whether the disposal or provision is for consideration or otherwise and whether the service provided can be availed of only by a section of the public".
[27] See ss. 3(2) and 4 of the Equal Status Act 2000.

bodies to make their services accessible to all persons with disabilities. Under the terms of this Act, for instance, public buildings were to be made accessible as far as practicable[28] to persons with disabilities, services for people with disabilities were to be mainstreamed so as to correspond to those offered to the general public[29] and communications made orally or in writing by public bodies were to be expressed as far as practicable in a form which was accessible to their recipients.[30] Significantly, agencies of the Irish criminal justice system - the Gardaí, the Courts Service and the DPP - have not been exempt from these obligations and they have all engaged in efforts to adjust their services and premises in recent years in order to render them more accessible to persons with disabilities. However, while the efforts we have witnessed recently to improve the infrastructure of Irish courthouses and Garda stations through the introduction of wheelchair ramps and the induction loops, as well as to provide information about the legal process in an accessible format, are to be strongly commended, there remains considerable scope for Ireland's criminal justice agencies to recognise the unique ways in which persons with a learning disability experience crime and the Irish criminal justice process. After all, as one representative from an Irish disability organisation recently intimated, "accessibility isn't just getting in and out of the building".[31]

Chief amongst the outstanding obstacles which learning disabled crime victims face within the modern Irish adversarial legal system is the general paucity of disability-specific offences that are enshrined in Irish statute. In contrast to the fervency with which Irish policy makers have in recent years criminalised emerging patterns of deviancy targeted at members of the general population, there has been a striking absence of policy intervention with regard to the spectrum of offences criminalising conduct which exploits persons with a learning disability.[32] The Prohibition of Incitement to Hatred Act 1989, for instance, fails to recognise disability as an

---

[28] Section 25 of the Disability Act 2005.
[29] Section 26 of the Disability Act 2005.
[30] Section 28 of the Disability Act 2005.
[31] Edwards, Harold and Kilcommins (Cork: 2012): 113.
[32] For instance, the new Criminal Law (Sexual Offences) Act recognises a host of new criminal offences aimed not only at protecting children against grooming and from the threat of online predators, but also at tackling child abuse material. The Act criminalises the purchase of sexual services in Ireland for the first time. See Department of Justice and Equality, 'Minister Fitzgerald Publishes the Criminal Law (Sexual Offences) Bill 2015' (Department of Justice and Equality, 23 September 2015) <www.justice.ie/en/jelr/Pages/PR15000487>, accessed 11 April 2017.

actionable ground for a hate crime offence in this jurisdiction.[33] Accordingly, while it is an offence to incite hatred against a group of persons on account of their race, colour, nationality, religion, ethnic or national background, their membership of the traveling community or their sexual orientation; Irish law does not recognise disablist hate crime as a substantive offence which is punishable through our courts.[34] This lacuna in Ireland's criminal law calendar is a significant cause for concern given the high rate of disablist hate crime which has been found to prevail in England and Wales. Recent figures released by the Home Office put the number of disablist hate crimes at 3,629 for the period 2015/2016. This figure corresponds to a 44% rise in the level of disablist victimisation recorded for the period of 2014/2015 (n = 2,515) and a staggering 108% increase on the level of hate crime recorded during the period 2011/2012 (n = 1,748).[35]

While there is no official monitoring framework in place for recording the rate of disablist hate crime experienced in Ireland, a recent case study analysis carried out by the Hate and Hostility Research Group at the University of Limerick identified incidents of criminal damage, harassment and assault as constituting clear examples of disablist hate crime.[36] Speaking in the context of persons with learning disabilities, Jim Winters has intimated that these episodes of victimisation serve to exacerbate the bonds of social exclusion which persons with learning disabilities routinely confront in their daily lives:

> Unfortunately, the way our society is structured, the approach to people with an intellectual disability is one of quite often segregation and congregation and exclusion of the mainstream of society. So you can imagine that if a person with an intellectual disability who is participating on the fringes of society, if you like, and who isn't accepted into mainstream society through systemic discrimination, that's when they're a victim of crime or a victim of abuse that that further marginalises them.[37]

---

[33] As of October 2014, 12 EU member states (Austria, Belgium, Croatia, Finland, France, Hungary, Lithuania, Netherlands, Romania, Slovenia, Spain and the United Kingdom) explicitly recognised a disability bias motivation in their criminal law. For a greater contextual analysis of Ireland's hate crime framework in light of the protection regime of other EU member states, see Haynes and Schweppe (2015).

[34] In seeking to redress this lacuna in Ireland's criminal offences calendar, the Irish Council for Civil Liberties has prepared a draft, Criminal Law (Hate Crime) Amendment Bill 2015. For further information, see: www.ul.ie/hhrg.

[35] Hannah Corcoran and Kevin Smith, *Hate Crime, England and Wales, 2015/16* (London: Home Office October 2016): 8.

[36] Haynes and Schweppe (2015): 18.

[37] Haynes and Schweppe (2015): 26.

Moreover, to the limited extent that Irish policymakers have taken some steps towards statutorily protecting persons with learning disabilities from criminal behaviour, these efforts have been sporadic and disjointed, characterised by a normative inconsistency in how they construct the identity of these victims. At a basic level, Irish policymakers have struggled to reconcile the principle of individual autonomy with their desire to protect vulnerable members of society from exploitation. Accordingly, the legislation which shapes a learning disabled crime victim's interaction with the Irish criminal justice system is characterised by disjuncture whereby the enforcement of oppresive measures is justified through paternalistic political rhetoric which is grounded in individualised notions of incapacity.[38] In this light Ireland's criminal process can be seen to have largely remained immune to the best efforts of social scientists to construct disability in social terms or to recognise it as a product of disabling structures in society.

It has been suggested that the root of this paternalistic legislative approach can be traced back to a stubborn subscription by Irish policymakers to an outdated, medicalised understanding of disability which focuses almost entirely on an individual's impairment.[39] The difficulty associated with this overtly pathological construction of these victims has been succinctly encapsulated by Edwards in the following terms:

> One of the paradoxes that faces people with disabilities in terms of gaining recognition within the (Irish) criminal justice system is that becoming visible as a 'victim' necessarily means buying into a set of discourses and identity that go against everything people with disabilities and the disability movement have fought for; that is, the right to autonomy, independence and self-determination.[40]

Until very recently, the most troublesome statutory instrument in this regard was section 5 of the Criminal Law (Sexual Offences) Act 1993 which explicitly criminalised the act of engaging, or attempting to engage, in sexual intercourse or buggery with persons who had a 'mental impairment'.[41] While under the terms of the Act, no criminal offence was committed if the parties were married to each other or if the victim was shown to be capable of living independently and protecting him or herself against abuse, the provision did not recognise consent as a valid defence

---

[38] Edwards (2014): 685, 685.
[39] For a discussion of this point, see Edwards (2014).
[40] Edwards (2014): 685, 692.
[41] For a detailed critique of this provision, see Alan Cusack, "The Right to Love: Over- and Under-Criminalisation in the Sexual Autonomy of Persons with Intellectual Disabilities" *Human Welfare* 4 (2015) 8.

to the offence. Accordingly, prior to the introduction of the Criminal Law (Sexual Offences) Act 2017, persons with learning disabilities were faced with the threat of criminal prosecution under Irish law if they engaged in either of these two prohibited sexual acts with a person to whom they were not married. Aside from its obvious perpetuation of pathological and pejorative terminology, this provision was reproachable on grounds that it both under-criminalised and over-criminalised this sensitive area of sexual agency. In relation to the latter argument, the Act was rightly criticised by the Irish Law Reform Commission for failing to recognise that persons with a learning disability can engage in consensual sexual activity:

> A regrettable effect of section 5 of the 1993 Act is that, outside of marriage context, a sexual relationship between two 'mentally impaired' persons may constitute a criminal offence because there is no provision for consent as a defence in respect of a relationship between adults who are both capable of giving a real consent to sexual intercourse.[42]

Although no known prosecutions were taken under the Act, its existence on Ireland's statute book until 2017 was strongly criticised - most notably by Inclusion Ireland - for cultivating a fear amongst care workers, family members and persons with a learning disability of engaging in any act which might be considered to facilitate such sexual activity.[43] In the words of the then Senator Catherine Zappone, the Act perpetuated a "chilling effect" whereby persons with learning disabilities within Irish society were fearful of forming relationships.[44]

In addition, in relation to the latter argument - the theory that the Act under-criminalised this area of sexual autonomy - Section 5 was criticised for offering insufficient protection for persons with learning disabilities.[45] Indeed, as the Act only applied to sexual intercourse and buggery, there was an obvious gap whereby the instrument failed to criminalise unwanted sexual contact more generally. The tragic consequences of this legislative gap were acutely illustrated in the case of *The People (DPP) v*

---

[42] Law Reform Commission, *Consultation Paper on Vulnerable Adults and the Law: Capacity* (Dublin: Law Reform Commission 2005) 141.
[43] Inclusion Ireland, "Law Relating to People with an Intellectual Disability must be Updated - Inclusion Ireland" (Inclusion Ireland, 31 January 2008) available at: <http://www.inclusionireland.ie/content/media/6/law-relating-people-intellectual-disability-must-be-updated-inclusion-ireland> accessed on 11 April 2017.
[44] Carl O'Brien, "Senator Launches 'Right to Love' Bill for People with Intellectual Disabilities" *The Irish Times* (Dublin, 11 June 2014).
[45] See, for instance, Shane Kilcommins, Claire Edwards and Tina O'Sullivan, *An International Review of Legal Provisions and Supports for People with Disabilities as Victims of Crime* (Dublin: Irish Council for Civil Liberties 2013): 26.

XY.[46] In this case, the accused was alleged to have forced a woman with a learning disability to perform oral sex with him. As this form of sexual conduct did not come within the scope of section 5 of the Act, the accused was charged with an offence under section 4 of the Criminal Law (Rape) (Amendment) Act 1990. On this issue, White J., in his judgement, noted that "The Oireachtas when they introduced the 1993 Act did not fully appreciate the range of offences needed to give protection to the vulnerable". In the particular circumstances of this case, given that there was no evidence of assault or a hostile intent on the part of the accused, the trial judge directed the jury to acquit the defendant stating that it was not appropriate for the judiciary to fill the 'lacuna in the law'.

From an international perspective, section 5 of the 1993 Act was arguably in breach of Article 23 of the UN Convention on the Rights of Persons with Disabilities which expressly requires state parties to take "effective and appropriate measures" to eliminate discrimination against persons with disabilities "in all matters relating to marriage, family, parenthood and relationships, on an equal basis with others".[47] In addition, it was also arguably in contravention of the principle of equal recognition as enshrined in Article 12 of the Convention given that it failed to respect the decision-making autonomy of persons with learning disabilities in the same way the decisions of non-disabled persons were respected.[48] In recognising these failings, section 5 of the 1993 Act was repealed by the Irish legislature in March 2017 by section 24 of the Criminal Law (Sexual Offences) Act 2017. Following the enactment of the 2017 Act, it is now an offence for any person to engage in a sexual act with an individual who does not have the capacity to consent to the act by reason of a learning disability.[49] In addition, the Act criminalises the sexual exploitation of individuals with learning disabilities by persons in authority.[50] While this new legislative framework unquestionably strikes a better balance between respecting the sexual agency of persons with learning disabilities on the

---

[46] *The People (DPP) v XY* (Central Criminal Court, 15 November 2010; The Irish Times, 16 November 2010).

[47] Alan Cusack, "The Right to Love: Over- and Under-Criminalisation in the Sexual Autonomy of Persons with Intellectual Disabilities" (*Human Rights in Ireland*, 3 December 2014) <www.humanrights.ie/mental-health-law-and-disability-law/the-right-to-love-over-and-under-criminalisa...> accessed 11 April 2017.

[48] The UN Committee on the Rights of Persons with Disabilities in its Draft General Comment on Article 12 expressly states that an individual's mental capacity cannot be used as a justification for restricting his or her legal capacity which includes freely and autonomously engaging in expressions of sexuality. See UN Committee on the Rights of Persons with Disabilities, *General Comment on Article 12: Equal Recognition before the Law* (Geneva: Committee on the Rights of Persons with Disabilities April 2014) para. 31.

[49] Section 21 of the Criminal Law (Sexual Offences) Act 2017.

[50] Section 22 of the Criminal Law (Sexual Offences) Act 2017.

one hand and safeguarding them from undue sexual exploitation on the other, it has nevertheless been sharply criticised by Flynn for representing a missed opportunity by Ireland's legislature to embrace a disability-neutral approach to this sensitive issue which would avoid perpetuating individualised notions of personal tragedy:

> There should be no separate offence targeting victims with disabilities who lack the capacity to consent to sex. If someone engages in sexual intercourse with a person who does not consent to it (for example because the person lacks capacity to consent) then this constitutes rape and should be prosecuted as such. Therefore, the new offences introduced in Part 3 should be removed, along with the existing, discriminatory section 5 of the Criminal Law (Sexual Offences) Act 1993 which they seek to replace.[51]

Both the 2017 Act, and its 1993 predecessor are not, however, the only legislative instruments to bear witness to the paternalistic and pathological manner by which victims of crime with learning disabilities have traditionally been constructed by Irish policymakers. Section 19 of the Criminal Evidence Act 1992, for instance, provides that "a person with a mental handicap" is entitled, on an equal basis with child witnesses, to apply for a range of special accommodations in court. While the recognition of a right for persons with learning disabilities to use these legislative supports is welcome, the pejorative phraseology which was used to give effect to this right is regrettable. As the Law Reform Commission[52] and Miriam Delahunt[53] have pointed out, the terms ‹mental handicap› and ‹mental impairment› are now widely recognised as being pejorative in nature; contributing to an oppressive and outdated account of persons with a learning disability. Moreover, the design of the legislation makes it clear that the priority for its architects in securing the introduction of these measures was to address the ostensible needs of child witnesses, not witnesses with a learning disability. As such, the 1992 Act represents a clear case of legislative infantilisation whereby Irish policymakers effectively analogised the testimonial experience of persons with a learning disability

---

[51] Eilionóir Flynn, "The Final Countdown: Ireland's Ratification of the UN Convention on the Rights of Persons with Disabilities" (*Human Rights in Ireland*, 31 January 2017) < http://humanrights.ie/mental-health-law-and-disability-law/the-final-countdown-irelands-ratification-of-the-un-convention-on-the-rights-of-persons-with-disabilities/> accessed on 11 April 2017.

[52] Law Reform Commission, *Vulnerable Adults and the Law* (Dublin: Law Reform Commission 83-2006): 77.

[53] Miriam Delahunt, "Issues in Respect of Support Measures for Witnesses with an Intellectual Disability in the Irish Criminal Justice System" *Irish Journal of Legal Studies* 5(1) (2015): 51, 53.

to that of children. Not only is this practice morally or symbolically reproachable in the sense of concretising paternalistic constructions of persons with a learning disability, but it is procedurally reproachable in the sense that it can set in motion a whole train of negative assumptions which undermine a complainant's credibility.[54]

2. Neglect at an Operational Level

Given the striking absence of crime victims with learning disabilities at a central legislative policy level in Ireland, it is hardly surprising that the framework of supports which is available to them at an operational level in this jurisdiction is underdeveloped. Indeed, out of the significant volume of political literature that has emerged on the issue of victim inclusion in the Irish criminal process only one substantive commitment has been made with regard to meeting the specific needs of crime victims with disabilities. The commitment - which is given by An Garda Síochána within the Victims Charter - takes the following simple form: "If you have any form of disability we will take your special needs or requirements into account".[55] This insipid commitment stands in marked contrast to the much more derivative and positive undertaking which the criminal justice agencies of England and Wales offer in the *Code of Practice for Victims of Crime*.[56] According to the terms of the Code, vulnerable and intimidated crime victims in England and Wales are legally entitled to receive an "enhanced service" from the jurisdiction's principle criminal justice agencies who must respect their eligibility to receive a range of supports.[57] The plurality of supports which are available to vulnerable crime victims under this framework throws into sharp relief the paucity of Ireland's operational commitments in this area.

While the promulgation of binding disability-specific commitments by Ireland's criminal justice institutions might still be some distance off, there is nevertheless some evidence to suggest that these agencies are

---

[54] Janine Benedet and Isabel Grant, "Hearing the Sexual Assault Complaints of Women with Mental Disabilities: Evidentiary and Procedural Issues" *McGill Law Journal* 52 (2007): 515.
[55] Department of Justice and Law Reform, *Victims Charter and Guide to the Criminal Justice System* (Dublin: Victims of Crime Office, Department of Justice and Law Reform, 2010) 17. This commitment is reiterated in the Garda Charter which provides, "We will ensure that our services meet the needs of all people regardless of gender, marital status, family status, age, religion, disability, sexual orientation or membership of the traveller community". See An Garda Síochána, *The Garda Charter : Working with Our Communities* (Dublin: An Garda Síochána, 2012): 2.
[56] Office for Criminal Justice Reform, *The Code of Practice for Victims of Crime* (London: Office for Criminal Justice Reform, 2005).
[57] Office for Criminal Justice Reform, *The Code of Practice for Victims of Crime* (London: Office for Criminal Justice Reform, 2005): para. 1.1-1.12.

now becoming aware of the unique way in which victims of crime with disabilities encounter crime and the criminal process. A clear example of this was a publication by the Committee for Judicial Studies of a guide for the Irish judiciary in 2011 entitled, *The Equal Treatment of Persons in Court: Guidance for the Judiciary*. In setting out best practice standards in the treatment of various categories of witnesses in court, this guide contains a dedicated section which provides "guidance on [the] appropriate treatment of persons with disabilities".[58] Similarly, policy co-ordinators within An Garda Síochána have, through the body's internal memoranda, evinced a growing concern for addressing the needs of persons with disabilities in recent years. Although it is difficult to obtain up-to-date information with regard to the official approach of An Garda Síochána towards victims of crime with disabilities,[59] the force's *Diversity Strategy and Implementation Plan (2009/2012)* sets out a range of specific commitments which it has given in order to meet its obligations under the Disability Act 2005, the Equal Status Acts 2000-2015 and the Employment Equality Acts 1998-2015. Foremost amongst these commitments, is an undertaking to develop and implement a 'Garda Síochána Disability Policy', to improve its "policing service to the public who have specific needs" and to develop "competence, expertise and external linkage to promote internal inclusion of those with disabilities and external response to citizens with disabilities".[60]

Both the Courts Service and the Office of the Director of Public Prosecutions have been less enthusiastic in their operational manifestos about meeting the needs of crime victims with disabilities. For instance, while the Courts Service had produced two insightful exploratory guides on how the court process operates in Ireland, *Going to Court* and *Explaining the Courts*, neither communication has been designed specifically with the needs of persons with a learning disability in mind.[61] Similarly, the Office of the DPP has produced four distinct documents in recent years which set out in detail the formalities associated with Ireland's prosecution process.[62]

---

[58] Committee for Judicial Studies, *The Equal Treatment of Persons in Court: Guidance for the Judiciary* (Dublin: Committee for Judicial Studies, 2011): 124.

[59] As experienced by this author. See also Edwards, Harold and Kilcommins (2012): 46.

[60] An Garda Síochána, *Diversity Strategy and Implementation Plan 2009-2012: Beyond Legal Compliance* (Dublin: An Garda Síochána, 2009): 16.

[61] Courts Service, *Going to Court: A DVD and Booklet for Young Witnesses* (Dublin: Courts Service of Ireland, 2012); Courts Service, *Explaining the Courts: An Information Booklet* (Dublin: Courts Service of Ireland, 2010).

[62] Office of the Director of Public Prosecutions, *The Role of the DPP* (Office of the Director of Public Prosecutions, 2015); Office of the Director of Public Prosecutions, *Going to Court as a Witness* (Office of the Director of Public Prosecutions, 2016); Office of the Director of Public Prosecutions, *Guidelines for Prosecutors* (Office of the Director of Public Prosecutions, 2016); Office of the Director of Public Prosecutions, *Policy on the Giving of Reasons for Decisions not to Prosecute* (Office of the Director of Public Prosecutions, 2008); Office of the Director

None of these publications however contain a specific commitment to responding to the individuated needs of crime victims with a disability.

On a practical level, one of the most damaging repercussions of this politics of neglect has been to foster an operational inertia amongst Irish criminal justice agencies with respect to the introduction of disability-awareness training. Strikingly, none of the principle stakeholders involved in Ireland's adversarial trial programme - not the Office of the DPP, nor the Courts Service, Law Society, Bar Council of Ireland nor the Judicial Studies Committee - recognise mandatory disability awareness training programmes for their members. While this paucity of specialist knowledge is worrying, it is not entirely surprising given the lack of knowledge which has been found to prevail amongst Irish criminal justice agencies with respect to the needs of mainstream victims. A recent study by McGrath, for instance, showed that 51% of members of the legal profession were unfamiliar with the provision of the Victims Charter;[63] while another separate report found that there was «an insufficient awareness of the Crime Victims Helpline» within the Irish legal community.[64] Similar concerns have also been raised with respect to the training practices of An Garda Síochána and, as far back as 1996, the Commission on the Status of People with Disabilities recommended that "Disability awareness training should be provided to all Gardaí and other persons working in this area as part of their general training".[65]

Unlike their colleagues in the Courts Service and the Office of the DPP, however, members of An Garda Síochána have over the course of the past decade proactively acknowledged their need for specialist training in responding to the specific needs of persons with disabilities. To this end, a 'Diversity Works' training scheme was launched in 2006 with a view to providing participants with strategic leadership competency in managing diversity both in the workplace and in the community.[66] Importantly, this programme was developed as a cross-border initiative with the co-operation of the PSNI which had previously enjoyed considerable success

---

of Public Prosecutions, *How We Make Prosecution Decisions* (Office of the Director of Public Prosecutions, 2015); Office of the Director of Public Prosecutions, *How to Request Reasons and Reviews* (Office of the Director of Public Prosecutions, 2015).

[63] Anthony McGrath, "The Living Victims of Homicide: Analysing the Needs and Concerns of the Co-Victims of Homicide within the Irish Criminal Justice System" (Cork: Unpublished PhD Thesis, University College Cork, 2009).

[64] Kilcommins et al (2010): 92.

[65] Commission on the Status of People with Disabilities, *A Strategy for Equality: Report of the Commission on the Status of People with Disabilities* (Dublin: Stationery Office, 1996): 63.

[66] European Union Peace II Garda Síochána / PSNI Diversity Works Programme 2006. See also, Special EU Programmes Body, "PSNI and An Garda Síochána Launch Cross Border Diversity Training" *Your EU* (Spring 2016): 10.

in cultivating a greater understanding of the needs of persons with learning disabilities amongst its members.[67] According to the Minister for Justice and Equality, this programme - which was developed in co-ordination with the National Disability Authority - emphasises the importance for every Garda who is required to deal with a disabled member of the public to take their time, to be flexible in their approach, to avoid assumptions of incapacity or helplessness and to proactively inquire about the type of assistance he or she requires.[68] Additionally, in order to provide directive guidance to its investigating officers, An Garda Síochána has recently published two detailed instructive manuals which set out best practice forensic standards which are to be followed when interviewing vulnerable witnesses.[69] Significantly, these protocols make it clear that persons with learning disabilities who have been the victim of a sexual or violent offence must only be interviewed by specially trained members of the gardaí in one of a number of strategically located, purpose-built interview suites.[70]

However, while each of these operational policy initiatives and awareness-raising training programmes have played a significant role in mitigating the systemic ableism which has traditionally informed police practice in Ireland, there remains considerable scope for improvement in this area. Emerging reports, for instance, suggest that there is a serious lack of standardisation in practice amongst Gardaí.[71] It would seem that while disability-awareness training may well be a constituent element of the modern Garda College curriculum, not all members of the force

---

[67] A 2001 study of a policing training event in Northern Ireland found that it had led to a positive shift in attitudes amongst members of the police force towards persons with an intellectual disability, see Andrew Bailey, O. Barr and B. Bunting, "Police Attitudes towards People with Intellectual Disability: An Evaluation of Awareness Training" *Journal of Intellectual Disability Research* 45(4) (2001): 344. For more background information on the establishment of this training programme, see Christopher Gordon, "Managing Diversity in the Garda Síochána", *An Garda Communique* (December, 2007): 10, 14.

[68] Parliamentary Questions, 10 March 2015 (PQ 329). Efforts have also recently been undertaken to introduce disability awareness training for recruit Gardaí as part of the 'Policing with Communities' module which is delivered by the Garda College in Templemore as part of the B.A. in Applied Policing degree. See, An Garda Síochána, *Written Submission to the Working Group on the Protection Process* (An Garda Síochána, 27 February 2015) available at: <http://www.justice.ie/en/JELR/An%20Garda%20S%C3%ADoch%C3%A1na.pdf/Files/An%20Garda%20S%C3%ADoch%C3%A1na.pdf > accessed on 11 April 2017.

[69] An Garda Síochána, *Garda Síochána Policy on the Investigation of Sexual Crime, Crimes against Children and Child Welfare* (Dublin: An Garda Síochána, 2013); National SATU Guidelines Development Group, *Recent Rape / Sexual Assault: National Guidelines on Referral and Forensic Clinical Examination* (Dublin: Health Service Executive and Department of Justice and Law Reform, 2014).

[70] An Garda Síochána, *Policy on the Investigation of Sexual Crime* (2013) 13, 61.

[71] See, in particular, Mary Carolan, 'Damages for Man with Autism 'Treated Despicably' by Gardaí' *The Irish Times* (Dublin, 2 February 2016). See also Edwards, Harold and Kilcommins (2012); Kilcommins, Edwards and O'Sullivan (2013); Bartlett and Mears (2011).

have shared equally in the benefits of such tuition.[72] Nor, would it seem, have all members of the Gardaí familiarised themselves equally with the best practice forensic standards which have been set down by Garda management with respect to interviewing vulnerable witnesses.[73] As a result of this plurality in the level of disability awareness within the force, the response which will greet a learning disabled crime victim upon reporting an incident of criminal victimisation at a Garda station cannot be predicted. As one victim support organisation intimated as part of a recent Irish study, "Victims of crime's experience depends on the individual Garda that they meet - some are terrific, some are fantastic and some are not, and there are huge barriers when you meet up with them".[74]

As the primary gatekeepers of Ireland's criminal justice system, members of An Garda Síochána enjoy unparalleled influence over the procedural trajectory of a complaint. Moreover, as first responders to alleged incidents of victimisation, they are uniquely placed to shape a complainant's initial impression of the Irish criminal justice process. For these reasons, the capacity of members of An Garda Síochána to respond appropriately, sympathetically and respectfully to the concerns of learning disabled complainants at the initial, often traumatic, reporting stage is a major factor in shaping their overall experience of the criminal justice system. And yet, notwithstanding these significant risks, Edwards et al.'s study provides anecdotal evidence of inappropriate Garda interviewing etiquette:

> One of those interviews, I think it took nine solid hours...now that has to be noted somewhere as that wasn't appropriate. This was one young woman who has an intellectual disability who was ready to pull out on hour one...she felt so - so violated that she needed to be - the acknowledgement needed to be given that yes that was wrong.[75]

---

[72] A recent newspaper report, for instance, indicated that while autism awareness training for members of an Garda Síochána is shortly to be rolled out nationwide, at present courses have only been made available in Waterford, Galway and Dublin. See Kitty Holland, 'Educating Gardaí about Autism: 'It's not a Temper Tantrum" *The Irish Times* (Dublin, 7 March 2017). Additionally, it is notable that no specific refresher training on diversity is available to graduates upon completion of the B.A. in Applied Policing. See *Written Submission to the Working Group* (An Garda Síochána, 27 February 2015) 2.

[73] As of June 2012, only 80 members of an Garda Síochána had received training on how to conduct interviews with individuals with intellectual disabilities. There were as few as 8 interviewers located in the entire Southern Region of Ireland on that date. See Parliamentary Questions, 26 June 2012 (PQ 433).

[74] Edwards, Harold and Kilcommins (2012): 107.

[75] Edwards, Harold and Kilcommins (2012): 108.

Bartlett and Mears noted similar findings in their 2011 study where one respondent commented as follows:

> I was sexually abused for seven years of my life. I did go to the Gardaí but they handled it very, very badly and I had to go to the papers so that they would take the situation I was in seriously. The Gardaí eventually put me in touch with the Rape Crisis Centre in my area. They said I didn't have a case and I wasn't raped so they said they weren't the people to help me because they were dealing with people who had it worse than me.[76]

Although negative accounts of this nature have gained prominence in recent years, they cannot accurately be said to be truly representative of the approach of all members of An Garda Síochána. Some respondents interviewed by Edwards et al., for instance, relayed entirely positive accounts of their encounter with members of An Garda Síochána. One social worker, for example, gave the following positive account:

> I found them to be extremely understanding... I felt very appropriate in the way they dealt with it, with the woman - very sensitive, and if she didn't understand all the questions they would rephrase them and they would allow me to step in to rephrase the questions asked, and when she came up with the statement, they gave her lots of time to rework it.[77]

Patently then, the task for Ireland's criminal justice agencies on an operational level is to standardise their practices so that all vulnerable victims of crime can receive the same significant level of support described in this account. The Gardaí's clear and meaningful commitment to elevate its policies and training programmes to better respond to the individuated needs of persons with disabilities is a particularly positive step in the right direction. The time has now come for other criminal justice agencies in Ireland to follow suit.

Professional Neglect of Persons with Disabilities as Victims of Crime

1. Poor Identification of Victims of Crime with Learning Disabilities

Given the striking absence of victims of crime with disabilities at a central policy level in Ireland, it is not altogether surprising to find that

---

[76] Bartlett and Mears (2011): 68-69.
[77] Edwards, Harold and Kilcommins (2012): 107.

their individuated needs are overlooked on a professional level by the country's principle criminal justice agencies. At the pre-trial stage of proceedings, this professional culture of deprioritisation is evident not only from the ostensible difficulty which members of An Garda Síochána encounter in positively identifying and conceptualising persons with learning disabilities as victims of crime, but also in how they and their counterparts in the Office of the DPP, respond to such incidents of victimisation once a positive identification has been made. While reliable empirical insights on the diagnostic practices of An Garda Síochána are notably scarce, international research suggests that police forces across the common law world struggle to accurately identify vulnerable witnesses.[78] In a study of accused persons, for example, carried out on behalf of the Royal Commission on Criminal Justice, it was found that members of the police force in the United Kingdom identified just 4% of a sample of suspects as vulnerable whereas an independent estimate of the same group put this figure at the higher rate of between 15 and 20%.[79]

Significantly, a similar pattern was identified by Burton et al. in their dedicated Home Office study on the treatment of vulnerable and intimidated witnesses in England and Wales. In this study of 500 respondents, the researchers noted that the percentage of witnesses officially identified as being vulnerable or intimidated was 9%. While this figure corresponded with the 7-10% prevalence rates of vulnerable and intimidated witnesses identified by criminal justice agencies in the earlier *Speaking Up For Justice* study, it was significantly lower than the 45% of respondents who self-identified during telephone screening interviews as potentially being vulnerable or intimidated for the purposes of qualifying for special measures.[80] Beyond illustrating the presence of an alarming disconnect between the expectations of witnesses and the approach of England's justice institutions, this figure is significant in the sense of revealing a gross misunderstanding amongst officials of what vulnerable and intimidated witnesses look like. In ultimately holding that 24% of those sampled could legitimately be categorised as falling within

[78] Rosie McLeod, Cassie Philpin, Anna Sweeting, Lucy Joyce and Roger Evans, *Court Experience of Adults with Mental Health Conditions, Learning Disabilities and Limited Mental Capacity Report 2: Before Court* (Ministry of Justice, 2010); Jennifer Keilty and Georgina Connelly, "Making a Statement: An Exploratory Study of Barriers Facing Women with an Intellectual Disability when Making a Statement about Sexual Assault to Police" *Disability and Society* 16(2) (2001): 273; Timothy Howard and Stephen Tyrer, "People with Learning Disabilities in the Criminal Justice System in England and Wales: A Challenge to Complacency' *Criminal Behaviour and Mental Health* 8 (1998): 171.
[79] Gisli Gudjonsson, Isabel Clare, Sue Rutter and John Pearse, *Persons at Risk during Interviews in Police Custody: The Identification of Vulnerabilities* (London: HMSO 1993).
[80] Burton, Evans and Sanders (2006): vi.

the vulnerable and intimidated category of witnesses, the researchers came to the conclusion that "even on the most conservative estimates, fewer than half of all [vulnerable and intimidated witnesses] are identified as such by [criminal justice] agencies".[81]

Recent Irish research would appear to suggest that legal professional bodies in this jurisdiction also experience significant difficulty in properly identifying vulnerable witnesses. It is now clear, for instance, following Edwards et al.'s research that no uniform understanding of disability exists amongst Ireland's criminal justice agencies. While some stakeholders in this study appeared to subscribe to a functional test of capacity for diagnostic purposes, others appeared to favour a less pathological framework based on a subject's degree of social mobility. For instance, the diagnostic approach of one respondent was put in the following terms: "We use the NDA definition. If it interferes basically with your working life, or your social life, em, we just go by what the NDA says", whereas another respondent framed the approach as follows: "I tend to go with the functional and situational definition of capacity, that's where I start from".[82] Inconsistent understandings of this nature with respect to the ontological indices of impairment pave the way for inconsistent criminal justice responses to incidents of disablist victimisation.

Worryingly, however, the dangers associated with such an ad hoc classification approach appear to be largely unacknowledged by central stakeholders in the Irish justice process. In expressing contentment at the lack of a consistent definitional approach to this issue, one policy operative justified this professional ethos of neglect on the following basis: "Because it's not a central issue, and to be honest... that's the blunt fact of it".[83] This avowed lack of any strategic approach in Ireland to identifying victims of crime with disabilities is illustrative not only in a sense of exemplifying once again the mainstream values of the Irish criminal justice apparatus, but also in the sense of suggesting that, in some instances at least, criminal justice agencies fail to appreciate the procedural significance which attaches to a witness's categorisation as vulnerable.

Without making a proper identification of witnesses who are likely to be vulnerable or intimidated, it is not possible for the police or prosecutors to go on to ask the harder question of what support, if any, should be provided to them in court. Nor, moreover, is it possible for them to adapt their forensic approach in their initial dealings with learning disabled

---

[81] Burton, Evans and Sanders (2006): 24.
[82] Edwards, Harold and Kilcommins (2012): 102.
[83] Edwards, Harold and Kilcommins (2012): 103.

crime victims in order to properly account for their cognitive difficulties. Such failings of professional pre-trial practice, it is submitted, have the potential to seriously prejudice the prosecution case in court. Indeed, the early identification of witnesses with a learning disability by the police or the DPP is vital if the testimonial supports and competency concessions set down in Part 3 of the Criminal Evidence Act 1992 are to have the best chance of achieving the objectives set out for them.[84] Moreover, such early identification is vital if Ireland is to meet its obligations under Article 22 of the EU Victims Directive which obliges all Member States to ensure that victims receive a timely and individual assessment in accordance with national procedures to identify specific protection needs and to determine whether and to what extent they will benefit from special measures in the course of criminal proceedings.[85]

2. Poor Attitudinal Response to Victims of Crime with Learning Disabilities

While properly identifying victims of crime with learning disabilities is an essential pre-requisite to realising their rights of equal access to justice, it is not a means to an end in itself.[86] Without the consequential adoption by the responding criminal justice agency of an approach that is sensitive to their impairment, the meaningful advantages associated with this correct identification can be entirely lost. And yet, emergent research suggests that criminal justice institutions routinely adopt a disproportionately dismissive attitude towards complaints raised by persons with a learning disability.[87] A clear example of this trend can be found in MIND's report, *Another Assault*, where it was revealed that 60% of respondents with mental

[84] Burton et al. noted in their study that "Many [vulnerable and intimidated witnesses] were identified for the first time by the Witness Service when they arrived at court, which was often too late for them to benefit from measures". See Burton, Evans and Sanders (2006): 11.

[85] Directive 2012/29/EU of the European Parliament and of the Council of 25 October 2012 establishing minimum standards on the rights, support and protection of victims of crime, and replacing Council Framework Decision 2001/220/JHA 2001/220/JHA [2012] OJL 315.

[86] "Even when the general intellectual status and handicap of an individual is detected correctly, the judgements of those subject's abilities in the practical task of answering questions does not follow this detection. This has important implications, for it does not support the view that if only the mentally handicapped can be identified, then they will be dealt with and judged appropriately". See Bryan Tully and David Cahill, *Police Interviewing of the Mentally Handicapped: An Experimental Study* (London: The Police Foundation, 1984): 2-3.

[87] See, for instance, Hoong Sin et al. (2009); Keilty and Connelly (2001); James K. McAfee, Judith Cockram and Pamela S. Wolfe, "Police Reactions to Crimes Involving People with Mental Retardation: A Cross-Cultural Experimental Study" *Education and Training in Mental Retardation and Developmental Disabilities* 36(2) (2001): 160.

health problems who reported a crime felt that the appropriate authority did not take the incident seriously.[88]

Very many theories have been proposed to explain the embedded prevalence of this ableist attitude amongst criminal justice professionals. One explanation which has been suggested by a number of commentators is that there persists amongst members of the police force an enduring perception that witnesses with disabilities are inherently less reliable than those drawn from the general population. In Keilty and Connelly's Australian study, for instance, we find one police officer openly evincing a distrustful approach to the testimony of a learning disabled complainant: "I think she just...exaggerated things and things got very big and she thought about it a lot. One little incident she would keep exaggerating that incident".[89] In England and Wales, meanwhile, we find one respondent in McLeod et al.'s study openly recounting the skeptical manner by which she was addressed by the police: "You feel you have to prove yourself a lot to them. In some respects I felt they didn't believe me at first...so that kind of upset me a bit".[90]

It appears that some police officers also entertain an additional perception that learning disabled crime victims are inherently less credible than their able-bodied counterparts. Accordingly, it is not uncommon for police to adopt a policy of investigative inertia on the basis of an assumption that a vulnerable victim's account would not be plausible to a jury in court even if all the necessary formalities around investigation and prosecution were observed. This prematurely dismissive attitude has been expressly denounced by Keilty and Connelly on the basis that it denies vulnerable crime victims the opportunity to meaningfully articulate their lived experience of victimisation:

> It is premature to consider whether a person has capacity to give evidence in a court at the point of deciding whether or not to take a statement or to charge the accused. A complainant is entitled to give her version of the complaint and to have it fully investigated, irrespective of whether the complaint proceeds further.[91]

Such a dismissive approach, it must be appreciated, is not merely symbolically disempowering, it is also instrumentally disempowering in the sense of unjustifiably depriving the jury of testimony which it might otherwise have found to be persuasive. In one relatively recent study on

---

[88] MIND (2007) : 2.
[89] Keilty and Connelly (2001): 273, 281.
[90] McLeod et al., *Report 2: Before Court* (2010): 5.
[91] Keilty and Connelly (2001): 273, 283.

this issue, for instance, it was found that juror attitudes were not negatively influenced by the disclosure of a witness's impairment and, in fact, jurors were more likely to convict an accused in cases where the alleged victims were described to them as "mildly mentally retarded".[92] It is clear then that police officers should guard against second guessing matters of credibility and fortitude in their investigative responses to reports of disablist victimisation.[93]

In Ireland meanwhile, two recent quantitative research endeavours point to the subtle subsistence amongst Irish prosecutors of a similarly dismissive professional attitude towards allegations of criminal wrongdoing which are raised by persons with learning disabilities. In the first of these studies, Hanley et al. noted, from a study of rape files received by the DPP between 2000 and 2004, that out of a total of 78 cases which involved a complainant with mental illness only two were prosecuted.[94] In a separate study, meanwhile, Hamilton found that out of 17 cases involving a learning disabled crime victim which were classified as rape by the DPP Prosecution Policy Unit between 2005 and 2007, only four were eventually prosecuted, whilst another one case was withdrawn.[95] Similar entrenched ableist assumptions have also been found to prevail amongst members of An Garda Síochána. This exclusionary ethic was particularly evident in the following account of one respondent to a survey conducted by Bartlett and Mears:

> The police let me down in some regards by not investigating more fully and the saddest thing is rape, mutilation and attempted murder is not exactly a grey area. There was a lack of information from the police and constant worry of being murdered.[96]

Almost identical sentiments were unearthed just over a year later in Edwards et al.'s study where one service provider openly admitted that "Getting [a case] past the guards to the DPP then sometimes is a problem

---

[92] Bettie L. Bottoms, Kari L. Nysse-Carris, Twana Harris and Kimberly Tyda, 'Juror's Perceptions of Adolescent Sexual Assault Victims who have Intellectual Disabiliites' *Law and Human Behaviour* 27(2) (2003) 205.

[93] Staggeringly, a study by Mencap in 1997 estimated that there were some 1,400 suspected cases of sexual abuse against persons with intellectual disabilities in the United Kingdom a year but only a quarter were investigated by the police and less than 1% were prosecuted successfully. See Mencap, *Barriers to Justice* (London: Mencap, 1997).

[94] Conor Hanly, Deirdre. Healy and Stacey Scriver, *Rape and Justice in Ireland: A National Study of Survivor, Prosecutor and Court Responses to Rape* (Dublin: The Liffey Press 2009).

[95] James Hamilton, 'Sexual Offences and Capacity to Consent: A Prosecution Perspective' (Annual Conference of the Law Reform Commission, Dublin, 7 November 2011).

[96] Bartlett and Mears [2011] 68.

- it stops a lot of the time".[97] Another interviewee, meanwhile, operating within Ireland's social care services, gave the distinct impression that members of the Irish police force entertain a mainstream bias in their construction of witnesses which cannot easily be countered when they are confronted by a complainant which does not conform to their 'ideal victim' subjectivity:

> And people with severe profound disability who have been assaulted by family members or others - because they're not a credible witness it stops...the person themselves being the victim won't be able to stand up in court and say this person did this, this and this to me, and the Gardaí say look there's no point in taking this to the DPP so it just stops again.[98]

Beyond perpetuating a culture under-reporting amongst victims and an ethos of under-prosecution amongst criminal justice institutions, this attitudinal neglect for the needs of complainants with disabilities at the pre-trial stage of Ireland's criminal process reinforces traditional constructions of inferiority. In effect, by failing to proactively respond on a consistent basis to reports of disablist victimisation, the gatekeepers of the justice process unwittingly perpetuate a perception that such offences are less serious than those committed against the general population. Consequently, victims of crime with learning disabilities find themselves caught up in a self-perpetuating cycle of neglect whereby, in the absence of a dedicated training programme to draw professional attention to their individuated needs, they are forced to assume an invisible status within the criminal justice process.

Procedural Neglect of Persons with Disabilities as Victims of Crime

1. Poor Investigative Interviewing Practices

Instrumentally speaking, there is little value in a police officer identifying and approaching in an attitudinally-inclusive manner crime victims with a learning disability if, in the officer's subsequent procedural duties, he adopts a method of inquiry which is blind to the lived experience of intellectual impairment. As we have already seen, the forensic practices which are followed by police officers and prosecutors in the immediate aftermath of an incident of criminal victimisation can have a dramatic influence on the shape which the formal response of these criminal justice agencies assumes. The first element of this response will inevitably take the form

---

[97] Edwards, Harold and Kilcommins (2012) 109.
[98] Edwards, Harold and Kilcommins (2012) 110.

of an investigative interview. The significance of this pre-trial procedural formality should not be underestimated and very often what a complainant says, and how they say it, at the reporting stage of a criminal investigation forms the basis of a series of significant procedural decisions taken by the police and prosecution service around whether or not to carry out a full investigation of a complaint. The interview process, for instance, will yield a preliminary narrative of events, will inform the police's identification of corroborating witnesses, will facilitate early determinations around witness competence and credibility and will provide valuable insights for the DPP in terms of the testimonial supports which a witness might be likely to require in court. And yet, notwithstanding the formative influence which the investigative interview exerts over the trajectory of the ensuing criminal justice response, international research suggests that criminal justice stakeholders routinely approach this formality without having due regard to the heightened cognitive and communicative challenges which crime victims with learning disabilities face in constructing a clear and consistent victimisation narrative.[99]

It is well-documented that persons with learning disabilities have been found to have broad deficits in the area of memory encoding, storage and retrieval.[100] Consequently, such witnesses have been found to encounter significant difficulty in providing spontaneous accounts of eyewitness events.[101] Moreover, emerging evidence from the field of cognitive psychology suggests that a large proportion of these witnesses are susceptible to a range of additional debilitating psychological vulnerabilities which can significantly impair their capacity to deliver a narrative account which corresponds to reality. Numerous studies, for example, have found that individuals with learning disabilities are more suggestible, more acquiescent, more likely to confabulate and more

---

[99] McLeod et al., *Report 2: Before Cour t* (2010); Keilty and Connelly (2001); Edwards, Harold and Kilcommins (2012); Sanders et al. (1997).

[100] Carol L. Brown and R. Edward Geiselman, "Eyewitness Testimony of the Mentally Retarded: Effect of the Cognitive Interview" *Journal of Police and Criminal Psychology* 6 (1990): 14; Douglas K. Detterman, "Memory in the Mentally Retarded: in Norman R. Ellis (ed.), *Handbook of Mental Deficiency: Psychological Theory and Research* (Hillsdale: Earlbaum, 1979).

[101] Tully and Cahill (1984); Nitza B. Perlman, Kristine I. Ericson, Victoria M. Esses and Barry J. Isaacs, "The Developmentally Handicapped Witness: Competency as a Function of Question Format" *Law and Human Behaviour* 18 (1994): 171; Rebbeca Milne, Isabel Clare and Ray Bull, "Using the Cognitive Interview with Adults with Mild Learning Disabilities" *Psychology, Crime and Law* 5 (1999): 81.

likely to engage in nay-saying than their counterparts within the general population.[102]

There is also evidence to suggest that such witnesses are more likely to obfuscate generic details about an alleged incident such as names, times and dates,[103] that they will entertain a final option bias in response to closed-multiple choice questions,[104] that their knowledge of the legal process is poor and that they struggle routinely to comprehend legal terminology.[105] Additionally, each of these psychological vulnerabilities can be significantly exacerbated by a range of environmental factors associated with the setting in which a witness's narrative is elicited. It is particularly apparent from the research which exists in this area, that a witness's responses will be biased by both the status of the interviewing actor and the formality of the venue in which the exchange is taking place.[106]

However, while these insights from the field of cognitive psychology raise serious questions about the factual reliability of any testimony elicited from witnesses with a learning disability, they should not be interpreted as giving cause to automatically discredit a witness simply by virtue of his or her intellectual impairment. There is, as Gudjonsson points out, no empirical basis for treating as unreliable the evidence of a witness simply because its author presents it with a number of psychological vulnerabilities: "Persons with moderate learning disability may well be able to give reliable evidence pertaining to basic facts, even when they are

---

[102] Isabel H. Clare and Gisli H. Gudjonsson "Interrogative Suggestibility, Confabulation and Acquiescence in People with Mild Learning Disabilities (Mental Handicap): Implications for Liability in Police Interrogations" *British Journal of Clinical Psychology* 32 (1993): 295; G.H. Gudjonsson and L Henry, 'Child and Adult Witnesses with Intellectual Disability: The Importance of Suggestibility' (2003) 8 *Legal and Criminological Psychology* 241.

[103] M.R. Kebbell, C. Hatton, S.D. Johnson and C.M.E. O'Kelly, 'People with Learning Disabilities as Witnesses in Court: What Questions Should Lawyers Ask?' (2001) 29 *British Journal of Learning Disabilities* 98; N. Beail, 'Interrogative Suggestibility, Memory and Intellectual Disability' (2002) 15 *Journal of Applied Research in Intellectual Disabilities* 129; M. Ternes and J.C. Yuille, 'Eyewitness Memory and Eyewitness Identification Performance in Adults with Intellectual Disabilities' (2008) 21 *Journal of Applied Research in Intellectual Disabilities* 519.

[104] L.W. Heal and C.K. Sigelman, 'Response Biases in Interviews of Individuals with Limited Mental Ability' (1995) 39(4) *Journal of Intellectual Disability Research* 331.

[105] K.I. Ericson and N.B. Perlman, 'Knowledge of Legal Terminology and Court Proceedings in Adults with Developmental Disabilities' (2001) 25(5) *Law and Human Behaviour* 529.

[106] G.H. Gudjonsson, G.H. Murphy and I.C.H. Clare, 'Assessing the Capacity of People with Intellectual Disabilities to be Witnesses in Court' (2000) 30 *Psychological Medicine* 307; M.R. Kebbell, C. Hatton and S.D. Johnson, 'Witnesses with Intellectual Disabilities in Court: What Questions are Asked and What Influence do They Have?' (2004) 9 *Legal and Criminological Psychology* 23; G.H. Gudjonsson and J. Gunn, 'The Competence and Reliability of a Witness in a Criminal Court: A Case Report' (1982) 141 *British Journal of Psychiatry* 624.

generally highly suggestible and prone to confabulation".[107] The central controlling factor, it would seem, which shapes the factual integrity of a learning disabled witness's account is the manner in which he or she is questioned about an alleged incident. Broadly speaking, the dominant research in this field would appear to indicate that the more specific the question asked, the less factually accurate the ensuing response.[108] Thus, whereas open questions (e.g. What happened?) tend to yield a highly accurate, if somewhat factually incomplete, response; closed questions have been found to elicit a more detailed response which is less factually precise. This phenomenon was recognised by Perlman et al. who arrived at the following conclusion following their empirical research in this area: "In contrast to the more open-ended recall formats, it appears that less accurate reports are obtained with more focused recall questions for both groups, but particularly for the developmentally handicapped group".[109]

In acknowledging then that the responses of witnesses can be systematically biased by question wording, Geiselman et al. developed a reflexive model of police interviewing which was specifically designed to improve response accuracy. This model, known as the cognitive interview, encourages the respondent to contextualise the event by 'reliving' the incident.[110] To this end, the eyewitness is asked to recall details about the event in four ways: (1) by reinstating the context surrounding the target event; (2) by exhausting the witness's memory for the event; (3) by recalling events in different orders and (4) by changing the storytelling perspectives. Crucially, in facilitating this nuanced recall of events, the interviewer is obliged to have recourse exclusively to open questions and to keep interruptions to a minimum. While Fisher and Geiselman, two of the model's principle architects, have been unequivocal in their belief of its deductive richness - claiming in one study, for instance, that the technique elicited up to 65% more relevant crime data than traditional interrogative techniques deployed by US police officers[111] - other studies have suggested that the technique should be approached with some caution. Brown and Geiselman, for instance, found that while the cognitive

---

[107] G.H. Gudjonsson, *The Psychology of Interrogations and Confessions* (Wiley 2003) 334. See also Ternes and Yuille [2008] 519.

[108] M.R. Kebbell and C. Hatton, 'People with Mental Retardation as Witnesses in Court: A Review' (1999) 37(3) *Mental Retardation* 179; H. Dent, 'An Experimental Study of the Effectiveness of Different Techniques of Interviewing Mentally Handicapped Child Witnesses' (1986) 25 *British Journal of Clinical Psychology* 13.

[109] Perlman et al. [1994] 181.

[110] R.E. Geiselman, R.P. Fisher, I. Firstenberg, L.A. Hutton, S. Sullivan, I. Avetissian and A. Prosk, 'Enhancement of Eyewitness Testimony: An Empirical Evaluation of the Cognitive Interview' (1984) 12 *Journal of Police Science and Administration* 74.

[111] R.P. Fisher and R.E. Geiselman, *Memory Enhancing Techniques for Investigative Interviewing - The Cognitive Interview* (Charles C. Thomas 1992).

interview, as compared to a standard police interview, yielded 32% more accurate information, it produced a disproportionate increase in the level of personal confabulations.[112]

An alternative model, developed by Yuille et al., has sought to overcome these narrative inaccuracies by taking a funnel approach to questioning whereby the interviewee is initially asked to provide a free narrative of the event witnessed before they are asked more specific, non-leading questions.[113] Beyond serving to minimise the risk of narrative confabulation, this 'stepwise semi-structured interview' model has been found to elicit more unbiased accounts than traditional interview methods.[114] Moreover, in adopting a staggered questioning approach, the model resembles (albeit lacking the direct emphasis on rapport-building) the 'special care questioning technique originally developed by Tully and Cahill as an alternative to the cognitive interview.[115] While it is clear then, that the precise approach which police should adopt when interviewing vulnerable individuals remains a matter of some contention, there appears to be one outstanding common truth to which all of the aforementioned interrogative models subscribe, namely that the performance of a witness with a learning disability can be greatly improved if appropriate, non-leading question strategies are employed which emphasise the primacy of free-narrative recall.

Significantly, these calls for specialist interviewing techniques have not gone unheard in England and Wales. In 2002 the Home Office published the *Achieving Best Evidence* guidance note which was intended to "assist those responsible for conducting video-recorded interviews with vulnerable, intimidated and significant witnesses, as well as those tasked with preparing and supporting witnesses during the criminal justice process".[116] In drawing on the insights of the aforementioned theorists, as well as the work of Jones and McQuiston, this guidance document advocates the adoption by the police of a 'phased approach' when interviewing children and vulnerable adults.[117]

---

[112] C.L. Brown and R.E. Geiselman, 'Eyewitness Testimony of the Mentally Retarded: Effect of the Cognitive Interview' (1990) 6 *Journal of Police and Criminal Psychology* 14.

[113] J.C. Yuille, R. Hunter, R. Joffe and J. Zaparniuk, 'Interviewing Children in Sexual Abuse Cases' in G.S. Goodman and B.L. Bottoms (eds.), *Child Victims, Child Witnesses: Understanding and Improving Children's Testimony* (Guilford 1993) 95.

[114] S. Porter, J.C. Yuille and A. Bent, 'A Comparison of the Eyewitness Accounts of Deaf and Hearing Children' (1995) 19 *Child Abuse and Neglect* 51.

[115] Tully and Cahill (The Police Foundation 1984).

[116] Ministry of Justice, *Achieving Best Evidence in Criminal Proceedings: Guidance on Interviewing Victims and Witnesses, and Guidance on Using Special Measures* (Ministry of Justice 2011) 1.

[117] D. Jones and M. McQuiston, *Interviewing the Sexually Abused Child* (Gaskell 1988).

One of the lead architects of the ABE guidance note, Ray Bull, has praised this investigative interviewing protocol for demonstrating, "that the findings of psychological research are very relevant to good interviewer performance and can have a profound positive influence on 'what works' in the investigative interviewing of vulnerable witnesses".[118] However, while Bull is certainly correct in recognising the formidable impact which psychological insights have had on a policy-design level in England and Wales, it is important that the reformative impact which they have had on the ground is not overstated. Recent evidence emerging from England and Wales, for example, appears to indicate the presence of a significant disconnect between theory and praxis in the interviewing techniques applied in cases involving vulnerable witnesses. One study carried out on behalf of the Home Office shortly after the launch of the ABE protocol concluded that the interviews were conducted in only a minority of cases (only in 33% of cases involving adult witnesses who were vulnerable or intimidated and in only 25% of child cases).[119] Moreover, in cases where the ABE protocol is formally invoked, research suggests that it does not follow that a vulnerable interview will automatically be questioned according to these best practice standards. Westcott and Kynan's research is particularly illuminative in this regard.[120] Following an analysis of 70 transcripts, it was noted that while police interviewers were able to deliver the four phases of the ABE framework in the recommended order, there were broad deficits in how the majority of them conducted the free narrative phase.

This insight has been confirmed in practice through a number of recent cases in the English courts. In *Re M (A Child: Failure to Comply with Achieving Best Evidence)*[121], for instance, we find Judge Bellamy at Leicester Family Court delivering a stinging criticism of the police's poor approach to staging an ABE interview with a young witness:

> This is not the first occasion on which it has been necessary for me to criticise Leicestershire Police for the way in which it has conducted an ABE interview of a young child. It is also not the first occasion

---

[118] Ray Bull, "The Investigative Interviewing of Children and Other Vulnerable Witnesses: Psychological Research and Working/Professional Practice" *Legal and Criminological Psychology* 15 (2010): 5, 5.
[119] Burton, Evans and Sanders (2007): 1, 11. This finding is particularly surprising given that a presumption in favour of a video interview exists for child witnesses. See Youth Justice and Criminal Evidence Act 1999, section 21.
[120] Helen Westcott and Sally Kynan, "Interviewer Practice in Investigative Interviews for Suspected Child Sexual Abuse" *Psychology, Crime and Law* 12(2006): 367.
[121] *Re M (A Child: Failure to Comply with Achieving Best Evidence)* [2014] EWFC B 141.

when I have come to the conclusion that an ABE interview is so significantly flawed that it is of no evidential value.[122]

Meanwhile, in the more recent family court case of *Re E (A Child)*[123], Lord Justice McFarlane, on appeal, was heavily critical of the decision by a trial judge to rely on a police interview which fell significantly short of the ABE conditions:

Insofar as the judge referred to these matters at all, she dismissed them as matters of concern and held that the interviews held the conditions required by the ABE guidance. I'm clear that such a conclusion was simply not open to the judge. The departures from the ABE guidance required the judge to engage with a thorough analysis of the process in order to evaluate whether any of the allegations that the children made to the police could be relied upon.[124]

In Ireland, meanwhile, the main policy protocol which delineates best practice standards in the conduct of investigative interviews with vulnerable complainants is An Garda Síochána's *Policy on the Investigation of Sexual Crime, Crimes Against Children and Child Welfare*. As the title suggests, this guidance document appears to have been developed with the dominant intention of meeting the needs of child witnesses, rather than the needs of witnesses with a learning disability. This impression is reinforced by the guidance note's introductory paragraph which makes no reference to meeting the individuated concerns of complainants with a learning disability: "This policy document outlines the procedures that Garda members will adhere to when investigating crimes of a sexual nature and suspected child abuse".[125] In addition, the document assumes a disempowering, paternalistic tone which fails to acknowledge and respect the personhood of members of this vulnerable victim constituency:

---

[122] *Re M (A Child: Failure to Comply with Achieving Best Evidence)* [2014] EWFC B 141, para. 108. Some of the police failings in this case included the use of leading questions, the lack of any sign of planning, the lack of any evidence of an attempt to establish ground rules for the interview, a failure to explore whether the witness knew the difference between telling the truth and telling lies, and a failure to follow the very clear guidance about the way in which the interview should be closed.

[123] *Re E (A Child)* [2016] EWCA Civ 473.

[124] *Re E (A Child)* [2016] EWCA Civ 473, para. 37.

[125] An Garda Síochána, *Investigation of Sexual Crime* (2013): 8. It should be noted, however, that there is an acknowledgement in the 'Policy Statements' section of the protocol that the document is to apply to interviews with complainants who have an intellectual disability. However, this acknowledgement is drafted in a manner which implies that it was included as an after-thought to the document's primary function of setting standards in the field of interviewing child witnesses.

"Written consent form must be obtained from the parent/guardian in advance of any interview being conducted with a child or person with an intellectual disability".[126]

Aside from perpetuating infantilised notions of persons with learning disabilities as victims of crime, this protocol is objectionable for the limited scope of its instructions. Not only does the policy recognise a strict offence-eligibility criterion whereby its guidance is limited to investigative interviews associated with crimes of a sexual nature, but it also recognises a strict interviewee-eligibility criterion whereby Gardaí are only obliged to follow the instructions when interviewing vulnerable complainants, not vulnerable suspects.[127] This ostensible procedural bias towards exclusively addressing the needs of vulnerable complainants would appear on its face to offend the principle of equality of arms and, in cases involving an equally vulnerable accused, it may have the unintended consequence of dissuading police officers from following best interview practice. Indeed, recent research emerging from England attributed the general reluctance amongst members of the police force to invoke the standards set out in the ABE protocol to a fear that, in so doing, they would be manifestly acting in a manner which prejudices the fair trial rights of an accused:

> The issue of parity between the victim and defendant seems to influence whether the police decide to record an interview for use as evidence in chief. Prosecutors, and even the police, often take the view that it would be unfair to provide a measure to help a prosecution witness that is statutorily barred to the defendant even when it would be equally helpful to him or her.[128]

It is also notable that the policy is far less prescriptive in its guidance than the ABE investigative interview protocol which applies in England and Wales. Indeed, in stark contrast to the detailed, phase-specific instructions of the latter guidance note, the Gardaí's policy only contains the vaguest of undertakings in the direction of following proper process. Accordingly, while the protocol sets out a number of ostensibly positive commitments such as a guarantee, for instance, that "the interviewing of children under the age of 14 years or persons with an intellectual disability

---

[126] An Garda Síochána, *Policy on the Investigation of Sexual Crime* (2013): 77.

[127] That the instructions have been designed for the purpose of meeting the needs of sexual offence complainants is clear from paragraph 33.3.5: "Specialist interviewers will not interview suspects. It is vital that the skills developed by specialist interviewers are maintained and not compromised by the model of interviewing required for suspect interviews". Moreover, paragraph 33.4.4 provides unequivocally that "the interview suites will not be used for any purpose other than the interviewing of complainants".

[128] Burton, Evans and Sanders (2007): 1, 12.

will at all times be actioned as a matter of priority"[129] and that «under no circumstances will a member who has not received [specialist] training attempt to interview a person who is under 14 years of age or with an intellectual disability regarding a sexual offence or offence involving violence or the threat of violence»,[130] it provides very little in the way of detailed guidance to ensure that the promised interviews are carried out in a meaningfully effective manner.[131] Indeed, the only thetical instructions which the document provides with regard to the practical exercise of interviewing complainants with a learningdisability is that those members of An Garda Síochána tasked with this duty should be "mindful of this additional sensitivity"[132] and should carry out the interview in «plain clothes unless circumstances dictate otherwise»[133].

Given the prescriptive vagueness of these directions, it is hardly surprising to learn that there is a distinct disjuncture between theory and praxis in the conduct of investigative interviews with complainants with learning disabilities in Ireland. It became obvious to Edwards et al. in their review of the Irish criminal process that there was a distinct lack of standardisation in Garda practice whereby some complainants with a disability were approached in an ontologically-sensitive manner while others were subjected to a gruelling interrogative experience. An example of the latter can be found in the following account which was recorded as part of the study:

> The minute detail of the incidences and there were a few - there were a number of incidents, dates, times - the Guard in question had no understanding of – 'well how long ago did that happen?' and 'what time was it?' and 'you said it was such another time', and I'm behind her back saying, 'stop that, you know, you can't do that'.[134]

---

[129] An Garda Síochána, *Policy on the Investigation of Sexual Crime* (2013): 71.

[130] An Garda Síochána, *Policy on the Investigation of Sexual Crime* (2013): 13.

[131] Although few details of the interview process are set down in the *Policy*, it would appear from other sources that specialist victim interviews are to be conducted by two specially trained members of An Garda Síochána in specifically-designed 'dedicated interview suites'. It is expected that one interviewer will occupy a passive role in the process. He or she will remain outside of the room but will be in radio contact with the active interviewer. The passive interviewer's role is to make sure that the active interviewer conducts in the interview in accordance with the *Garda Síochána Interviewing Model*. The interview process is taped and a transcription of the exchanges is subsequently prepared. See, generally, Kevin Sweeney, 'The Changing Nature Of Police Interrogation in Ireland' (Limerick: unpublished PhD thesis, University of Limerick, 2016).

[132] An Garda Síochána, *Policy on the Investigation of Sexual Crime* (2013): 34.

[133] An Garda Síochána, *Policy on the Investigation of Sexual Crime* (2013): 72.

[134] Edwards, Harold and Kilcommins (2012): 108.

Conclusion

Much of the discourse in Ireland which surrounds the topic of addressing the individuated needs of vulnerable witnesses has focused on the procedural formalities of the Irish trial. While, it goes without saying that the exchanges which take place in court have a commanding influence on the shape of a jury's verdict, it is important to recognise that these exchanges are themselves the product of a series of sophisticated determinations which take place at an earlier stage of proceedings. Indeed, in many respects, it is the decisions that are taken outside the four walls of the courtroom which have the greatest influence on whether or not a vulnerable crime victim's right of equal access to justice will be meaningfully realised in a given case. At the pre-trial stage of proceedings, for instance, a complainant takes the initial decision to report an offence, the police investigate the matter, the complainant's vulnerabilities are identified and communicated to interested stakeholders, important decisions about competence, credibility and fortitude are taken, and suitable testimonial supports are put in place for the complainant's courtroom appearance. A disjuncture, at any stage of this chain of proceedings may cast fatal doubt, not merely on the likelihood of securing a criminal conviction, but on the wider prospect of a trial being heard with respect to a given allegation of disablist victimisation.

And yet, for all the determinative influence which these pre-trial interactions exert over the trajectory of criminal proceedings, they have attracted little in the way of targeted political, professional or procedural attention from the principle stakeholders of Ireland's criminal justice process. Owing to a mainstream bias in how Irish criminal justice institutions construct victim identities, the individuated needs of complainants with learning disabilities have gone largely unmet and unrecognised within the investigative and reporting formalities which comprise Ireland's pre-trial process. A politics of neglect, conceived at a policy level, has permeated both professional attitudes and procedural practices alike with the result being that neither members of An Garda Síochána nor prosecutors within the DPP are adequately sensitised to the lived experience of intellectual disability to be in a position to meaningfully identify and respond to the ontological realities of intellectual impairment. The outstanding consequence of this embedded politics of neglect has been to concretise the invisible status of victims of crime with learning disabilities in Ireland who are at once both disempowered and disincentivised from reporting criminal offences owing to a lack of accessible information about the procedural formalities involved and a justified skepticism about the exacting credibility barriers which the prosecution process will entail.

CHAPTER 14

Balancing accessibility and authority:
Towards an integrated approach to vulnerability in the criminal courts

Dr. Jessica Jacobson

The subject of this chapter is provision for vulnerable court users – both defendants and witnesses, including complainants – in the criminal courts. Over the course of the chapter, I will make the argument that tackling vulnerability on the part of court users should be regarded as an **integral part of the core business of the criminal courts**.

There are four parts to this discussion. First, I will provide a brief overview of the evolution of provision for vulnerability in the criminal courts. Secondly, I will consider the question of how vulnerability should be defined. The third part of the chapter will discuss what an 'integrated' approach to tackling vulnerability in the criminal courts would entail. The chapter will then conclude with a discussion of whether an integrated approach to tackling vulnerability, of the kind suggested here, would run the risk of undermining the authority of court proceedings.

The evolution of provision for vulnerability in the criminal courts

Provision for vulnerability in the criminal courts has evolved in a piecemeal fashion since, in 1989, the *Pigot Report* was published by the Home Office,[1] and proposed that pre-recorded evidence-in-chief and cross-examination of child witnesses should be admissible in court. Ten years after this, the Youth Justice and Criminal Evidence Act (YJCEA) 1999 introduced eight 'special measures' to assist witnesses identified as 'vulnerable' or 'intimidated'. These measures permit use of screens around the witness stand; evidence by live video-link; evidence in private; removal of wigs and gowns; pre-recorded evidence in chief; pre-recorded cross-examination; intermediaries in court; and communication aids.

Most of the above provisions were implemented in 2002, with use of intermediaries implemented in 2004. However, it was not until 2014 that the first pilots of pre-recorded cross-examination (under section 28 of the YJCEA) commenced in three areas – a full 25 years after the *Pigot Report* had originally recommended the introduction of such a measure. At the time of writing, a phased expansion of pre-recorded cross-examination to other courts, for certain limited groups of complainants, is planned.

---

[1] Home Office, *Report of the Advisory Group on Video Evidence*, Chairman HHJ Thomas Pigot QC, (London: Home Office, 1989).

Alongside the implementation of special measures for vulnerable and intimidated witnesses, statutory provision for vulnerable defendants has evolved at a slower pace. As originally formulated, the YJCEA explicitly excluded defendants from access to its measures for witnesses (albeit vulnerable defence as well as prosecution witnesses were eligible). Since then, however, the legislation has been amended so as to extend two of the measures to defendants: a 'vulnerable accused' can give evidence to the court by a live link under certain circumstances (section 47 of the Police and Justice Act 2006), while section 104 of the Coroners and Justice Act 2009 provides for vulnerable defendants to have the assistance of an intermediary when giving evidence. The latter provision has not yet been implemented, although a court can use its inherent powers to appoint an intermediary to assist a defendant at trial.

Legislative change is only part of the picture of evolution of provision for vulnerable court users. Over the past five years in particular, a growing body of rules, directions and guidance has sought to raise practitioners' awareness of the issue of vulnerability and ultimately to change the ways in which vulnerable people are dealt with by the courts. Vulnerability is a prominent theme in the current Criminal Procedure Rules and Practice Directions;[2] for example, the importance of facilitating witness and defendant participation, including by helping both groups of court users 'to give their best evidence', and ensuring that defendants 'can comprehend the proceedings and engage fully with his or her defence' is highlighted in the specific Practice Direction on 'Vulnerable people in the Courts'.[3] A wide array of practitioner guidance is available through The Advocate's Gateway website, launched in early 2013.[4]

Practical reform encompasses the development of the 'ground rules approach', whereby there is an expectation that the court should make directions on how a vulnerable witness is to be questioned at the outset of a trial; and, more generally, the imposition (through case law and other guidance) of limits on aggressive or manipulative styles of cross-examination.[5] Some specialist training for practitioners has recently been introduced, including a new national training programme for advocates on dealing with vulnerable witnesses.[6] A related development is the proposed

---

[2] October 2015, amended July 2017.
[3] Criminal Practice Directions I: General matters: 3D: Vulnerable people in the Courts.
[4] https://www.theadvocatesgateway.org/.
[5] Particularly significant here was the case of Barker [2010] EWCA Crim 4; see also Criminal Practice Directions I: General matters: 3E: Ground rules hearings to plan the questioning of a vulnerable witness or defendant.
[6] See https://www.icca.ac.uk/advocacy-the-vulnerable/national-training-programme-2016 -18.

reform of the 'fitness to plead' framework, with recommendations for reform having been put forward by the Law Commission, to which a final response from government is awaited.[7] And across the criminal justice system as a whole, the expansion of criminal justice liaison and diversion schemes, based variously in police stations and courts, is intended to ensure prompt identification of and response to vulnerabilities among suspects and defendants.[8]

The motivations underlying these various strands of policy and practice reform can be broadly understood as relating to three, interlinked imperatives. The first of these is the imperative to bolster individuals' legal rights – including the right to a fair trial – and access to justice, allied to a recognition that the exercise of the right to a fair trial and access to justice imply capacity to engage actively with the justice process and not simply to play a passive role within it. Secondly, the development and implementation of measures to address vulnerability within the criminal justice system are part of a wider public policy agenda to promote social inclusion and equality. Thirdly, it is increasingly recognised that the criminal courts – like other public bodies – have safeguarding responsibilities with respect to all vulnerable people appearing in them; more generally, there is a growing sense that the courts have a moral obligation to reduce court users' anxiety and distress.

In the absence of wide-scale research into the day-to-day work of the courts and experiences of court users, it is difficult to assess the extent to which the reforms outlined above have resulted in significant and tangible changes in practice.[9] It is much harder still to say whether provision for vulnerability has had the effects of enhancing access to justice, social inclusion, and the welfare of individuals appearing in the courts. Nevertheless, there are indications from research, as well as from anecdotal evidence collected by the author and colleagues, that there has been real change to the way in which vulnerable people are treated in court. Provision of special measures for vulnerable witnesses is a frequent occurrence in the courtroom, and research has found that the measures are welcomed by witnesses, although delays and practical hitches are

[7] See https://www.lawcom.gov.uk/project/unfitness-to-plead/.
[8] See   https://www.england.nhs.uk/commissioning/health-just/liaison-and-diversion/about/.
[9] The author and colleagues Penny Cooper, Gillian Hunter and Amy Kirby are currently undertaking research funded by the Nuffield Foundation which is exploring both policy and practice in relation to vulnerability in the courts.

commonplace.[10] It has also been observed that advocates are increasingly adapting their style of questioning and, particularly, cross-examination of vulnerable witnesses and defendants to the individuals' needs – thanks in no small part to the influence of intermediaries and ground rules hearings.[11] From the perspective of the judiciary, there would appear to be growing awareness that the work of the intermediary, for example, is 'an essential part of the delivery of a fair trial'.[12]

Defining vulnerability

Any consideration of provision for vulnerability in the criminal courts should consider the question of who are the 'vulnerable' court users to whom this provision applies. Reflecting the somewhat disjointed way in which reform has taken place, there is no single, standard definition of vulnerability in existing policy and guidance.

Vulnerable and intimidated witnesses under the YJCEA

Section 16 of the YJCEA arguably contains the most explicit definition of a vulnerable court user, in making special measures available for prosecution and defence witnesses who are vulnerable on the grounds that they are aged under 18 or, if adults, 'the quality of evidence ... is likely to be diminished' on account of a 'mental disorder', 'significant impairment of intelligence or social functioning', or 'physical disability' or 'physical disorder'. Under Section 17, 'intimidated' witnesses are eligible for most special measures on grounds of 'fear or distress' relating to testifying.

Youth

Youth – that is, being under the age of 18 – is generally treated as an objective social characteristic that signifies vulnerability in and of itself, with respect to both witnesses and defendants. All witnesses aged under

[10] See, for example, Mandy Burton, Roger Evans and Andrew Sanders, *An evaluation of the use of special measures for vulnerable and intimidated witnesses* (London: Home Office Findings 270, 2006); Corinne Charles, *Special Measures for Vulnerable and Intimidated Witnesses: Research exploring the decisions and actions taken by prosecutors in a sample of CPS case files* (London: CPS, 2012); Jessica Jacobson, Gillian Hunter and Amy Kirby, *Inside Crown Court: Personal experiences and questions of legitimacy* (Bristol: Policy Press, 2015).
[11] See, for example, Joyce Plotnikoff and Richard Woolfson, *Intermediaries in the criminal justice system: improving communication for vulnerable witnesses and defendants* (Bristol: Policy Press, 2015); Emily Henderson 'Communicative competence? Judges, advocates and intermediaries discuss communication issues in the cross-examination of vulnerable witnesses', *Criminal Law Review* (2015): 659-678.
[12] HHJ Michael Topolski QC 'A Postscript' in *Addressing Vulnerability in Justice Systems*, eds Penny Cooper and Linda Hunting (London: Wildy, Simmonds & Hill, 2016): 151.

18 at the time of the hearing are automatically eligible for special measures under the YCJEA.

Young defendants – that is, those aged between ten, which is the age of criminal responsibility, and 18, the age at which an individual becomes an adult in the eyes of the law – are largely treated as a distinct sub-group within the wider population of defendants. They fall within the remit of the youth justice system, the 'principal aim' of which is defined in statute as the prevention of offending by children and young people (section 37(1) of the Crime and Disorder Act 1998). Additionally, all courts have a statutory duty to 'have regard to the welfare' of every child or young person who comes before them 'either as an offender or otherwise' (section 44 (1) of the Children and Young Persons Act 1933). The vast majority of cases involving young defendants are dealt with by the Youth Court, a specialist type of magistrates' court which is less formal than adult courts (for example, the general public are not permitted to attend hearings, and defendants are called by the first names and are allowed to sit with their advocate or supporters rather than in the dock); and there is a distinct sentencing framework for young offenders.

Vulnerable adult defendants

As noted above, vulnerable defendants are not encompassed by most of the YJEA's special measures; hence the Act, as originally formulated, did not include a definition of vulnerability with respect to defendants. However, the subsequent extension of the live link and intermediary provisions saw vulnerable defendants defined in similar terms to vulnerable witnesses: that is, with reference to 'mental disorder' or another 'significant impairment of intelligence and social function' rendering the defendant 'unable to participate effectively as a witness giving oral evidence in court'.

Vulnerability in the Criminal Practice Directions

The importance of facilitating witness and defendant participation is highlighted in the specific Criminal Practice Direction on 'Vulnerable people in the Courts', which cites the YJCEA definition of a vulnerable witness. It is also noted that this definition is by no means exhaustive, since *'many other people* giving evidence in a criminal case, whether as a witness or defendant, may require assistance' [emphasis added];[13] but no definition is offered for this wider concept of vulnerability, or criteria by which an individual's vulnerability might be assessed.

---

[13] Criminal Practice Directions I: General matters: 3D: Vulnerable people in the Courts, 3D.1-3D.2.

Developing a broader understanding of vulnerability?

The above brief overview of major definitions of vulnerability in the criminal courts makes it clear that the 'vulnerable' are by no means a single, easily identifiable sub-group within the general population of court users. There are, rather, various overlapping sub-groups of court users for whom differing types and levels of provision for vulnerability are made available.

These vulnerable sub-groups of court users are potentially very large.[14] And with growing knowledge and awareness of the kinds of psychological, intellectual or emotional needs that can impact an individual's capacity to function effectively in the courtroom, so these sub-groups – in a sense – become larger. Moreover, it is evident that the complexity and formality of the court process is such that many or even most people who enter the courtroom as laypeople can find the experience extremely intimidating, confusing and alienating, whether or not they have any kind of pre-existing 'mental disorder' or 'impairment'.[15]

This means that drawing a line between individual court users who are 'vulnerable' and those who are 'not vulnerable' becomes an increasingly difficult and arbitrary process. A further question that arises is whether, to the extent that any such line is drawn, those who are deemed 'not vulnerable' might be disadvantaged by the fact that special provision is made available to those deemed 'vulnerable'.

Accordingly, it can be argued that vulnerability will be most effectively tackled if the concept is understood in a broad sense as having three dimensions. These dimensions, which in practice will often be interlinked, are:

1. Personal attributes of the court user which impede participation in the court process, such as a mental health problem, impairment or physical disability;

2. Experiences of the court user which reflect particular aspects of the criminal case; for example, where the alleged offence is especially serious or distressing and may have profound implications for the individual's life;

---

[14] Data on the characteristics of the general court user population are lacking; however, for a brief overview of some of the existing evidence pointing to high levels of mental health problems and learning disabilities or difficulties among defendants, see Jenny McEwan, 'Vulnerable defendants and the fairness of trials' *Criminal Law Review* 2 (2013): 100-113.

[15] See, for example, Jacobson et al, *Crown Court*.

3. Fear, distress or disturbance associated with the court process itself, and particularly the highly formal and complex nature of proceedings.

An integrated approach to tackling vulnerability

The broader definition outlined above suggests that vulnerability should not simply be seen as a set of psychological, social or physical attributes that an individual brings with him or her into the courtroom. Rather, vulnerability is manifest in many different ways throughout the court (and the wider criminal justice) process; indeed, as the third 'dimension' makes clear, vulnerability can be *created by* the court process. In other words, it is important to recognise that the courtroom is host not only to 'vulnerable people', but also 'vulnerable moments' which can be experienced by any court user.

It follows from this that dealing with vulnerability should not be regarded as some kind of 'add-on' to routine court business, which entails little more than making *specific adjustments* – for example, by implementing the statutory special measures – in response to the *specific needs* of those individuals who are deemed vulnerable. Tackling vulnerability is better seen as an integral part of the core business of the courts, meaning that court proceedings should be conducted in a manner that is sensitive to the manifestations and effects of vulnerability in all its guises. To achieve this will doubtless require far-reaching, systemic change to the court process – such that, for example, efforts are made to enhance the clarity of court proceedings and the language of the courtroom; to reduce the ritual and theatricality of proceedings; to alter the physical lay-out of courtrooms; and to prohibit aggressive and manipulative styles of cross-examination.

Greater clarity

Much of what goes on in court is difficult for any layperson to understand. Legal concepts are complex, and the language used by the professionals in court is often technical, convoluted and jargon-filled. In the course of many criminal cases, it is inevitable that some of the exchanges between professionals will focus on technical and legal issues that are largely impenetrable to non-lawyers; and even the core, substantive issues addressed by a case may raise complicated questions of law. Nevertheless, it has been widely recognised that clarity of communication is essential if laypeople are to engage in a meaningful way with, rather than being largely passive spectators of, the court proceedings that concern them. The need for greater use of simpler language in court has been highlighted in recent reviews of youth proceedings,[16] while guidance on vulnerability more generally has also pointed to the significance of this issue.[17] That the benefits of clearer communication would extend beyond those who are typically described as 'vulnerable' to all laypeople who enter the courtroom cannot be disputed, especially if it is borne in mind that – as has long been documented by psychologists[18] – situations of stress can disrupt cognitive capacity, including in relation to comprehension.

Reducing ritual and theatricality

The ritual and theatricality of proceedings are frequently commented upon by those who research the criminal courts. For example, much of Carlen's description dating to more than four decades ago still applies today, when she refers to the

> Portrayal of an inviolate and necessary justice ... aided in the higher courts by rigid rules of ceremony and by the traditional ceremonial costume. There, men and women well trained in legal rhetoric monopolise the stage, and the acting is often worthy of the best traditions of the theatre.

In magistrates' courts, she writes, the character of proceedings tends towards the 'farcical'; yet here, too, the setting is 'very formal and ritualistic'.[19] The author and colleagues have observed in the Crown Court that ritual, theatricality and what is often perceived as a kind of game-playing by advocates can be intimidating and alienating for court users, and can contribute to the great sense of disconnect between the 'us' of the court professionals and the 'them' of the laypeople in the courtroom.[20]

---

[16] Lord Carlile of Berriew CBE QC, *Independent Parliamentarians' Inquiry into the Operation and Effectiveness of the Youth Court* (London: Houses of Parliament, 2014); Charlie Taylor, *Review of the Youth Justice System in England and Wales* (London: Ministry of Justice, 2015); Ali Wigzell, Amy Kirby and Jessica Jacobson, *The Youth Proceedings Advocacy Review: Final Report* (London: BSB and CILEx Regulation, 2015).

[17] See, for example, Advocacy Training Council, *Raising the Bar: the handling of vulnerable witnesses, victims and defendants in court* (London: Advocacy Training Council, 2011).

[18] For example, for reviews of research on the impact of stress on cognitive function in the context of the military and the work of health professionals respectively, see Jennifer Kavanagh 'Stress and performance: a review of the literature and its applicability to the military', Technical Report (Santa Monica, California: Rand, 2005); Vicki R. LeBlanc, 'The effects of acute stress on performance: implications for health professions education', *Academic Medicine*, 84: 10 (2009): S25-S33.

[19] Pat Carlen, *Magistrates' Justice* (London: Martin Robertson, 1976): 37.

[20] Jacobson et al, *Crown Court*; see also Amy Kirby 'Effectively engaging victims, witnesses and defendants in the criminal courts: a question of "court culture"?', *Criminal Law Review* 12 (2018) 949-968.

Existing provision for vulnerability provides some scope for creating a less elaborate, more informal atmosphere in the courtroom: for example, removal of wigs and gowns in the Crown Court are permitted under the YJCEA special measures and by the Criminal Practice Directions; and there is an explicit expectation that proceedings in the Youth Court are conducted with less formality than in the adult courts. But wider efforts to reduce the level of formality and elements of ceremony and extravagant or playful performance in court proceedings may well have the effect of making those proceedings feel more accessible and meaningful to all involved in them.

Amending the physical lay-out of the courtroom and reducing use of the dock

The sense of theatre and ceremony associated with court proceedings is often enhanced by the physical structure and environment of the court. The courtroom is a physical space which, it has been noted, acquires an almost 'sacred' character; this is a space in which, as in cathedrals, individuals feel that they must 'lower their voice, duck their heads, and tiptoe around once they enter'.[21] Change to the physical set-up, like change to the procedural aspects of criminal cases, might also help to promote court users' sense of active engagement with proceedings. In the Youth Court, for example, there is a general expectation that the magistrates or district judge should sit as at the same level as all others in court, and (as noted above) that defendants can be seated with his or her advocates or supporters rather than in the dock.

Use of the dock in adult courts has been the subject of increasing comment among some reformers, researchers and practitioners. It is argued that the location of defendants in the dock can be a serious impediment to their effective participation in court proceedings, particularly as the dock tends to be situated at the rear of the court, meaning that the advocates typically have their back to defendants, and defendants' capacity to hear and communicate is further compromised by the growing use of security screens as part of the dock. Hence the argument is made that the dock should not be routinely used, but only where there is an identified security risk.[22]

---

[21] T. Scheffer, K. Hannken-Illjes and A. Kozin, *Criminal Defence and Procedure: Comparative Ethnographies in the United Kingdom, Germany, and the United States* (Basingstoke: Palgrave Macmillan, 2010): 141.

[22] For example, JUSTICE, *In the Dock: reassessing the use of the dock in criminal* trials (London: Justice, 2015); Linda Mulcahy 'Putting the Defendant in Their Place: Why Do We Still Use the Dock in Criminal Proceedings?', *British Journal of Criminology* 53: 6 (2013): 1139-1156.

New styles of cross-examination

Change to the ways in which vulnerable witnesses and defendants are cross-examined has been referred to above as one of the practical manifestations of the growing awareness of the issue of vulnerability in the criminal justice system. Increasingly, limits are placed on the kinds of questions that advocates can ask of those who are vulnerable, and the style in which they ask them, in the wake of

> thirty-odd years of empirical research [which] have demonstrated that conventional cross-examination, with its preponderance of suggestive and confusing questioning tactics, is a veritable 'how not to' guide for obtaining best—that is to say, full and accurate—evidence from vulnerable witnesses.[23]

There now appears to be a general acceptance among practitioners that 'conventional' approaches to cross-examination are inappropriate – in terms of the potential impact on both the quality of evidence obtained and the well-being of the individual – when a vulnerable person has taken the witness stand. There is, however, less agreement about whether the shortcomings of conventional cross-examination, particularly in its more manipulative or aggressive forms, apply to all witnesses and not just those deemed vulnerable. The tension between ensuring robust challenge to a witness's testimony and providing the witness with the protection or support he or she needs cannot be easily resolved; but there would seem to be a clear 'need for formal scrutiny of assumptions about cross-examination'.[24]

Benefits of an integrated approach to tackling vulnerability

There is no intention to suggest here that the proposed broad, systemic changes to the court process would make it unnecessary to put in place specific adjustments for some court users' specific needs. Adjustments would still be required for the minority of court users who have the most significant vulnerabilities. But that minority of court users would be *smaller*, and the required adjustments would be *more effective*, if their context is a court process which is easier for everyone to engage with. Furthermore, an integrated approach to tackling vulnerability should help to ensure that no kind of trade-off is implied between the rights of the 'vulnerable' and the rights of the 'non-vulnerable', or between the rights of one group of court

---

[23] Henderson, 'Communicative competence', 659.
[24] Plotnikoff and Woolfson, *Intermediaries*, 307.

users (such as defendants) and the rights of another (such as victims or witnesses).

It was argued in the first section of this chapter that aspirations relating to such broad social goods as access to justice, social inclusion and welfare underlie much of the existing provision for vulnerable people in the criminal justice system. A truly integrated approach to tackling all facets of vulnerability in the criminal courts should help to advance all these aspirations still further.

Striking a balance between accessibility and authority?

Is there a risk that court reforms focusing on accessibility and engagement could undermine the solemnity and sense of the authority of court proceedings? These proceedings, after all, are not meant to be a part of mundane, everyday life. As an arena in which far-reaching decisions about individuals are made – decisions which, moreover, are intended publicly to uphold the wider social and moral order – the criminal courts form their own small and distinctive world. The rituals of the courtroom, and the formality and elaborateness of court processes, language and architecture, all arguably help to reinforce what has been referred to as the 'delicate separateness' of the court business.[25] As many commentators have pointed out, the theatrical and ritualistic nature of court process is not an accident but, in a sense, is intrinsic to the process. For example, it has been argued with respect to trials that they are:

> the re-enactment of a conflict … They exploit iconic props as crucial clues to the unfolding of the narrative, and often rely on space, staging, costume, and spectacle in an attempt to bring back to life the dramatic event they are attempting to recount. Trials and theatre … share an underlying structural similarity or have overlapping functions…: both are forms of conflict resolution through aesthetic and ritual means; both serve the consolidation of community through public scapegoating, ostracism, and expulsion; both act as vehicles for social catharsis.[26]

However, recognition that the 'drama' of the criminal trial may serve some important functions does not necessarily imply that a more engaging and accessible court process would be less authoritative. In fact, it can be argued that reforms aimed at making proceedings easier to understand

---

[25] Nigel Fielding, *Courting Violence: Offences Against the Person Cases in Court* (Oxford: Oxford University Press): 53.

[26] Julie Stone Peters 'Legal Performance Good and Bad', *Law, Culture and the Humanities*, 4 (2008): 180-1.

and to participate in would have the effect of reinforcing, rather than undermining, the seriousness with which participants take the process. The greatest threat to the court's authority, perhaps, is where proceedings are conducted in a way that is marginalising, alienating or largely comprehensible. The following comments by witnesses and defendants – derived from empirical studies of the Crown Court and Youth Court undertaken by the author and colleagues[27] – demonstrate that the court user role can easily become that of passive viewer of a spectacle deemed highly confusing, intimidating or even bizarre:

> The justice is a law unto itself. It doesn't make any rhyme nor reason. ... It's all trickery. (Witness, Crown Court)

> Well, it's posh innit? The courts are posh. It's all posh to me, everyone in wigs; everyone talks in this funky language. (Defendant, Crown Court)

> [The lawyers] should remember: it's not a game. They're playing with people's emotions and people's lives, and they're there to get a bloody prosecution. It's not a human rights exercise or a game. With some of these barristers, I think they see it as a game. (Complainant, Crown Court)

> [My lawyer] was reading out of a book; he kept going into the book and then talking like: 'In section 21 we see... like we found this out and this is not real, this cannot be happening and lalala, you've got these rights and stuff.' Proper ridiculous. I had no clue, me, I just stood there and stayed white and nearly cried. (Defendant, Youth Court)

> All the people that were talking, I couldn't understand ... They asked me if I understood – I just said yeah. ... I just wanted to get it over with, and that. I didn't want them to think I was being rude or something. (Defendant, Youth Court)

The research findings of procedural justice theorists – who explore the ways in which legal authorities interact with the public, and the consequences for compliance with the law – strongly suggest that in the situation in which court users perceive themselves to be no more than passive spectators, the legitimate authority of the court is called into question. Procedural justice theory points to the direct link between

---

[27] Jacobson et al, *Crown Court*; Wigzell et al, *Youth Proceedings Advocacy Review*.

perceptions of justice process as *legitimate*, and *direct experiences* of the process as a fair one, and one within which they are treated with respect and given a voice.[28] Accordingly, court reforms in support of accessibility and engagement provide the courts with a route towards authority that is more likely to be regarded as legitimate and less likely to be regarded as oppressive or arbitrary, or exercised in a somewhat whimsical fashion.

Finally, it is important to consider the implications for the issues discussed in this chapter of government's current modernising agenda for the justice system, central to which is the wide-scale programme of court closures and a growing emphasis on 'virtual' court attendance. It may be that some of the traditional barriers to access to and engagement with the criminal courts will be broken down as a result of the ongoing changes and associated rethinking of 'what is a court?'.[29] Greater use of video-link technology permits the appearance in court of individuals who would struggle for any reason to appear in person; and certain aspects of formality and ritual may be difficult to sustain alongside 'virtual justice'. However, there is also a danger that *new* barriers to access and engagement will arise. In particular, while virtual attendance at court provides for easier access in a literal sense, it also poses its own particular challenges to meaningful communication between the court and the individual at the other end of the video-link.[30] In other words, technological 'solutions' to difficulties of access can potentially become technological 'problems', and the importance of an integrated approach to tackling vulnerability – at the heart of which is an intense and profound focus on accessibility and engagement – may be all the more important at a time of rapid and far-reaching change to the very nature of court proceedings.

---

[28] Procedural justice theory has been largely associated with the work of Tom Tyler and colleagues in the United States; for example, Tom R. Tyler, *Why People Obey the Law* (Princeton: Princeton University Press, 2006); Tom R. Tyler and Yuen J. Huo *Trust in the Law: Encouraging Public Cooperation with the Police and Courts* (New York: Russell-Sage Foundation, 2002). For specific consideration of procedural justice theory as it relates to the courts see, among others, Tom R. Tyler 'Procedural Justice and the Courts', *Court Review*, 44 (2008): 25-31.

[29] JUSTICE *What is a court?* (London: JUSTICE, 2016).

[30] For discussion of implications of the government's modernisation agenda for the work of the criminal courts see, for example, Jenni Ward, *Transforming Summary Justice: Modernisation in the Lower Criminal Courts* (London: Routledge, 2016); Jane Donoghue, 'The Rise of Digital Justice: Courtroom Technology, Public Participation and Access to Justice', *Modern Law Review* (in press).

Bibliography

Advocacy Training Council. *Raising the Bar: the handling of vulnerable witnesses, victims and defendants in court*. London: Advocacy Training Council, 2011.

Burton, Mandy, Evans, Roger and Sanders, Andrew. *An evaluation of the use of special measures for vulnerable and intimidated witnesses*. London: Home Office Findings 270, 2006.

Carlen, Pat. *Magistrates' Justice*. London: Martin Robertson, 1976.

Carlile, Lord. *Independent Parliamentarians' Inquiry into the Operation and Effectiveness of the Youth Court*. London: Houses of Parliament, 2014.

Charles, Corinne. *Special Measures for Vulnerable and Intimidated Witnesses: Research exploring the decisions and actions taken by prosecutors in a sample of CPS case files*. London: CPS, 2012.

Donoghue, Jane. 'The Rise of Digital Justice: Courtroom Technology, Public Participation and Access to Justice'. *Modern Law Review* (in press).

Fielding, Nigel. *Courting Violence: Offences Against the Person Cases in Court*. Oxford: Oxford University Press.

Henderson, Emily. 'Communicative competence? Judges, advocates and intermediaries discuss communication issues in the cross-examination of vulnerable witnesses'. *Criminal Law Review* (2015): 659-678.

Home Office. *Report of the Advisory Group on Video Evidence* (Chairman HHJ Thomas Pigot QC). London: Home Office, 1989.

Jacobson, Jessica, Hunter, Gillian and Kirby, Amy. *Inside Crown Court: Personal experiences and questions of legitimacy*. Bristol: Policy Press, 2015.

JUSTICE. *In the Dock: reassessing the use of the dock in criminal trials*. London: Justice, 2015.

JUSTICE. *What is a court?* London: JUSTICE, 2016.

Kavanagh, Jennifer. 'Stress and performance: a review of the literature and its applicability to the military'. Technical Report. Santa Monica, California: Rand, 2005.

Kirby, Amy. 'Effectively engaging victims, witnesses and defendants in the criminal courts: a question of "court culture"?'. *Criminal Law Review* (forthcoming).

LeBlanc, Vicki R. 'The effects of acute stress on performance: implications for health professions education'. *Academic Medicine*, 84: 10 (2009): S25-S33.

McEwan, Jenny. 'Vulnerable defendants and the fairness of trials'. *Criminal Law Review* 2 (2013): 100-113.

Mulcahy, Linda 'Putting the Defendant in Their Place: Why Do We Still Use the Dock in Criminal Proceedings?'. *British Journal of Criminology* 53: 6 (2013): 1139-1156.

Peters, Julie Stone. 'Legal Performance Good and Bad'. *Law, Culture and the Humanities,* 4 (2008): 179-200.

Plotnikoff, Joyce and Woolfson, Richard. *Intermediaries in the criminal justice system: improving communication for vulnerable witnesses and defendants.* Bristol: Policy Press, 2015.

Scheffer, T., Hannken-Illjes, K. and Kozin, A.. *Criminal Defence and Procedure: Comparative Ethnographies in the United Kingdom, Germany, and the United States.* Basingstoke: Palgrave Macmillan, 2010.

Taylor, Charlie. *Review of the Youth Justice System in England and Wales.* London: Ministry of Justice, 2015.

Topolski, Michael. 'A Postscript'. In *Addressing Vulnerability in Justice Systems,* edited by Penny Cooper and Linda Hunting. London: Wildy, Simmonds & Hill, 2016.

Tyler, Tom R.. *Why People Obey the Law.* Princeton: Princeton University Press, 2006.

Tyler, Tom R.. 'Procedural Justice and the Courts'. *Court Review,* 44 (2008): 25-31.

Tyler, Tom R. and Huo, Yuen J.. *Trust in the Law: Encouraging Public Cooperation with the Police and Courts.* New York: Russell-Sage Foundation, 2002.

Ward, Jenni. *Transforming Summary Justice: Modernisation in the Lower Criminal Courts.* London: Routledge, 2016.

Wigzell, Ali, Kirby, Amy and Jacobson, Jessica. *The Youth Proceedings Advocacy Review: Final Report.* London: BSB and CILEx Regulation, 2015.

CHAPTER 15

Advocating PEACE: Will it make people cross?

Professor Ray Bull and Dr. Andy Griffiths

As pointed out by the Prison Reform Trust "There is a general recognition in law that defendants must be able to understand and participate effectively in the criminal proceedings of which they are a part" (Jacobson and Talbot, 2009, 2). This chapter overviews that in England and Wales the police service has extensively modernised how suspects should be questioned following several examples of poor practice some decades ago. It then reviews the government's official guidance on the interviewing of vulnerable witnesses, noting that defendants (including innocent ones) are witnesses to what took place at relevant times. Following on from this it presents some currently available advice to advocates on how to cross-examine. It then provides some recent examples of poor/bad questioning in court of vulnerable defendants. Relevant and recent advice from the United Nations is then described. This is followed by some comments regarding training of professionals regarding enabling defendants to participate effectively.

When the Police used to get it wrong

The history of policing in the UK over the last 35 years has been dominated by large scale and significant changes to pre-trial investigative powers. These changes have been manifested in pieces of legislation that have altered police powers, citizens' rights, or both. In particular, the Police and Criminal Evidence Act (PACE, 1984), the Criminal Procedure and Investigations Act (CPIA, 1996), and Youth Justice and Criminal Evidence Act (YJCE, 1999). These legislative changes have helped to transform police procedure, from common law administrative guidance to a clear set of rules designed to improve the integrity of the evidence presented to Courts. A theme underpinning every one of these changes is the influence of psychology and the use of empirical evidence to inform them. In fact, these changes pre-date by some decades the much more modern movement known as Evidence Based Policing (Sherman, 2015), which seeks an empirical evidence base for all police activity. In this regard police conduct in relation to the interviewing of victims, witnesses and suspects is some thirty years ahead of other areas of police work, and can provide a useful background to the debate surrounding effective ways to communicate with vulnerable defendants.

A brief explanation of the influence of psychology is beneficial at this point in order to provide context for discussing its role in where the police have been found at fault and how this information may prove useful in consideration of where the legal profession could reflect on its own practices. The Phillips Royal Commission on Criminal Procedure (Philips, 1981) broke new ground in utilising evidence provided by psychologists, declaring that empirical evidence would underpin its findings rather than 'arguments from principle unsupported by specific verifiable evidence' (Philips, preface; in Royal Commission on Criminal Procedure, 1981). This was in contrast to an earlier Royal Commissions shortly before on eyewitness identification (Devlin Committee, 1976).

The most logical explanation for the Phillips' commission stance would appear to be the involvement of psychologists as expert witnesses in assessing the interrogations of suspects by police officers in then contemporary miscarriage cases. The commission initiated real time observational studies of police questioning (Irving and Hilgendorf, 1980; Softley, 1980) as part of its evidence collection, and in considering and accepting the psychological evidence presented subsequently, moved psychology from external dispassionate observer to interested policy maker within the British legal system. The resulting legislation (PACE, 1984) and accompanying Codes of Practice (in particular Code C: the treatment and questioning of suspects) transformed police questioning of suspects from a vague and heuristic process governed by Judges Rules (St. Johnston, 1966; Softley, 1980) to a very much more formal process that recognised concepts of oppression and unfairness (s.76 & s78 PACE, 1984). It also laid down regulations such as a maximum duration of questioning (Code C12.7), and mandatory audio recording (Code E3.1) that were designed to prevent further miscarriages. As we now know, these codes/rules subsequently served to highlight skill deficiencies in the police that required a nationwide training program to rectify (PEACE, see below).

In essence, what the evidence presented to the Commission revealed was the complexity of communication within the legal context, where the vulnerabilities of individuals were not always recognised and how significant certain issues such as bias (Ask and Granhag, 2005) were within the adversarial justice system.

Such developments within the UK system have resulted in significant changes throughout the pre-trial process, both before and after charge, in the way that police officers are mandated to gather evidence and reveal same (CPIA, 1996). The UK's evolution in this regard, however, has not yet been mirrored globally, in other adversarial systems, though relevant developments have taken place nationally in New Zealand and in parts of

Australia and Canada. In particular, the US is still experiencing miscarriages (see www.innocence project.org) that are caused by similar issues to those that led to the UK's changes.

Below we provide examples of cases where ignorance or some other human frailty on behalf of investigator or counsel exacerbated a problem for a vulnerable defendant resulting in a miscarriage of justice and serving as an example of what not to do.

Colin Lattimore and others

The recriminations from this case, and subsequent judge led enquiry (Fisher, 1977) led to the Royal Commission of Criminal Justice under Sir Cyril Phillips (1981). Colin Lattimore, Ronal Leighton, and Ahmet Salih were convicted on the basis of their confessions of killing Maxwell Confait and setting fire to his flat. Those convictions were overturned on appeal (R v Lattimore (1975) 62 Cr. App. Rep. 53 CA). Lattimore and Leighton had been charged with the murder of Confait, and Salih with the arson (Eddleston, 2009). The ages and intellectual abilities of the defendants were very relevant to the Court of Appeal's decision; Lattimore was 18, had an IQ of 66 and was illiterate, Leighton, was 15, had an IQ of 75 (considered borderline intellectual functioning), while Salah was 14 at the time of questioning and English was his second language (Gudjonsson, 2003). The case was a watershed moment in British justice, and the police officers involved in obtaining the confessions received much criticism (Fisher, 1977; Gudjonsson, 2003). However, it is worthy of note that the judges and barristers involved in the original trial were also criticised for their lack of grasp of the issues around the vulnerability of the defendants, as was Lord Fisher for not addressing this issue in his report (*HC Deb 13 April 1978 vol 947 cc1807-18*).

Fisher compounded this blinkered approach by concluding that at least one of the three defendants must have been involved in the crime in order for that person to furnish the others with the details provided in the confessions (1977). He totally overlooked or dismissed the possibility that the police themselves could have contaminated the defendants' confessions with their case knowledge during the interviews (Gudjonsson, 2003). In 1980 two different individuals were charged, tried and convicted of the crime (Naughton, 2013).

This notable miscarriage was caused by a premature conclusion drawn by police detectives concerning the guilt of their suspects, the blind pursuit of confessions which supported their single hypothesis, and then the inability of the trial advocates, and reviewing judge (Fisher) to see beyond the confessions, even when there was contradictory pathology evidence (Eddleston, 2009). It was only the pressure of Lattimore's father and the efforts of his local Member of Parliament that drew enough attention to force an appeal and the independent enquiry with its far-reaching affects.

George Thomas Heron

This case is significant because, unlike the Confait case, Heron was not cleared on appeal, but acquitted by a jury after His Honour Judge Mitchell refused to admit his confession into evidence, due to the nature of the police questioning (Griffiths and Milne, 2006). It is also significant because the case came after PACE (1984), and showed the development of the judiciary's approach to deficient police questioning techniques. Significantly, the interviews were audio recorded so the court had access to the actual content of the interview and not merely to a written summary produced afterwards. Heron initially made no comment in interview until the senior officer in the case took over questioning. The transcripts show his leading approach, which resulted in the evidence being excluded.

For example -

Q. Did she struggle a bit then George?

Yeah

Q. George, George, did she start to struggle then?

A little yes.

Q. Did you hit her, did you; did you hit her then George?

I can't recall hitting her then.

Q. She didn't want to go into the building did she at the finish?

No

Q. Why was she knocked out before you took her inside?

No

Q. Did you slap her?

Yeah

Q. You did?

So then you pushed her through the window, ad through the hole whatever it is?

Just helped her through.

Q. If you's left her there she would have run away wouldn't she?

Yeah

Q. Did she go in first or not, howay George you've just about told us everything haven't you, George, well what happened come on.

Despite the ruling of the trial judge, it is noteworthy that the senior detective in the case sought to defend the police conduct stating that, in the absence of strong forensic evidence, "in a difficult case there is no use pussyfooting around" (Pithers, 1993).

Dean Lyons

As stated above, the UK is by no means alone regarding a failure to recognise vulnerability, although it does appear to have encountered these issues earlier than other countries. In Ireland the case that led to a major change was that 1997 of Dean Lyons.

Lyons initially attended a Garda station voluntarily in relation to a murder enquiry, and quickly confessed to the crime, in the first of four interviews. He also subsequently confessed to a second, linked murder. His initial confessions have been described as lacking in detail (Birmingham, 2006), however, Lyons subsequently signed a statement written by a Garda officer, which did contain more detail that corresponded to the details of the crimes. A file of evidence was presented to the Director of Public Prosecutions (DPP) with the police recommending that Lyons be tried for murder. Lyons was remanded into custody where he repeated his confessions to prison staff, other prisoners, and even his own legal team. However, before he could be tried, another suspect's confession to the same crimes caused further examination of Lyons' confessions and the charges were discontinued.

The case resulted in an official enquiry (Birmingham, 2006). This found that Lyons was not responsible for the crimes, was mentally vulnerable, and had a history of lying. The report concluded that he was able to learn information that he included in his final confession from the officers interviewing him, through their leading questions. This, along with the willingness of most of the enquiry team to believe his confession, resulted in a situation where a miscarriage of justice was only narrowly averted. In contrast to Lattimore and Heron, whose confessions were coerced, Lyons's confession was voluntary, most probably caused by a desire for notoriety (Gudjonsson, 2003). The Lyons case has resulted in wholesale changes to Garda interview practice, with training provided to all officers along the lines of the PEACE model (see below).

Robert Davies

Davies was an immature 17 year old with emotional and learning difficulties interrogated by police who suspected him of involvement in the murders of a young mother and her two-year-old daughter. There was no forensic or physical evidence to implicate Davies, but the officers repeatedly told him there was (https://www.law.umich.edu/special/exoneration/Pages/casedetail.aspx?caseid=5058).

For example -

Detective " You need to think about where you were, because we know exactly where you were."

Davies " I'm trying to think, I was with my mother and her boyfriend."

Detective " No, you weren't, we know where you were."

Davies " I was not there."

Detective " Its not that big of a deal to say you were there Robert… if you can work with me, …then that gives us something to tell the Judge."

After 6 hours Davies confessed to peripheral involvement, thinking he would be taken home, but he was charged and taken to Court. Davies' confession was compounded when, on legal advice, he offered a guilty plea at trial in order to minimize his sentence, meaning that the interrogation was never challenged. It was only years later when one of the actual offenders admitted that Davies took no part in the crime that a campaign to obtain Davies' release commenced – led by the lawyer who represented him at trial. The second author of this chapter submitted a deposition in the case, providing evidence about the unreliability of Davies' confession. Davies was fully pardoned in 2016 and awarded significant compensation for the 13 years that he spent in gaol.

Although the common factor in all these cases is police malpractice or lack of professionalism, it is noticeable that the cases also highlight ineffective representation by defence counsel and ignorance by judges and advocates, indicating a widespread lack of knowledge across the criminal justice systems in several countries.

The development of PEACE

In 1999 in one of the UK's most respected national, daily newspapers ('The Guardian') a journalist/documentary producer wrote:

"In 1982, when I was 19, I saw a disturbing and raw documentary about Thames Valley Police that always stayed with me. Three male detectives interrogated a woman who reported that she had been raped earlier that day. Its brutality and cold-heartedness caused a sensation...possibly the most savage encounter between police and public ever recorded on television...the detectives had been taught this approach at police college and interviews like this were happening everywhere...".

In 2017 in another of the UK's most respected national, daily newspapers ('The Times') a male victim of rape wrote:

"In 2014, knowing that I was going to be interviewed by someone official while being tape recorded was a frightening prospect...I feared the police would not take me seriously, but I couldn't have been more wrong...the police have been kind, attentive, sensitive and respectful. They were relaxed and friendly, yet also professional." Later in court "...to hear the guilty verdict was hugely important to me."

What are the likely explanations for this huge change in police interviewing from 1982 to 2014? One leading contender is the massive development that occurred between these two dates in the way the UK police conduct their questioning/interviewing. Around 25 years ago the police service in England and Wales began a major step forward in terms of adopting an innovative 'investigative interviewing' approach to the seeking of justice. This change involved a number of highly experienced police investigators forming a working party (in 1990) to develop up to date training on interviewing/interrogating (informed by relevant research within psychology and related disciplines). In light of their deliberations they recommended what they called the PEACE model/approach. This change began in 1992 and it involved guidance documents and training courses that all police interviewers in England and Wales should attend and which contained much research-based cognitive and social psychology (Milne and Bull, 1999) that was (and still is) presented in 'everyday language'.

Draft reports of the 'early' research studies (conducted soon after the recording of interview with suspects became mandatory in 1986) found low levels of skills regarding the interviewing of suspects. This led the senior London police officer Tom Williamson to convene (in 1990) a different small working party involving psychologists (including Eric Shepherd, Stephen Moston and the first author of this current chapter, RB) that produced in 1991 an (unpublished) overview of aspects of psychology that were thought likely to be useful to the improving of such interviewing/ interrogating. This overview was made available by Tom Williamson to the national team of detectives that was developing 'PEACE'. Once that team of detectives had written their guidance documents they sent drafts of these to RB asking if they had "...got the psychology correct?" – They indeed had.

To accompany the PEACE model senior police chiefs published seven principles underpinning the new approach (that is itself based on the concept of investigative interviewing - Milne and Bull, 1999) (see www.app. college.police.uk/app-content/investigations/investigative-interviewing) including:

1. The aim of investigative interviewing is to obtain accurate and reliable accounts from victims, witnesses or suspects about matters under police investigation. To be accurate, information should be as complete as possible without any omissions or distortion.

2. Investigators must act fairly when questioning victims, witnesses or suspects. People with clear or perceived vulnerabilities should be treated with particular care, and extra safeguards should be put in place.

What does the PEACE method involve?

PEACE is an acronym for:

P	Planning and Preparation
E	Engage and Explain
A	Account
C	Closure
E	Evaluation

(for a full explanation of the PEACE method/framework see Milne and Bull, 1999 and www.app.college.police.uk/app-content/investigations/ investigative-interviewing; also see the 2013 document entitled 'Advice on the structure of visually recorded witness interviews' that is available online at http://library.college.police.uk/docs/APPREF/ACPO-Witness-Interview-Structure-2013.pdf.)

It is within the account phase that questions are put to interviewees (whether suspects, witnesses or victims). Within this phase guidance is provided in the 2013 document on how to do this effectively, namely, "Each relevant topic not adequately covered in the witness's initial account should be expanded using ...open-ended and specific-closed questions

(question types as described in chapter 3 of Achieving Best Evidence)".
See below for more on Achieving Best Evidence – Ministry of Justice 2011.

This phenomenal development constituted an evolution (perhaps a revolution) away from coercive, dominating interrogation practices that are still being practised in many countries.

This 'sea change', described as the PEACE approach is now being followed in an increasing number of organisations around the world - and was in 2016 recommended to the United Nations by its Special Rapporteur (see below).

With regard to vulnerable interviewees, this PEACE approach seems to make very good sense in the experience of both authors of the current chapter. For example, quite a few years ago now (in the early 1990s) Becky Milne and the first author (RB) were asked by a major police force to assist them in their interviewing of residents in a home for vulnerable adults who may have been physically abused by the owners/directors of that residence (see the 'Independent Longcare Inquiry', Department of Health, 1998). Within this investigation first of all the police asked a clinical/forensic psychologist to advise them as to which of the residents would likely be able to communicate in an investigative interview setting. The police then interviewed the most likely person and immediately couriered by police motorcycle that video recorded interview to the University of Portsmouth where Becky and RB were at that time worked. Later on that very day we sent feedback on the quality of the interviewing to the investigative team who did their best to take it on board when the next day interviewing another resident. Again that video recording was promptly sent to Becky and RB for comment – and so on. The outcome of this investigation was that the female director of the care home was sent to prison and male owner committed suicide on the day before he was due to be charged by the police.

In our 1999 book entitled 'Investigative interviewing: Psychology and practice', at the end of our chapter on 'Interviewing vulnerable people' the first author of the current chapter (RB) wrote "This chapter overviews what is presently known on this topic. Sadly, we know very little... no methodologically rigorous research exists...interview...vulnerable people...who are in most need of our support. Something must be done about this" (128). Nowadays a substantial body of relevant research exists to guide how valuable victims/witnesses should be interviewed by police/ questioned in court (e.g. not asked suggestive or leading questions – with which they often comply), and thus the police service has been making attempts to improve their interviewing of such persons, at least here in the UK. For example, Code C (paragraph 11C) of the Codes relating to the Practice Police and Criminal Evidence Act 1984 states that "Although… people who are…vulnerable are often capable of providing reliable evidence, they may, without knowing or wishing to do so, be particularly prone in some circumstances to provide information that may be unreliable, misleading or self-incriminating. Special care should always be taken when questioning such a person."

However, there are still parts of our justice system in which that 1970s domineering style seems to remain and which involves a substantial number of vulnerable persons (who often have limited powers of communication and understanding).

Vulnerability and the vulnerable part of ABE

For example, Johnston et al. (2016) found that two thirds of a sample of adolescent defendants (average age 16 years) had listening-comprehension skills below the norm for ten year olds and that almost half had a diagnosis of attention deficit hyperactivity disorder (ADHD). Similarly, in their overview Young et al. (2011) noted regarding ADHD that, whereas the rate in the general population is around 3%, UK prison studies have found rates of over 40% for youths and 20% for adult males (a proportion of whom would have been cross-examined).

The organisation Barnado's has reported that of children in the youth justice system 60% have significant speech, language or communication difficulties, around 25% have a learning disability, and over 30% young people in police custody have a mental health disorder. (See http://www. barnardos.org.uk/what_we_do/our_work/youth_justice.htm) For a review of language impairments among youth offenders see Anderson, Hawes, and Snow (2016) and for an overview of how and why youths' developmental immaturity renders them vulnerable to questioning see Cleary (2017).

In England and Wales police interviewers receive training as how to interview these vulnerable people. Indeed, one of the seven principles upon which the PEACE approach is founded (see above) is that people with clear or perceived vulnerabilities should be treated with particular care, and extra safeguards should be put in place. This training is based on an extensive government guidance document that is commonly referred to as 'ABE' (i.e. 'Achieving best evidence in criminal proceedings: Guidance on interviewing victims and witnesses, and guidance on using special measures' (Ministry of Justice, 2011). The original 2002 version of this substantial guidance was commissioned to be written by a team led by Professor Graham Davies and the large section on how to interview vulnerable people was written by the first author of the current chapter.

Achieving best evidence

Among the advice in that section of ABE it is noted that a considerable proportion of vulnerable people will require that their interviews go at a slower pace than do other witnesses. This is because many of them will have a slower rate of understanding, and/or thinking and/or replying than do other people. Both research and best practice have found that interviewers will need:

- to slow down their speech rate
- to allow extra time for the person to take in what has just been said
- to provide time for the person to prepare a response
- to be patient if the person replies slowly
- to avoid immediately posing the next question
- to avoid interrupting.

Some vulnerable people, even more so than ordinary people, may feel shame or resentment about being interviewed, especially on personal matters. Therefore, interviewers should be aware that asking someone to provide information frankly and in detail about personal matters (e.g. involving sex) is asking the person to do something in a manner that they may have learned to avoid. The interviewer should inform the person of why she/he is being asked to give a detailed account and that doing so, in that situation, is not breaking with convention. It is important to carefully explain to the person that it is his/her account that is required. This is particularly important with particularly vulnerable people, some of whom will be under the impression that the interviewer somehow already knows what happened and that their role, therefore, is merely to confirm what the interviewer says (e.g. to conform to authority).

It should be explained that if the interviewer asks a question that the person does not know the answer to (but understands), the interviewer would be really happy for the person to indicate "I don't know". Vulnerable people can spend much of their lives trying to appear competent and therefore may be especially unwilling to admit "I don't know" unless they are assisted to realise how good it is to say this (when appropriate).

Research findings consistently have shown that improper questioning of vulnerable people is a greater source of distortion of their accounts than are their memory deficits. ABE notes that vulnerable "witnesses when recalling negative events may initially be more comfortable with peripheral matters and may only want to move on to more central matters when they feel this is appropriate. Therefore, interviewers should resist the temptation prematurely to 'get to the heart of the matter'. They should also resist the temptation to speak as soon as the witness appears to stop responding, and they should be tolerant of pauses, including long ones, and silences. They should also be tolerant of what may appear to be repetitious or irrelevant information from vulnerable witnesses. Interviewers must try to curb their eagerness to determine whether the interviewee witnessed anything untoward." (76).

Some vulnerable people may be particularly compliant in that they will try to be helpful by going along with much of what they believe the interviewer 'wants to hear' and/or is suggesting to them. Research has often found that some vulnerable people often acquiesce to 'yes/no' questions. That is, they answer such questions affirmatively with "Yes" regardless of question content. This can even occur even when an almost identical 'yes/no' question is asked subsequently but this time with the opposite meaning. However, this is not solely due to the interviewee. The way in which the interview is conducted (e.g. in an authoritative way) and the nature of the questions asked (e.g. suggestive or too complex) are likely also to influence the extent of such unconditional positive responding. Similarly, sometimes 'nay-saying' (repeatedly responding with "No") will occur, particularly for questions dealing with matters that are socially disapproved of/social taboos.

Questions that have a 'yes/no' format can very often be transformed into questions that have an 'either/or' format. Such 'either/or' questions, by avoiding 'yea-saying' or 'nay-saying', more frequently elicit reliable responses from vulnerable people than do 'yes/no' questions. Even so, a small proportion of people seem always to choose the latter of the two alternatives offered by 'either/or' questions. If an interviewee appears to be doing this, the interviewer should phrase some of the 'either/or' questions so that the first alternative is the one which more likely fits in with the account the witness is giving. Also, it would often be good practice to add "or something else" to the end of an 'either/or' question.

Both research and best practice have found that vulnerable interviewees may well have great difficulty with questions unless these:

- are simple

- do not contain jargon

- do not contain abstract words and/or abstract ideas

-   contain only one point per question

-   are not too directive/suggestive

-   do not contain double negatives.

Because vulnerable witnesses in particular will experience difficulty if the interviewer 'topic hops', when questioning a witness interviewers should ask the various types of questions about one issue, before proceeding to ask questions about another. This would be good practice in terms of how memory storage is organised. When this occurs, the questioning on each issue should normally begin with an open question, though some particularly vulnerable people may not be able to cope with such questions and specific or closed questions may be necessary. To assist the person the interviewer should indicate a change of topic by saying, for example, "I'd now like to ask you about something else".

Although some particularly vulnerable people may not be able to provide information in response to open questions, they may be able to respond to specific questions. However, interviewers may be aware that specific questions should not unduly suggest answers to the witness. If specific questions are asked it is advisable whenever possible, to follow them up with an open-ended question. Specific questions vary in their degree of explicitness and it is always best to begin with the least explicit version of the question. The more specific the questions become the more likely they are to produce errors.

ABE notes that,

"At the beginning of the use of closed questions interviewers should try to avoid using ones that contain only two alternatives (especially yes/no questions) unless these two alternatives contain all possibilities (e.g. 'Was the person male or female?'). If questions containing only two alternatives are used, these should be phrased so that they sometimes result in the first alternative being chosen and sometimes in the second alternative." (76).

and that,

"In addition to legal objections, research indicates that interviewees' responses to leading questions tend to be determined more by the manner of questioning than by valid remembering.... leading questions should only be used as a last resort, where all other questioning strategies have failed to elicit any kind of response. On occasions, a leading question can produce relevant information which has not been led by the question. *If this does occur, interviewers should take care not to follow up this question with further leading questions. Rather, they should revert to open or specific questions." (77).*

and that,

"It cannot be over-emphasised that responses to leading questions referring to central facts of the case that have not already been described by the witness in an earlier phase of the interview are likely to be of very limited evidential value in criminal proceedings." (77).

Current advice to advocates on how to cross-examine

While some important developments have recently begun to take place with regard to the police questioning of vulnerable people (such as in the ABE guidance mentioned above), if vulnerable suspects subsequently seek to give evidence at court they can still sometimes face being cross-examined in a domineering and coercive manner. Such a manner is designed to be challenging for non-vulnerable people and thus it may well be more likely to present greater difficulties for vulnerable suspects. For example, among current online guidance on cross-examination it is stated that,

"Asking only leading questions is perhaps the oldest rule… it is a good one…allows the cross-examiner to be forceful…" (see http://www.readingschools.org/userfiles/215/Classes/7206/the%20 ten%20commandments%20of%20cross%202014.pdf?id=1620) and "Use leading questions which legitimately call only for a 'yes' or 'no' answer" (see https://www.yumpu.com/en/document/ view/11449308/a-checklist-of-winning-cross-examination-concepts-and-techniques).

Among the best-selling books on advocacy is 'The Devil's Advocate: A short polemic on how to be seriously good in court' by Iain Morley (2010). On the relevant publisher's website at http://www.sweetandmaxwell. co.uk/Catalogue/ProductDetails.aspx?productid=552390&recordid=5295 it is stated that,

"The Devil's Advocate, a best-selling advocacy manual in both the UK and the Commonwealth, brings a fresh approach to the Do's and Don'ts of good advocacy. Written with humour and style, the title explains clear techniques, taking the reader through the practical application of advocacy step-by-step. The Devil's Advocate has quickly become the leading handbook and practical guide to advocacy in any adversarial courtroom, in any country, to be read and carried about by any advocate."

and that,

"...the book of my dreams, the Titanic of the advocacy world (even though it is modestly sized)...Iain Morley has bridged the gap between reading about advocacy and how you actually do it... [the book is] warmly welcomed and should be in every white wig box."

in 'The Barrister'

"Quite simply [this] is the best book of its kind. Indeed it is the only book of its kind… Buy this book. Study it. You won't regret it." in 'Science & Justice'.

Within this book Morley states that "Rightly or wrongly, adversarial advocacy is not really an enquiry into the truth. Perhaps the adversarial system should be about finding out what really happened. But it isn't." (12). He adds that "Advocates try to win their cases within the rules, irrespective of the truth,.. (13). This contrast with one of the fundamental aspects of the 'PEACE' approach (see above).

Morley also states that "…if defending, we know what areas to cross-examine…Do we want the witness to appear a liar, or simply mistaken, or just likeably unreliable?" (83). Morley further notes that "Cross-examination is all about bending perception", "Always ask leading questions", "Never ask an open question" (157-158) and "Never, ever…ask the witness to explain" (161).

Interestingly, toward the end of his book Morley says that "On the continent of Europe…a more inquisitorial style…Cross-examination is not allowed, as it is thought it might erroneously place suggestions in the mind of the witness…" (236).

In his book Morley emphasises "…strive…to win, but always…within the rules" (15) – so perhaps it is 'the rules' that need to be changed?

The potential effects of poor/bad questioning of vulnerable defendants

It is acknowledged that, ultimately defendants with learning disability are at greater risk of wrongful conviction (Jacobson and Talbot, 2009: O'Mahony, Marchant, and Fadden, 2016). Therefore, the manner in which they behave when giving evidence is crucial to their receiving a fair trial. The legal provision for witnesses to give evidence by live link is also available to defendants, but appears rarely used (Fairclough, 2016). In the case of a defendant with an intellectual disability or communication difficulty, the fact that this legal provision is rarely utilised may result in the defendant, on Counsel's advice, either not testifying, or testifying 'live' poorly, and a jury gaining a negative impression of the defendant's innocence.

In the latter situation, the manner of examination and cross-examination will be crucial to the impression that the defendant gives to the Court, and there is little current research on this topic. The consensus of decades of research on police interviews, either with witnesses or suspects, is that not all police officers are naturally good communicators. Some are prone to using leading language which influences the information they receive, particularly from those considered more vulnerable (Powell, Wright, and Clark, 2010). It is not unreasonable to assume that lawyers, barristers, and judges will display a similar range of 'natural' abilities. A study of fifty legal defence firms, conducted in the same era as early UK research on police officers questioning techniques, found similar issues of defence solicitors influencing defendants' pleas by the manner in which they explained the trial process to them (McConville, Hodges, and Bridges, 1994).

If a defendant does give evidence, an advocate's manner of questioning will contribute to their perceived credibility. Questioning is a multi-faceted element of communication (Hargie, 2006), too broad for complete discussion in this chapter. However, we will use three examples to demonstrate this point.

Repeat questions can cause interviewees to contradict themselves (Andrews and Lamb, 2014), and a recent study on their use by lawyers in Scottish courts with child witnesses (Andrews and Lamb, 2017) found widespread use of this question type by all lawyers, but more so by defence lawyers in conjunction with suggestive prompts. Research has for years shown that child witnesses are more likely to give contradictory answers after repeated questions especially those that are leading (Andrews and Lamb, 2014). Although such research has been conducted with child witnesses, the potentially negative effects of this poor questioning can be extrapolated to adult defendants with intellectual disability. Defendants with autism may be either overly compliant or blunt and aggressive in the face of examination of this type (Cooper and Allely, 2017).

Police training has warned of the dangers of *multiple questions* (Shepherd and Griffiths, 2013) since the implementation of PEACE, on the basis that this affects the reliability of the information in the response. Examples of similar multiple questioning can be seen in recent examples of cross-examination:

Prosecution Counsel: *How did you first see Mr X? What was he doing?*

Defendant: *He was on his motorbike.*

Prosecution Counsel: *Did he stop? Did you ask him to stop or did anything happen?*

Defendant: *Yeah, I asked him nicely* (O'Mahony, 2012).

Complex questions should similarly be avoided, but examples of these can also be found -

Prosecution Counsel: *And whether or not you might be schizo or schizophrenic, as far as you are concerned, it has got absolutely nothing to do with it. Is that right?*

Defendant: *I'm sorry, can you repeat that question because I can't understand it.*

(O'Mahony, 2012)

A strong argument that supports why vulnerable defendants will struggle to comprehend complex or clumsy examination or cross-examination is to point out that many adults with no intellectual disability also struggle in the same circumstances (Kebbell, Evans, and Johnston, 2010: Henderson, 2014). Indeed, the UK police realised many years ago that not only vulnerable people but all interviewees require great skill on the part of the questioner/interviewer. This crucial point has been recognized by the United Nations, as mentioned below.

The recent United Nations recommendation

We would like to share with you some of what a United Nations special rapporteur (in fact a Law Professor) wrote in his 2016 report for the UN (that is available at http://antitorture.org/wp-content/uploads/2016/09/Report_A-71-298_English.pdf).

In the section of his report on how to communicate with people who may be involved in or planning wrong-doing he stated that,

"The Special Rapporteur…advocates the development of a universal protocol identifying a set of standards for non-coercive interviewing methods and procedural safeguards that ought, as a matter of law and policy, to be applied at a minimum to all interviews by law enforcement officials, military and intelligence personnel and other bodies with investigative mandates." (2).

When mentioning this "universal protocol" the UN Special Rapporteur noted that "Encouragingly, some States have moved away from accusatorial, manipulative and confession-driven interviewing models with a view to increasing accurate and reliable information and minimizing the risks of unreliable information and miscarriages of justice" (13) and that "The essence of an alternative information-gathering model was first captured by the PEACE model of interviewing adopted in 1992 in England and Wales...investigative interviewing can provide positive guidance for the protocol..." (12).

Is now the time for those not only who interview vulnerable suspects but also those who examine in court vulnerable suspects to take on board this recommendation from the United Nations?

Training issues

People only need training if they do not already regularly behave in ways in line with the training. The original PEACE pilot training program was assessed as being a success (McGurk, Carr, and McGurk, 1993). However, a more extensive national evaluation (Clark & Milne, 2001) found less evidence of improvement. The difference between these two evaluations may be explained by the facts that:

- The 1992 pilot course was attended by volunteers whereas the later national program sought to train all officers, the implications being that (i) not all police have the potential to benefit from interview training and (ii) more experienced officers might have been more resistant to change due to embedded 'bad habits'

- Handpicked trainers delivered the pilot course, whereas due to its size, the national program was cascaded through several levels (i.e. the original trainers taught other trainers, who then trained others, etc.). This approach diluted the impact.

- A major evolution of the PEACE approach was the recognition that not all police officers can become skilled interviewers and thus a tiered system was introduced (Griffiths and Milne, 2006) within which officers receive graded levels of training commensurate with their skills and abilities. The development of these levels of training included the involvement of psychologists and lawyers. This updated approach has produced tangible improvements (Griffiths and Milne, 2006; Walsh & Bull, 2010, 2012a, 2012b).

Conclusion

In 2017 Cooper and Allely made the point regarding vulnerable people that "Findings from research, far from being a reason to set the bar very low for lawyers, emphasise the need for lawyers to become adept at asking questions..." (42). Currently, it is likely that the cross-examining of some vulnerable defendants has made them feel cross/annoyed and thus diminished their respect for the criminal justice system, which is likely to influence negatively their future behaviour and that of their friends/ family. As Arndorfer, Malloy, and Cauffman (2015) pointed out in the USA, although it is impossible to modify some factors that have already influenced people's perceptions/beliefs about the police and justice system, it is possible to modify their perceptions in the future by making their treatment more humane (as police interviewers in the UK have already achieved).

In order to practise/profess as a Forensic Psychologist one has to be registered. Registered psychologists should not practise outside of their competencies. In his 2017 report Rees states that "...a court must also take into account the fact that an advocate...will have satisfied himself or herself before continuing to act...that the training...enables him or her to conduct the case in accordance with proper professional competence" (419). Thus, advocates should only practise within their competencies.

The Court of Appeal in *Lubemba* recognised that "The trial judge is responsible for controlling questioning and ensuring that vulnerable witnesses and defendants are enabled to give the best evidence they can. The judge has a duty to intervene therefore if an advocate's questioning is confusing or inappropriate". However, should it be left up to judges to do this or should the training of advocates be good enough that judges very rarely have to do this?

In the April 2007 practice direction issued by The Lord Chief Justice mentions measures to be adopted to assist vulnerable defendants to understand and participate in court proceedings including what is said by advocates including that cross-examination is conducted by questions that are short and clear. In the Consolidated Criminal Practice Direction section on the treatment of vulnerable defendants it is stated that "All possible steps should be taken to assist a vulnerable defendant to understand and participate in those proceedings. The ordinary trial process should, so far as necessary, be adapted to meet those ends." and "Throughout the trial the court should continue to ensure, by any appropriate means, that the defendant understands what is happening and what has been said by those on the bench, the advocates and witnesses." and "The court should ensure, so far as practicable, that the trial is conducted in simple, clear language that the defendant can understand and that cross-examination is conducted by questions that are short and clear". (See http://www.justice.gov.uk/courts/ procedure-rules/criminal/practice-direction/part3#id6328221).

In 2013 Lord Chief Justice Judge stated that "...the objective of cross-examination is to investigate the truth by questions which must be clearly understood by the witness...". This is similar to one of the principles of the PEACE method mentioned above.

In our opinion, it is right for society to deem that the needs of vulnerable witnesses/victims are a priority – and much has been achieved in this regard with regard to their police interviewing to obtain best evidence. Thus, now would seem the time for us all to turn our attention more to the needs and best treatment of vulnerable suspects. As far as we are aware almost no relevant research has been conducted on this particular topic. Is now the time for a guidance document on 'Achieving Best Treatment' (ABT) for vulnerable defendants?

We wish to dedicate this chapter to the memory of Nina Westera who tragically died in her early forties in 2017 due to a particularly aggressive type of cancer. Not only as a police officer did she have deep involvement in training all officers in New Zealand in the PEACE method, but she also subsequently achieved a PhD on how best to present in court the testimony of vulnerable people.

References

Anderson, Stavroola, A.S., David, J. Hawes, and Pamela C. Snow. 2016. "Language impairments among youth offenders: A systematic review." *Children and Youth Services Review*, 65: 195–203.

Arndorfer, Andrea., Lindsay, C. Malloy, and Elizabeth Cauffman, E. 2015. "Interrogations, confessions, and adolescent offenders' perceptions of the legal system". *Law and Human Behavior*, 39: 503-513.

Andrews, Samantha J., and Michael E. Lamb. 2014. "The effects of age and delay on responses to repeated questions in forensic interviews with children alleging sexual abuse." *Law and Human Behavior*, 38: 171-180.

Andrews, Samantha J., and Michael E. Lamb. 2017. "Lawyers question repetition and children's responses in Scottish Criminal Courts." *Journal of Interpersonal Violence*, published online 26.08.17. (accessed September 1st, 2017).

Ask, Karl, and Par Anders Granhag. 2005. "Motivational sources of confirmation bias in criminal investigations: the need for cognitive closure". *Journal of Investigative Psychology and Offender Profiling,* 2, 43-63.

Birmingham, George. 2006. "Report of the Commission of Investigation (Dean Lyons Case)" http://www.justice.ie/en/JELR/Dean%20Lyons%20 Commission%20of%20Investigation.pdf/Files/Dean%20Lyons%20 Commission%20of%20Investigation.pdf (accessed August 1, 2017).

Clark, Colin, and Rebecca Milne. 2001. *"National evaluation of the PEACE Investigative Interviewing Course. (Report No. PRAS/149)".* London: Police Research Award Scheme.

Cleary, Hayley, M.D. 2017. "Applying the lessons of developmental psychology to the study of juvenile interrogations: New directions for research, policy, and practice." *Psychology, Public Policy and Law,* 23, 118-130.

Cooper, Penny, and Clare Allely. 2017. "You can't judge a book by its cover: evolving professional responsibilities, liabilities, and 'judgecraft' when a party has Asperger's Syndrome." *Northern Ireland Legal Quarterly, 68,* 35-58.

Criminal Procedure and Investigations Act (CPIA). 1996. http://www. legislation.gov.uk/ukpga/1996/25/contents.

Department of Health. 1998. *The Independent Longcare Inquiry.* London: Department of Health.

Devlin Committee. 1976. *"Report of the Committee on Evidence of Identification in Criminal Cases",* Cmnd 338 134/135, 42 April.

Eddleston, John J. 2009. *"Miscarriages of justice: Famous London cases."* Barnsley: Wharncliffe.

Fisher, Sir Henry. 1977. *"Report of an enquiry by the Hon. Sir Henry Fisher into the circumstances leading to the trial of three persons on charges arising out of the death of Maxwell Confait and the fire at 27 Doggett Road, London SE6."* London: HMSO.

Griffiths, Andy, and Rebecca Milne. 2006. "Will it all end in Tiers?" In *Investigative interviewing: Rights, research, regulation,* edited by Tom Williamson. Chichester: Wiley.

Gudjonsson, Gisli. H. 2003. *"The psychology of interrogations and confessions."* Chichester: Wiley.

Hargie, Owen. 2006. *"The handbook of communication skills."* Hove: Routledge.

Henderson, Emily. 2014. Did you see the broken headlight? Questioning the cross-examination of robust adult witnesses. *Archbold Review, Issue 10.*

Irving, Barry, and Linden Hilgendorf. 1980 "Police interrogation: The psychological approach." *Royal Commission on Criminal Procedure, Research Study No. 1.* London: HMSO.

Jacobson, Jessica J. and Jenny Talbot. 2009. *"Vulnerable defendants in the criminal courts: A review of provision for adults and children."* London: Prison Reform Trust.

Johnstone, K., Prentice, K., Whitehead, H., Taylor, L., Watts R., & Tranah, T. 2016. Assessing effective participation in vulnerable juvenile defendants. *Journal of Forensic Psychiatry and Psychology, 27,* 802-818.

Kebbell, Mark R., Laura Evans, and Shane D. Johnson. 2010. "The influence of lawyers' questions on witness accuracy, confidence, and reaction times and on mock jurors' interpretation of witness accuracy." *Journal of Investigative Psychology & Offender Profiling, 7:* 262-272.

The Rt Hon. The Lord Judge. 2013. *"The evidence of child victims: The next stage."* Bar Council Annual Reform Lecture. Available at http://www.barcouncil.org.uk/media/241783/annual_law_reform_lecture_rt_hon_the_lord_judge_speech_2013.pdf.

Lubemba [2014] EWCA Crim 2064; {2015] 1 Cr. App. R. 12 (p. 137) at [44]

McConville Mike, Jacqueline Hodgson, and Lee Bridges 1994. *"Standing accused: The organization and practices of criminal defence lawyers in Britain."* Oxford: Clarendon Press.

McGurk, Barry J., Michaal J. Carr, and Debra McGurk. 1993. *"Investigative interviewing courses for police officers: An evaluation (Rep. No. 4)."* London: Police Research Group, Home Office.

Ministry of Justice. 2011. Achieving best evidence in criminal proceedings: Guidance on interviewing victims and witnesses, and guidance on using special measures. Available at www.cps.gov.uk/publications/docs/best_evidence_in_criminal_proceedings.pdf.

Morley, Iain. 2009. *"The devil's advocate: A short polemic on how to be seriously good in court (second edition)."* London: Sweet and Maxwell.

Naughton, Michael. 2013. *"The innocent and the criminal justice system: A sociological analysis of miscarriages of justice."* Basingstoke: Macmillan.

O'Mahony, Brendan. 2012. "Accused of murder: supporting the communication needs of a vulnerable defendant at court and at the police station." *Journal of Learning Disabilities and Offending* Behaviour, 3: 77 – 84.

O'Mahony, Brendan, Ruth Marchant, and Lorna Fadden. 2016. "Vulnerable intermediaries and justice." In *Communication in investigative and legal contexts edited by* Gavin Oxburgh, Trond Myklebust, Tim Grant, and Rebecca Milne. Chichester: Wiley.

Philips, Sir Cyril. 1981. *"The Royal Commission on Criminal Procedure."* Cmnd 8092. London: HMSO.

Pithers, Malcolm. 1993. "Uproar after acquittal in Nikki Allen murder case not guilty verdict ends six week trial in which judge refused to admit alleged confession on interview tape as evidence". *The Independent.* November 19th 1993. http://www.independent.co.uk/news/uk/uproar-after-acquittal-in-nikki-allen-murder-case-not-guilty-verdict-ends-six-week-trial-in-which-1505896.html.

Police and Criminal Evidence Act. 1984. http://www.legislation.gov.uk/ukpga/1984/60/contents.

Powell, Martine, Rebecca Wright, and Susan Clark, S. 2010. "Improving the competency of police officers in conducting investigative interviews with children." *Police Practice and Research, 3*: 211–226.

Rees, T. 2017. R. v Rashid (Yahya). *Criminal Law Review, 5,* 418-421.

Royal Commission on Criminal Procedure. 1980. "Police Interrogation. The Psychological Approach: A case study of Current practice; Research studies No. 1 and No. 2." London: HMSO.

Shepherd, Eric, and Andy Griffiths. 2013. "Investigative interviewing: The conversation management approach." Oxford: Oxford University Press.

St. Johnston, Thomas, Eric. 1966. Judges' rules and police interrogation in England today. *Journal of Criminal Law and Criminology,* 1-12.

Sherman, Lawrence, W. 2015. "A tipping point for "Totally Evidenced Policing": Ten ideas for building an evidence-based police agency." *International Criminal Justice Review, 25,* 11-29.

Softley, Paul. 1980. with assistance from David Brown, Bob Forde, George Mair & David Moxon. "Police interrogation: An observational study in four police stations." Royal Commission on Criminal Procedure. Home Office Research Study No. 61. London: HMSO.

Walsh, Dave, and Ray Bull. 2012. "Examining rapport in investigative interviews with suspects: Does its building and maintenance work?" *Journal of Police and Criminal Psychology, 27*: 73-84.

Walsh, Dave, and Ray Bull. 2012. How do interviewers attempt to overcome suspects' denials? *Psychiatry, Psychology and Law, 19*: 151-168.

Walsh, Dave, and Ray Bull . 2010. What really is effective in interviews with suspects? A study comparing interview skills against interview outcomes. *Legal and Criminological Psychology, 15:* 305-321.

Young, Susan, Marios Adamou, Bianca Bolea, Gisli Gudjonsson, Ulrich Muller, Mark Pitts, , Johanes Thome, and Philip Asherson. 2011. "The identification and management of ADHD offenders within the criminal justice system: A consensus statement from the UK adult ADHD Network and criminal justice agencies." *BMC Psychiatry, 11*: 32.

Youth Justice and Criminal Evidence Act. 1999. http://www.legislation. gov.uk/ukpga/1999/23/contents.

POSTSCRIPT

'Mind the gap'

In all courts and tribunals early identification of participants' needs, effective communication between participants and a sharing of best practice and experiences are key. To support this, The Advocate's Gateway (TAG) has pioneered free and accessible guidance by and for justice system professionals. The work of TAG has been gaining international interest and recognition since its inception in 2012. Those of us involved in the development of TAG could hardly have imagined its impact and TAG is extraordinarily grateful for the support it has received from so many leading and influential individuals.

The 2017 *Access to Justice for Vulnerable People* conference, funded by The Council of the Inns of Court (COIC), further promoted, on an international platform, the sharing of best practice and experiences. TAG started small. In six years, much has been achieved and the intention is to keep working collaboratively with those who are best placed to inform discussion and practice in justice systems around the world. As The Rt Hon. Lady Dorrian so eloquently put in her opening address at the 2017 conference, justice does not need to be compromised by measures that are there to protect the vulnerable. Justice is enhanced by such measures.

Those who study developments in England and Wales will know only too well that the issues surrounding access to justice and effective participation of witnesses and victims in criminal proceedings have been high on policy and reform agendas for years. A seismic shift has already taken place in criminal courts; many amendments have been made in both legislation, policy and procedure bringing us to where we are today. Recently for example, The Legal Aid, Sentencing and Punishment of Offenders Act 2012 introduced a new provision to include child immigrants as vulnerable for the purposes of obtaining funding assistance.

Several factors have assisted this sea-change and continue to do so. The introduction through legislation and development of the role of the intermediary is now well documented. It is the 'special measure' that has made the most significant difference in recent years. The primary purpose of the intermediary role is to improve the quality of the evidence offered in proceedings; the role is now more universally understood, and its use is more common. Overseas the value of the role is being realised, for example, in Australia and New Zealand and in South America and the Caribbean.

Advocates and the judiciary now have various tools such as the Equal Treatment Bench Book, advocacy training courses and the toolkits on The

Advocate's Gateway. But a person's first contact with the criminal justice system is primarily the police. Fortunately significant advances in the training of officers and the implementation of liaison and diversion services have also assisted in achieving earlier identification of vulnerability and the ability for more appropriate interventions.

Change is not only happening in the criminal justice system. In our first book, following the 2015 international conference *Access to Justice for Vulnerable People*[1], my co-editor wrote about family court proceedings and how they were lagging behind in accommodating child and vulnerable adult witnesses and about the recommendations of the working group co-chaired by Ms Justice Russell. We are delighted that Ms Justice Russell has written the preface to this volume and that the working group's report has now given rise to the 2017 revisions to the Family Procedure Rules and Practice Directions.[2] Another example of progress is the new 2018 edition of the Equal Treatment Bench Book (ETBB);[3] changes in it reflect practice developments in the courts and tribunals to ensure effective and meaningful participation of all court users. The Rt Hon. Sir John Gillen, on discussing the scope of the current measures in Northern Ireland for disabled people, highlights that a "positive action" may be required to remove barriers to effective communication and participation, as well as modifications to the environment of the court.

However, legal practitioners still face significant challenges not least because public resources are scarce and particularly so in the criminal justice system. Lore Mergaerts et al presents research that has been carried out in the Belgium system investigating the current practices of criminal defence lawyers in identifying a suspect's vulnerability. These authors identify the important role of the criminal defence lawyer in early identification and highlight the lack of knowledge and clear unequivocal approach to vulnerability in that system. Dr. Jessica Jacobson uses the terms "access" and "engagement" when she reflects on the findings of intensive research carried out with court users in England, in particular, those who are vulnerable. She discusses, despite new "wide-scale" innovations being made such as virtual court attendance, this invariably erodes the traditional engagement that a person would have if they attended court. Rather, what is required Dr. Jacobson explains, is the need for the courts to consider vulnerability and 'vulnerable moments' in the context of general court business, recognising

---

[1] Penny Cooper & Linda Hunting 2016, *Access to Justice for Vulnerable People*, Wildy, Simmonds & Hill Publishing, London.

[2] *The Family Procedure (Amendment) Rules (2018)* http://www.legislation.gov.uk/uksi/2018/440/made (accessed May 25, 2018).

[3] Judicial College (2018), *The Equal Treatment Bench Book 2018* https://www.judiciary.uk/wp- content/uploads/2018/02/ETBB-February-2018-v15.08.18.pdf (accessed March 19, 2018).

there is a need for all court proceedings to be alive to the 'manifestations and effects of vulnerability in all its guises'.[4] There is no 'magic bullet' and no such thing as 'one size fits all' when it comes to the needs of vulnerable people who come in to contact with the justice system. We know that 'true equal treatment may not always mean treating everyone in the same way'.[5]

In this new volume, Dr. Alan Cusack examines the question of whether equality and therefore, access to justice, is adequately considered for vulnerable people who come in to contact with justice systems. He argues, that the question of equality begins well outside of the court room, starting with the persons very first encounter with a justice system, the police. The research carried out by Penelope Gibbs and Transform Justice, gives an illuminating insight about unrepresented defendants, and how in turn, this can lead to multiple disadvantages and vulnerabilities within criminal proceedings. Their conclusions provide several recommendations to support this ever-increasing group in an era of austerity. Professor Ray Bull and Dr Andy Griffiths set out what is known about how a vulnerable person is likely to respond when interviewed, and techniques which should be deployed to enable more accurate, effective communication and gathering of evidence.

Research and practitioner experience tell us that very often, vulnerable witnesses and defendants have been left excluded and bewildered when they have come in to contact with a justice system. In his chapter John Horan, a barrister, argues that disability law itself may foster inequality and make those who are disabled feel demeaned. He draws attention to the great need for judges (and others) to be educated more fully about the needs of disabled people. Dr. Anton van Dellen similarly considers the available protections for individuals with physical disabilities in light of both administrative and judicial decision making. Disability takes many forms. Someone who is profoundly deaf and requires the communication assistance of deaf professionals, is another form of vulnerability which requires specific expertise. It is extremely rare for an advocate to have experience in these matters, and Dr. Sue O'Rourke and her co-writers explain succinctly the need for distinctions and adaptations to be made between spoken language and sign language interpreting in proceedings.

Vulnerability does not necessarily mean a disability. Dr. Hugh Asher highlights the issues of vulnerable women offenders, already from often very chaotic and dysfunctional, abusive backgrounds, and how factors particular to them can make the giving of evidence an extremely

---

[4]   See p. 225.
[5]   Ibid., page 3.

challenging process. Dr. Allely et al discuss the importance of raising a greater awareness and recognition of men and women with autism symptomology in the prison estate. Professors Ellison and Munro consider the impact of trauma on victim participation.

The need to adjust for linguistic and cultural requirements and differences is not exclusive to those who may already have been regarded as 'vulnerable'. In her chapter, Felicity Gerry QC provides an insightful discussion of the provisions that exist and the experiences of vulnerable indigenous Australian people in the judicial system. It is intended that the work of The Advocate's Gateway, and publication of its toolkits, raises awareness in general about effective participation and helps improve courtroom practices for the benefit of all. Mr. K.G.M. van Dijk-Fleetwood-Bird discusses the "invisible disability" of language disorders and its prevalence in the juvenile justice system. She argues that undetected severe language problems have wide implications on factors such as right to a fair trial and access to justice.

Research, case law and practitioner experience have informed the development of all TAG toolkits as well as each and every valuable contribution to this new volume. My co-editor, Professor Penny Cooper, has been an 'anorak' in the development of toolkits and best practice. Her work is informed by her experiences in legal practise, observing numerous trials involving vulnerable people, academic research, training intermediaries, training judges and not least by her experience as the parent of a person with autism. I share her commitment and in a similar way, as the sister of a vulnerable person with complex needs, I bring my own personal experience to the TAG mission of improving access to justice for court participants, particularly those who are vulnerable and at risk of unfair treatment.

TAG, and certainly the 2017 conference, have provided a forum for individuals to share their ideas and best practice on an international footing, across a variety of disciplines. Long may we continue to have these discussions, and long may we endeavour to close the gaps in access to justice that exist for all vulnerable people.

'For Aaron'

Linda Hunting
November 2018